France before the Romans

France

306 illustrations, 8 in colour

contributors
GERARD BAILLOUD · JACQUES BRIARD
OLWEN BROGAN · GLYN DANIEL
MAX ESCALON DE FONTON · F. R. HODSON
CHARLES McBURNEY · STUART PIGGOTT
R. M. ROWLETT · DENISE DE SONNEVILLE-BORDES

before the Romans

Edited by
Stuart Piggott · Glyn Daniel
Charles McBurney

THAMES AND HUDSON

Chapters 2-5 translated from the French by Margaret Brown

Designed and produced by Thames and Hudson, London
Filmset by Imprimerie de la Tribune de Genève, Switzerland
Text printed by Camelot Press Ltd. Southampton, England
Colour illustrations printed by Henry Stone Ltd., Banbury, England
Monochrome illustrations printed by BAS Printers Ltd., London, England
Bound by Leighton Straker Bookbinding Co. Ltd., London, England

© Thames and Hudson Ltd, London 1973
English edition © Thames and Hudson Ltd, London 1974

ISBN 0 500 05017 1

Contents

Preface   8

STUART PIGGOTT AND GLYN DANIEL

1   From the Beginnings of Man to *c.* 33,000 BC   9

CHARLES McBURNEY
University of Cambridge

Setting the scene: geographical and chronological framework · The role of France in
the growth of early prehistory · The Lower Palaeolithic and the initial population of
France · The Middle Palaeolithic stage · Conclusions

2   The Upper Palaeolithic: *c.* 33,000 – 10,000 BC   30

DENISE DE SONNEVILLE-BORDES
Centre National de la Recherche Scientifique, Bordeaux

Natural environment · The Upper Palaeolithic industries · The life of the hunter-fishers

3   From the End of the Ice Age to the First Agriculturists:
    10,000 – 4000 BC   61

MAX ESCALON DE FONTON
Centre National de la Recherche Scientifique, Marseilles

The Epipalaeolithic · The Mesolithic · The Early Neolithic · The relationship between
the natural environment and the cultural succession · Conclusions

4   The First Agriculturists: 4000 – 1800 BC   102

GERARD BAILLOUD
Centre National de la Recherche Scientifique, Paris

The Early Neolithic · The Middle Neolithic · The Late Neolithic and the Chalcolithic

5 Bronze Age Cultures: 1800 – 600 BC   131

JACQUES BRIARD
Centre National de la Recherche Scientifique, Rennes

The introduction of metallurgy · The birth of Bronze Age cultures (1800-1500 BC)
The culmination of Bronze Age cultures (1500-1200 BC) · Transition and change (1200-1000 BC) · Urnfields and the Atlantic Bronze Age (1100-800 BC) · Into a fresh era: the change from bronze to iron (800-600 BC)

6 From 600 BC to the Roman Conquest   157

F. R. HODSON
Institute of Archaeology, University of London

R. M. ROWLETT
University of Missouri, Columbia

Massalia: the literary and archaeological evidence · The sixth century BC
The fifth century BC and after · Conclusions

7 The Coming of Rome and the Establishment of Roman Gaul   192

OLWEN BROGAN
University of Cambridge

Gallia Transalpina · The campaigns of Caesar · The fashioning of Roman Gaul
Production and trade · Religion

8 Summary and Conclusions   220

GLYN DANIEL
University of Cambridge

STUART PIGGOTT
University of Edinburgh

Bibliography   224

Sources of illustrations   232

Index   234

In Memory of Dorothy Garrod

Preface

This book was planned by the late Professor Dorothy Garrod and ourselves many years ago. When she died in 1969, Dr Charles McBurney kindly and readily took over her editorial responsibility, not only for his own chapter (Chapter 1), but for Chapters 2 and 3 by Madame Denise de Sonneville-Bordes and M. Escalon de Fonton. One of us (S.P.) has been responsible editorially for Chapters 4 and 5 (by Gérard Bailloud of Paris, and Jacques Briard of Rennes) and the other (G.D.) for Chapter 6 (by F. R. Hodson of the Institute of Archaeology in the University of London, and Ralph M. Rowlett of the University of Missouri, Columbia) and Chapter 7 (by Lady (Olwen) Brogan, of Cambridge). At the end of the book we have added some minor personal comments of a general nature.

We are most appreciative of the willingness of the writers of the seven chapters – four French, three English and one American – to co-operate in this endeavour, and their patience through the long delays that have been involved. Mr John Trevitt acted for a while as assistant and adviser to the Editors; his work was then taken over by the editorial staff of Thames and Hudson. This book would not have seen the light of day without their painstaking and skilled care, and we are most grateful to them. The maps have all been drawn with his customary and characteristic skill by Mr H. A. Shelley.

STUART PIGGOTT
GLYN DANIEL

From the Beginnings of Man
to *c.* 33,000 BC
CHARLES McBURNEY

**Setting the scene: geographical
and chronological framework**

The importance of dating past events both relatively and absolutely was early recognised as a prime objective of prehistoric studies; realisation of the significance of the geographical setting is a more recent development. Today few seriously interested in studies of the past are content to ask merely what happened and when. In prehistory as in history there is a widening of the focus of interest beyond the merely descriptive to the investigation of basic causes. It is in this area above all that geography plays a leading part.

Yet it must be admitted that special difficulties attend the reconstruction of the wider environment of early cultures, and nowhere more so than in the earliest periods of all. Not merely is there the difficulty shared with later periods of abstracting the effects of recent historical society upon the environment, but there is in addition the task of appreciating the profound influence of extensive changes in climate and topography – especially notable in France – throughout the immense periods of time involved.

Some of the geographical features of France most
1 likely to be relevant to the prehistoric record are however sufficiently obvious. In a general geographical sense present-day France and Spain together represent the extremity of a broad habitable zone which, under natural conditions, would be clothed with meadowland and mixed deciduous and coniferous forest. France alone represents about one tenth of the total area of this zone. The southern margin of France forms a narrow corridor of contrasting Mediterranean-type ecology with a northward extension up the Rhône valley. The high ground of the Massif Central serves to separate this territory from the Atlantic littoral where a broad zone from the Loire to the Pyrenees combines the characteristics of both the main northern belt and the Mediterranean zone. The high plateau of Burgundy offers a less marked but still perceptible separation between the northern end of the Rhône basin and the Paris basin with the regions adjacent to the east and west. In the far south and southeast the Pyrenees and Alps form a major barrier to intercourse with Spain and central Europe respectively.

That these topographical features played a palpable part in canalising the spread of culture and fostering

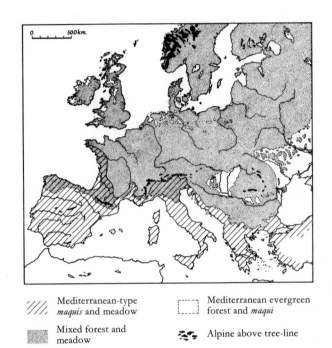

///// Mediterranean-type
       maquis and meadow

[----] Mediterranean evergreen
       forest and *maqui*

::::: Mediterranean evergreen
Mixed forest and
       meadow

Alpine above tree-line

1 Main vegetational zones of Europe

local variants will become apparent at many stages in French prehistory, and can already be detected in the archaeological record of the Pleistocene and early post-glacial epochs.

It should be noted that during this epoch environmental conditions often differed appreciably from those of the present day. The most drastic contrasts were of course associated with the intensely cold glacial episodes known as 'glacial maxima'. It is now clearly demonstrated that the earliest arrival of man in France and Europe pre-dates at least three such maxima. At their climax these were sufficiently severe to induce permanently frozen ground or 'permafrost' conditions as far *2* south as the Loire (Poser 1947). Comparable conditions are hardly found today outside the Arctic and high Alpine regions. Among further major effects two were of special importance to human geography. The first was the spread of glaciers to form ice-caps such as are now found in Greenland and Iceland. The main ice-cap was in northern Europe and covered at its maximum an

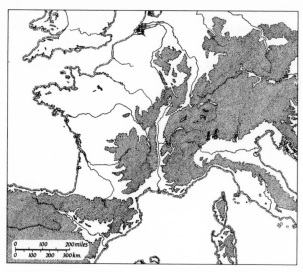

2 *Topography of France in relation to southwestern Europe: stippled area over 366 m. (1200 ft) above sea-level*

area from Scandinavia south towards a line extending roughly east-southeast from the Thames valley to the middle Don in central Russia, north of the Caspian.

A second, far smaller, ice-cap spread radially from the Alps, leaving a non-glaciated corridor in central Europe some 200 miles wide from north to south. Still smaller mountain glaciers of relatively trivial extent occurred in the Pyrenees, the Massif Central, the Carpathians, the Appenines, and elsewhere. The result of all these was of course to intensify the general trend of the climate and produce secondary consequential changes in geology and topography of almost equal importance to man. Thus the accumulation of moisture in the form of ice on land led to a world-wide lowering of the sea-level, extending the coastline to seaward and on repeated occasions actually joining Britain to the Low Countries and hence to France. Conversely the recurrent melting of ice during the interglacials gave rise to heightening of the sea-level to, on occasion, 30-40 m. above the present. This in turn resulted in the submergence of the estuarine reaches of river valleys and substantial topographical changes.

During the glacial maxima much of northern France, together with the greater part of central and east central Europe south of the ice sheet, were subject to the deposition of great blankets of wind-blown dust 3 known as 'loess'. These imply conditions of strong winds coupled with low humidity and consequently low vegetation-cover, all features confirmed by the microscopic study of fossil pollen contained in them and in contemporary formations. Thus multiple environmental changes contingent on the climate affected in turn the distribution of plant, animal, and human communities and the nature of the cultural response. Yet, broadly speaking, a subdivision into three ecological territories remains valid for France at this time despite changes of emphasis at the glacial peaks; the northern

province was characterised by steppe species and connected with similar environments in Britain and central Europe, the southwesterly province graded into substantially more genial conditions and acted even at the height of the glacial maxima to some extent as a refuge area for more warmth-adapted species, and no doubt human cultures as well. Finally, studies of fossil pollen have shown that the Mediterranean province to the southeast continued to share the relatively greater degree of warmth and dryness of other regions of the circum-Mediterranean sphere, even during the cold 2 climates of the ice age (Firbas 1939).

While the more particular effects on man of these periodic changes, in as far as they can be detected or suspected, will be discussed in the course of the detailed accounts to follow, it may be useful to tabulate briefly at this point what is known of the succession and duration of the episodes and their current nomenclature. It should be added that the picture has changed considerably over the last decade from that familiar from earlier textbooks. This is a result both of substantial advances in method and of the accruing volume of research. Particularly notable has been the development of a variety of radiometric methods of time measurement, which now overlap to provide at least an outline 4 chronology in years for much of the material. Up to a short time ago it had been widely accepted that the sequence was a good deal simpler and more clearly established than the table would suggest. Two factors in particular have underlined the need for us to give the matter further consideration. The first was the advent

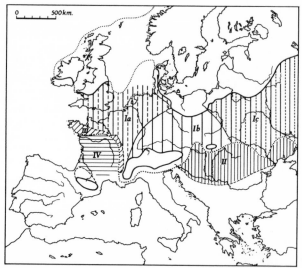

3 *Climatic and vegetational zones in western Europe during the last glacial maximum (after West 1968). Ia, permafrost with little summer warmth. Glacial-maritime province. Ib, permafrost with least summer warmth. Ic, glacial-continental province. II, permafrost with warmer summers and forest vegetation. III, no permafrost but little summer warmth and forest vegetation. Maritime tundra vegetation. IV, maritime climate with forest vegetation*

DESCRIPTION	ALPINE AREA	NW EUROPE	BRITAIN	EUROPEAN USSR	RADIOMETRIC TIME ESTIMATES (terminal dates BP[1])
Last Glacial	*Würm*	*Weichsel*	*Weichsel*	*Waldai*	10,000
Last Interglacial	Riss-Würm	Eem	Ipswichian	Mikulino	70,000
Penultimate Glacial (Late stadial)	*Riss*	*Warthe*	*Gipping?*	*Moscow*	100,000
Interstadial (Early stadial)	? *Riss*	Saale-Warthe Saale	? *Gipping*	Odinzovo Dniepr	125,000 170,000
Penultimate Interglacial	Mindel-Riss	Holstein	Hoxnian?	Lichwin	> 200,000
Ante-Penultimate Glacial	*Mindel*	*Elster*	*Lowestoft?*	*Oka*	> 300,000
Ante-penultimate Interglacial	Gunz-Mindel	Cromerian	Cromerian	Belovezhsky	
Ante-penultimate Glacial	*Gunz*	*Menapian*	*Beestonian*	*Apsheron*	
Earlier Glacial and interglacial stages					

4 Outline of European glaciations

of a serious basis for time estimate, and the second the unexpected discovery that the deep sea bottom preserved a far more continuous record of climatic change throughout the Pleistocene than most terrestrial sequences. Whereas the latter are necessarily broken by the very nature of the geological events they reflect, the former embody an unbroken record in the slow but continuous accumulation of fine deposits of ooze. These oozes are found on analysis to be composed largely of stratified remains of microscopic organisms, capable of giving biological and chemical evidence of temperature change coupled with physical (mainly radioactive) evidence of their age.

Thus while many difficulties still remain to be resolved sufficient progress has now been made in linking the terrestrial indications of various geological events to the directly dated temperature record of the sea bottom. This in turn has had a profound effect on our whole picture of the changing world of ice-age man. Perhaps the most significant single contribution is the resultant time-perspective and the way it affects certain crucial events in the evolution of human culture.

The main alterations to the traditional scheme have been the addition of a multiplicity of earlier cold stages of more or less comparable duration and extent (Emiliani 1961), together with a growing realisation of the importance of lesser oscillations termed 'interstadials' in the case of the milder sub-phases. As a recent summary has put it: 'the correlation of pre-Eemian interglacials across Northern Europe is not clear, because of the problematical nature of the interval between the Saale-Warthe and Dniepr-Moscow glacial advances' (West 1968). Nevertheless the new evidence is undoubtedly giving rise to a much more realistic picture of the environmental complexity of early human settlement throughout western Europe.

The role of France in the growth of early prehistory

In the minds of most laymen and not a few specialists in other branches of prehistory, France ranks as the *fons et origo* of the earliest Stone Age studies, that is to say of

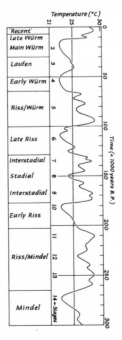

5 Temperature changes of the European later Middle and Upper Pleistocene as recorded in deep-sea cores and dated by Ph/Th (after Emiliani 1961 and West 1968)

[1] Considerably higher dates have been offered by Shackleton and Opdyke, 1973. – Ed.

the whole vast period preceding the Neolithic and the invention of agriculture. Although there is indeed much truth in this point of view, and this chapter will be mainly concerned with enlarging upon it, it is essential at the outset to point to some of the landmarks of current work outside France, and indeed to some lesser-known discoveries as well, which all help to place French researches and discoveries in a more precise perspective.

To take perhaps the most famous contribution of all, that of Boucher de Perthes establishing the coexistence of tool-making man with a wide range of extinct mammals, there can be no serious doubt that his publications *On the Creation* (1838), (quoted in Bibby 1957) and his later and more famous *Antiquités Celtiques* (1847) laid the foundations for the realisation of human antiquity by the great majority of scientists. Although de Perthes was by no means the first to arrive at this idea, and it is difficult at this distance of time to be certain how far he did so independently, the fact is that its general acceptance owes more to his determined advocacy and sustained field observations than to any other worker.

Nevertheless he worked at a time when, for two generations at least, the same ideas had been stirring in other minds. John Frere's prophetic suggestion in 1799 (based on his discovery of hand-axes at Hoxne, Suffolk) is perhaps the most explicit and percipient: 'The situation in which these weapons were found may tempt us to refer them to a very remote period indeed; even beyond that of the present world', but a generation or more later, in the decade immediately preceding the publication of *Antiquités Celtiques*, R. A. C. Austin (1838) announced the discovery of flint implements and bones of extinct animals *in situ* beneath stalagmite in Kent's Cavern near Torquay, Devon, and similar claims had been made by Schmerling in Belgium and Tournal (Lyell 1868) in southern France. It is true that sceptics countered their claims by a variety of objections. Among these (ignoring Frere's perfectly valid observations) was the supposed lack of similar traces outside caves. Already at this time the widespread occurrence of gravels of fluviatile origin in the neighbourhood of modern rivers but at higher levels and clearly far older, containing abundant remains of extinct mammalia, was widely recognised. Dean Buckland had explained this circumstance as due to the effects of the Biblical Flood; for this reason the gravels were referred to as 'diluvium', and accordingly any remains geologically preceding them as 'antediluvian'.

Thus de Perthes was already aware, at the outset of his researches, of the geological antiquity of some of the fluviatile deposits of the Somme basin.[1] Nor was the idea of the artificial nature of hand-axes as such new in his day. Their earliest recognition as signs of human activity goes back at least to the seventeenth century; and although such ideas were sporadic and may have been unknown to de Perthes at the time, they neverthe-

[1] The publications of Dr Rigollot (1819 for instance) on the nature of the contained mammalian fauna can hardly have failed to have been on his shelves at the time.

less serve to show that the deduction that hand-axes were artifacts was not in itself a very difficult one even at this time. Nevertheless it would be doing de Perthes less than justice to suggest that his realisation of the contemporaneity of man-made artifacts with very ancient geological deposits was not in many respects an independent one. Apart from this, what we owe him above all is the energy with which he propagated his notions and forced them upon contemporaries bound by preconceptions and prejudices. He thus achieved what was undoubtedly one of the great revolutions of natural philosophy, destined to open the vast landscape of prehistoric researches perhaps more effectively than any other single worker concerned with human past.

It should be added that a measure of his success was certainly due also to the exceptional richness of the deposits with which he was primarily concerned. In the Somme valley and adjacent regions of the Seine basin, both easily recognisable prehistoric artifacts and exceptionally clear geological successions containing them are abundant. Indeed it is only within the last generation, and to a considerable extent within the last decade, that discoveries in other regions both within and outside France have begun to replace the Somme as the standard framework for the earliest stages of human development. L. de Lamothe, V. Commont, H. Breuil, F. E. Zeuner, W. B. Wright, and more recently, F. Bordes, are among the names of well-known specialists who have successively erected systems of prehistoric chronology of wide import on the evidence collected from this area. Were all the lecture courses, popular books, and learned papers written on the subject to be gathered together they would certainly run to many thousands and fill a substantial library. The terms Chellean, Abbevillian, and above all Acheulean, known to all with even the vaguest acquaintance with prehistory, derive from find spots in this area. Recognised before the end of the century, with more or less reason or even no reason at all they have since been applied to finds as far apart as southern Africa and India. Thus, subsequent to the pioneering work of de Perthes, the work of many specialists combined to assign to this area of gravel pits and alluvial deposits, scarcely 200 × 100 km. in extent, a central place in the development of early world prehistory. Among these perhaps the most influential of all, after de Perthes himself, was the Abbé Henri Breuil. This great figure in European prehistory, whose opinion for many years carried more weight than that of any other prehistorian alive at the time, had made his initial reputation in the study of Upper Palaeolithic art in the caves of southwestern France and Spain, and in the study of cave stratigraphy in the same general region. It was indeed mainly owing to his efforts that many misleading ideas that dogged the early development of Palaeolithic archaeology were swept away. In a sense, on the tide of these successes he turned confidently to the analysis of problems of the Lower and Middle Palaeolithic in northern France soon after the First World War. Even if the last twenty years or so have seen the abandonment of many of his cherished conceptions, it remains nonetheless a fact that the impetus of Palaeolithic researches owes a great deal to his energies and enthusiasm at this time.

Basically this phase in the development of the subject opens towards 1900 with the geological researches of L. de Lamothe (1911, 1918) and Ch. Depéret (1906, 1918), and the still valuable if less publicised fieldwork of V. Commont (1909, 1910a and b), devoted mainly to the painstaking linking of archaeological finds with meticulously observed geological profiles. The most important contribution of the first two, destined to have widespread repercussions, was their newly developed hypothesis of world-wide fluctuations in sea-level. These were destined to become an important and permanent element in our understanding of Quaternary events in general, although there was at first considerable confusion regarding the true nature and causation of these phenomena. When Breuil proposed his synthesis, combining the geological and archaeological results available in the first two decades following the First World War, two further concepts had already begun to take shape. Before the work of Lamothe and Depéret, the existence of high-level marine deposits (and to a lesser extent buried terrestrial formations below sea-level) of comparatively recent Quaternary date had been not infrequently observed, but it had been widely supposed that all were due to localised movements of the earth's crust. The new contribution lay in massive evidence showing that in addition to purely localised movements of the land against a stable sea there were also independent movements of the sea. These were registered geologically in stable areas of coastline in many areas throughout the world during the greater part of the Pleistocene, and reached an amplitude on occasion of some hundreds of feet.

This radical discovery, although today a commonplace of Quaternary geology, took time to achieve general acceptance; even today the precise amplitude and sequence of the fluctuations is the subject of continuing discussion. Clearly the practical issue in any particular case – the correlation, say, of two widely separated archaeological finds each related to a given sea-level – must turn on 'tectonic stability', that is to say the extent to which localised crustal movement can be eliminated in each case. In the nature of things it is to be expected that although progress in these studies enables a clear-cut statement in some instances, in others the evidence may simply not exist to dispel all uncertainty one way or the other.

At the time of which we are speaking, immediately following the First World War, an increasing number of the younger generation of both archaeologists and geologists were eagerly espousing the new ideas. Among the first was Henri Breuil (1932, 1934, 1936, 1937, 1939), soon to be followed by the English geologist, W. B. Wright (1939), F. E. Zeuner (1945) of Germany and an impressive array of workers in cognate fields. Some of these, it must be allowed, seem at this remove to have shown more enthusiasm than caution, and this might on occasion be claimed for each of the three

referred to by name. At the time continuing opponents of international standing included the veteran French palaeontologist, Marcelin Boule, and his faithful pupil, Raymond Vaufrey.

Two new aspects of this work which also emerged about this time and served to encourage the protagonists of the application to archaeology, were the realisation that (1) major high sea-levels (where they could be substantiated) were specifically indicative of warm interglacial conditions, while (2) substantial low levels indicated the cold conditions of glacial maxima.

The significance of this discovery lay above all in its potential for direct correlation between widely separated prehistoric finds and their dating with reference to the newly established multiple peaks of climate change during the Ice Age. This latter concept, the 'polyglacial' theory as it was termed, had gradually come to replace the 'monoglacial' theory of the late-nineteenth-century geologists, mainly as a result of the classic researches of A. Penck and E. Brückner (1901-1909) on the glacial history of the Alps in the early years of this century. By the end of the First World War their new scheme had come to be widely accepted among Quaternary specialists, and the work of correlating biological evolution and the broad subdivisions of the Palaeolithic with the new framework had already begun. To some of the older workers in the field such as Boule, this task appeared to offer few difficulties. At about this time he published the categoric pronouncement that the earliest traces of man and a number of fossil species of mammal could not conceivably go back farther than the beginning of the Last Interglacial (or 'Eemian Period' to use present-day nomenclature). In fairness it should be borne in mind, when attempting to understand these pioneering debates, that up to this time (despite some inspired guesses, like that of Lyell) nothing resembling an acceptable time-scale of dates in years for these events of earth-history as yet existed. With these in mind it is today easy to see that biological events such as the evolutionary changes in the earliest species of elephant associated with man could not possibly have taken place during the 30,000-40,000 years now known to have been occupied by the Eem.

Lamothe had distinguished the last high sea-levels of the Pleistocene as occurring at 60 m., 30 m. and 18 m. in descending order of age. On studying the topography of the Somme valley he came to the conclusion that the river had regraded its bed in response to these, leaving a shelf or 'terrace' flattening out downstream to meet each of these levels at its mouth. These terraces were subsequently abandoned by the river when the general sea-level fell during the succeeding (glacial) episode. Only one terrace could be recognised in almost its entirety – that reaching the sea at about 30 m. above its present level. It maintained a profile roughly parallel to the modern river, and together with its fluviatile cover was referred to as the sheet of St Acheul. Two others surviving in parts could be projected to reach the sea at about 50 m. and 18 m. respectively below the present sea-level. These last were the sheet of the Ferme de *6*

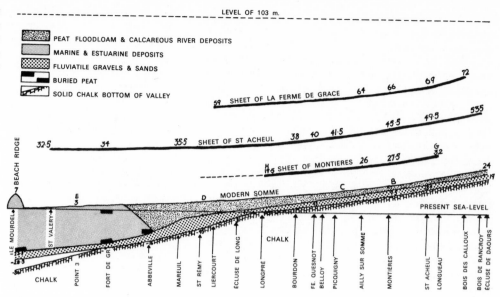

6 Longitudinal section of terraces of the Somme after de Lamothe (1918). The sheet of La Ferme de Grâce carries the oldest traces

LEVEL OF 103 m.

PEAT FLOODLOAM & CALCAREOUS RIVER DEPOSITS
MARINE & ESTUARINE DEPOSITS
FLUVIATILE GRAVELS & SANDS
BURIED PEAT
SOLID CHALK BOTTOM OF VALLEY

59 SHEET OF LA FERME DE GRACE 64 66 69 72

32·5 34 35·5 SHEET OF ST ACHEUL 38 40 41·5 45·5 49·5 53·5

11·5 SHEET OF MONTIERES 26 27·5 G 32 24

BEACH RIDGE

MODERN SOMME

PRESENT SEA-LEVEL

CHALK

ILE MOURDEL · ST VALERY · POINT 3 · FORT DE GR · ABBEVILLE · MAREUIL · ST RÉMY · LIERCOURT · ECLUSE DE LONG · LONGPRÉ · BOURDON · FE. QUESNOT · BELLOY · PICQUIGNY · AILLY SUR SOMME · MONTIÈRES · ST ACHEUL · LONGUEAU · BOIS DES CALLOUX · BOIS DE RANCROY · ECLUSE DE DAOURS

CHALK

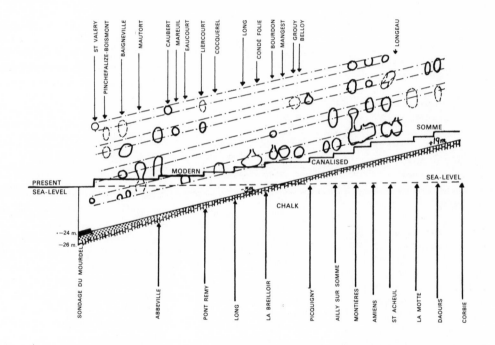

7 Profile of the 30 m. terrace of the Somme (after Commont)

ST VALERY · PINCHEFALIZE-BOISMONT · BAIGNEVILLE · MAUTORT · CAUBERT · MAREUIL · EAUCOURT · LIERCOURT · COCQUEREL · LONG · CONDE FOLIE · BOURDON · MANGEST · GROUY · BELLOY · LONGEAU

SOMME

CANALISED +19m

MODERN

PRESENT SEA-LEVEL

SEA-LEVEL

CHALK

−24 m.
−26 m.

SONDAGE DU MOURDEL · ABBEVILLE · PONT REMY · LONG · LA BREILLOIR · PICQUIGNY · AILLY SUR SOMME · MONTIÈRES · AMIENS · ST ACHEUL · LA MOTTE · DAOURS · CORBIE

Grace and of Montière respectively. Commont followed a somewhat similar system of interpretation and, in the course of many years of fieldwork on ballast pits attributable to the terraces, and collation of earlier workers' discoveries, noted the presence of Lower Pleistocene mammals and (possibly later) hand-axes on the Upper or Ferme de Grace terrace, further hand-axes with a Middle Pleistocene fauna on the Middle (St Acheul) Terrace, while the earliest Middle Palaeolithic occurred with Upper Pleistocene forms on the Lower (Montière) Terrace. The latter was further subdivided by Breuil and others into two subsidiary features called the higher and lower Low terraces respectively.

In reaching his pioneering chronology for the early settlement of France, Breuil accordingly relied on three recent discoveries: the polyglacial theory of Penck and Brückner, the theory of glacially controlled eustasis (or sea-level change), and finally the correlation of fluviatile deposits in river estuaries with sea-levels and hence with specific phases of the Ice Age. It was in this latter area that he was to offer a number of original suggestions that held the field for many years. After embarking on a number of purely geological investigations aimed at explaining the mode of formation, weathering, subsequent displacement and so forth, in a word the geological history of the various tool-bearing deposits of the terraced deposits of the Somme, he proposed a detailed comprehensive scheme. This in effect arranged the numerous and varied exposures yielding man-made tools into some twenty separate stages, extending over the last three main episodes of Penck and Brückner's scheme of glacial maxima. In terms of modern chronometric results this indicated a duration for human occupation in the Somme valley (and hence by implication of western Europe) of some 300,000-400,000 years – say roughly five times as long as Boule's original conception would have implied.

Breuil's scheme for this vast increase in antiquity of well known types of archaeological find was as tenaciously opposed by his contemporaries as had been Boucher de Perthes' in his day. This opposition was still continued in some quarters long after research outside France had amply confirmed the general reasonableness of his contentions. To say this however is not to endorse the validity of all the arguments he used, some of which may today be regarded as fragile, to say the least. Among these latter must be placed the extent to which he pushed the newly developed 'eustatic' reasoning. In this he was by no means alone and the same criticisms could equally be levelled at workers such as F. E. Zeuner and W. B. Wright in his later years. Briefly it would be said by most geologists now that they sought to use the undoubted effects of sea-level change to explain geological events too far removed from the sea itself and hence falsified the dating of a certain number of archaeologically important sites.

Nevertheless the broad principles that all these workers, and Breuil in particular, sought to pioneer, undoubtedly led the way to many modern conceptions of prehistory and prepared the ground to an important degree for the full application and acceptance of many current discoveries, especially in the field of absolute time measurement.

A less fortunate outcome of Breuil's own work, and one which may be claimed to have had the reverse effect was, curiously enough, his treatment of the actual archaeological material itself, although it is only fair to add that some of his discredited conclusions owed not a little to the climate of opinion of his day. Broadly speaking the least valid of his conclusions were in the field of classification and cultural interpretation. They may be said to have sprung from an altogether too 'geological' approach to what were essentially cultural issues. One effect of the new long chronology was to spread out the archaeological finds over a much longer time span. This in turn encouraged Breuil to see in any observable differences of tool-type or technology the characteristics of 'stages' in cultural evolution, valid by implication over wide areas and vast intervals of time.

Neither Breuil nor any other prehistorian of his generation seems really to have thought through the full import of such a concept, let alone applied the scientific tests appropriate to fundamental propositions of this kind. That his ideas should have taken so firm a root and exerted so lasting an influence requires indeed some special explanation. Two factors can be recog-

nised. On the one hand most Palaeolithic archaeologists of the day were impressed by the typological subdivisions established for the later periods of prehistory. On the other hand there was also the profound and continuing influence of the concept of biological evolution. Evolution was by this time a fact which no thinking prehistorian could fail to take into account, and it seemed an obvious corollary that cultural evolution should have followed the same general pattern as anatomical, and consequently that orderly stages in the unfolding of human culture were to be expected.

On the strength of these premises, Breuil proceeded to subdivide the sequence of changes in the Lower and Middle Palaeolithic of the Seine basin into some 15 phases: Abbevillian (previously Chellean), Clactonian I-II, Acheulean Stages I-VI, Levalloisian Stages I-VI. Although the precise features of the stages were never published in detail other than by the illustration of 'representative' specimens, (the notion of quantitative assessment simply did not exist at this time) Breuil was fully prepared to use his classifications in relatively distant territories such as Italy, Belgium, Germany, etc.

Several criticisms of this scheme would occur to most workers today. The first concerns allowance for sheer accidental random fluctuation in relation to the total number of specimens in each sample. To this must be added at least some allowance for functional variation, such as the differences to be expected between seasonally occupied sites, butchering sites, settlement sites and so forth. It is only when these and other disturbing factors have been offset that most modern workers would wish to deduce possible distinguishing features of separate traditions or evolutionary states within a tradition. Still less would they think of extending any but the very widest categories across huge areas and formidable geographical barriers in the manner that seemed natural to Breuil and his contemporaries. In the last resort it is probably the advent of viable time estimates over the past decade that is bringing about the greatest changes in this type of research. The realisation that the duration of relatively trivial differences in tool-kits would have to be spread over periods from 20,000 to 50,000 years has inevitably led to the abandonment of the cultural aspect of Breuil's interpretation and emphasised the necessity for an altogether more sophisticated and flexible approach, even if at the time of writing no finality in this respect has yet been achieved. Among early criticisms of Breuil's sequence were those of F. Bordes on both typological and stratigraphic grounds. If many of these still carry considerable weight, others do not. Today Breuil's long chronology probably stands better supported than it did at the time he proposed it.

A few instances will serve to show this. The first concerns the date of very early traces of man, Breuil's 'Abbevillian' stage in the Somme basin. Breuil (1939) placed this in a warm period shortly before the Mindel (ante-penultimate) glacial maximum. In this stratigraphical position in his terrace sequence Breuil thought that he could also show association with the final representatives of an early mammalian fauna known as the Villafranchian, which was independently dated to the period in question. A similar association between the earliest traces of man in Germany, in this case a human mandible, had long before been noted at Mauer. The general proposition of tool-making man in Europe at this time has recently been confirmed – by human fossils associated with a different type of artifact, at the site of Vértesszöllös in Hungary. Again, a few artifacts of a possibly similar kind have been geologically dated to the same period in the cave site of Vallonet in southern France. Finally, the precise type of tool for which Breuil made his claim in the Somme, a crude form of hand-axe, is now certainly known to have been widely current both at and before this time in tropical and northern Africa.

There is thus little left of the various *a priori* criticisms levelled at Breuil's conclusion on this particular highly significant issue, and it seems hard to deny world priority to his suggestion.

A second point in his chronological scheme of almost equal significance concerns an important cultural watershed in the European Palaeolithic succession, namely the replacement of the simple original method of flake-tool manufacture by the more effective and economic process known as 'prepared core' technique. This in fact distinguishes the later or Middle Palaeolithic from the Lower Palaeolithic in most classifications. Under favourable conditions the distinction can be confidently recognised even on a small sample of specimens, as Breuil clearly demonstrated. Here again however discussion arose on the correct stratigraphical position, and the criticisms have continued into relatively recent published works. Before Breuil's initial exposition of the Somme it had been widely accepted that the cultural event in question dated at earliest from the beginning of the Last or Würmian Glacial phase. The whole taxon of industries distinguished in this way had up to this time been known collectively as 'Mousterian'. To Breuil must go the credit of drawing attention at the outset to a readily definable distinction between 'Mousterian' artifacts and a related variant which he termed 'Levalloisian'. He was the first to note that whereas the former were mainly to be found in cave sites in hilly country, the latter were concentrated to a considerable degree in open sites in the low-lying regions on either side of the English Channel and neighbouring regions. He believed that the two manifestations were interrelated but concluded that the Levalloisian was the earlier and to a large extent ancestral stage, and he ascribed it to the cold phase immediately *preceding* the Last Interglacial; in other words to late Riss. This ageing of a well known cultural episode by a whole glacial cycle found many critics and was indeed attacked by F. Bordes as lately as 1951 in his well-known paper 'L'évolution buissonnante' already mentioned. Final proof of its correctness has however recently been made available from the Thames (Kerney and Sieveking, 1970) and with it confirmation of much of his stratigraphic system.

Thus Breuil's contribution to Lower and Middle Palaeolithic studies in the Somme, even if it contained some features which have been eventually discarded, embodied totally new findings which played no small part in the eventual development of the subject and mark a substantial breakthrough in many respects.

Nevertheless, despite these qualifications, the work of F. Bordes after the Second World War produced further valuable re-orientation of basic ideas and approach. Starting with two well-known monographs, *Les limons quaternaires du bassin de la Seine* (1954) and *Le complexe Moustérien* (with F. Bourgon, 1951) he and his co-workers have added enormously to the body of data bearing on what is now known as the Middle Palaeolithic complex. The originality of his approach resides both in his analytical methods and in his interpretations. A lively and continuing discussion has arisen, in the course of which many divergent points of view have been expressed. Yet even his most stringent critics would not wish to deny that he has brought an order and systematic approach to Middle Palaeolithic researches which they largely lacked up to this time. Briefly, he abandoned Breuil's whole scheme of numbered stages for both Acheulean and Levalloisian, substituting a new set of industrial groups which he conceives as being practised simultaneously, forming a branching rather than a unilinear pattern of evolution. It would be hard to imagine a more radical reappraisal from the typological point of view of Breuil's standpoint.

A further interpretation developed by Bordes concerns the change to the Upper Palaeolithic, characterised by a variety of well-marked technological innovations together with re-orientations of tool-form. For Breuil the advent of the Upper Palaeolithic was best explained as the introduction of an exotic tradition developed outside the area of southwest Europe, and probably (in his estimation) due to a human strain indistinguishable from modern man, as opposed to the sharply differentiated Neandertal type responsible for the Mousterian. This 'invasion hypothesis' has been strongly criticised by many authors in recent years, although still supported implicitly or explicitly by others. Whatever the truth of the matter may eventually prove to be, there can be no doubt as a matter of historical fact that Bordes' work, based entirely on his classification of the lithic industries, has been extensively used to support the opposite point of view, namely that modern man and his cultural tradition developed indigenously in southwestern France.

These in broad outline were the main phases in the development of French thought regarding the Lower and Middle Palaeolithic which may serve as a brief introduction to our account of the present stage reached by investigations.

The Lower Palaeolithic and the initial population of France

We have seen that in its day the sequence gradually worked out for the Somme and adjacent areas of northern France served as the standard conception of early human development virtually throughout the world. If this is no longer the case it is due not so much to any major shift in the interpretation of the French evidence, as to the great strides made in Palaeolithic researches elsewhere. In fact we have seen that many pioneering suggestions put forward by certain French workers of the past, for long criticised and opposed by their colleagues, have turned out to be fully justified. What has altered above all is the context of these finds and the way they have now been joined in a synthesis which lends them further and more precise significance than they previously possessed.

In no field of enquiry is this more strikingly the case than that concerned with the initial peopling of southwestern Europe by man. It should be obvious today that such a problem involves something more than the usual generalities of prehistoric and proto-historic discussions. In seeking to understand the peopling of a new area at any time during the past 30,000 years it is probably adequate, at any rate at the outset, to think in terms of comparable events that can be studied over recent historical times. But when dealing with events as vast as those under consideration, other factors of a basically biological nature must also be taken into account. These arise in part from the time-scale. It is in this field especially that the discoveries of the past decade or so play a highly significant role, above all those in Africa. The initial discovery was that of a substantial period or culture phenomenon in this area *preceding* the first appearance of hand-axes in the record, and characterised by the very much simpler and less specialised artifacts known as pebble-tools. These were simply, more or less randomly flaked jagged edges produced by bold trimming of natural pebbles. Suspected since the early twenties, these were not satisfactorily demonstrated to be man-made till L.S.B. Leakey's researches at Olduvai in northern Tanzania early in the 1930s. At first these were regarded as representing an event of the same order of magnitude as the hand-axe techno-complex itself. The date of the culture interface was estimated to be roughly the same as Breuil had suggested for the earliest hand-axes in the Somme, i.e. linked to a loosely defined phase of mammalian evolution terminating the so-called Villafranchian epoch of the Lower Pleistocene.

It was not until radio-active time estimates (based on the potassium: argon ratio in volcanic minerals) became available, that it was realised that the new 'stage' was nothing less than the opening epoch of human culture as such which lasted considerably longer than the whole of the subsequent process of human development down to the present. This was subsequently confirmed in northern Africa by the recent geological researches of P. Biberson. The real significance of this immense gestatory period resides not only in its sheer duration but also in the implications that arise from it.

Thus, if we compare the period involved to the known rates of evolution in other animals, we can hardly avoid the conclusion that human evolution itself was an important factor in the pattern of cultural change. In 1952 F. Bourdier announced the discovery of a single flake of apparently artificial origin *in situ* in a very high-level fluviatile deposit in the Somme, truncated by (and hence antecedent to) that containing the association claimed by d'Ault du Mesnil (1893) between terminal Villafranchian mammals and crude hand-axes. It would follow that this highly probable human artifact type belongs at latest to a late Lower Pleistocene age. This first find, not inconsistent with the Mauer mandible referred to above, was soon followed by two others which seem to clinch the matter fairly conclusively. The first of these was of geologically dated occupation traces in the cave of Vallonet, in Provence (de Lumley 1963). Here in a deposit preserved by exceptionally favourable circumstances, underlain by evidences of a cold climate and succeeded by a high sea-level no less than 106 m. above the present, was a rich and typical mammalian fauna of Villafranchian (that is to say clearly Lower Pleistocene) type associated with four highly probable chipped stone artifacts. They comprise one flake and three artificially trimmed nodules. The former is reported to show indications of having been struck from a pebble-tool of the type associated with Australopithecine hominids in east Africa and with typical Villafranchian mammals in Algeria.

If these two recent finds were to be fully substantiated they would strongly suggest that the first human beings to reach Europe were the contemporaries of the later Australopithecines of east Africa. They could conceivably belong to the evolved variant termed by some palaeontologists *Homo habilis*. Both the term and the concept are however subject to discussion at the present time, so that it would be unwise to press this conclusion too far as yet, but the possibility is certainly an interesting one. The period suggested would be perhaps most reasonably estimated as in the order of a million years, if account is taken of two circumstances. First, that approximately three-quarters of a million years ago the capacity to make recognisable hand-axes was already a widespread characteristic of African hominids. This could accordingly provide a not unreasonable limit for the earliest group of settlers in Europe, who seem to have been ignorant of this tool form. A world sea-level in the order of 100 m. above the present is attested in many parts of the world, and although not so far directly dated radiometrically, is everywhere an event of great antiquity and nowhere later than the Lower Pleistocene in palaeontological terms.

Secondly, if it is accepted that the most likely point of entry for prehistoric immigrants from Africa lay across the Straits of Gibraltar, then one would expect central Europe to be peripheral to such a movement and to subsequent movements from the same source, and hence to be the ultimate area of survival of each earlier wave of expansion. That this was in fact the case is strongly suggested by the finds at Vértesszöllös. Here a rich assemblage of artifacts in a purely 'pebble-tool' tradition are associated with a local and undoubted late Villafranchian type of micro-mammalian fauna known as the Biharian. Fragmentary associated human remains represent a type of man certainly more advanced than *Homo habilis*, but perhaps of comparable status to the earliest hand-axe makers in Africa, to judge from preliminary reports. Elsewhere in central Europe the rarity of hand-axes of all forms especially those of primitive technique, is notorious, whereas reports of early dated pebble-tools are accumulating. A group from an early geological horizon at Sedlec near Prague is a case in point.

It would seem to follow that, despite their exiguous nature, recently discovered evidences for a pre-hand-axe using group in Europe substantially earlier than the penultimate glacial are neither *a priori* unreasonable nor unexpected.

Another problem is posed by the date and character of the earliest hand-axe makers themselves. In some ways this is a still more elusive issue. Even if we grant, as we surely must, that a likely minimum age for the beginning of this episode is *c.* 400,000 BP, say perhaps during or shortly before the Mindel glaciation of the Alps, it must be confessed that closer positive indications are still tenuous. A date of 350,000 for Mindel has been obtained by the K/A method (Shotton 1966) for an apparent geological equivalent in the Rhine valley, at some distance from the relevant moraines in the Alps. It is not as yet possible to confirm this figure owing to uncertainty inherent in geological correlations of this kind, and to further uncertainties in the chronometric reading itself. This is based on a K/A ratio and although the validity of this method in principle has been clearly confirmed by independent tests, the fact remains that 'rogue' determinations can and do still occur. Nevertheless a general figure exceeding 200,000 BP for what may still be referred to as the 'Mindel-Riss Interglacial' has now been estimated by two alternative methods, so that the order of magnitude at least of Mindel is no longer in serious doubt. On the other hand we have as yet nothing like a detailed picture of the complex of episodes included under the terms of both 'Riss' or 'Mindel'. That at least one glacial advance (and probably several) comparable in extent to Riss and Würm took place at about this time has long been clear. It is also virtually demonstrated that the Villafranchian mammals did not outlast the episode however we define it. It follows that if the association claimed by d'Ault du Mesnil between crude hand-axes and a terminal Villafranchian fauna on the 40 m. terrace of the Somme at Abbeville could be finally confirmed, then a minimum date in the order of 350,000 would have to be accepted with all that that implies for the earliest hand-axe makers elsewhere in Europe.

Unfortunately, despite various claims and a brief re-excavation by Breuil in 1935, the question of the association, let alone the typological status of the artifacts in modern terms, still remains unsettled. Nor can the issue be indirectly settled from evidence elsewhere. The very existence of a typological stage of the kind envisaged by Breuil still has to be proved conclusively anywhere in Europe, notwithstanding the fact that it is certainly attested in Africa and probably in southwest Asia as well. Indeed until the statistical method of D. A. Roe (first proposed in 1964) became available virtually the only approach was one based on a hypothetical evolutionary sequence. Thus while the nature and variation of human tools made during the Mindel-Riss is becoming rapidly clearer as a result of new methods of analysis, and the high degree of skill in toolmaking throughout the greater part at least of this long period is evident, only scattered indications are available to suggest the nature of a possible earlier phase in Europe itself. A remarkable elephant-butchering site discovered in the last century at Ambrona in the Upper Ebro valley in northern Spain has recently been re-excavated and found to contain a rather massive hand-axe assemblage with auxiliary tools and bones *in situ*. This is now assigned by K. A. Bützer (1964) to the period immediately preceding the interglacial in question, *i.e.* to late Mindel. The fauna is certainly more evolved than that found at Abbeville, and the tool assemblage likewise more evolved than that claimed by d'Ault du Mesnil.

No assemblages exactly like those at Ambrona have in fact ever been recovered from any European site, though isolated specimens falling within the supposed range of variation have been reported from time to time from geologically early horizons. A specimen from a very early terrace of the upper Thames at Hanborough in Oxfordshire is a case in point (W. J. Arkell 1947, etc.). At one time a true assemblage from an apparently pre-Mindel-Riss formation known as the Caversham Channel, between Reading and Marlow on the middle Thames, was claimed to show typologically archaic features. Both the character and the dating have subsequently been called in question, and the situation at the time of writing is still not clear. Again on the basis of Roe's new method of analysis (Roe 1964) a single hand-axe assemblage from Farnborough in a possibly pre-Mindel-Riss horizon shows typological distinctions which separate it from the remaining certainly Mindel-Riss finds and are more in accord with those claimed for Abbeville.

In conclusion it cannot any longer be said with confidence that an 'Abbevillian' (or as an older generation would have called it, 'Chellean') stage was ever practised in Europe. This remains a possibility but no more. Pre-Mindel-Riss hand-axe manufacture of some kind is, all things considered, likely despite the uncertainty of its archaeological distinguishing features. It is quite possible that when finally isolated it will turn out to be more similar to the later assemblages than used to be supposed. Although the developmental antecedents of this industrial form were certainly registered in Africa, it seems possible that they may not have reached Europe till a relatively advanced stage of development, some time during or immediately after the Mindel glaciation.

As to the later development of the auxiliary tools associated with hand-axes, here again it is to be noted that time-honoured evolutionary notions, repeated in scores of textbooks since the beginning of the century,

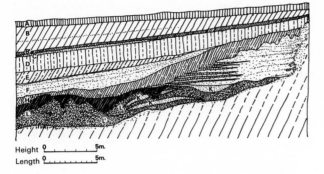

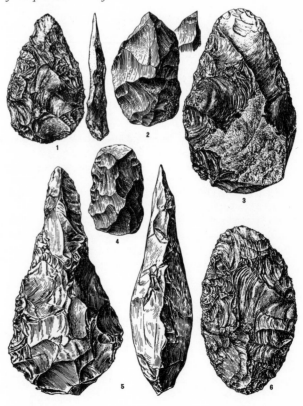

8 *Section of the 30 m. terrace of the Somme (after Commont). The workshop site comes from Layer H. A-B, loess; D, weathered loess; E, older loess; F, H, slope deposit with solifluction; L, K, fluviatile*

have evaporated under the closer scrutiny of modern research. An example is offered by the history of a remarkable workshop site at St Acheul discovered by V. Commont in the Somme shortly before the First World War and published posthumously by F. Bordes (1953). Known in the literature as the Atelier Commont, it offered a concentrated scatter of implements evidently the traces of a single camp-site occupied by one hunting group for a few days or weeks. When re-examined and published from the original field notes by F. Bordes, it appeared that one of the most striking features were the variety and relatively high finish of the tools ranging from large highly finished hand-axes to relatively small and delicate trimmed flakes. All would appear to have been made and used by one group of hunters at one time. Individually and collectively these implements would certainly have been regarded as 'late' in the supposed evolutionary succession as originally conceived, and assigned in time to the Last Interglacial or even the early part of Würm. In fact their geological context is such that they cannot be later than an early stage of Riss, since they occur in a terrestrial formation *overlying* fluviatile gravels of Last Interglacial date but *underlying* a loess of certain Rissian age.

Outside France an almost identical assemblage is that already mentioned from Hoxne where traces of multiple settlements are associated without question to an unmistakable Mindel-Riss interglacial flora. Clear evidence from mollusca in the Thames valley shows that a land connection between Britain and the Low Countries was established for a short period at least, at or close to this time. The evidence comes from Swanscombe on the '100 ft' or Boyne Hill terrace of the Thames, widely ascribed to the same geological age and conditions as the fluviatile gravels underlying the Atelier Commont on the Somme. The associated industry at Swanscombe also shows many of the same typological characteristics.

It is furthermore of great interest that at both Swanscombe and another site of the same age, Steinheim an der Murr in southwestern Germany, fossil remains reveal that the type of man responsible for the industries possessed an interesting combination of 'modern' features together with others of archaic character typical of an earlier stage of human evolution. Collectively these fossil finds demonstrate that by this time the prehistoric population of southwest Europe had reached an advanced stage of anatomical evolution rapidly approaching that of modern man – *Homo sapiens sapiens.*

It is interesting to compare this anatomical condition to that of the makers of the earliest hand-axes in Africa (at Olduvai in east Africa and Ternifine in Algeria) a quarter or half a million years earlier. These belonged to the so-called *Homo erectus* stage, with a substantially smaller brain and a whole range of muscular and other anatomical features more closely related to man's early hominid ancestors. It would accordingly seem that active anatomical evolution was in progress during the very long period that hand-axes were in current use. J. S. Weiner and B. G. Campbell (1964) estimate (partly on the basis of K/Ar readings) a time interval between these two forms of the order of 150,000-200,000 years.

Given a substantial human population freely interbreeding throughout western Europe, an evolutionary change of the order indicated by the two sets of fossils seems not unreasonable.

It is remarkable that throughout the time of which we are speaking there is extremely little sign of basic

9 *Hand-axes from Commont's workshop site. Note variations from pointed to oval forms*

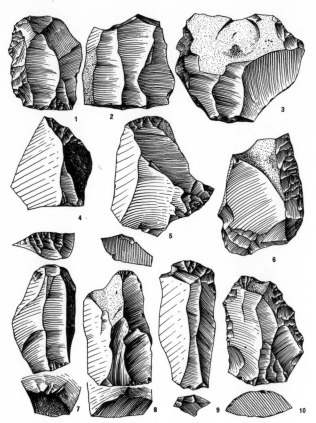

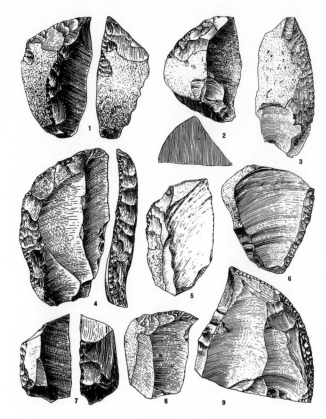

10 Commont's Acheulean workshop site : scrapers on flakes. Note wide generally plain striking platforms and thick cross-sections. Mostly terminal scrapers

11 Commont's workshop site : side-scrapers and backed flake knives. Note massive cross-section of no. 2

cultural change either in the form of the tools or in the methods used for their production. This applies equally to the hand-axes themselves and to the smaller tools made from trimmed flakes. In the main the latter comprise simply flakes with one convex or straight or occasionally irregular (denticulated) edge. There is no unequivocal sign of a 'point' suitable for mounting in a shaft or handle, such as occurs commonly in the following Mousterian period.

A kill site of this period at Lehringen in southern Germany has however produced a 4.2 m. wooden spear with fire-hardened point and carefully shaped shaft, and the tip of a second comes from a contemporary deposit near Clacton-on-Sea. From these observations it seems likely that at least a proportion of the struck flakes which normally accompany hand-axes (that is to say, wherever adequate search has been made) were intended for wood-working and the manufacture of heavy hunting weapons.[1] Little is known at present of the function of the hand-axes themselves. From sites such as Ambrona we can see that they were in regular demand and were frequently discarded on kill and

butchering sites, especially those of large animals such as elephants. From their form alone they were of course totally unsuitable as weapons. A few microscopic tests carried out by the writer have so far shown no traces of the highly characteristic kind left by working hard substances. The latter however frequently occur on both hand-axes and flake tools of more or less the same shape and size as those of the Acheulean at a later date. In general the cutting of soft substances such as meat or hide seems to leave no microscopic traces of any kind.

The geographical dispersal of stone industries of Acheulean type, with or without dating evidence throughout France, is beginning to be relatively well known. They appear in general to be significantly commoner along the low-lying river valleys of the Atlantic watershed, and grow rapidly more scarce as one ascends to higher ground or passes eastwards into the Rhône basin. Although by no means unknown in the Rhône basin, they do not show anything like the concentrations noted particularly to the northeast of France, especially in the Paris basin. There it is estimated that already by 1900 in the Somme valley and adjacent area more than twenty thousand specimens had actually been recognised in the course of some half a century's research, to say nothing of the immense numbers that must have

[1] In Africa shaped wooden clubs with prepared hand-grips have been reported (Clark 1969) from the Acheulean at Kalambo Falls.

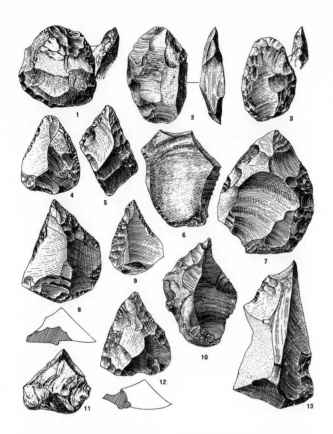

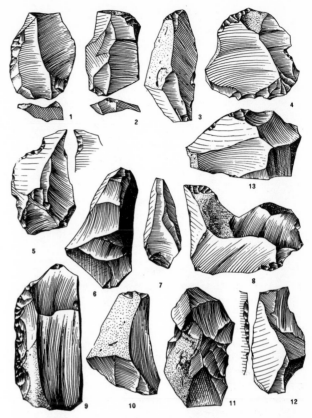

12 Commont's workshop site : double-sided scrapers

13 Commont's workshop site : various trimmed flakes. Note coarse primary flake 10, typical discoid prepared core

passed unnoticed. As one passes to the southwest along the coastal plain, find-spots continue to be recorded in appreciable numbers, although the conditions for research and preservation are not perhaps quite so favourable. Thus for geological reasons large exploitations of gravel and above all brick-earths are not so numerous. Nevertheless finds occur and are recorded from far upstream in the Garonne basin and the foothills of the Pyrenees. Here the industries are no longer made of flint but of the local crystalline rocks such as quartz and other crystalline stones. Further finds to the south across Spain link the French sites spatially to the immensely richer find areas of Africa.

The fact that the recorded finds thin out perceptibly as one passes eastwards into the Rhône basin, may be contrasted with their relative scarcity in the Italian peninsula. Eastwards again across the high ground in the Balkan peninsula they are virtually unknown, although human habitation in this area, as already pointed out, is of great antiquity. Much intensive search has established that a similar rarity can be positively deduced for the areas north and east of Belgium. To the north of the Seine basin however in southern Britain, which as we have noted was repeatedly joined to the continent, the density of finds is approximately that of northeastern France.

This distributional pattern alone is a strong argument in favour of an African origin and a point of entry specifically across the Straits of Gibraltar. It is unfortunate that so far there should be relatively little published research in this field from the Iberian peninsula, but such finds as have been made available, taking into account the amount of research, argue for a wide distribution and a density of the same order as that of, say, the Garonne basin. Various other details point in the same direction, such as the prevalence of the typical African 'cleaver' form of hand-axe in southwestern France and Spain, the early geological date suggested (if not as yet conclusively demonstrated) by the sequence of raised beaches along the Portuguese Atlantic coast, and finally a number of detailed resemblances between the probable succession in the last-named area and that established recently on the Atlantic coast of Morocco at Casablanca.

All in all, the many different types of indicator converge to offer a picture of human life in France during the epoch approximately 150,000 to 400,000 years ago, in which France lies at the centre of an area of vigorous colonisation stemming ultimately from northwest Africa. It is true that palaeontological evidence shows that at no time during this period were the two land-masses actually linked by a continuous land-bridge, but it should be noted that during glacial maxima, such as the Mindel, the width of the Straits would have been no more than 3-4 miles. Swimming is by no means the sophisticated behaviour pattern it is sometimes represented to be; on the contrary it is common to many non-aquatic genera including other primates, and there is no reason why primitive man should have been less capable in this respect, or less moved to colonise new territories, than other mammalian species. In any event, the occurrence would not have to be frequent over the immense time periods involved, in order to establish viable and vigorous populations bringing with them patterns of socially maintained behaviour.

It can hardly be denied that this view of the situation provides a reasonable explanation; economic, consistent with the known facts, and one which should be susceptible of test as information increases.

The Middle Palaeolithic stage

It is a curious and intriguing fact that after the long period just discussed, in all areas occupied by hand-axe makers, a profound modification occurs at a date somewhere between (in round figures) 100,000 and 150,000 years ago. The change is everywhere of a comparable nature, and affects a whole range of industrial practices. One noticeable feature is an overall reduction in tool size. This is a general tendency which becomes obvious if one compares, say, a group of hand-axes from a Mindel-Riss Interglacial (or equivalent age-group) with a group from the early Würm. A similar tendency has recently been reported in the east Mediterranean (Gilead 1970). The size trend with regard to flake-tools is again similar. These were long thought to be a special property of the Middle Palaeolithic; they have now been shown to occur in quantity as early as the Mindel-Riss Interglacial in some (but possibly not all) tool assemblages. From the late Riss onwards they form the dominant tool class numerically.

In respect of size the distinction between the two stages is one of degree rather than of kind. In another respect however the reverse is true, namely in the primary processes of flake-tool manufacture – those aimed at the production of 'blanks' destined to be trimmed into standardised or more specialised forms. The new method of production has been named 'Levallois' or more generally 'prepared core' technique. The observable characteristics have been studied quantitatively by the present writer, and by F. Bordes, from metrical and class-analytical points of view respectively. An interesting point which arises from the former is that the new technique not only provided manifestly greater control of form than earlier techniques but resulted in an important economy of raw material (of the order of 30-40%). This is equally true of both the European and south and east Mediterranean collections studied by the writer.

In the older method of manufacture a series of large flakes was struck off the margins of a natural nodule or fragment by a simple method characteristically resulting in an angle between striking platform and bulbar surface on flakes of about 110°-115°. The striking platforms on the flakes were normally wide and the removals tended to alternate from side to side of the nodule in such a way that each negative scar provided the smooth surface for the platform of the next and so on. In practice it can be easily shown that the mechanical properties of flint, chert, and some crystalline rocks are such that using this method of production of large serviceable flakes makes little demands on manual dexterity. It is however, as just mentioned, relatively more wasteful of raw material (and hence of the effort of collecting it). The new method about to be described demands greater skill but once it has been mastered results in a net saving of effort by providing both a greater ratio of sharp cutting edge per cubic unit of raw material and simultaneously greater control over the outline of the resulting flake. For instance in one variant a domed form was imparted to a core, known to prehistorians as a 'tortoise core', which yields a smoothly oval flake comparable to the 'ovate' form of many hand-axes of the Lower Palaeolithic, but very much sharper and more effective for cutting purposes. Another form of core is suitable for the production of regular triangular flakes coming to a sharp point, with a relatively thin butt. A third, more rectangular shape facilitates the removal of narrow blade-like flakes suitable for knife-like functions and still more economical of raw material in ratio of cutting edge to volume. Perhaps the commonest form of prepared core, however, is that known as the 'discoid', applied to the production of smaller, less regular flakes which none the less also yield considerable economy of raw material. It is specially suitable for the provision of standardised blanks for reworking into such common forms as those known as 'Mousterian side-scrapers' and 'Mousterian points'.

14
16 : 1-5
15 : 1-4

The basic factors which link all these devices are two: first the realisation that the outline of a flake can be largely predetermined on the parent block or 'core', and secondly the careful intentional preparation of the striking platform. This greatly facilitates removal from many of the core shapes in question. Such processes must of course have been slowly evolved by trial and error, and socially transmitted through practical demonstration. A remarkable fact is the relative speed with which they emerged after so long a period of apparent stagnation, or at the most extremely slow development. Another interesting feature is the consistency with which particular technical and typological variants were practised over relatively restricted areas and limited phases of time. There would seem to be valid evidence here, in such 'clustering' of characteristics within a time-space framework, for the socially conditioned communication of habits and ideas. In reaching such an explanatory model of a broadly 'cultural' nature it is of course necessary to eliminate other possible explanations, as far as the data allow. Here it must be frankly admitted that specialists differ widely in their assessment. At one end of the scale is the attitude of most early workers, such as Breuil's, described above, where virtually every demonstrable difference between two or more assem-

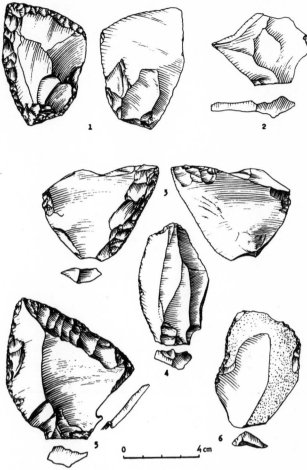

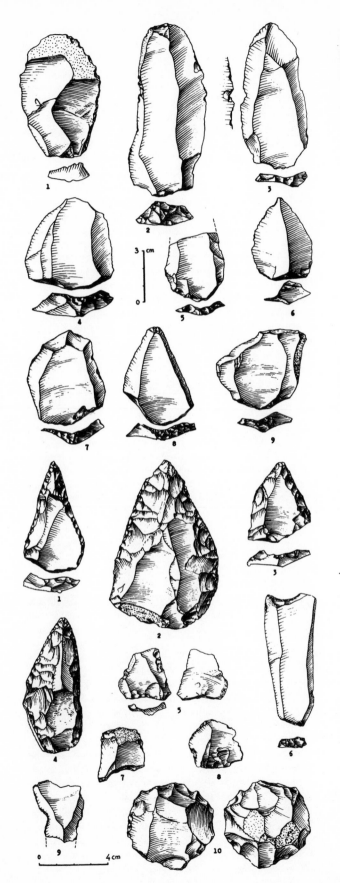

14 Open site of Les Gros-Monts, Nemours. Mousterian with Levallois tendencies. Note thin cross-section, preparation of striking platforms, and carefully struck points

◄ *15 Les Gros-Monts : 1-4, trimmed points ; 5-9, various trimmed flakes ; 10, typical discoid prepared core*

16 Les Gros-Monts : double and single side-scrapers

blages of artifacts was interpreted as reflecting an underlying difference of social tradition or 'culture'. That this attitude has still not been replaced in the minds of some writers is evident (Collins 1970). Others attempt to explain virtually all differences that can be observed in successive or alternating horizons as due to immediate *ad hoc* response to some individual and passing necessity.

A necessary prerequisite to effective testing of these suggestions is of course a systematic descriptive method which allows objective evaluation of the attributes, typological and technological, of the assemblages to be interpreted. There can be little doubt that F. Bordes' method of class analysis has gone far to achieve this preliminary purpose.

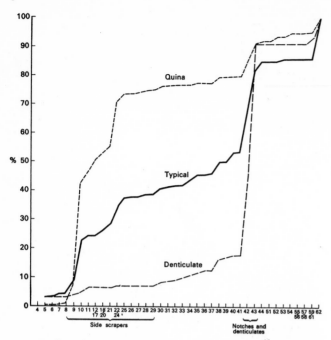

100
90
80   Quina
70
60
% 50   Typical
40
30
20   Denticulate
10
0

4 5 6 7 8 9 10 11 12 13 18 21 22 23 26 27 28 29 30 31 32 33 34 35 36 37 38 39 40 41 42 43 45 51 52 53 54 55 57 59 60 62
                17 20   24   56 58 61

Side scrapers   Notches and
                                                          denticulates

17 Cumulative graphs showing differential frequencies of artifact types numbered according to the system of F. Bordes, to illustrate his theoretical classes of industry

17 In essence his method is as follows. All the products of a given assemblage are divided into separate classes defined both by their morphological characteristics and method of manufacture. Special attention is applied to flakes whose initial form on parting from the parent core has been modified by subsequent trimming or 'retouch'. These are divided into no less than sixty-odd separate classes. The percentages of all classes are then calculated and comparison with another assemblage is carried out on their basis. For ease of visual comparison each assemblage is habitually expressed in the form of a cumulative frequency diagram. While it is clear that within the limits of the objectivity with which specimens are assigned to each class (or, to put it differently, the effective definition of the separate classes) such a system does indeed provide a basis for detailed differentiation between assemblages, the significance of such differentiation, even granted these assumptions, is not equally obvious. The terms of this problem may be appreciated from a brief description of the main characteristics of the artifacts in question.

The overwhelming majority of the recognisable implements made during the period in question used the same basic technique. A large chip or 'flake' was struck off the parent core. The outline and the angle of incidence of the sharp edges were then modified by repeated strokes with a pebble or bone hammer (most probably unmounted and simply held in the hand). Much of the classification used by Bordes and others concerns the shape of the modified outline and other edge characteristics. A few of the forms produced by this trimming or 'retouching' process compare reason-

ably closely to known categories of implement seen in use by recent primitive hunters; others do not, and accordingly their separation into 'types' is a purely subjective process imposed on the collection by the classifier and quite probably bearing only the vaguest connection with the intentions and distinctive work actions of the original maker. Nevertheless it is clear, as already said, that even such arbitrary classification does at least serve to supply a detailed description of the visible characteristics of any given assemblage provided that the classes are adequately defined and applied in the same fashion in each case.

An idea of the appearance of such an industry is given by fig. 14. Figs. 14-16 shows flakes or blanks for working *14-16* up into retouched tools. The upper or 'dorsal' surface prepared by primary flaking on the core is shown in each case, together with a detailed view of the characteristically prepared surface at right angles to the dorsal surface, which was destined to receive the blow which detached the flake from the core. It was the careful preparation of this 'striking platform' which formed an important element of the new Middle Palaeolithic technology, and together with higher precision in delivering the detaching blow at the requisite spot and angle, made it possible to take advantage of the preparatory shaping on the 'prepared core'.

Figs. 15-16 give an idea of the sort of variation in the *15-16* form of the retouched flakes normally observed at this stage of the Palaeolithic. It will be seen that both pointed and saw-like forms occur, presumably designed in part with a view to cutting or penetrating use respectively, together with others in which the retouch merely takes the form of an isolated concavity or notch. Since sharply pointed wooden spears are known to have been in use it may be conjectured that the last were on occasion used to smooth a spear shaft or handle. More than this it is hard to say in explanation of the function of these ancient lithic tool assemblages of the Middle Palaeolithic; although in the subsequent Upper Palaeolithic the resemblance to the equipment of recent hunters is so strong that classification of intention and function can be attempted with much greater assurance. Nevertheless, despite the arbitrary nature and uncertain basis in theory of his form of analysis, Bordes believes that it indicates the simultaneous presence in the Garonne basin in a total area of approximately 19,500,000 hectares, of no less than seven independent cultural traditions. These would have been practised in his estimation by separate communities exploiting the same territory and environment, without mutual exchange of ideas or practices over a period now known to be in the order of 30,000-40,000 years. The statistical evidence for three such variants is summarised as an example of Bordes' method in the cumulative diagrams shown in fig. 17. The frequencies of two of the attri- *17* butes used for the cumulative curve are shown in figs. 18, 19, the scraper and Quina indices. It may be noted *18-19* that the total area involved in this highly specialised cultural explanation of a typological situation is geographically less than that exploited by many single

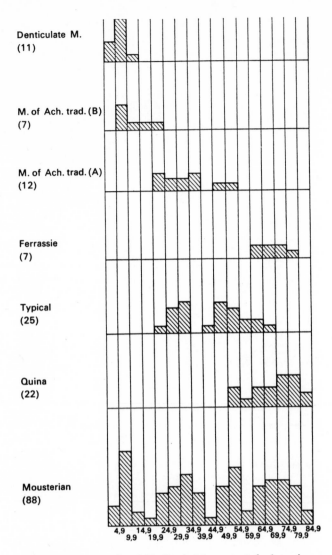

Denticulate M.
(11)

M. of Ach. trad. (B)
(7)

M. of Ach. trad. (A)
(12)

Ferrassie
(7)

Typical
(25)

Quina
(22)

Mousterian
(88)

4,9   14,9   24,9   34,9   44,9   54,9   64,9   74,9   84,9
   9,9   19,9   29,9   39,9   49,9   59,9   69,9   79,9

18 Frequency graphs of F. Bordes' 'scraper index' to show differential occurrence in his classes of industry

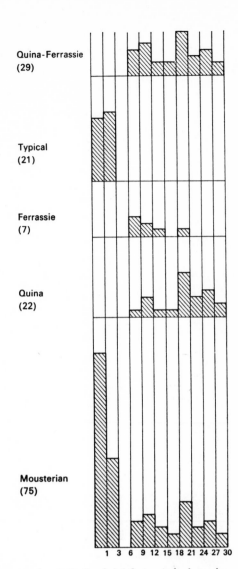

Quina-Ferrassie
(29)

Typical
(21)

Ferrassie
(7)

Quina
(22)

Mousterian
(75)

1   3   6   9   12   15   18   21   24   27   30

19 Frequency graphs of F. Bordes' 'Quina index' to show differences in his industrial classes

communities living with a comparable technology and economy in recent times. A few such occupied territories are in the order of a third or half as great but these do not overlap in the manner apparently implied by Bordes' conception. Again, wherever (as in the case of some Eskimo groups) the territory occupied by a single group can be plotted over a length of time, it proves to be fluid and the duration in time is measured in centuries or at most a few millennia rather than the decimillennia envisaged by Bordes.

For these and other reasons many palaeo-ethnologists approach the explanatory model offered by Bordes with considerable reservations, and feel it necessary to examine all other feasible possibilities before accepting a conception so far removed from any situation that has actually come under ethnographic observation. Several such alternatives have in fact been worked out in considerable detail. They may be conveniently discussed under two headings: 'functional' and 'diachronic'.

The principal exponents of the 'functional' model are Drs L. and S. Binford (1966), and L. G. Freeman (1966). Taking as their point of departure the numerical data published by Bordes, these workers have sought to analyse the characteristics of the many assemblages available using sophisticated statistical techniques, notably various forms of what is known as 'multivariate analysis'. In one experiment they examined simultaneously the relative frequencies of 40 of Bordes' tool classes in 17 separate finds distributed from southwest Asia to the Atlantic coast of France. The result showed that certain groups of tools had a marked tendency to occur together, forming clusters or 'factors'. On examination the elements composing the factors suggest by their forms that they could reasonably represent the equipment needed for specific types of activity such as butchering of animal carcasses, maintenance and repair of the large wooden spears, antler clubs, etc. that we know were among the hunting

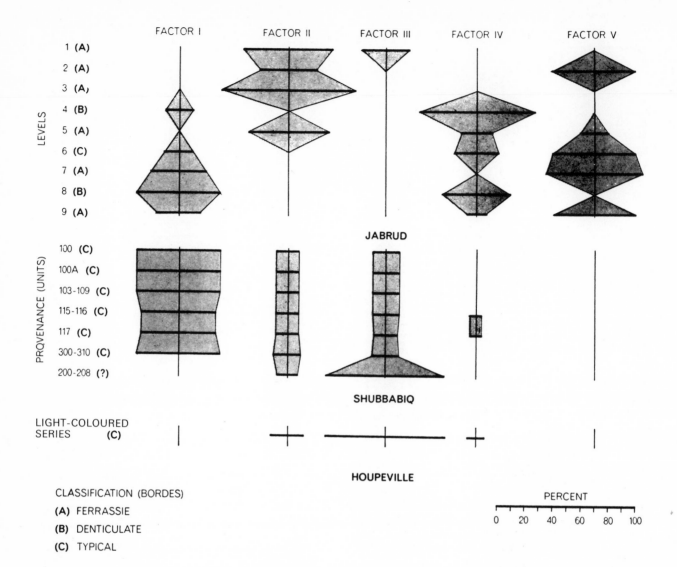

FACTOR I   FACTOR II   FACTOR III   FACTOR IV   FACTOR V

LEVELS

1 (A)
2 (A)
3 (A)
4 (B)
5 (A)
6 (C)
7 (A)
8 (B)
9 (A)

JABRUD

PROVENANCE (UNITS)

100 (C)
100A (C)
103-109 (C)
115-116 (C)
117 (C)
300-310 (C)
200-208 (?)

SHUBBABIQ

LIGHT-COLOURED
SERIES   (C)

HOUPEVILLE

CLASSIFICATION (BORDES)

(A) FERRASSIE
(B) DENTICULATE
(C) TYPICAL

PERCENT

0   20   40   60   80   100

20 *Diagram to show the differential occurrence of the various tool groups or 'factors' obtained by statistical and computer* *analysis of a series of Mousterian industries by L. G. and S. R. Binford*

weapons, or such base-camp activities as food and clothing preparation. (We have of course no direct evidence of clothing, although it is hardly conceivable that human life could have been maintained without it in more northerly regions during much of this epoch.)

On further analysis the contents of individual layers in various stratigraphical successions are often found to correspond largely to one or more of these common factors, to the virtual exclusion of others. This suggests that particular sites may have been repeatedly used for specific purposes, and that much of the variation observed in the tool inventories is to be explained in this way rather than by supposing the existence of watertight cultural traditions practised independently by different communities over long periods within the same territories. At the time of writing the debate continues, but the 'diachronic' type of explanation is also being actively explored.

According to this the main explanation for variation in tool class frequencies would reside neither in contemporary individual traditions nor in short-term activity oscillations, but in successive developmental stages of wide-spread common traditions. Here again common-sense considerations and the development of new methods of archaeological analysis have both played a part, using once again the data thrown up by Bordes' method. A further contributing factor has been improved methods of field excavation, whereby a closer chronological subdivision or 'resolution' of individual dug units is achieved. Although recent C14 data suggest that in most cave and rock shelter deposits it is unrealistic to suppose that a given scatter of artifacts isolates a pattern smaller, say, than the combined effects of some fifty or a hundred occupations, nevertheless there is every reason to believe that greater 'resolution' of data has in fact been made possible. In open sites on the

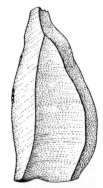

TYPICAL BORER

BEC

NATURALLY BACKED KNIFE

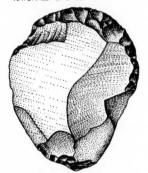

TYPICAL END SCRAPER

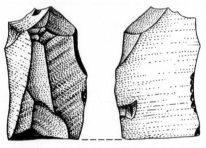

ATYPICAL BURIN

21 *Example of the various tools comprising a single 'factor' as shown in fig. 20*

other hand there are of course many cases where individual occupations can be identified with some confidence. None has yet been reported in any detail from France but central and eastern Europe have provided good examples that show the context of lithic assemblages similar to those of the French Middle Palaeolithic.

One may quote as an example the locality of Salzgitter-Lebenstedt near Hannover close to the contemporary ice-cap. Here a scatter left by a single group of hunters at one camp site reveals an elongated bone-littered area of 15 m. × 6-7 m. with an outlying fringe scatter of flint tools and debris. A second scatter made later in the same locality is of similar dimensions. In neither case is there any very clearly discernible pattern such as has been found in connection with a number of Upper Palaeolithic settlements (e.g. those from Czecho-slovakia and Bavaria). A more recent find in the USSR

of the same approximate date however, at the locality of Molodova I in the Dniestr valley (Chernysh 1959) does show the only clearly patterned scatter associated with Mousterian-type stonework so far known. It shows a circular zone of bones and mammoth tusks and skulls enclosing a space some 8 m. in diameter with numerous small hearth places and a dense concentration of flint-work, tools and debris. None of these sites or others like them appear to show so far the sort of specialised assemblage that a strict interpretation of the Binfords' functional hypothesis might lead us to expect; but it is only fair to say that too few specifically identified activity areas have been examined for this purpose.

Main characteristics of Bordes' groups

I CHARENTIAN GROUP
(a) *Quina sub-group*
Side-scrapers – high (*c.* 50%)
Transverse variant – high
Quina variant – high
Hand-axes – low
Backed knives – low
Levallois technique – low

(b) *Ferrassie sub-group*
Side-scrapers – high
Transverse variant – low
Quina variant – moderate
Hand-axes – rare or absent
Backed knives – rare or absent
Levallois technique – high

II TYPICAL MOUSTERIAN
Side-scrapers – variable
Transverse variant – low
Quina variant – rare or absent
Hand-axes – rare or absent
Backed knives – rare or absent
Levallois technique – variable

III MOUSTERIAN OF ACHEULEAN TRADITION
(a) *Sub-group A*
Side-scrapers – moderate, variable
Quina variant – rare or absent
Hand-axes – variable (*c.* 8%)
Backed knives – moderate to high
Levallois technique – variable
Denticulates: moderate to high

(b) *Sub-group B*
Side-scrapers – low
Quina variant – nil
Hand-axes – low
Backed knives – high
Other Upper Palaeolithic-like types – moderate
Levallois technique – variable
Denticulates – high

IV DENTICULATE MOUSTERIAN
Side-scrapers – low
Quina variant – nil
Hand-axes – nil
Backed knives – low to nil
Levallois technique – variable
Denticulate – high to every high

When considering the newly formulated diachronic view of the French Middle Palaeolithic it is necessary to examine some of the features of Bordes' supposed 'cultural' groups. In a recent summary he instances their distinguishing characters as he conceives them as shown in the table on the preceding page:

In a recent study of Mousterian variants in the northern part of the Garonne basin (the Périgord) P. A. Mellars (1969) has shown that a long stratigraphical sequence registered at the site of Combe Grenal (Bordes 1966) suggests the following chronological succession of Bordes groups:

(a) Temperate episode, early Würm (or more probably late Eem); Typical Mousterian.

(b) Very cold climax (probably early Würm climax): first Ferrassie then Quina.

(c) Milder episode (probably the so-called Moorshoofd or Hengelo interstadials of Würm): Denticulate followed by return to Typical.

(d) Minor cold oscillation (possibly that separating Hengelo from the subsequent Denekamp mild period but in any case much milder than the preceding cold climax: Mousterian of Acheulean tradition.

Mellars further claims that in twelve other sites in this area the succession of Mousterian of Acheulean tradition on Quina or Ferrassie can also be observed. This last contention does not however seem as clearly established to the present writer as Mellars claims, and is specifically contested by Bordes. A non-hand-axe variant (possibly typical Mousterian) clearly overlies for instance the Mousterian of Acheulean tradition in the lower rock-shelter at the eponymous site of Le Moustier, and no less than two such layers occur in a similar relative position in the not far distant Pyrenean site of Abri Olha. The same occurs to the west of the Pyrenees in the famous north Spanish site of Castillo, near Santander. Moreover a few hand-axes of a similar kind occur as early as late Riss in the Channel Islands site of Cotte de St Brelade (Jersey) which was joined to the mainland of France at that time. Again it may be recalled that the original contention of the older writers on the Somme was consistently in favour of a major hand-axe horizon at the *beginning* of the formation of the younger (Würmian) loess with the form becoming rarer higher up (Breuil's Levallois stages V-VI).

In addition mention should be made of an interesting statistical analysis of a sample of Bordes' data carried out by F. R. Hodson (1969) using a multivariate process of 'distancing' which expresses degrees of resemblance giving equal weight to all variables involved.

The results appear in the form of a scale of resemblance or 'seriation' that is not inconsistent with Mellars' hypothesis. Furthermore if the stratified Charentian successions at four well recorded sites in the Périgord (La Ferrassie, Chadourne, Puymoyen, Roc-en-Pail) are examined separately a certain harmony of variation can be observed as Mellars has pointed out (1969). In all four the attributes of Levallois technique, facetted preparation of striking platforms, and frequency of blades decrease with time, whereas transverse side-scrapers increase. These tend to show that some degree of evolutionary trend within this group is at least a possibility, though it would perhaps be necessary to eliminate environmental factors in a systematic fashion before the idea could be considered as rigorously tested.

Finally, the writer in his turn has tried statistical techniques on a stratified succession of late Rissian date in the cave site of La Cotte de St Brelade (Jersey) mentioned above. The object was to test a further frequently mooted possibility, namely the effect of raw material on lithic typology and technology. This site offers a unique opportunity to do this since it was occupied during a period of rising sea-level when the sources of good quality flint and chert were being gradually submerged by the sea, and accordingly inhabitants were being progressively forced to use inferior local raw materials. Using the well known statistical device of partial correlations and pursuing the matter further with the more elaborate method of principal component analysis it transpires that a whole range of basic characters such as the size of tools and their relative frequency and even their shapes were far more closely associated with the availability of raw material than with the passage of time. In other words it seems likely that many factors other than pure evolutionary trend were responsible for the observed variation in Middle Palaeolithic tool assemblages in France.

The whole matter would seem to be in need of far more systematic treatment before an agreed explanation or set of explanations is likely to emerge. There is one point however that does seem to stand out more clearly and is likely to strike the reader of this work, as he compares this chapter with the next; namely, that despite their enormous abundance, the wide time span of their occurrence and intensive research, these lithic assemblages of the Middle Palaeolithic do *not* fall into anything like the same well defined type of geographical and chronological patterning which so manifestly characterises the subsequent Upper Palaeolithic epoch in the same area. Although it may be that some degree of evolutionary change may ultimately become detectable, or even more than one such trend as postulated by Bordes, there seems little likelihood that this material will ever yield a sequence as well defined say as the Aurignacian-Solutrean-Magdalenian (to say nothing of minor but equally firmly established subdivisions) which so clearly marks the changes in industrial habits from the thirtieth millennium onwards over wide areas of France. To the writer at least it seems abundantly evident that the whole pattern of Middle Palaeolithic industrial variation is separated by a profound taxonomic contrast from all that took place after it.

In the short space of two or three thousand years at most the whole patterning of lithic assemblages in space and time underwent a profound change from the unstructured to the structured, from a condition totally unlike that of modern primitive communities to one which could be paralleled in almost any area where men continued to live by hunting and fishing and gathering down to recent times.

Does this change reflect an equally profound change in the nature of the underlying social mechanisms (of which of course the archaeology is but the material expression), and through the social organism to the underlying potentialities of the men responsible? Does it in fact represent nothing less than the replacement by ethnic movement of an ancient human strain of fundamentally more limited capacity by men essentially like the races of today? Is it, in a word, the displacement by our direct ancestors of a relict strain of Neandertal type? The present writer remains frankly convinced that it is. Mme Bordes in the following chapter urges the contrary. The reader must form his own opinion of the present state of the debate. It is unlikely however that the issue will remain indefinitely in suspense; the progress of radiometric dating and the increasing use of objective methods of classification can hardly fail to bring out the truth of the matter one way or the other in due course.

Conclusions

The most recent discoveries now make it more than a reasoned possibility that human beings made their first appearance on French soil somewhere in the order of half a million to a million years ago, at a time when human physical evolution was already well advanced in Africa, and traditionally conditioned industrial behaviour or 'culture' of a distinctively human kind was already beginning to take shape.

These first Europeans, the inhabitants of France among them, were equipped at the outset with only the barest rudiments of such (cultural) behaviour patterns. As far as the recorded evidence goes, we do not positively know that they had made much progress towards standardised equipment though they were able at least to sharpen stones effectively by fracture. A similar industrial status is known to have lasted more than a million years in Africa.

Standardised multi-purpose tools in the form of the so-called hand-axes made their first appearance in Europe, specifically in the west and southwest, in France and Spain, at a date that has yet to be accurately determined but is probably in the order of 300,000 to 500,000 years ago. It was thus substantially later than present indications suggest for Africa. Subsequent cultural evolution of this and associated tool-forms are not yet satisfactorily established in Europe although beginning to come to light in the stratigraphical record of Africa, and perhaps the Middle East. The territory occupied in Europe seems mainly to have been river- and lake-sides, where big game such as elephant, rhinoceros, hippopotamus and smaller mammals were not infrequently killed, sometimes with long wooden spears shaped with the aid of flint implements and hardened in the fire. No mountain occupation is attested at this time.

The general pattern of human activity in France, which seems to have been a main focus for human habitation, as well as other parts of Europe remained basically unchanged till the relatively rapid emergence of a distinctly lighter, more sophisticated and more efficient equipment produced by substantial improvements in technology about 125,000 ± 25,000 BP. This, defined in cultural terms, is the beginning of the Middle Palaeolithic. Human strains seem to have been variable but are on the average distinctly more evolved and closer to modern man than the makers of the earliest hand-axes say in Africa or their contemporaries in the Far East. Traditional taxonomy groups them under the heading of Neandertal man rather than *Homo erectus* (who appears to have been associated with the earliest tools in Europe). In brain size they are fully equivalent to modern man but still show certain features of skull structure and muscular insertions which link them to their predecessors rather than ourselves. Whether their brains were structurally and functionally the same as ours is difficult to decide but the geographical and chronological patterning of their industries suggests processes of cultural evolution and variation differentiated to a significant degree from those of modern man completely evolved, who is first certainly attested at or soon after 33,000 BP.

2

The Upper Palaeolithic:
c. 33,000–10,000 BC
DENISE DE SONNEVILLE-BORDES

The Upper Palaeolithic in Europe lasted some twenty thousand years, a period far shorter than the time which had elapsed since man first appeared there, but nonetheless long by comparison with subsequent human history. Palaeolithic man now reached his highest level of achievement, manifested particularly in France, an outstanding centre of cultural development throughout the period. The most striking aspects are widely known from the paintings, engraving and sculpture which abound alike on cave and shelter walls and on loose objects found among archaelogical material. This artistic creation is only one manifestation, albeit the most spectacular, of human progress at this time. Other evidence, of technical advances, population expansion and social organisation, contributes to a more detailed appreciation of man's accomplishment in France, and helps to elucidate it. Such technical and mental 'mutations' did not everywhere develop so dynamically. Alongside regions which were reservoirs of population and ideas lay empty or sparsely peopled zones, untouched by the main currents.

There has long been debate over the criteria which define the Upper Palaeolithic and distinguish it from the preceding Middle Palaeolithic or Mousterian, and hence over the date of its first appearance. The differentiation is not always as clear as at first believed. It is conceded that the appearance of anatomically modern man, *Homo sapiens sapiens*, as distinct from Neandertal man, and the invention of techniques hitherto unknown, or little-used, coincide sufficiently to serve in association to define a new period. There is, however, no abrupt break with the Middle Palaeolithic. Palaeontology has dismissed Neandertal man as having no possible organic link with *Homo sapiens*. Yet certain Neandertal finds, for example those from La Ferrassie in the Dordogne, do show some modern traits, such as an incipient chin as illustrated on this page. In France, the oldest representative of *Homo sapiens sapiens* is the Combe-Capelle man (Dordogne) who was found in a Lower Perigordian layer at the beginning of the Upper Palaeolithic. Combined with his modern characteristics there are still certain primitive traits (Piveteau 1962). This same Lower Perigordian still contains a number of Mousterian tools, so that it is impossible to isolate it archaeologically from final Mousterian. It must be allowed that, in France, the one proceeds partially from the other (Bordes 1958a).[1]

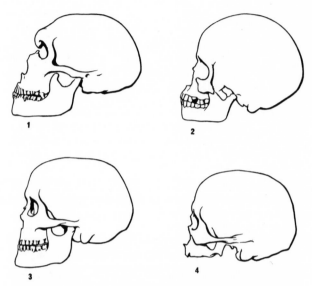

1 *Palaeolithic man. Neandertal Man: 1, La Ferrassie. Homo sapiens: 2, 'negroid' adolescent of Grimaldi race, Grotte des Enfants, Grimaldi; 3, male of Cro-magnon race, Grotte des Enfants, Grimaldi; 4, male of Chancelade race, Raymonden, Chancelade (1 and 4, after Boule and Vallois 1952; 2 and 3, after Piveteau 1957)*

Despite these connections, indicative of probable origins, which it is advisable neither to ignore nor to underestimate, the Upper Palaeolithic emerges as an extremely novel complex of cultures. These are well differentiated from each other, but share various inventions and, if one may so express it, 'motivations', which separate them sharply from both the Mousterian and the subsequent Mesolithic cultural epochs. New is the emphasis on such tools as end-scrapers and burins, made on elongated flakes known as 'blades'. Contrary to a now outmoded opinion, however, blades were not the sole basis of the lithic industries. In the early Perigordian, Aurignacian, early Solutrean and early Magdalenian, tools made on undifferentiated flakes are frequent or even predominant. By contrast blades and bladelets are overwhelmingly preponderant in the evolved Perigordian, Upper Solu-

[1] While the views expressed in this paragraph are shared by some other prehistorians, they are not as yet universally accepted by Palaeolithic specialists. – Ed.

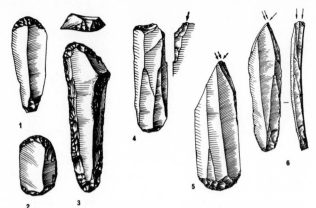

2 End-scrapers and burins: 1, simple, untrimmed scraper on blade; 2, double end-scraper; 3, Aurignacian scraper on blade; 4, burin on truncation; 5, burin-scraper; 6, dihedral burin. Drawings by P. Laurent

trean and Middle and Upper Magdalenian. What is novel is the development of specialised tools. End-scrapers and burins, borers and truncated forms are also present in the Middle Palaeolithic and even in the final Acheulean, but from now on they are prepared in a multiplicity of ways. On double and composite implements two or more similar or different tools are worked on a single piece, in a great number of combinations, such as the burin-scraper, the multiple borer, etc. Although the relative numbers of these different types vary considerably between cultures, a basic community of forms lends remarkable typological unity to the Upper Palaeolithic (Sonneville-Bordes 1960 and 1966).

Special tools confined to particular industries were constantly being invented, for example the thick scrapers of the Aurignacian, the backed points of the Perigordian, or Solutrean foliate forms. Some belong solely to one phase of an industry, such as 'Noailles' burins, the tanged points of the evolved Perigordian, the willow-leaf points of the final Solutrean, and the shouldered points of the terminal Magdalenian. The working of bone, antler and ivory, which was practically unknown in Mousterian times, becomes highly developed, and applied for instance to the manufacture of relatively specialized implements such as arrow straighteners, spear throwers or detachable harpoons. Such objects of stone and bone, weapons and tools whose exact purpose for the most part escapes us, reach a special status of significance. They are some of the best preserved evidence for the activities of fossil man. Since they are so specific we are better able to date the levels containing them than during the Middle Palaeolithic.

Artistic development reflects social life and the organisation of leisure; it is also possible to deduce something of the thoughts of individuals and communities on the relationship of man to the world of nature, and even to the occult. Increase in the number of graves and funerary rites is another aspect of these preoccupations, allowing us to read to some extent the minds of these very ancient societies (Sonneville-Bordes 1959).

(margin references) 2:4   2:2; 10:3   :5; 22:2-3   13:2-9; 9   18-19   10:6; 9:6   19:3   24:2-3   12; 23   28   30

CHRONOLOGICAL FRAMEWORK

The chronology of the Upper Palaeolithic is established by relating its stratigraphic subdivisions to the phases of the glacial period; for instance, by studying the profiles of silts and loess in open-air sites and the layered sequences of deposits in caves and rock-shelters. Carbon 14 dates will, in theory, give still greater precision (Movius 1960, 1961 and 1966). The beginning and end of the epoch and its estimated duration of some twenty thousand years are in fact fixed only approximately, and for France mainly by reference to the archaeological sequence observed by excavation at the key sites of La Ferrassie and Laugerie-Haute. The broad succession is as follows: Aurignacian, Solutrean, Magdalenian and Azilian.

The Upper Palaeolithic developed during the close of the last great Quaternary glaciation, the Würm, more

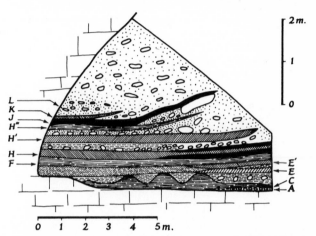

3 Section of La Ferrassie (after Peyrony 1934). Situated on Departmental Route no. 32 between Savignac de Miremont and Le Bugue. The site consists of one cave (Upper Palaeolithic), a small (Mousterian) rock-shelter and a large shelter (Mousterian and Upper Palaeolithic). The large rock-shelter was excavated by Capitan and Denis Peyrony. Collections in Musée de Saint-Germain-en-Laye and Musée des Eyzies.

Peyrony's section *(reading from the base)*
A-D – Mousterian levels: A – some bifacial tools; C and D – fine Mousterian of Ferrassie type. Burials of Neandertal men (1909)
E – reddish layer; early Perigordian of Châtelperron type
E' – grey layer with earliest Aurignacian
F – reddish-brown layer: typical Aurignacian I (bone points with split base)
H – dark-brown layer: Aurignacian II (flattened, lozenge-shaped bone points)
H' – Aurignacian III layer (lozenge-shaped bone points with oval section)
H" – Aurignacian IV (biconical bone points)
J – Upper Perigordian with Font-Robert points (period Va)
K – Upper Perigordian with truncated flints (period Vb)
L – limestone accumulation with some traces of Upper Perigordian with 'Noailles' burins (Period Vc)
Talus of limestone accumulation
Dating (F. Bordes)
Layers B-C (Mousterian): glacial stadial Würm II
Layer E: interstadial Würm II-III
Layers F-K: Würm III stadial, with a period of cold at the start (Aurignacian levels), followed by a warmer period (Perigordian levels)
At the end of Würm III, the rock-shelter was filled up

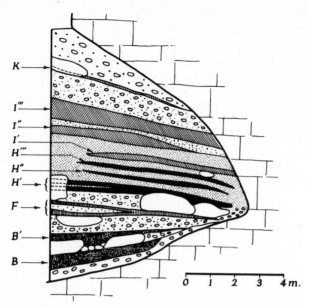

4 *Section of Laugerie-Haute, east (after E. and D. Peyrony 1938). Huge site on the road from Les Eyzies to Périgueux, on the right bank of the Vézere (180 m. long by 35 m. wide). Explored in 1863 by Lartet and Christy, followed by numerous excavators, including Hauser. Bought by the state after the First World War, and excavated scientifically by Denis and Elie Peyrony from 1921 onwards (collections in Musée des Eyzies). New excavations by Bordes beginning in 1955.*

There are two excavation sites, east and west:

Laugerie-Haute sections (Denis Peyrony)
B and B' – Perigordian III levels (Final Perigordian of F. Bordes)
D – present only on the west site (Aurignacian V or Final)
F – present only on the east site (proto-Magdalenian)
H', H", H'" – Solutrean: Lower (unifacial points), Middle (laurel-leaf points) and Upper (shouldered points)
I', I", I'" – Lower Magdalenian: I (*raclette* scrapers), II (triangular flints), III (bone rods with semicircular section)
K – at the east site, hoard of Magdalenian V (barbed bone points)
Dating (F. Bordes)
The lower layers up to HJ (Middle Solutrean) are composed of dry accumulations and rock-fall from the roof, representing a cold climate (end of Würm III)
Layers H" and H'" (Middle and Upper Solutrean) and I', (Magdalenian I) are more earthy and contemporary with a warmer and more humid climate (interstadial between Würm III and Würm IV). The upper layers, with rock accumulation, represent the return of a very cold and dry climate, with Würm IV
C14 datings (east site)
Lower Solutrean: 18,700 ± 300 BC. Proto-Magdalenian: 19,785 ± 250 BC

precisely during its last two stadials, Würm III and Würm IV. Early Perigordian is everywhere found in the interstadial Würm II-III, a period of climatic amelioration between the two secondary advances, or stadials, Würm II and Würm III. Radiocarbon dates are at present inexact beyond say 33,000 years. 33-32,000 BC might be proposed for the first appearance of the early Perigordian. Aurignacian and Perigordian occupy the greater part of the Würm III advance. The beginning of typical Aurignacian falls about 30,000 BC, and evolved Perigordian about 26,000 BC. Solutrean begins at the

end of Würm III, about 19-18,000 BC and ends during the interstadial Würm III-IV. The Lower Magdalenian, which follows it during this interstadial, starts about 15,000 BC. Middle and Upper Magdalenian occupy Würm IV, the final stadial of Würm, ending about 10,000 BC with the advent of the temperate Allerød oscillation. The Azilian which derives from the Magdalenian belongs to post-glacial times.

GEOGRAPHICAL DISTRIBUTION
The boundaries of human occupation in France varied throughout the Upper Palaeolithic in response no doubt to natural environmental and climatic conditions and also, perhaps to an increasing degree, to the changing vitality of social groups responsible for the successive cultures of this long period. These boundaries never exactly correspond to those of modern France, but they at times coincide with certain of the great natural frontiers, such as rivers and mountains, which have always been barriers. The Pyrenees and the rivers Loire, Garonne, Rhône and Durance are the obstacles which limited certain cultures, or which these barely transgressed. During the twenty thousand years in question the only region consistently occupied without a break was that lying between the Loire and the Garonne, with the highest occupation density in the Périgord, in the valleys of the Dordogne and Vézère. All Upper

5 *Classic sites of the Upper Palaeolithic in France. 1 Le Placard. 2 Les Vachons. 3 Fourneau du Diable. 4 Chancelade. 5 Badegoule. 6 Font-Robert. 7 Noailles. 8 Pech de la Boissière. 9 La Gravette. 10 Jean-Blancs. 11 Combe-Capelle. 12 Brassempouy. 13 Isturitz. 14 Aurignac. 15 Mas d'Azil. 16 Gourdan. 17 Châtelperron. 18 Solutré. 19 Grimaldi. 20 Arcy-sur-Cure. 21 Cirque de la Patrie. 22 Beauregard. 23 Pincevent*

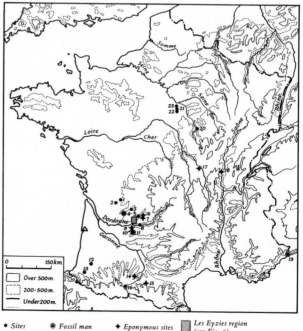

• *Sites*　⊙ *Fossil man*　✦ *Eponymous sites*　▨ *Les Eyzies region (see Fig. 7)*

1 Laussel, Dordogne: detail of the 'Venus' with horn.

2   Les Combarelles, Dordogne: reindeer engraved on the cave wall.

3   *Equus caballus gallicus* (Prat 1968). Magdalenian horse in black, Le Portel, Ariège.

4   *Saïga tatarica*: a, present-day; b, Magdalenian engraving at Gourdan, Haute-Garonne.

5 La Marche, Vienne: human figure on a rock.

6 Heads of horses, with offset outline; Magdalenian, Isturitz, Basses-Pyrénées.

7 Wounded bison, painted in black. The two arrows at the side are red. Niaux cave, Ariège.

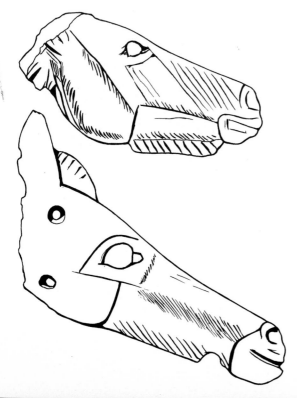

51

8 La Mouthe, Dordogne: sandstone lamp with engraved ornament on the back.

9 Abri du Poisson, Dordogne: fish carved on the roof of the shelter.

10 Raymonden, Chancelade, Dordogne: engraved bone.

11 Richard (alias Grotte des Eyzies): rib decorated with engravings of ibex, with detail.

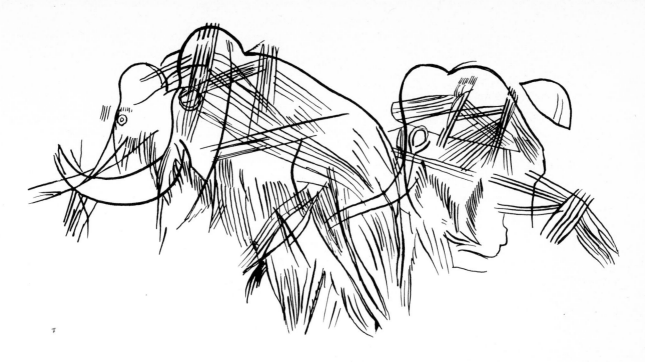

12 Mammoths and 'roof-shaped' signs (traps?) engraved in the Bernifal cave, Dordogne.

13 Rouffignac, Dordogne: paintings of mammoths, from the frieze of eleven (detail).

14 Rouffignac, Dordogne: central rhinoceros from
the frieze of three (detail).

SITES	STRATA OR SPECIMENS	INDUSTRIES	CLIMATE (WARM / COLD — DRY / WET)	CLIMATE PHASES
LES MARSEILLES — COUZE	B• a H	Magdalenian VI		
	a b	Magdalenian V		
	c• d• e f	Magdalenian IV		
East 2•g h• i• 3 j•		Magdalenian III		
	4• k 5• 6• l 7 8	Magdalenian II		Progressive oscillations of Würm IV
	9 10• 11 12• 13 14• 15 16• 17	Magdalenian I { Id Ic Ib Ia }		
West 0•	18• 19 20•	Magdalenian 0		
1• 2• 3•	21• 22• 23•	Final Solutrean		Interstadial Würm III-IV
4• 5• 6• 7•	24 25• 26• 27• 28•	Upper Solutrean		
8• 9• 10• 11•	29• 30•	Middle Solutrean		Regressive oscillations of Würm III
12a• 12b• 12c• 12d•	31• 32	Lower Solutrean		
13• 14 15	32(?)	Protosolutrean		
16• 17	34• 33 35	Aurignacian V		Major phase Würm III B
18 19	36• 37	Protomagdalenian		
21• 20 22 •23	38• 39 40• 41 42•	Perigordian VI		Würm III A / Würm III B oscillation
LE TROU DE LA CHÈVRE	3• 5• 6• 7•	Upper Perigordian		
	8 9•	Typical Aurignacian (III?)		Major phase of Würm III A
	10			
	11• 12•	Typical Aurignacian (II?)		Progressive oscillations of Würm III
	13 14•	Lower Perigordian		
	15• 16• 17• 18•			Interstadial Würm II-III
	• = Hearths			

LAUGERIE-HAUTE (site label spanning the central strata)

6 *Evolution of climate during the late Würmian in the Périgord (after Laville 1964)*

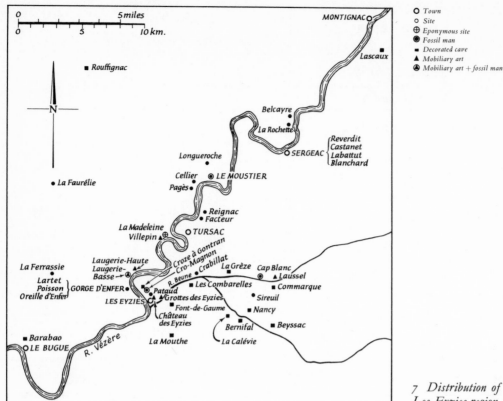

7 *Distribution of Palaeolithic sites in the Les Eyzies region (Dordogne)*

Palaeolithic cultures are represented here, in their principal and variant forms. This is the region of the classic stratigraphies, evidence for the complete Upper Palaeolithic sequence in France, correlating archaeological industries with their natural environment. This occupation of a naturally defined area did not occur in Mousterian times, and must be attributed to the growth of truly organised societies (Sonneville-Bordes 1963b).

Natural environment

PERIGLACIAL PHENOMENA

Upper Palaeolithic France was subjected to glacial conditions even more rigorous than those of the late Middle Palaeolithic. The great Scandinavian glacier extending across the north of Europe did not reach France, but its proximity brought periglacial conditions to the wide plains of the Paris basin. At times of glacial advance they were swept by violent winds laden with fine loess dust, which was deposited like a blanket over large areas. These tempests precluded all animal and human life in these regions which were transformed into deserts. In more temperate phases when the temperature rose to some extent and rainfall increased, the deposition of loesses stopped or was reduced. Shrub vegetation replaced arid steppe, and large animals, herbivores and pachyderms became established and were exploited by the human hunters. A phase of this kind occurred during Würm III, and is reflected in cave deposits by a scree horizon in which evolved Perigordian occurs (Bordes 1954).

There was minor glaciation in the Massif Central and in the Pyrenees, and a large Alpine glacier advanced down the valley of the Rhône, reaching the vicinity of Lyons. However, from the beginning of Würm III the glaciers began to retreat. Periods of maximum cold do not in fact correlate with the maximum extension of the ice, and the Upper Palaeolithic which experienced the most intense cold correlates with a recession of the glaciers. This process released water which resulted in a rise in the sea-level, which had been greatly lowered during the preceding period. On the Provence coast the final transgression registered hardly appears to exceed the present level of the Mediterranean (Bonifay 1962).[1]

CLIMATE

The climatic sequence of the Upper Palaeolithic in the Périgord has been established from studies of cave and shelter deposits, in particular at Laugerie-Haute (Bordes 1958b, Laville 1964). A sequence of archaeological material allows the levels to be dated. Abundant faunal remains confirm this and elaborate conclusions have been drawn from the sedimentology. Mild climatic conditions are attested by clayey, earthy, or even clearly sandy, water-laid layers. By contrast, periods of dry cold when frost action caused exfoliation from the cave walls, which flaked off and split into sharply angular

[1] Evidence elsewhere, notably in north Italy, however, suggests that the Mediterranean level was still substantially below that of the present (Blanc 1936), perhaps by as much as 80 m. (Bloom 1971). – Ed.

42

fragments, gave rise to accumulations of loose scree with no admixture of earth; these are interpreted as the debris of thermoclastic weathering. The framework so 6 established for the Périgord is applicable within limits to the rest of France, allowing of course for the modifications demanded by differences in topography.

The exact chronological positions of certain episodes termed 'interstadials' (Göttweig, Paudorf, Lascaux, Arcy) are not accurately known. The correlations which have been proposed between these and the Périgord succession are between purely climatic episodes established in regions of very different latitude and phases relating to sedimentary sequences. They are unconnected with industries and consequently lack the check provided by archaeologically dated levels.

From the consistent indications based on the study of fossil pollen (palynology) and sediments during the Upper Palaeolithic in the Périgord it would appear that a series of milder and more humid oscillations, sometimes even clearly temperate, occurred at the beginning and end of the major cold phases Würm III and Würm IV. Each glacial phase developed through a series of oscillations culminating in considerable periods of great cold and dryness. Similarly, towards the end of these glacial phases interglacial improvements in temperature built up through successive oscillations.

FAUNA

Several species of large, cold-loving mammals such as mammoth and woolly rhinoceros, already known from Mousterian times survived into the Upper Palaeolithic. Protected against the cold by their thick coats, they are 2 associated with reindeer in the food debris of the hunters. As the cold lessened, however, reindeer retreated and temperate species returned or increased. When the proportion of reindeer had become insignificant, horse predominated, or more rarely, large bovines, such as ox or bison, or the red deer Cervus elaphus (Prat 1968).

Other associated Arctic species are the musk-ox, collared lemming, Arctic fox, hare, and wolverine together with snow-partridge and snowy owl. In addition there are Alpine species, now found only at higher altitudes – marmot, chamois, and two species of ibex 11 (the Alpine Capra ibex and the Pyrenean Capra pyrenaica). Formidable carnivores, such as bears, lions and hyenas, also lived in the caves.

The fauna of the Upper Palaeolithic was thus little different from that of the Mousterian, apart from a few 4 innovations. The saïga antelope (Saïga tatarica), previously practically unknown in France, appeared on the shores of the Atlantic to the southwest. Like the spermophile antelope to which it is related, it is typical of arid steppe conditions with relatively warm summers and cold winters, as in central Asia where it is found today. Herds roamed the hills of the Charente and the Gironde, without venturing much into the broken uplands of the Périgord.

At the beginning of the Upper Palaeolithic a species of horse, Equus caballus germanicus, remarkable for its elongated head, solid build, massive limbs and broad hooves, is present in Aurignacian and Perigordian levels. In the course of Würm III it gives place to Equus caballus gallicus (Prat 1968), a short-headed horse like a 3 pony, with short thick-set limbs and easily recognisable in the paintings and engravings on the cave walls.

VEGETATION

By the microscopic study of fossil pollen from habitation sites and by establishing the present-day distribution of the plants involved and their ecology and climatic tolerance, palynology is able to reconstruct the contemporary floral environment of Palaeolithic life. Work on late Würm material in France is still sporadic and chiefly centred on Arcy-sur-Cure (Leroi-Gourhan 1967) and Laugerie-Haute (Paquereau, unpublished).

It was previously held that Arctic-type tundra, with mosses, lichens, dwarf birch and willow and the creeping mountain avens (Dryas octopetala) growing on a frozen subsoil, covered the whole of France. In point of fact these species, which occur in northern Europe and in mountain regions, were absent from southwestern France, except in rare cases. Even in the Upper Palaeolithic, when glacial cold reached its maximum intensity, France, on account of its latitude, never experienced the long polar nights and the extreme obliquity of the sun's rays which nowadays determine the establishment and extent of tundra in Arctic regions (Bordes 1968).

In periods of more favourable climate with higher temperatures and humidity forest species return or increase. Scotch pine (Pinus silvestris) returned to northern France, associated with birch and hazel. In the southwest pine and hazel were accompanied by such warmth-loving species as lime, elm, beech, maple, ash and, rarely, oak. At times when climatic improvement was most marked the trees formed woods and light forests, along with considerable hazel copses, with temperate undergrowth including ivy, blackthorn, hawthorn and, on calcareous soils, box and juniper, as well as numerous ferns. Along the watercourses plantations of willow and alder grew up, and in the pools and meres there were reeds and rushes, ranunculus and floating and submerged plants, such as the water-lily (nymphaea). Between the forest zones and thickets lay grassland and there was an abundance of heather and bilberry. All in all, this vegetation was adapted to relatively temperate conditions.

During the very cold and dry phases of Würm III and Würm IV trees and temperate plants disappeared. They were replaced by grasses, characteristic of open prairie and steppe. At certain periods steppe, dotted with helianthemum and artemisia but without trees or shrubs, doubtless covered the whole of Europe, including France. During the final oscillations of Würm IV, the Late Glacial stage, there were two warmer intervals, named Bølling and Allerød, which C14 dates to 12-11,000 and 10,500-10,000 BC. They are characterised by a growth of Scotch pine and birch, accompanied in the southwest by some deciduous trees. In between these oscillations there were periods of great cold, the 'Dryas phases' of the Scandinavian researchers. In France,

Geology	Glacial phases (cold periods)	Interglacial phases (more temperate periods)	Dates (approximate)	CULTURES		INDUSTRIES (characteristic forms)		HUMAN FOSSILS	ART
PLEISTOCENE	WÜRM IV		10,000	AZILIAN		flat harpoons, Azilian points, thumb-nail scrapers, geometric microliths		Rochereil	painted pebbles
				MAGDALENIAN	VIb	harpoons with double row of barbs, 'parrot-beak' burins, shouldered points, Laugerie-Basse and Teyjat points, bone points, *plus* in the upper levels (VIb) Azilian points and geometric microliths			
					VIa				Limeuil, Teyjat (VI)
					V	harpoons with single row of barbs, bone points, semicircular wands, spear-throwers		Laugerie-Basse Chancelade St-Germain-la-Rivière Cap Blanc	La Madeleine (IV, V, VI)
			12,000		IV	harpoon prototypes, forked base points, semicircular wands			carved outlines (IV) Cap Blanc (III)
					III	grooved bone points, semi-circular wands, delicate long bone points			
			15,000		II	bone points with conical or pyramidal base, bladelets, triangles, denticulated triangles			
		Interstadial Würm III-IV			I	bone points with oval section, with bevelled or pointed base, and grooved spike motif, raclettes, star-shaped borers, transverse burins with notch and lateral retouch			
			17,000	SOLUTREAN PROTO-SOLUTREAN	final upper middle lower	laurel-leaf points, Solutrean arrowheads, willow-leaf points, shouldered points, bladelets laurel-leaf points unifacial points unifacial points		Roc de Sers	Roc de Sers Fourneau du Diable
				AURIGNACIAN V		bone points with simple bevel and grooves			
			18,000	PROTO-MAGDALENIAN		retouched blades		Abri Pataud	decorated *bâton*
	WÜRM III		20,000	UPPER PERIGORDIAN	VI Vc Noailles Vb trunc. el. Va Font-Robert IV GRAVETTE IV FONTENIOUX	truncated pieces Noailles burins truncated elements Font-Robert points Gravette points	flat burins, backed bladelets, uneven scrapers on flakes, arrowheads, Gravette points		'Venuses'
			25,000	AURIGNACIAN	IV III II I	biconical bone points oval bone points lozenge-shaped bone points split base bone points	Dufour bladelets, 'beaked' burin, flat-nosed scraper, retouched blades, notched blades	Cro-Magnon Grimaldi negroids	painted and engraved rocks: Abri Blanchard, Abri Cellier, La Ferrassie, Laussel
			30,000						pigments, personal ornaments, notched bones and stones
		Interstadial Würm II-III	40,000	LOWER PERIGORDIAN	"II" LES COTTÉS I CHÂTELPERRON	Chatelperronian and Les Cottés points *plus* Mousterian tools, ochres, incised objects of bone and ivory, pierced teeth		Combe-Capelle	
				MOUSTERIAN				Neandertal	

8 Evolution of the Upper Palaeolithic in France (after A. Roussot)

flora analogous to that of the cold northern steppe is not found in the southwest.[1]

8 The position of Upper Palaeolithic industries in relation to this climatic sequence can now be summarized (Bordes 1958; Laville 1964 and fig. 10). Early and Lower Perigordian occur in reddish deposits, clayey or sandy in texture indicative of extremely high humidity and a fairly moderate temperature.

The Aurignacian which follows undoubtedly appeared a little before the third stadial of Würm, but it is only in the course of the intense dry cold of Würm III, with its Arctic fauna, that Aurignacian I developed fully. It grew milder, with fauna adapted to the more temperate conditions, during Aurignacian II. Subsequently the cold returned, and frost-induced rock-falls continued until the end of the Aurignaco-Perigordian cycle, though there was one short milder and more humid oscillation, contemporary with the occurrence of 'Noailles' burins in the Perigordian. The Aurignaco-Perigordian industries were followed by the Solutrean towards the end of the same cold and dry phase, as attested by a zone of angular debris in the cave deposits, but later less uniform conditions obtained with a fauna dominated by reindeer.

This regressive oscillation in Würm III was followed by the inception of a marked interstadial, Würm III-IV. Rise in temperature and increased humidity began during the Upper Solutrean, but fully temperate conditions were not re-established until the development of the Lower Magdalenian, reflected in the cessation of frost-action and deposits of angular scree and in the accumulation of water-laid clays. From Middle Magdalenian times onwards there appeared premonitory indications of the last and most intense cold period, Würm IV, which developed during the Upper Magdalenian. With it went a gradual increase in desiccation, which was particularly suited to the saïga antelope.

At the end of the Magdalenian more temperate and humid conditions set in, a prelude to post-glacial times and the final disappearance of cold fauna from France. The Reindeer Age had come to an end.

Upper Palaeolithic industries

The works of Henri Breuil (1912) and Denis Peyrony (1933, 1936, 1946) during the first half of the twentieth century established the sequence of Upper Palaeolithic industries on a firmer basis in France than in any other European country. Peyrony's excavations at Les Eyzies, La Ferrassie (1934) and Laugerie-Haute (D. and E. Peyrony 1938) form the foundation of a classification which statistical analysis has confirmed in its general validity

[1] I am grateful to M. M. Paquereau for providing me with all this material, much of it unpublished, on vegetation.

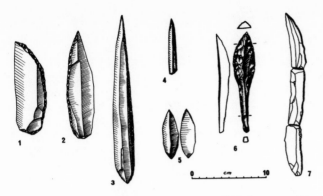

9 *Flint points from the Perigordian: 1, Châtelperron point or knife; 2, Les Cottés point; 3, Gravettian point; 4, micro-Gravette point; 5, dart ('fléchette'); 6, Font-Robert point; 7, associated truncated flints (after Peyrony 1934, fig. 88). Drawings by P. Laurent*

(Sonneville-Bordes 1959). Preliminary or complete publication of modern excavations in France since the Second World War, particularly in the key region of Périgord and the surrounding Corrèze, Vienne and Charente (Sonneville-Bordes 1959 and 1966), and various monographs – on the French Solutrean by P. Smith (1966), the Palaeolithic in Ardèche by J. Combier (1967), the Upper Palaeolithic in the Ile-de-France by B. Schmider (1968) and M. Escalon de Fonton's work on the Mediterranean Midi – confirm and complete the classic framework for the Upper Palaeolithic in France.

AURIGNACIAN AND PERIGORDIAN

The cycle of Aurignacian and Perigordian industries occupies the beginning of the Upper Palaeolithic. H. Breuil (1912) regarded this as the linear development of a single culture, the Aurignacian. This he subdivided into levels, first with Châtelperron points, which are flint points with curved backs, then with split-base bone points and finally with Gravettian points, slender flint points with straight backs. Peyrony's lifetime of excavation at numerous sites in the Dordogne, especially at La Ferrassie and Laugerie-Haute, allowed him to distinguish among this material two industrial complexes: the Perigordian, which comprises those levels with backed flint points and the Aurignacian *sensu stricto* in the levels with bone points.

Work by F. Bordes (1958b) at Laugerie-Haute and H. Movius (1960 and 1966) at the Abri Pataud – vast rock-shelters at Les Eyzies on the right and left banks of the Vézère respectively – verify the general validity of this distinction. However, the chronology of material between the top of the Aurignacian layers and the base of the Lower Solutrean remains to be determined.

Lower Perigordian (= Chatelperronian or Castelperronian. Eponymous site: the cave of Châtelperron, Allier)

The passage from Middle to Upper Palaeolithic in all probability emanated from the Mousterian in its most progressive branch, the Mousterian of Acheulean tradi-

tion, at least in France which is the only country in Europe to have, albeit in limited number, early or Lower Perigordian deposits initiating its Upper Palaeolithic. Provided that we take into account only stratigraphically proved sequences it is impossible to deny that Lower Perigordian material is transitional in character, although given to novelty. The characteristic tool is a flint point with the curved back steeply retouched, the Châtelperron point or knife. 'Archaic', Mousterian-type tools – side-scrapers, serrated flints and Mousterian points – are abundant in the oldest layers. They later become fewer, and there is a proportional increase in end-scrapers, burins and borers, often indifferently worked. At Arcy-sur-Cure (Yonne) a fair variety of worked bone is associated: points, perforated teeth, notched bones and bone-cut pendants (André Leroi-Gourhan 1964). Alongside this traditional early Perigordian there is a variant freer from Mousterian influ-

10 *Flint implements from the Perigordian group: 1, scraper; 2, denticulated flint (Lower Perigordian); 3, double burin; 4, bitruncated backed blade, La Gravette; 5, angle-burin on trimmed blade, Laugerie-Haute (proto-Magdalenian); 6, 'Noailles' burin; 7, backed bladelet; 8, flake scraper, La Gravette (Upper Perigordian). Drawings by P. Laurent*

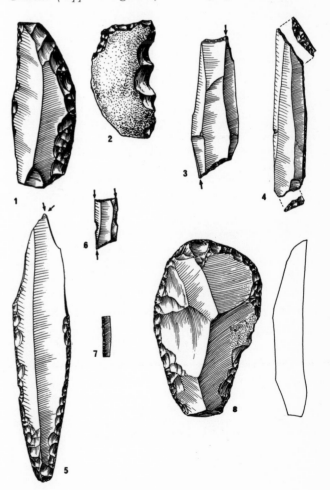

11 Tomb of the 'negroids' at the Grotte des Enfants, Grimaldi (after Verneau 1912)

in France succeeded and absorbed it. Far more abundant than the Lower Perigordian, the Aurignacian was frequently established at new sites. It is characterised by fine bone work abundant and diversified: awls, polishers, perforated batons and objects incised with regular lines, 'marques de chasse' or hunting tallies. The bone *20:1* points (often termed spear-points: *pointes de sagaie*) evolved during the long period of Aurignacian development from phase I to V. The split-base points of *6* Aurignacian I are notable: flat and elongated, of more *12:1* or less triangular outline, with a cleft at the base. With Aurignacian III came the invention of a forked base. *12:2* The very late final variant Aurignacian V at Laugerie-Haute contained spear-points with a simple bevelled end, unique in the Palaeolithic, and on which the bone *12:3* canals can be seen.

The lithic industry is very different from the Perigordian and in its early phases is characterised by finely made invasive scale-like trimming, reminiscent of that of the Mousterian of Quina type. This was used in the *13:1*

9:2 ence (Pradel 1963) which has curved-back points with the base worked as a scraper, called Les Cottés points (from the Les Cottés Cave, Vienne).

No representational art is yet known from the Lower Perigordian.

Though more have recently been found, sites are few. They lie between the rivers Loire and Yonne and the Pyrenees, with an outpost on the Mediterranean coast at Grimaldi, though material is practically unknown in *5* the valley of the Rhône. The zone of greatest intensity and variety is between the Yonne, Loire, and Garonne.

The oldest *Homo sapiens sapiens* in France dates from this period. At the Roc de Combe-Capelle shelter (Dordogne), lying in a grave in the Lower Perigordian layer and adorned with marine shells, was a relatively short man (about 1.60 m.) with fairly primitive characteristics: strong eyebrow ridges and a poorly defined chin.[1] The *11* two 'negroid' skeletons found at Grimaldi in the lower layers of the Grotte des Enfants, near Menton, are of approximately the same period. An old woman and an adolescent boy were lying side by side in a pit in a contracted position; Verneau (1906-12) compared them to Bushmen and Hottentots owing to certain morphological features – though rather short in stature the legs were very long, the face broad and short, with very *1:2* wide nose with a basal depression, prognathous jaw and massive teeth. This 'negroid' interpretation has now been abandoned; the skeletons are doubtless simply a local variant of the common European Upper Palaeolithic stock (Piveteau 1957, 1962).

Typical Aurignacian (eponymous site: the cave of Aurignac, Haute-Garonne)
There is no archaeological continuity between the Lower Perigordian and the typical Aurignacian which

12 Upper Palaeolithic bone points: 1, split-base point, Aurignacian I, La Ferrassie; 2, forked base point, Aurignacian III, La Ferrassie; 3, point with single end bevel, Aurignacian V, Laugerie-Haute; 4, spear with single bevel, Magdalenian III, Laugerie-Haute (east); 5, spear with incised lines, Upper Solutrean, Fourneau du Diable; 6, large spear, Perigordian with 'Noailles' burins, Gavaudun; 7, large spear with double-bevel, Magdalenian VI, La Madeleine. Drawings by P. Laurent

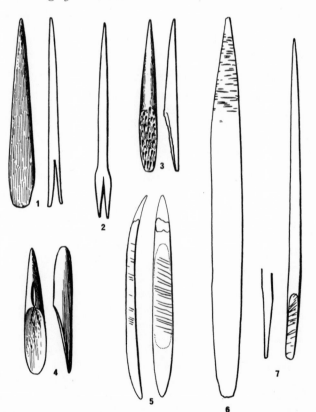

[1] The true sapient character of this specimen is however in no serious doubt. – Ed.

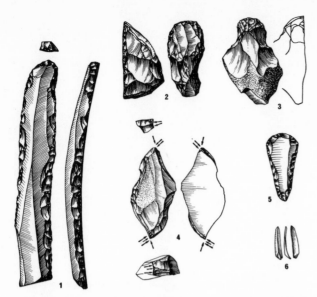

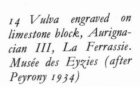

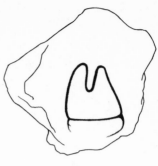

14 Vulva engraved on limestone block, Aurignacian III, La Ferrassie. Musée des Eyzies (after Peyrony 1934)

13 Aurignacian flint implements: 1, Aurignacian blade scraper; 2, carinated scraper; 3, nosed scraper; 4, 'beaked' burin; 5, fan scraper; 6, Dufour bladelet. Drawings by P. Laurent

manufacture of large, freely trimmed blades, sometimes strangulated. Distinctive scrapers, carinated and nosed, *13:2-3* were worked on thick flakes or nodules by a delicate lamellar retouch. Bladelets called Dufour bladelets (after those from the Dufour cave, Corrèze), worked with an *13:6* alternating, semi-abrupt retouch, which are known throughout the Upper Palaeolithic, occur here in their most typical form and in large quantities. As the Aurignacian develops, retouched blades disappear, the proportion of end-scrapers grows less while that of burins, *13:4* characteristically beaked burins, increases. Typical Aurignacian is very strongly represented between the Loire and the Pyrenees, but far less evident in the Rhône valley, penetrating to Mediterranean France only at Grimaldi.[1]

The first animal paintings, in red and black, appear during the early Aurignacian, and the first engravings are found on blocks of stone fallen from the roof of rock-shelters. The engravings, which are deeply incised and at times amount almost to reliefs, generally depict animals, imperfectly rendered and difficult to interpret. The best is undoubtedly a deer engraved in dotted depressions from the Abri du Renne at Belcayre (Dor- *14* dogne). In the same period are found human vulvae in association with cupmarks and engraved lines, deeply incised on stone blocks in the shelters of La Ferrassie, Le Poisson and Cellier in the Dordogne. This motif is unknown at later periods (Sonneville-Bordes 1965).

Multiple burials have been found in the Aurignacian layers at Cro-Magnon and Grimaldi. The skeletons were powdered with red ochre and adorned with neck-

laces and bracelets of shells, perforated teeth and occasionally fish vertebrae. They belong to the Cro-Magnon race (named from the Cro-Magnon shelter at Les Eyzies, Dordogne), which was tall in stature (1.80 m.), with robust, flattened tibia, and very large hands, long, narrow skull, broad and short face, high forehead, very wide, subquadrangular orbital apertures, high cheekbones, delicate, narrow nose and well-defined chin. *1:3*

Upper Perigordian (= Gravettian. Eponymous site: the shelter of La Gravette, Dordogne)

In southwestern France and in the Pyrenees Aurignacian deposits are overlain by layers with Upper Perigordian, characterised by the presence, in variable proportions, of a flint point with a straight back trimmed by abrupt retouching. This is the Gravettian point. Due to the *9:3* complexity of the industries and their successions it is not possible to establish a definitive scheme of cultural development during this period, which lasted until the Solutrean. Modern excavations at Laugerie-Haute (Bordes 1958b) and the Abri Pataud (Movius 1960, 1966) have contributed many details and also modifications to the chronological framework of post-Aurignacian industries near Les Eyzies, the region of western Europe where it appears in its most complete and complex forms. The stratigraphical successions of the two sites appear to be complementary.

Without going into detail it can be said that a connection between the Lower and Upper Perigordian is confirmed by the existence in both assemblages of flint points with the back blunted by steep retouch, the Chatelperronian and Gravettian points respectively with *9:1, 3* the Les Cottés point as an intermediary. This connection, *9:2* however, is not admitted by all archaeologists. Distinguishing features of the Upper Perigordian are the excellence of the technique for detaching blades, the poor execution or absence of secondary work on tools of all types, the abundance of burins, which are often *10:3* multiple, and the appearance of backed bladelets. Bone *10:7* work is not abundant and shows little variety. In the *12:6* course of successive stages of Upper Perigordian development specialised tools appear and disappear, as they were invented and then abandoned: darts in *9:5* association with large flake scrapers, truncated flints, *10:8, 4* tanged Font-Robert points (Font-Robert cave, Cor- *9:6* rèze) and tiny, multiple 'Noailles' burins (Noailles *10:6* cave, Corrèze).

[1] Though found outside France down the northwestern Italian coast and in Spain. – Ed.

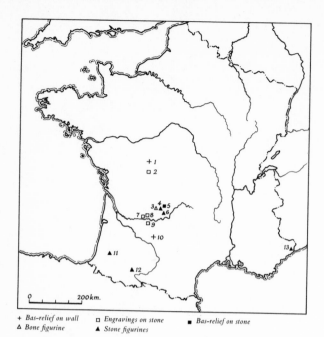

15 Distribution map of Upper Palaeolithic portrayals of women. 1 Angles. 2 La Marche. 3 Laugerie-Basse. 4 Tursac. 5 Laussel. 6 Sireuil. 7 Couze. 8 Lalinde. 9 Termo-Pialat. 10 La Magdeleine (Penne). 11 Brassempouy. 12 Lespugue. 13 Grimaldi

+ Bas-relief on wall   □ Engravings on stone   ■ Bas-relief on stone
△ Bone figurine   ▲ Stone figurines

It is curious that Font-Robert points and 'Noailles' burins show different distributions. The points are concentrated between the Loire and the Garonne, outside this area they occur in the Macon region, in the Ile-de-France near Nemours (Cirque de la Patrie: Schmider 1968) and even in Belgium (Sonneville-Bordes 1961).[1] They are unknown on the French slopes of the Pyrenees (Méroc 1963), and so too in Spain. By contrast the more numerous 'Noailles' burins are widespread in the classic region between the Loire and the Garonne, they also occur in the French Pyrenees, but not in Spain, reach the Mediterranean at Grimaldi, but are so far unknown north of the Loire. The Rhône valley in this period was practising a quite different industry showing microlithic tendencies with fine flint work, microgravers and small shouldered points. These J. Combier (1967) has grouped under the name of Rhodanian.

It is now necessary to transfer to this period the little female statuettes which were once wrongly referred to as 'Aurignacian Venuses'. Very similar finds have been found in Italy, central Europe, the Danube valley and far to the east in the Ukraine. The human figures in a 1, I like style, mostly nude females, found engraved or 15 sculpted in low relief on blocks or slabs of stone (Laussel and Termo Pialat in the Dordogne), are doubtless of the same date. There are also animal engravings on small bone and stone objects, as well as works on 16 cave walls, engraved, painted or even sculptured, such as the unskilful deep engravings at Pair-non-Pair in the

Gironde and the fine fish in low relief at the Abri du 9 Poisson at Les Eyzies (Sonneville-Bordes 1965).

Human remains deriving from this period are very fragmentary.

PROTO-MAGDALENIAN
Above the final Perigordian at Laugerie-Haute and the Abri Pataud there were layers with an industry unknown as yet elsewhere, the proto-Magdalenian. How it relates to Aurignacian-Perigordian industries remains to be determined. It comprises large blade burins, 10:5 backed bladelets, fine and strongly trimmed blades, Gravettian points and microgravers. The overall typological affinities appear to relate it to Perigordian tradition (Peyrony 1933; Sonneville-Bordes 1959; Bordes and Sonneville-Bordes 1966). Bone objects are abundant. On a reindeer-antler baton from Laugerie-Haute, with a broken perforation at one end, there are engravings in low relief of, on one side, two opposed mammoths and on the other the hindquarters of a bison. This is the earliest example of naturalistic decoration on a small object known in France. The same industry discovered by Movius at the Abri Pataud contained no artistic work, but there were important human remains, especially those of an adolescent girl showing fairly close resemblance to the ancient Cro-Magnon type (Movius and Vallois 1960).

Throughout France Aurignacian and Perigordian industries are totally independent of each other and show no reciprocal influences in their composition, although the stratigraphies demonstrate that they developed parallel to one another for several thousands of years.[2] The limited distribution of the Lower Perigordian argues in favour of an origin somewhere between the Loire, the Yonne and the Garonne. If Peyrony's hypothesis that the Upper Perigordian developed by evolution from the Lower be maintained, it would seem reasonable that the transition took place in the classic zone between the Loire and the Pyrenees, the only area where deposits of both industries are found.

The wide distribution of the typical Aurignacian with split-base bone points between Hungary and the Atlantic shows that at this period France belonged to a

[1] But their reported occurrence in Britain has not been confirmed. – Ed.

[2] But not necessarily in this area. – Ed.

48

sort of European community, of which it formed only the Atlantic province. The primary area of the Aurignacian lies south of the Loire. A few sparse traces on the loess plains of the Paris basin are indicative of occasional passage, arising no doubt from the contacts established between the southern tribes and the Aurignacian group in the Belgian Ardennes. In the latest phases the zone of expansion contracted into the region of Périgord-Corrèze and Vienne. The late survival of Aurignacian V at Laugerie-Haute is consistent with this reduction in the culture's area.[1]

Alongside and in contrast, the Perigordian which had been rare in its early stages expanded in its evolved form to reach even the previously almost deserted region of Ile-de-France, at Cirque de la Patrie. No reason is apparent for the contrasted diffusion of assemblages with Font-Robert points towards the north and of those with 'Noailles' burins southwards, at the time when Perigordian sites reached their greatest density and extent. Except in the classic zone, the break is striking and general for the whole period from evolved Perigordian up to and including the Lower Solutrean. The rest of France was at this time a wilderness, as were the adjacent Spain and Belgium.[2]

SOLUTREAN (EPONYMOUS SITE:
SOLUTRÉ, SAÔNE-ET-LOIRE)
The Solutrean is the best defined of French lithic industries from a typological point of view and the most confined geographically. It occurs between the Loire where it is known only from a group of caves in the Mayenne, the Rhône which it does not cross, and the Pyrenees, with extensions into Catalonia in the east and Asturias in the west. It does not occur in Provence, where an industry with backed points, the Epiperigordian, takes its place (Escalon de Fonton 1966). There are three subdivisions: Lower Solutrean with unifacial points, Middle Solutrean with laurel-leaf points, and Upper Solutrean with notched and willow-leaf points. It is rare to find all three stages in superposition. They are present at Laugerie-Haute, but not at the eponymous site of Solutré.

17 The typical implements are worked with the flat and parallel-sided retouch termed Solutrean, which gives the industry its highly distinctive position in the evolution of Upper Palaeolithic techniques. For the first time, indeed, pressure-flaking was widely employed, sometimes for the manufacture of unifacial points and 18 laurel-leaves, which could also be made by percussion, but especially for notched points and the willow-leaf. The technique is difficult, time-consuming and laborious, but produces very regular flaking. It was carried by the Solutreans to a high degree of perfection, and was then abandoned to reappear again only in the

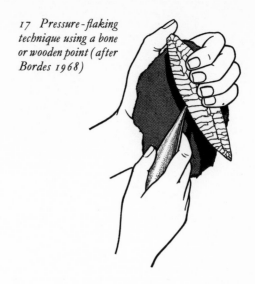

17 Pressure-flaking technique using a bone or wooden point (after Bordes 1968)

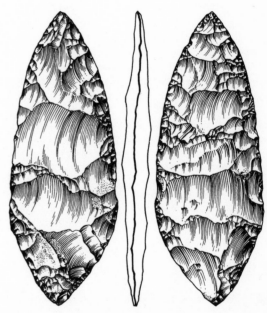

18 Large laurel-leaf worked by percussion-flaking, Solutré, Saône-et-Loire (after Combier 1967)

Bronze Age (Bordes 1968). Jasper works far better than flint by pressure-flaking and was often used by the Solutreans. They also discovered the technique of heating flint, which when raised to a temperature of 200-300°C in sand works more easily when pressure-flaked (Bordes 1968).

The Solutrean evolved through successive substitutions of the type fossils: unifacial points, then laurel-leaves varying greatly in size and at times notched, 19:1-2 tanged or with a wide indentation, as at the very curious site of Montaut in the Landes, and finally 19:5 shouldered points and willow-leaves. Once invented, 19:4,3 these diagnostic forms were at no point entirely abandoned. Material common to all phases shows little

[1] There is however some evidence for a special variant of this culture at this time north of the Alps and in the British peninsula (as it then was). – Ed.

[2] The lack of population at this time in the Rhône basin and Spain is not a view shared by all specialists. – Ed.

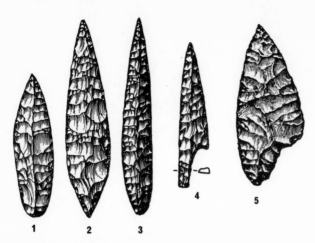

19 Typical Solutrean implements : 1, unifacial point, Lower Solutrean; 2, laurel-leaf point, Middle Solutrean; 3, willow-leaf point, Upper Solutrean; 4, shouldered point, Upper Solutrean; 5, laurel-leaf from Montaut. Drawings by P. Laurent

change. Mousterian types, side-scrapers and points, reappear after a break of thousands of years. Burins are rare and end-scrapers on blades fairly numerous, sometimes fan-shaped or with Solutrean flaking. Borers are relatively frequent and backed bladelets rare or absent, except in the final phase (Sonneville-Bordes 1960; Smith 1966).

The working of bone shows little variety. The Solutreans, however, invented an eyed needle in bone or ivory, just like those we use. They also made notched 20 : 2-3 objects – 'hunting tallies' – and bracelets.

Some regions were not reached by the Solutrean until its middle phase of development. Early Solutrean occurs only in the Périgord and in the Gard-Ardèche region, possibly also at Le Trilobite (Yonne). In its

middle phase, with the laurel-leaf, it reached the Pyrenees, penetrating into Spain, and appeared in the Rhône valley.[1] This is the time of its widest distribution. If these movements to the south were initiated by population pressure within the classic region, the bands who were dispersed on to the French slopes of the Pyrenees and along the Cantabrian coast would doubtless have lost contact with their point of origin. In fact some of the original forms invented in Spain – concave-base laurel-leaves and bone spear-points with a flattened middle obliquely scored with fine lines – are also found 12 : 5 on a few Pyrenean sites in France. Thus there was more contact between the two sides of the Pyrenees than between the north and south of the Garonne basin (Méroc 1956). The industry at Montaut (Landes), with shouldered leaf-points peculiar to the site, is perhaps 19 : 5 the result of geographical isolation. The final stage of Solutrean development, Upper Solutrean with shouldered points, is strikingly represented in the classic region, although its type fossil is known neither north of the Loire nor in the Rhône valley.

There has long been debate over the origins of the Solutrean. From technical analogies and distribution of bifacial work it was assumed that the culture originated in Hungary, in north Africa or again in Spain. These hypotheses are now entirely abandoned. The origins of the Solutrean should not be sought in central Europe, where the industry is not present, nor in Spain where only its latest phases are known. It cannot have arisen

21 Distribution map of Upper Palaeolithic sculptured friezes: 1 Angles. 2 La Chaire-à-Calvin. 3 Le Roc de Sers. 4 Fourneau du Diable. 5-8 Laugerie-Haute, Cap-Blanc, Commarque, Reverdit. 9 La Magdeleine (Tarn). 10 Isturitz. 11 Tuc d' Audoubert

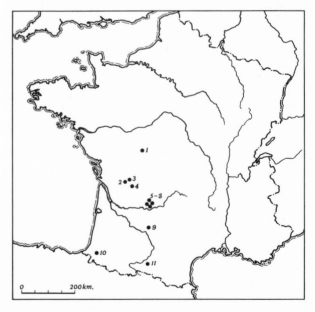

20 Scored objects ('hunting-tallies') : 1, Aurignacian, Abri Blanchard, Dordogne, Musée des Antiquités Nationales; 2, Solutrean, Laugerie-Haute (west), Musée des Eyzies; 3, ivory bracelet, Solutrean, Fourneau du Diable, Dordogne, Musée des Eyzies. Drawings by P. Laurent

[1] But only in the western sector; elsewhere the continuing tradition was Gravettian. – Ed.

outside the area bounded by the Loire, Rhône and Garonne, since it scarcely ever crosses the Loire or the Rhône and is found in the Pyrenees to the south only in its middle phase. This area, which produced the earliest Solutrean levels, must necessarily be its zone of origin. In other words the Solutrean, in its flint technique the most brilliant of cultures, is evidently autochthonous.[1]

21 Fine bas-reliefs, representing friezes of animals on blocks of stone, have been found in Solutrean deposits: Roc de Sers (Charente) and Fourneau du Diable (Dordogne).

No human remains are known, apart from some isolated teeth.

MAGDALENIAN (EPONYMOUS SITE: THE SHELTER OF LA MADELEINE, DORDOGNE)

Classification of the Magdalenian was established by H. Breuil (1912) on the basis of its bone tools, which occur in particular abundance and variety and are highly elaborated. Spear-points characterise its early stages (I-III) and harpoons the later (IV-VI). A complete, or almost complete, sequence on a single site is exceptional (Le Placard, Charente; Laugerie-Haute and Chancelade, Dordogne).

The oldest phase is marked by a technique of detaching flint flakes, which were used to make large and heavy utensils, notably burins, and by the presence of *22:2,1* star-shaped borers and a little scraping tool called a *raclette*, which is at times very abundant. Certain authors (Cheynier 1939; Allain and Fritsch 1967; Schmider 1968) isolate this phase under the term Badegoulian (Badegoule, Dordogne).

From the time of Magdalenian II-III, which contains *12:4* bone spear-points and rods of semicircular section, the relative proportion of flint tool types becomes remarkably constant, with burins always abundant, simple

blade scrapers less frequent, as well as composite tools and borers, and very numerous backed bladelets, some- *22:3, 6* times serrated. The prototypes of harpoons appear in the Upper Magdalenian (IV), then harpoons with a single row of barbs (V), and then two rows (VI). Their *23:4-7* size is very variable; most often they are made from reindeer antler and at times decorated with engravings. Some novel flint types appear, limited in distribution and ephemeral: 'parrot-beak' burins do not go beyond *22:4* the Loire and Rhône; flint points, of Laugerie-Basse *24:1-2* type and shouldered, occur in Vaucluse, but are unknown outside France. By contrast, several sites in the classic region of France have produced points with

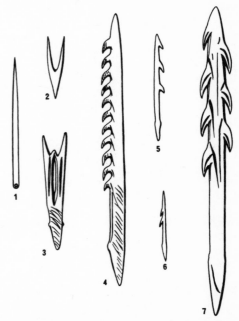

23 *Magdalenian bone implements: 1, eyed needle; 2, forked object, Raymonden, Chancelade; 3, fowling fork, Laugerie-Haute; 4-6, harpoons with single line of barbs (4, 6, Raymonden, Chancelade; 5, Fontalès); 7, harpoon with double line of barbs, La Madeleine. Drawings by P. Laurent*

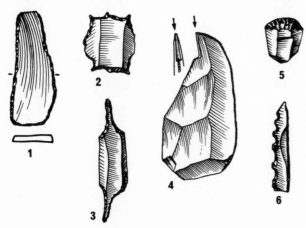

22 *Magdalenian flint implements: 1, scraper (raclette); 2-3, multiple borers; 4, 'parrot-break' burin; 5, end-scraper; 6, serrated, backed bladelet. Drawings by P. Laurent*

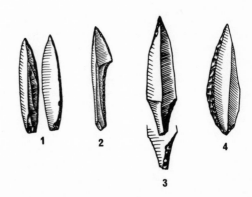

24 *Upper Magdalenian flint points: 1, point, Laugerie-Basse; 2, shouldered point; 3, Teyjat point; 4, Azilian point. Drawings by P. Laurent*

[1] This point of view, shared by P. Smith, is not universally accepted. While the fully evolved variant is undeniably a product of Périgord, more recent data including C14 dates can be held to support an ultimately central European origin on fresh grounds. – Ed.

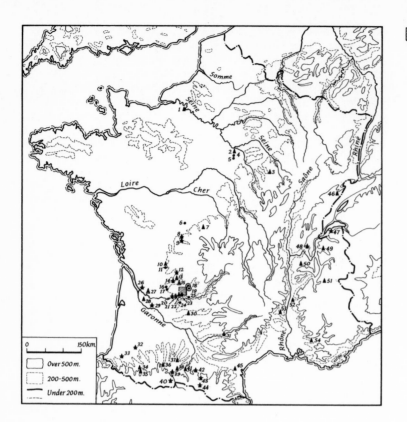

Les Eyzies region
(see Fig. 7)

		Site	Mobiliary art	Burial
Magdalenian	with raclettes	●	◆	◉
	Upper and Final	▲	♣	△

25 Magdalenian sites in France. 1 Gouy. 2 Pincevent. 3 Le Cheval. 4 Les Gros-Monts. 5 Beauregard. 6 La Pluche. 7 Saint-Marcel. 8 La Marche. 9 Le Chaffaud. 10 Mouthiers. 11 Le Placard. 12 Teyjat. 13 Fourneau du Diable. 14 Rochereil. 15 Chancelade. 16 Solvieux. 17 Gabillou. 18 Badegoule. 19 Lachaud. 20 Gare de Couze. 21 La Roche de Lalinde. 22 Le Soucy. 23 Cimeuil. 24 Jean-Blancs. 25 Pech de la Boissière. 26 Les Fées, Marcamps. 27 Saint-Germain-la-Rivière. 28 La Pique. 29 Fontarnaud. 30 Le Martinet. 31 Fontalès. 32 Sorde. 33 Isturitz. 34 Poeymaü. 35 Saint-Michel-d'Arudy. 36 Aurensan. 37 Les Harpons, Lespugue. 38 La Tourasse. 39 Gourdan. 40 Lortet. 41 Marsoulas. 42 Mas d'Azil. 43 Bédeilhac. 44 La Vache. 45 La Crouzade. 46 Arlay. 47 Veyrier. 48 Les Hoteaux. 49 Les Douattes. 50 Bobache. 51 Méaudre. 52 Soubeyras. 53 Oullins. 54 Adaouste

24:3 shoulder or a crude tang and truncated body which are identical with those from Switzerland and Germany, where they are found in quantity (Sonneville-Bordes 1963a).

What is the geographical extent of the Magdalenian? In order to answer this question it is necessary to distinguish between the archaic period, the early Magdalenian with *raclette* scrapers, and 'la belle époque' which began with Middle Magdalenian but *25* reached its full development only in Magdalenian VI. Distribution in the earliest phase is limited, bounded by an arc along the edges of the Massif Central, with a few traces in Burgundy, some shelters and open-air sites in Berry and Poitou and fuller and more extensive development in the south, in Charente, Gironde and above all in Périgord. Early Magdalenian does not cross the Garonne, except for an isolated excursion on to the left bank (reported by E. Monméjean), or the Rhône, though there were some notable open-air sites on the Beauregard plateau near Nemours in the valley of the Loing (Schmider 1968). It remains unknown to the north in the Ardennes and to the south in the Pyrenees. Thus the Magdalenian came to light in the limited area where the great Upper Palaeolithic cultures of western Europe had achieved their greatest density and continuity. But we have also to take into account the exceptional finds in the Loing valley. Previously the lands of the Paris basin north of the Loire had never been among the areas of dense population. Throughout the Upper Palaeolithic sparse collections of flints from deep in the loess or clays, comprising a few tools among

numerous waste blades and bladelets, do not suggest colonisation, but rather brief chance halts of people from adjacent areas south of the Loire or in the Ardennes, hastening across this cave- and shelter-less region, which wind, storm and dust made especially inhospitable. Nonetheless the Beauregard plateau doubtless served as a staging-point in the human advance towards the north, as B. Schmider has suggested (1968).

The limited distribution of early Magdalenian stands in contrast to the remarkable geographical expansion of the Upper Magdalenian. Sites multiplied beyond the regions occupied by the archaic industry. Towards the east they ring the Massif Central. On the right bank of the Saône-Rhône corridor they occupy the mouths of the tributaries which cut through the mountains and there are small groups throughout the Ardèche and Gard valleys. There is a spread into the valley of the Tarn and sites are well represented around the Lot. There was massive expansion along the valleys which penetrate the high lands of the Massif Central from all sides, notably along the natural corridors of the Loire and Allier (Delporte 1966). Southwards there was reoccupation of Pyrenean territory, which had stood abandoned since the end of the Solutrean, throughout the length of its northern slopes, with slight penetration into Catalonia and a broad advance into Cantabrian Spain as far as Asturias, along the Atlantic route already used by the Upper Solutrean. Northwards, regions of Belgium and trans-Rhenish lands were reoccupied, after remaining uninhabited throughout the Solutrean. Once the Rhône was crossed, the Jura and the Dauphiné were heavily colonised.

Much remains to be done to establish, with the requisite chronological precision, the stages and variety of reciprocal connections between these groups and those of south Germany and of Switzerland, which was now inhabited for the first time since the Mousterian period.

This geographical expansion was accompanied in its later stages by a marked diversification of equipment in northern regions away from the classic zone. This may be illustrated from the Magdalenian site of Pincevent in the Ile-de-France, on the alluvial plain of the Seine between its tributaries Yonne and Loing. Recent excavations have established successive occupation layers, dated by radiocarbon to about 10,000 BC. A high proportion of borers is a feature common to almost all Magdalenian series in Switzerland, Germany and Belgium and we can thus define a Germanic type of Magdalenian which is statistically distinct from the final Magdalenian of the classic zone (Sonneville-Bordes 1968). This feature also characterises the Pincevent material and relates it to the Rhenish Magdalenian (Leroi-Gourhan and Brézillon 1966).

Since the end of the Perigordian the Mediterranean coastlands, unaffected by Solutrean, had entered upon a cultural phase characterised by developments distinct

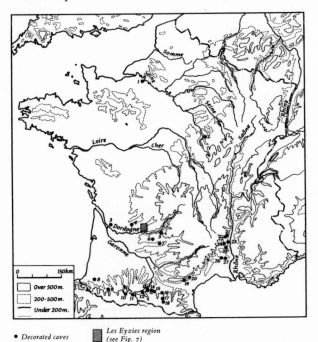

• Decorated caves

▪ Les Eyzies region (see Fig. 7)

26 *Upper Palaeolithic sites with cave art in France.* 1 Gouy. 2 Arcy-sur-Cure. 3 Pair-non-Pair. 4 Gabillou. 5 Roca-madour. 6 Cougnac. 7 Pech-Merle, Cabrerets. 8 Isturitz. 9 Etcheberri. 10 Labastide. 11 Gargas. 12 Montespan. 13 Tuc d'Audoubert. 14 Trois-Frères. 15 Mas d'Azil. 16 Le Portel. 17 Bédeilhac. 18 Niaux. 19 Sallèles-Gabardès. 20 Aldène. 21 Ebbou. 22 Le Colombier. 23 Le Figuier. 24 Oullins. 25 Chabot. 26 La Baume-Latrone. 27 Bayol

from those farther north. The Magdalenians did not reach there but were content to halt in Vaucluse on the right bank of the Durance. There was no crossing of the river apart from one exceptional excursion on to the left bank attested by harpoons in the Adaouste cave, relics of a raid which was probably short-lived (Escalon de Fonton 1966).

The area occupied by the Magdalenians was thus greatly increased between its archaic and final phases. Such expansion does not come about without population pressure, but we lack the most elementary data for producing even rough numerical estimates.

Another sign of vitality is the abundance of works of art of all types throughout the Magdalenian. This is the Golden Age of the Palaeolithic, a peak of true culture in the history of humanity, and in fact the first. Innumerable examples of artistic work engraved or sculptured on weapons and tools or on pieces of stone, bone or 5, 10 ivory, belong in this period, as do a great many of the paintings and engravings on rock walls, as well as those 26 sculptured friezes (Angle-sur-l'Anglin, Isturitz, Mou- 21 thiers) that are not Solutrean.

There is an increase in the number of graves, of women and children as well as of men. We also have a 42 good knowledge of Magdalenian man from numerous complete remains. The human type is the Chancelade man (from the Raymonden shelter, at Chancelade, Dordogne). The body was powdered with red ochre and tightly contracted, as though bound before burial. Granial capacity was very high (1710 cc), in excess of that of modern man. The distinguishing characteristics of this race are the height of the forehead, the ogival elevation of the cranium, projecting cheek bones and 1 : 4 very robust mandible. Height was moderate (1.60 m.). The type has been likened to the Eskimos, but this comparison is nowadays strongly contested (Piveteau 1957, 1962).

AZILIAN (EPONYMOUS SITE:
THE CAVE OF MAS D'AZIL, ARIÈGE)
Beginning in final Magdalenian levels there appear a small number of forms which foreshadow recent times: geometric microliths, curved-back points, as well as 24 : 4 small ogival thumb-shaped flake scrapers. These tools continue to develop in the period that follows, but this sees the end of the glacial era. The Azilian occupied the start of the post-glacial. It corresponds with a humid and temperate period in which the cold-climate fauna disappear. The material is improverished: backed points of Azilian type and small scrapers. Artistic work is mediocre: pebbles incised with geometric signs or painted with red and black dots and strokes. Sites are relatively few. With this the Palaeolithic comes to an end.

The life of the hunter-fishers

GAME
Upper Palaeolithic man lived by hunting, fishing and no doubt gathering. The game available had scarcely changed since Mousterian times, except for an incursion of saïga antelope, in herds which ranged over the 4

53

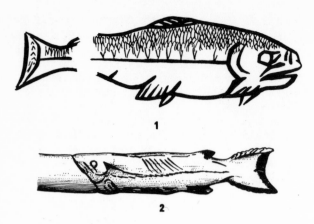

27 *Salmon engraved on a shaft : 1, Lortet, Hautes-Pyrénées (after Piette 1900) ; 2, Grotte Rey, Dordogne (after Breuil and Saint-Périer 1927)*

smoothly undulating lands of Charente and Gironde, and ventured far less often into the broken uplands of the Périgord. Weapons and tools were used for catching, killing, skinning and cutting up the animals whose remains abound on habitation sites, dismembered and with the bones splintered; they include large herbivores (horse, ox and bison), deer (reindeer and red deer), the large cats and other predators (lion, wolf, fox, bear, lynx), pachyderms (mammoth and rhinoceros), and ibex, boar, etc. These served as reserves of meat, but they also furnished bone, ivory and antler for weapons and tools and as a medium for decoration, teeth for necklaces and ornaments, leather and furs for clothing and straps, hair, ligaments and gut for ropes, fastenings and thread. These last perishable remains have not survived, but it is reasonable to assume they were used; there is further-more from the time of the Upper Solutrean the testimony of the eyed needle.

To these long recognised species we may add types of game which often escaped notice in the older excavations because their remains are small. Nowadays the bones and even the claws of birds, as well as fish bones and vertebrae, can be collected by sieving. These made an important contribution to diet, especially grouse, wild duck, snow-partridge and bustard, perch, trout, *27* pike and salmon. The crow and the eagle were used in time of famine. No doubt their feathers were utilised for ornament. This essentially carnivorous diet, of meat and other products such as marrow from long bones, was further supplemented by gathering wild berries (like bilberries), roots and nuts and by collecting wild honey and eggs, as among all hunting peoples, thereby making up for carbohydrate and other deficiencies.

WEAPONS

We can do no more than speculate about their possible function. Ethnographical comparisons, with Australian aborigines for example, tell us little, since the equipment of these societies is infinitely less varied, elaborate and complex than that of Upper Palaeolithic man. By study-

ing traces of wear and by experiment it is possible to set limits to interpretation (Semeenov 1964; Bordes 1967). It is assumed that scrapers were used for scraping skins, borers for piercing holes in leather or drilling stone or bone and burins for grooving, though doubtless these also served many other purposes, to judge from the extensive variety of types.

The use to which flint points were put seems easier to determine (Bordes 1967). They are the points of projectiles, probably the principal weapon of the hunters. In the early Perigordian this holds good for Chatelper-ronian points, the extremely sharp and effective Gravet-tian points and Font-Robert points, furnished with a tang to assist in hafting. In the Solutrean the same was true of the unifacial and the shouldered points; the *19* laurel-leaf was either a missile point or a knife. At the *18* end of the Magdalenian we may include Laugerie-Basse points, and especially points with shoulder or tang. *24*

Bone points were particularly developed in cultures which lack flint points and doubtless served the same function. The Aurignacian invented the split-based spear-point, where for the first time a male haft was *12:1* inserted into its terminal, a device not found again until the socketed forms of the Bronze Age (Bordes 1968). The final Aurignacian and Upper Perigordian saw the appearance of spear-points with simply bevelled ends, *12:3* which survived until the end of the Palaeolithic. The base is often striated, to help steady it against the shaft to which it was bound. The Magdalenians too used this *12:4* form, but they also invented spear-points with a double base bevel which was probably inserted into a fork in *12:7* the haft, as well as forked-base points. In addition they made harpoons, very varied in type, forked objects and *23:2-7* fish-hooks. It was necessary to straighten the shafts of javelins, etc. The well-known perforated batons were perhaps used for this purpose. They are lengths of *28* reindeer antler with a hole (or, rarely, several) bored through the junction with a tine, and sometimes striated. When these first appear in the Aurignacian they are plain; in the Upper Magdalenian, where they are numerous, they are frequently decorated with natu-ralistic or schematic engravings of, say, a row of animals (horse, ibex). There have been many suggestions as to their purpose, and one of these gave rise to the term '*bâtons de commandement*'.[1] Probably, as suggested above, they are straighteners for arrows and spears such as are used by present-day Eskimos.

28 '*Bâton de commandement*', *Magdalenian VI, La Madeleine (after Zervos 1959)*

[1] From their fanciful resemblance to an eighteenth-century army Marshall's ceremonial baton! – Ed.

All this relates to points in non-perishable materials, flint and bone. We know nothing of the advances and modifications which may simultaneously have changed or improved their wooden shafts, or of systems of fixing the point to them, by binding or glueing. It is unlikely that in France wood was ever entirely unobtainable. During the most rigorous steppe periods microclimates in sheltered valleys supported trees, which would provide shafts and handles, and at the same time firewood (Bordes 1968) found in hearths.

At first projectiles would seem to have been thrown by hand. During the Solutrean spear-throwers appear made from reindeer antler and these may well have been preceded by wooden ones which have now disappeared. The Palaeolithic spear-thrower engages by means of a male coupling. It consists of a shaft of varying length (generally about 50 cm. in ethnographic specimens) with a hook at one end. The butt of the

31 Sorcerer playing on a musical bow; engraving, Trois-Frères cave, Ariège (after Breuil 1952)

(Ariège) an engraving which is beyond doubt Magdalenian represents a sorcerer playing on a musical bow. *31* It is not known whether at this time man had progressed from this to the idea of a ballistic bow. In fact many of the small flint points could have served as arrowheads, rather than as javelin points.[1]

HUNTING METHODS

Hunting with missiles is attested by the presence of projectile points, spear-throwers and spear-points, as well as by cave art showing animals with lines on their flanks which are sometimes barbed. Collective expeditions, which call for organisation and planning, would have been indispensable for the capture of the more powerful predators and the pachyderms. Traps and snares were doubtless utilised: the hut-like designs enclosing the mammoth at Bernifal are perhaps representations of these. The enormous heap of horse carcasses, amounting to more than ten thousand head, found in the Upper Palaeolithic level at Solutré (Saône-et-Loire) is not easy to interpret. (It has been called a *'magma à chevaux'* – a midden of horse carcasses.) As the site lies at the foot of a rock overhang, it used to be supposed that the hunters surrounded the herds of horses on the plateau above causing them to stampede and hurl themselves over the edge of the cliff; but the idea of indiscriminate slaughter on this scale is now questioned. Natural catastrophe, such as at times affected the bison in the United States (in the Cheyenne valley: Thévenin 1943), may perhaps account for such a vast bone deposit; or, again, it may signify a slaughterhouse, analogous to the mammoth-slaughtering centres in central Europe at this time.[2]

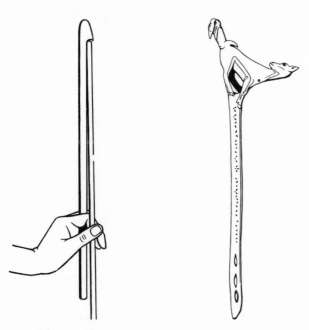

29 Use of the spear-thrower. Drawing by P. Laurent

30 'The fawn and the birds' spear-thrower, Magdalenian, Mas d'Azil, Ariège (after Péquart 1942)

spear to be thrown was placed against the hook and its shaft held in place along the stock. The throwing
29 motion is the same as in hurling a javelin. This method is known to the Eskimos and Australians; it increases the range of a projectile and its power of penetration. Spear-throwers are abundant in the Magdalenian. The stock or shaft is often decorated with engravings and
30 the hook sculptured into fine animal forms.

There are no portrayals of archers in the French Upper Palaeolithic (although they are abundant in Spanish cave art, which is nowadays assigned to a later period). However, in the cave of Les Trois Frères

1 The earliest direct evidence for the bow comes from water-logged deposits in northern Germany associated with the Ahrensburgian culture at about 8800-8000 BC. – Ed.

2 The regular exploitation of migrating herds, a feature of both American Indian and Eskimo life in recent times is another possibility. – Ed.

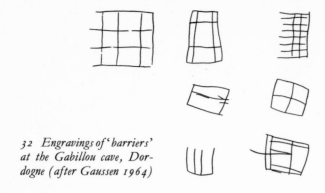

32 Engravings of 'barriers' at the Gabillou cave, Dordogne (after Gaussen 1964)

Some prehistoric paintings and engravings, for example at Gabillou and Lascaux, show what have
32 been interpreted as barriers or enclosures, a possible indication of hunting by driving the herds into artificially fenced-in areas. This leads one to consider the possibility of domestication, or rather semi-domestication, of the horse in Palaeolithic times. This was postulated at the beginning of the century by E. Piette (1906)
6 on the evidence of drawings of horses' heads found in Magdalenian levels in the Pyrenees. These show additional features which Piette interpreted as straps, halters and harness (which he referred to collectively as *chevêtre*).

33 Perigordian tent-footings, Corbiac, Dordogne: structure of layer 1A (excavations F. Bordes)

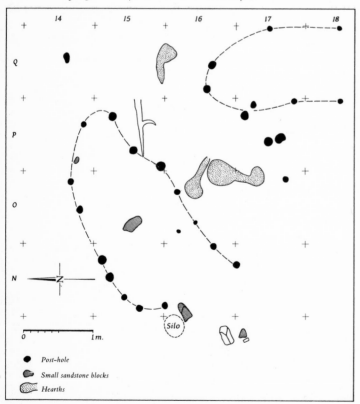

Post-hole
Small sandstone blocks
Hearths

The disputed '*querelle du chevêtre*' has continued through half a century and recently it has been revived by L. Pales and M. Tassin de Saint-Péreuse (1966) who demonstrate that in some instances the features are certainly secondary and could not be merely a schematic representation of either the superficial or internal anatomy of a horse (as occurs in some other instances).

HABITATION

It has long been thought that Palaeolithic man was an incessant nomad, continually moving in pursuit of the reindeer, like the Arctic Eskimos, Lapps and Samoyeds who follow its seasonal migrations. Modern studies of reindeer teeth, however, based on the date of their eruption and their state of wear, make it clear that the Quaternary reindeer in France was never a seasonal migrant (Bouchud 1954, 1959). In fact the reindeer found in the caves had been killed during each of the twelve months of the year, which means that the hunters who killed them lived at these sites throughout the year and did not abandon them seasonally.

At least relatively sedentary, they settled on the access slopes or near the mouth of caves and rock-shelters, preferably ones facing the sun, where they were assured of air, light and sunshine and an escape for the smoke of their fires. It is less usual to find them occupying the deep corridors of caves, as they did at Mas d'Azil, which is a veritable Magdalenian citadel on the right bank of the Arize (Ariège). Fires, which were fed with wood and bone, were frequently laid in hollows which had been scooped out, encircled by large stones and river pebbles. When the fire died down these stones which bordered the hearth gave out their stored heat by radiation. They may even have served to warm or boil liquids in leather or stone vessels, as among the present-day Eskimos.

Stone lamps were another invention of this period; they either consisted of a small cup hollowed out of a rough limestone block or took a more elaborate and ornamented form with a handle, and used fat as fuel. They enabled men to move about easily in the dark cave corridors, where quantities of them have been found, especially in decorated caves like La Mouthe, 8 Lascaux, or Gabillou.

There are few signs that the natural formation of the interior of the caves or shelters had been modified.[1] Works of art, colouring materials, bone and flint tools, hammer-stones, waste flakes and fragments of bone, all are piled pell-mell in the occupation layers and at times mixed with ash from the hearths. The publication of modern excavations at present in progress, in which the position of all objects found is being recorded, may perhaps disclose some domestic order, or working places. In the case of the La Marche cave, Vienne (in course of publication by Pales and Tassin de Saint-Péreuse), which has yielded engraved Magdalenian plaques in thousands, we should perhaps 5

[1] Some instances of post-holes have however been reported from a few sites. – Ed.

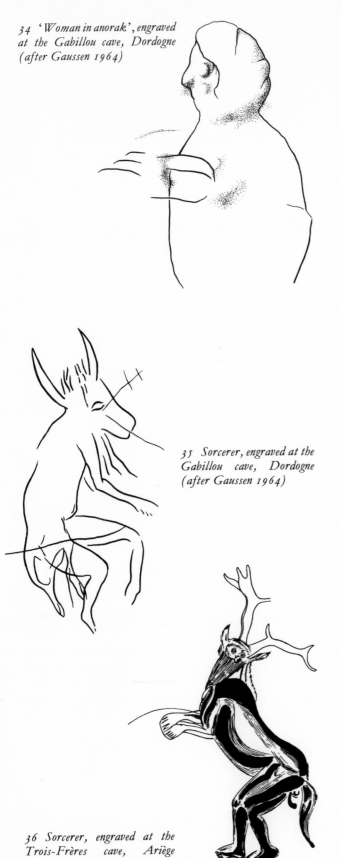

34 'Woman in anorak', engraved at the Gabillou cave, Dordogne (after Gaussen 1964)

35 Sorcerer, engraved at the Gabillou cave, Dordogne (after Gaussen 1964)

36 Sorcerer, engraved at the Trois-Frères cave, Ariège (after Breuil 1952)

37 An amorous pursuit: engraved on bone, Isturitz, Basses-Pyrénées (after Saint-Périer 1936)

adopt the hypothesis of a sort of 'Academy' or training centre, such as has already been suggested for the site of Limeuil in the Dordogne (Capitan and Bouyssonie 1924).

Certain open-air sites dated to the Aurignacian-Perigordian (Rabier and Corbiac en Bergeraçois, Dordogne) and to the Magdalenian (Solvieux, Dordogne; Pincevent, Seine-et-Marne) are at present being examined systematically. Their size varies from a few square metres to several hundreds. Some are paved with pebbles. They are the temporary camping sites of hunters, or seasonal stations that were used either one or several times, as at Corbiac (excavations by F. Bordes) and Pincevent (excavations by A. Leroi-Gourhan), to which men returned, by habit or tradition. Traces of post-holes, accumulations of flints and hearths are also features of open-air sites, as at Corbiac.   *33*

CLOTHING

With the eyed needle, made of bone or ivory and either round or flattened, thread could be drawn through materials. This points to the existence of sewn clothing, which was doubtless cut to shape. Unfortunately in the available representations men and women are almost always naked. The anorak figures in the engraved caves of Gabillou and Angle-sur-l'Anglin alone give some idea of the functional clothing which was worn at the time: it appears to be a heavy garment with a hood. *34* Necklaces, bracelets and anklets sometimes adorn the nude figures and confirm a taste for ornament which is *37* suggested by the shells, stones and pierced teeth found in all the graves. Colouring materials, black manganese dioxide and red iron oxide, found in lumps, sticks or as powder, were perhaps used for body painting. The animal skins worn by certain masked figures painted or engraved deep in the caves are taken to be a particular garb in which sorcerers and 'shamans' dressed up. *35-6* Confronted with an often rigorous climate and by tasks which required ease of movement Upper Palaeolithic man no doubt wore, at least in the open air, some functional garment of leather or fur, perhaps lined with down from birds, as do the Eskimos.

DEMOGRAPHY

Everything indicates that man adapted closely to his natural environment and showed remarkable inventive ingenuity. His cumulative advances right through the Upper Palaeolithic resulted in a 'population explosion' during the Upper Magdalenian. However, data are

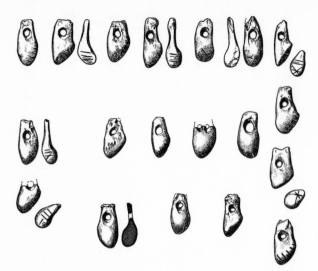

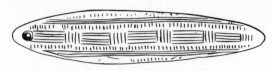

39 *Churinga or reverberating slat (bull-roarer) in reindeer antler with colour-wash of red ochre. Length 15.7 cm. Magdalenian, La Roche de Lalinde, Dordogne. Musée des Antiquités Nationales (after Zervos 1959)*

38 *Parts of a necklace: perforated deer canine teeth. Magdalenian grave at Saint-Germain-la-Rivière, Gironde. Musée des Eyzies. Drawings by P. Laurent*

40 *Seals engraved on a perforated 'bâton'. Magdalenian, Montgaudier, Charente (after Breuil and Saint-Périer 1927)*

lacking for a numerical evaluation of this phenomenon, which manifests itself in the density and richness of sites, the development of art and of burials, and in geographical diffusion. Even in this favourable period settlements remained widely scattered, with some zones of exceptional concentration. Out of the 400 Magdalenian sites 300, or three-quarters, are in southwestern France, 110 in the Périgord alone. One hardly dares venture an overall figure for France, but perhaps the population might be put at 200,000-300,000 (?) remembering that in 1788 the population of Australia was estimated at 300,000, that is between one and two individuals per square mile of the fully inhabited regions along the north coast and in the southeast. It should however be realised that natural conditions were far more rigorous and less favourable in Australia than in southwestern France during the Palaeolithic. The number in each group may be estimated at between twenty-five and thirty individuals, as among present-day primitive hunters (Bushmen, Australian aborigines), with rather a higher figure, perhaps a hundred, in very favourable instances. Present-day primitive peoples are in fact groups on the margin of subsistence, which was certainly not true of the Magdalenians in their prime (Sonneville-Bordes 1968).

These people buried many, though by no means all, of their dead in the caves and shelters. It is not known if distinctions of rank, age or sex determined the choice of grave. From statistical study of the seventy-six skeletons of determinable age and sex from all the Upper Palaeolithic graves in Europe, H. Vallois (1937, 1960, 1961) has concluded that expectation of life was low and infant mortality very high, as is usual among primitive people where fertility reaches its natural rate. Women died earlier than men, before the age of forty,

no doubt because of the risks of pregnancy and childbirth. The very few old men did not exceed the age of sixty.

DISEASE

Reasonable conjecture apart, we do not know what were the causes of death among Upper Palaeolithic people (Vallois 1934). The skeletons show no sign of rickets. The teeth are not decayed though at times they are extremely worn, right down to the roots, no doubt because they were used as tools, to soften skins and draw threads, as among the Eskimos. Trepanning was not practised in France at this time – it did not appear until later, in the Neolithic – neither was dental mutilation or avulsion.[1] Impressions of hands on the cave walls include some where fingers or joints are missing, sometimes seen as proof of voluntary or pathological mutilation. More probably, however, these resulted from flexing the fingers, perhaps indicating a sign language (Leroi-Gourhan 1967), or a magical practice.[2] In rare instances human remains have been adapted after death; thus, skull caps at Le Placard had been trimmed into cups and an infant jaw from Les Trois Frères had been perforated. This is evidence of magical beliefs rather than of cannibalism.

COMMUNICATION

Development of articulate speech must of course have taken place long before this period. But during the

[1] As occurred among the contemporary hunters of north Africa, for instance. – Ed.

[2] A sign language of hand gestures was practised by North American Indians. – Ed.

Upper Palaeolithic, man seems to have used representational signs for recording numbers and perhaps for transmitting messages. From the earliest Aurignacian, and more frequently in the Solutrean and Magdalenian, bones and pieces of antler are marked with repetitively incised lines, arranged in groups in many different ways. These 'hunting tallies', as they have been called, must relate to a system of enumeration for a subject which eludes us. Could it have been items of game, numbers of vanquished foes or phases of the moon? There are engraved symbols such as those on seventy *38* deer teeth from the necklace of the 'Lady' of Saint-Germain-la-Rivière (Gironde) – a Magdalenian skeleton powdered with red ochre and buried beneath a small 'dolmen'. Also from the final Magdalenian there are *10* little scenes engraved on bone (their meaning is obscure but perhaps they are a form of pictograph, like the bison scene from Le Château, Les Eyzies (Dordogne). The later painted pebbles of the Azilian have been interpreted by E. Piette as a sort of writing. The *31, 39* musical bow from Les Trois Frères and the 'churinga' from Roche de Lalinde are proof of an interest in music.[1]

MOVEMENT

Nothing is known of any system of exchange or barter. Nevertheless men did leave their local hunting grounds for distant excursions to the shores of the Atlantic and Mediterranean and shells from these seas are found on Périgord sites. Far more surprising are the remains of seal, an unusual animal to bring back or obtain by exchange. It was found at the Lartet shelter at Les Eyzies and at Chancelade near Périgueux. Several Magdalenian sites, such as Montgaudier, Sorde and *40* Isturitz, also contained drawings of seals.

MAGIC

In all probability the hunter will have sought to reinforce the effectiveness of his ingenious technical inventions by attempting to exercise power over nature, and in particular over his quarry – a power conferred by magical practices. (This has, however, been questioned by A. Leroi-Gourhan, 1964, 1965). Such practices were no doubt developed throughout the whole of the twenty millennia involved. Ethnological comparisons support a possible interpretation of positive and negative hand impressions, in red and black found on cave walls, as ownership signs. Sometimes these occur isolated (Font de Gaume), at other times they surround or impinge on figures of animals. H. Breuil attributed them to the archaic Aurignacian period. Women were not excluded from this remote hand magic: at Gargas (Ariège) and Pech-Merle (Lot) the diminutive versions suggest small female or infant hands. The rite was no longer practised during the later Magdalenian. The magic hands disappear from the deep caves, while by contrast animals,

wounded or pierced by darts, become more numerous. *7* Human figures, often grotesque, masked and clad in animal skins, must surely be sorcerers, perhaps members *35-6* of some sort of order.

WOMEN

The role of women in Upper Palaeolithic societies underwent an evolution in the course of the twenty millennia. The Venuses of the old Aurignacian-Peri- *1, I* gordian cycle are almost invariably representations of women with the heavy form that denotes pregnancy, perhaps the mother-goddesses of a fertility cult, unless they were sorceresses serving as charms or talismans by reason of the powers of exorcism often attributed to the feminine sex as such (Gobert 1968). The majority are figurines which could have been worn as a pendant. The reclining or recumbent women of the Magdalenian, engraved or sculptured on cave or shelter walls, or on blocks of stone as in the case of the Venus of Gare de *41* Couze, are a different matter. These are not pregnant and their function is perhaps more secular. The scene engraved on a bone at Isturitz would suggest this; it is *37* not known whether it depicts an erotic pursuit, a magical hunt or a sexual initiation rite (Saint-Perier 1936). Whatever their religious role, at no time was any discrimination shown to women in funerary rites. They

41 *Magdalenian engraving of a woman. On a limestone block at Gare de Couze, Dordogne. Musée des Eyzies (after Bordes, Fitte and Laurent 1963)*

---

[1] To say nothing of some finds of fine carved house flutes with multiple holes from a number of sites. – Ed.

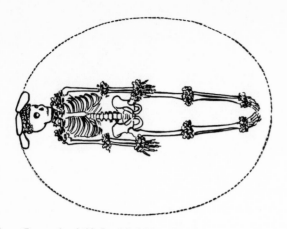

42 Grave of a child, La Madeleine, Dordogne (after Capitan and Peyrony 1928)

received the same protection and the same adornment as men, as did the child with which they are frequently associated. During the Magdalenian woman may even in certain instances have been accorded exceptional honours: at Le Placard, for example, a female skull was lying on a stone surrounded by one hundred and seventy shells, some perforated, while the 'Lady' of Saint-Germain-la-Rivière was, as mentioned above, protected by a 'dolmen', the only known Palaeolithic example of this type of monument. Again, at Sorde a woman was buried with a necklace of bear and lion teeth engraved with arrows, seal and fish. In the Upper Magdalenian at La Madeleine (Peyrony 1933) a child aged about seven was buried in a small grave, powdered with red ochre *42* and with bracelets and necklaces ringing its head, neck, elbows, wrists, knees and ankles, a testimony of tenderness and perhaps of a belief in supernatural life.

From the End of the Ice Age to the First Agriculturists:

10,000–4000 BC

ESCALON DE FONTON

The various changes which took place during this epoch, relatively short as it is, decisively conditioned the subsequent course of western prehistory. The period from *c.* 10,000 to *c.* 8000 BC saw the disintegration of the Upper Palaeolithic culture; it melted away, as it were, with the last ice and snows of the final glaciation. Hence the name Epipalaeolithic.

From *c.* 8000 to *c.* 6000 BC, what survived of the earlier cultural tradition was modified by a series of relatively rapid adaptations to the new conditions; virtually a new world emerged with the temperate climate. This epoch is known as the Mesolithic.

During the millennium that followed decreasing precipitation reduced available water supplies, and led, as might be expected, to the adoption of a less nomadic existence. Domestication of the indigenous wild sheep

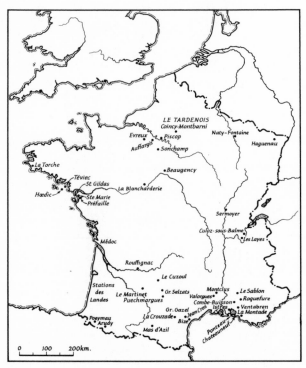

1 Map of France showing the prehistoric sites mentioned in the chapter

in the French Midi set prehistoric man on the path to a Neolithic way of life, heralded in many areas round the Mediterranean by the appearance in the archaeological record of Cardial pottery.

From *c.* 5000 to *c.* 4000 BC the hunting, fishing and pastoral peoples of the Mediterranean coast were increasingly adopting 'Neolithic' ways and acquiring the techniques of pottery-making and stone-grinding without any great modification of their other equipment. During this time the inhabitants of the hinterland of southern France, isolated from communication routes, continued in their traditional ways, ignoring the Neolithic innovations. In the north and northeast of France more and more newcomers from the east arrived among a still Mesolithic population, and became acculturated.

After the fourth millennium invasions and infiltrations followed one another in still more rapid succession, increasing the rhythm of change, adaptation and acculturation, which together make up what may be termed progressive cultural change. Between the tenth and fourth millennia the prehistoric world had in fact passed from a homogeneous to a heterogeneous, regionally specialised phase.

In order to analyse the causes of these changes and adaptations, and to distinguish the migrations, it will be best to study the events of each region against their ecological background. In this way the derivations and intrusions will emerge more clearly and the pieces of the puzzle can be put together in a truer perspective.

The Epipalaeolithic (10,000–8500 BC)

Origins

From an original centre in southwestern France the Magdalenian expanded towards the north, the northeast and the east, avoiding only the Mediterranean areas of the extreme southeast, south of the Durance, and possibly part of the Rhône valley. This was a region which had early been colonised by peoples passing along the Mediterranean coast (Sonneville-Bordes 1960; Escalon de Fonton 1966a).

If the Magdalenian, especially in its later phases, was unable to establish itself in Provence, this is because the country was already occupied by other peoples of different origin, characterised by an epi-Gravettian type of industry. This is also true at this period of Languedoc, the region on the west bank of the Rhône (Escalon de Fonton 1966a).

Reindeer were not present during the Upper Palaeolithic in lower Provence for ecological reasons, chief of which is the mountainous and broken character of the terrain. Consequently no reindeer-based culture could develop there and its place is taken by contrasting epi-Gravettian culture. This in turn, as the climate became warmer, gave rise to the Romanellian.

Romanellian (10,000-8500 BC)

The warmer conditions of the Allerød interstadial began about 10,400 BC in the French Midi.[1] The Romanellian site of Baume de Valorgues in the Gard (Escalon de Fonton 1966a) is dated by C14 to 10,390 BC, by which time reindeer and all other elements of a truly glacial fauna had disappeared. Remains of wild ass were found at this level, together with aurochs, red deer and, above all, rabbit. There were, however, no snail shells.[2]

This Romanellian may well have influenced the contemporary final Magdalenian in other regions, ultimately helping to promote its development into Azilian. In the period in question the Romanellian lithic element of material culture consists principally of very short end-scrapers, micro-Gravette points, Azilian 'points' (known as 'pen-knife' blades elsewhere), rare microliths such as lunates, triangles and unifacial points – all types which recur a thousand years later in the typical Azilian (Sonneville-Bordes 1960).

The stratigraphy of the Valorgues site provides the most complete and informative evidence to date for the Romanellian and the cultural condition that prevailed in the French Midi during the Allerød interstadial

18

2 Abri Capeau I at Lavalduc, Istres, Bouches-du-Rhône. Stratigraphic section. The Romanellian hearth is in layer 2. A first series of rock falls is visible corresponding to Dryas III, followed by more serious falls in the Boreal. The rock-shelter was then blocked

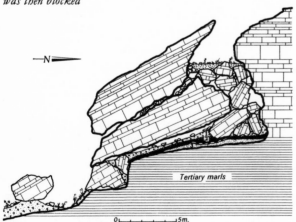

[1] That is to say somewhat earlier than for example in the Netherlands, owing to the more southerly latitude. – Ed.

[2] The snail formed an important element of diet at this time south of the Mediterranean. – Ed.

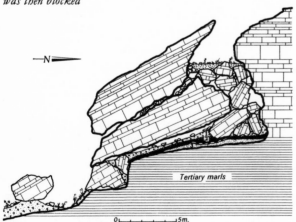

3 Abri Capeau I at Lavalduc. Final Romanellian industry, showing backed bladelets

(Escalon de Fonton 1966a). Four levels can be distinguished. Listed below in ascending chronological order, the percentages of ogival and typical end-scrapers taken together are an interesting indication of development.

Level I   (layers 25-19): 7.76%   (base level)
Level II   (layers 18-14): 9.54%
Level III (layers 13-10): 12.24%
Level IV   (layers 9-8): 23.40%   (top level)

Micro-Gravette points, rare or absent in the lower levels, increase in layer 8 to 10.4%. The same is true of backed bladelets, which increase from 5% at the base of the deposit to 19.4% at the top. Side-scrapers are abundant in the middle levels and so are Azilian points. The uppermost layer (layer 8), containing 13% of ogival scrapers, was found to have only 2% of Azilian points but 15% of atypical Gravettian points and micro-Gravette points, types which are very rare in the lower levels. On the other hand, the frequency of end-scrapers is in inverse ratio to burins, gradually changing from a proportion of 1:4 at the base to 4:3 in the final level.

Near the Rhône delta in Provence, the site of Abri Capeau at Lavalduc-Istres (Bouches-du-Rhône: Escalon de Fonton 1966c) produced an industry related to the Romanellian. Short end-scrapers on flakes and ogival

19

20

2

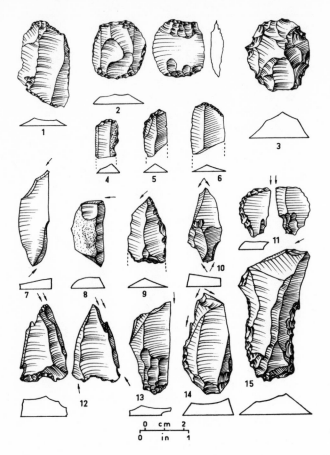

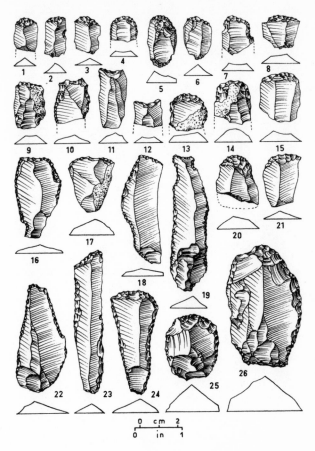

4 *Abri Capeau I at Lavalduc. Final Romanellian industry, showing scrapers and burins*

5 *Abri Capeau I at Lavalduc. Final Romanellian industry, showing end-scrapers*

3-5 scrapers together totalled 25% and this, with the abundance of backed bladelets (18%) and scarcity of Azilian points (about 0.94%), suggests comparison with the industry of the top level at Valorgues, despite the low proportion of Gravettian and micro-Gravette points (4.75%). This may represent a local variant. An assemblage 6 from the Abri de la Marcouline at Cassis about 20 km. east of Marseilles resembles the final Romanellian. Short end-scrapers on flakes and ogival scrapers account for 20% of the industry, and backed bladelets 7 for 21%. However, Azilian points are rare (1%) and micro-Gravette points (5%) and burins (3%) relatively few. While almost all types of burin are represented at Valorgues and the Abri Capeau, those at the Abri de la Marcouline are all formed on trimmed truncations. The proportion of scrapers to burins is very high (13:2), offering an even stronger contrast to the typical Azilian, where the figure is always below parity. C14 dates for the Romanellian obtained at the Abri Capeau were: 9750 BC; at La Baume de Valorgues (Saint-Quentin, Gard) layer 8, 10,140 BC, and layer 15, 10,390 BC.

Several sites in Provence have yielded a typical Romanellian industry. The Nicolaï rock-shelters at Saint-Marcel near Marseilles provide a particularly interesting stratigraphy. Towards the end of the Allerød

interstadial, among the snail shells which characterise the Romanellian deposits *Helix nemoralis* L. is predominant. Occupation layers during this period are separated by considerable falls of rock detached from the cliff overhang during the Dryas III phase. Immediately afterwards the character of the Romanellian begins to change with the progressive adoption of

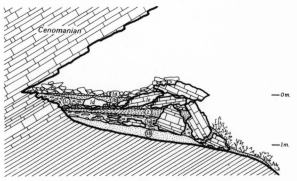

6 *Abri de la Marcouline, Cassis, Bouches-du-Rhône. Stratigraphic section. Layer 2: Romanellian. Rocks which fell during Dryas III can be seen covering the Romanellian in layer 2*

63

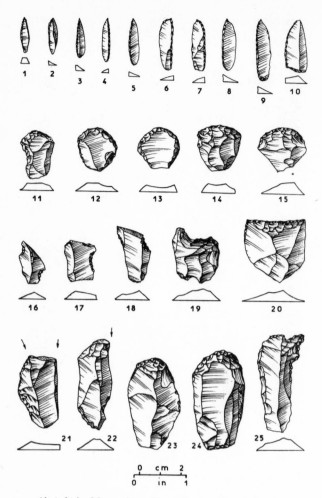

value, since early excavators did not always recognise this tool). Nonetheless it is certain that the influence of Romanellian material culture did reach as far as this region. The site of La Balme de Glos is most significant in this connection since it shows an undisturbed level with small round and ogival scrapers, 'pen-knife' blades, etc., lying below a layer of Upper Magdalenian containing reindeer, without traces of Azilian influence. The stratigraphy of this interesting site is as follows (numbered from the top downwards):

Layers	1–7:	Metal-using cultures
Layers	8–9:	Magdalenian (with reindeer)
Layers	10–11:	Romanellian (with reindeer)
Layer	12:	No industry, but fauna including reindeer

The bone industry of the French Romanellian did not include barbed or detachable harpoons; its forms are restricted to round-sectioned spear-points, sometimes with a few oblique and irregular striations near the base, and crude, atypical awls.

The only artistic products that have come to light are small oval pebbles painted a uniform red, and some bones engraved with fine but irregular lines which do not appear to be representational. No Romanellian burials are known.

Most frequently occupation sites are beneath rock-overhangs; there are also some open-air sites. There are no very large settlements, only the simple camping-sites

7 Abri de la Marcouline. Final Romanellian industry

coarse, serrated tools. This transitional phase is termed Romanello-Montadian and it is followed by further rock falls during the Boreal.

Nearer the Rhône at Istres the Abri Cornille presents a similar stratigraphy, though with richer cultural material. The same climatic and industrial sequences are apparent, with typical Romanellian developing during the Allerød interstadial and rock falls during Dryas III, while the industry is again transformed into a Romanello-Montadian (Escalon de Fonton 1966a). A little farther north at Mormoiron (Vaucluse) wide-spread open-air camping sites at Le Sablon contain a rich Romanellian industry.

It would further appear that the Romanellian spread northwards via the Rhône valley, as several sites in the Dauphiné have produced a typical industry of this kind (Bourdier and Lumley 1954, 1956) such as Colomb, Balme, Glos, La Passagère, Olette, Fontabert, Bobache and Saint-Roman. On all these sites the proportion of scrapers to burins is often higher than 4:1 and at times even greater. Burins at Glos, La Passagère, Fontabert and Bobache are very rare indeed (although these figures should not be taken at quite their face

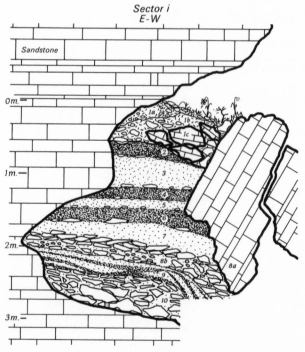

8 Abri Cornille, Istres-Sulauze, Bouches-du-Rhône. Layers 2–8: Montadian; layer 9: Romanellian. The rocks which fell on to the Romanellian during Dryas III can be seen (8a) and later those (1c) from the Boreal, over the Montadian

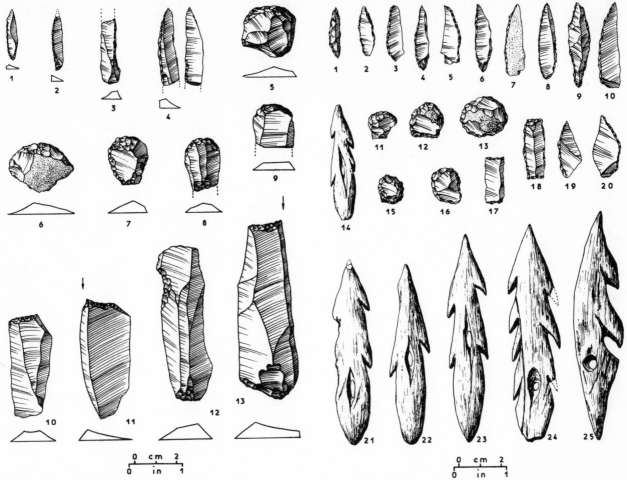

9 *Abri Cornille. Romanellian industry from layer 9 (Allerød)*

10 *Cave of Mas d'Azil, Ariège. Typical Azilian industry (after Péquart)*

of hunters, and some hut sites near water-sources. These huts, which contain one or more hearths, seem to have been very small. A considerable number of camping sites, and what may be huts, have been found in the region of Mormoiron (Vaucluse), on the Sablon plain, suggesting that the Romanellians returned frequently to this chosen area.

Azilian (9000–8500 BC)

The post-Würmian rise in temperature came relatively early in the Midi. It does not appear to have been uniform throughout the area, least so in mountainous or inland regions as opposed to the Mediterranean littoral. On the other hand, it has been shown that the absence of reindeer does not necessarily correspond to a complete cessation of cold conditions, since this animal had never become established on the mountainous coasts of Provence, where its place is taken by ibex, better adapted to the difficult terrain.

A combination of two factors seems to have maintained the reindeer in areas where it had once been dominant: the persistence of relative cold during the first part of the Allerød interstadial, and the favourable terrain of the great plains and wide valleys. The Magdalenian civilisation, based on the reindeer, was thus able to continue in certain areas where the reindeer had not entirely disappeared. This would seem to explain, for instance, why certain Magdalenian sites, such as the cave of La Vache (Ariège), are contemporary with Romanellian sites elsewhere in southeastern France at the beginning of the Allerød interstadial.

Sites yielding material transitional between final Magdalenian and Azilian are still few and their industries – of such potential interest to prehistory – are still imperfectly known. There is however one excellent example, the proto-Azilian of the La Vache cave (Malvesin-Fabre, Nougier and Robert 1950), in which a flint industry already very Azilian in style is associated with some flat, deer-antler harpoons of epi-Magdalenian type.

The Azilian flint industry is truly Epipalaeolithic, in the sense that it is virtually an extension of the final Magdalenian. The tools are obviously of the same forms, though smaller, and would seem to serve the *10-11* same purposes. Almost all types of burin are represented, but straight dihedral (alternately flaked) burins

65

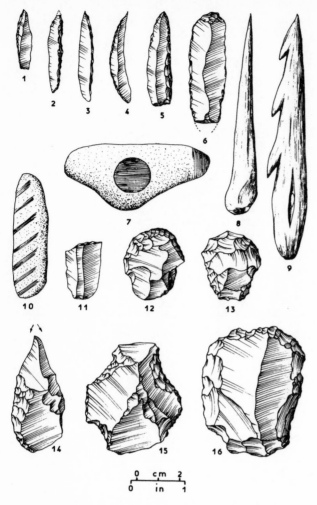

11 Cave of La Crouzade, Gruissan, Aude. 1-3, 7, 10-13: Azilian. Cave of Bize (Bize, Aude). 4-6, 8-9, 14-16: Azilian

where such categories as lunates and round scrapers are concerned; in their typology and technique these are strongly reminiscent of the same types in the final Magdalenian.

Azilian is found in all regions settled in the final Magdalenian, though there may be some slight regional differentiation related to ecological factors.

Whereas harpoons are unknown in the Romanellian and its parent epi-Gravettian, the Azilian, like the Magdalenian from which it derives, used them extensively for hunting and especially for fishing. Early Romanellians were in fact not fishers but hunters; only in a subsequent phase did they adapt themselves to fishing and they then used a barbed spear or dart armed with geometric microliths. Furthermore, it was round the Mediterranean that the barbed dart with microlithic flints first came into use, to spread in due course to the whole of Europe.

Azilian harpoons are made from deer antler and usually have two rows of barbs. These barbs are rather irregular and are formed by simple notching or angular indentations in the hard outer layer of the antler, cut in such a way that they scarcely stand out from the line of the edge. In the oval base of the harpoon there is a lenticular hole parallel to the long axis and worked not by boring but by incising, so that it looks something like a button-hole.

In artistic output the Azilian is richer than Romanellian. Among its painted pebbles there are some ornamented with abstract designs (dots, broken and undulating lines, etc.). Other pebbles have schematic engravings (Breuil 1955) which have not yet been clearly interpreted.

We should know more about Azilian graves had nineteenth-century excavators taken more care. At Mas d'Azil graves in simple pits contained skeletons still coated with red ochre (Piette 1892).[2]

General

Romanellian and Azilian merely prolong the regional Upper Palaeolithic industries from which they derive, the first in the Mediterranean zone and the second in Atlantic coastal and inland areas where the reindeer had formerly lived. In their basic way of life and means of subsistence the Upper Palaeolithic and the Epipalaeolithic closely resembled one another: men were hunters, fishers and gatherers. The equipment alone changed as a result of a change in the game hunted, from large animals during the Upper Palaeolithic to smaller game later. Wea ons and tools were evidently adapted accordingly, and it is worth bearing in mind in this connection that some forms of hunting such as rabbit-snaring would need no weapons at all. We need scarcely comment on the requirements of a snail-hunt!

(7% at Longueroche) and burins fashioned from truncated forms (6% at Longueroche) predominate.[1] But some sites, for example Villepin (Sonneville-Bordes 1960), have no burins at all. In general burins are far less abundant in the Azilian than in the Romanellian and markedly fewer than in the parent Magdalenian (where they often amounted to about 15% of the total). Truncated blades however are numerous (Longueroche 6%, Villepin 3%), and ogival scrapers (Longueroche 4%, Villepin 13%) and end-scrapers (Longueroche 4%, Villepin 24%) even more so. Statistically, however, the primary characteristic of the Azilian in southwestern France is the extreme abundance of backed bladelets (Longueroche 13%, Villepin 13%) and Azilian points (Longueroche 20%, Villepin 21%), coupled with a scarcity of micro-Gravette points (Longueroche 0.42%, Villepin 3%) and an almost complete absence of Gravettian points.

Flint implements of the Pyrenean Azilian are generally small, while in the Périgord forms are larger, especially

[1] These are respectively the 'bec de flûte' and 'angle burins' of some English authors and the Mittelstichel and Winkelstichel of some German authors. – Ed.

[2] As in the Palaeolithic – see chapter 2. – Ed.

If a difference in game made little change in the overall way of life, this does not hold for the art. The decorated caves of the Upper Palaeolithic may have been sanctuaries (Leroi-Gourhan 1958 a-c). Many could, for instance, have been cult places for initiation ceremonies, and their labyrinthine plans suggest possible sites for symbolic rites. Thus it may have been partly through the mediation of animal symbolism that the young initiates were accepted into the world of their elders. Animals are an integral part of the hunter's world, providing him with sustenance and representing his very way of life. Quite suddenly, however, these large animals which were the basis of the culture disappeared, to be replaced by a few deer and wild asses, but above all by rabbits and snails! And rabbit and snail catchers could scarcely initiate their children by displaying horse, reindeer and mammoth. The symbolism of union with the hunted, which had been basic to all previous tradition and ethos, would no longer serve as an effective expression of ideas.

Abstract signs alone would have retained their value and for this reason art might have been transformed in order to remain effective at the symbolic level; such was perhaps the attitude which prevailed among the men of the ancient world and through their enduring cultures. If there was a real break between the Upper Palaeolithic and the Epipalaeolithic it might well be reflected in the conversion to this symbolic and wholly non-representational art.

The subsequent stage in our series of ethnographic episodes deserves to be termed Mesolithic, since this was when the transition from the old world of hunters and fishers to the new world of shepherds and agriculture was effected. Man as a 'predator' lived in harmony with nature, controlled by and contributing to its equilibrium. Intellectually rather than materially dominant, he never attempted any dangerous modification of his environment. As a 'producer', and especially as an agriculturist, he was to find it necessary, in order to survive, to exterminate grazing animals and forest trees, thereby progressively upsetting earth's natural harmony.

The Mesolithic (8500–3000 BC)

Origins

Almost everywhere in France the Mesolithic was indigenous, that is to say it stemmed directly from a local Epipalaeolithic. Every Mesolithic industry reflects the style of its parent civilisation. Each variant of the Azilian changed into an Azilio-Sauveterrian and then into a Sauveterrian. Each type of Sauveterrian gave rise to a form of Tardenoisian. Some Tardenoisian, like that of the Mediterranean coast which derives from Romanello-Montadian and from Montadian, succeeded in evolving into the Neolithic stage through the domestication of sheep. Other Tardenoisian groups saw the arrival of Neolithic immigrants and adopted their ways, often after living alongside them in what is termed a proto-Neolithic phase.

Montadian and Castelnovian Tardenoisian

After the Allerød interstadial the Romanellian was rapidly transformed during the Dryas III[1] phase into a Romanello-Montadian, when the majority of its blade forms and backed bladelets were abandoned and there was a very marked increase in the number of serrated tools fashioned from thick flakes. Flints became increasingly crude, including the burins which were most frequently worked on a thick core-like flake, the parent nucleus being for detaching flakes, not blades. The resultant industries took on a somewhat 'Mousterioid' appearance.

Once the transformation was complete there were no more round or ogival scrapers, blades or backed points, but only robust composite tools, serrated, and on thick flakes. Some truncated flints, side-scrapers with convergent or even pointed outline (pseudo-Mousterian points) and crude burins were still produced. To these were added flints worked with wide deep indentations, Aurignacian-like strangulated forms on thin flakes, shouldered nosed scrapers and a few rare microliths, made by the microburin technique. This was a method of detaching microliths from a segment of blade by an oblique fracture across a prepared notch. Such notched pieces should not be confused with true notched tools, even though some blades prepared in this manner were abandoned before the final step in the operation had taken place.

The microliths of early and middle Montadian take the form of lunates and triangles, and were used as barbs for darts or arrows; they are always very small. The Montadian is found in Dryas III and in the pre-Boreal in lower Provence, between 8500 and 7000 BC (Escalon de Fonton 1966a).

Towards the end of the eighth millennium the Montadian lithic industry was enriched by the addition of

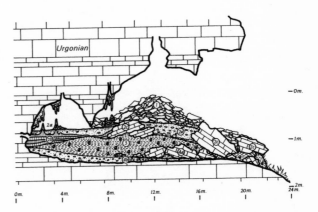

12 Grotte de la Montade, Bouches-du-Rhône: section. The Montadian industry in layer 3 (pre-Boreal) was covered by rock falls (2c) during the Boreal

[1] The last really cold phase in the glacial climate, often known as Younger Dryas. – Ed.

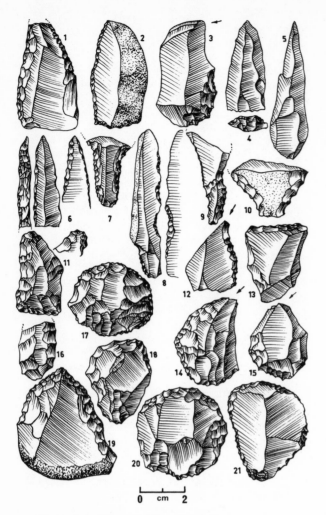

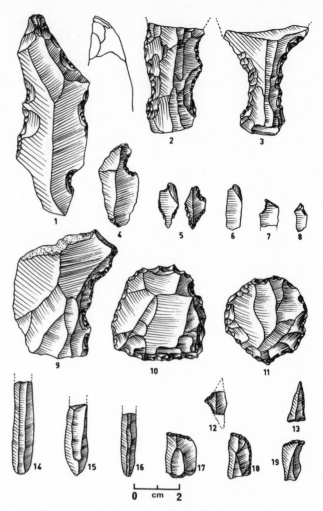

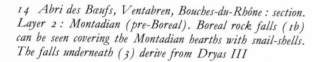

13 *Grotte de la Montade. Montadian industry*

15 *Abri des Bœufs. Montadian industry*

14 *Abri des Bœufs, Ventabren, Bouches-du-Rhône : section. Layer 2 : Montadian (pre-Boreal). Boreal rock falls (1b) can be seen covering the Montadian hearths with snail-shells. The falls underneath (3) derive from Dryas III*

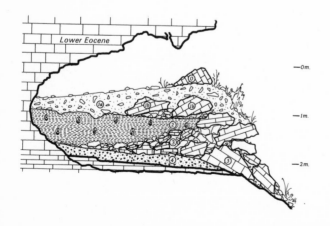

steeply trimmed trapezes, which were certainly used in connection with fishing. At this stage it passes into a proto-Castelnovian (Escalon de Fonton 1966a).

Early and middle Montadians were hunters, living on the edges of the great plain of La Crau near the Rhône delta (Escalon de Fonton 1956). Aurochs and wild ass, which were plentiful in the region, constituted their principal quarry. In the middle Montadian rabbit becomes increasingly abundant in occupation layers. Snail shells appear in the final Montadian, and in the pre-Boreal they form enormous heaps among the ashes in shelters and occupied caves.

The best stratigraphy to date is at the Abri Cornille at Istres (Bouches-du-Rhône). It contains (from the bottom upwards) Romanellian, Romanello-Montadian, *16-17* early and middle Montadian without snail shells, followed by upper Montadian with such shells, and finally proto-Castelnovian. The neighbouring site, the Abri de la Baume-Longue at Ponteau (Martigues, Bouches- *18* du-Rhône) has yielded an apparently transitional final Montadian variant or a proto-Castelnovian. A few kilo- *19* metres away the Châteauneuf-les-Martigues rock-shelter *15*

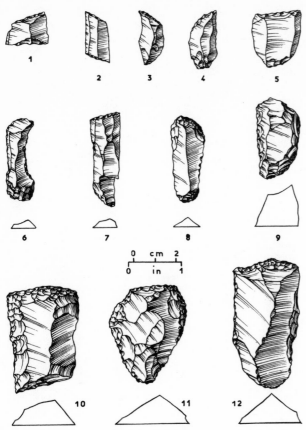

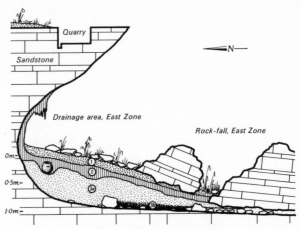

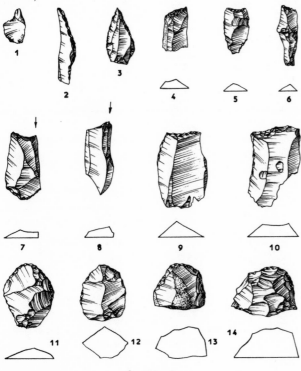

18 La Baume-Longue, Ponteau-Martigues, Bouches-du-Rhône : section. Layer 3b : final transitional Montadian, proto-Castelnovian ; rocks which fell during the Boreal are lying over the Montadian. Layer 2 : drainage concretions from a dried-up spring, which contained a Couronnian pot. The upper rock fall belongs in the sub-Boreal

16 Abri Cornille. Montadian industry from layer 4 (pre-Boreal)

17 Abri Cornille. Montadian industry from layer 2 (pre-Boreal)

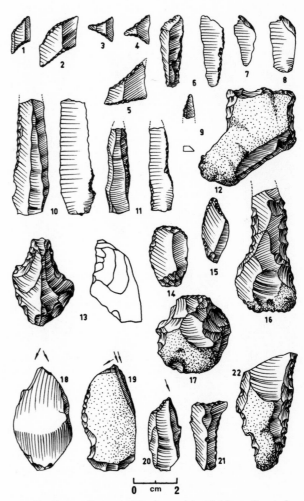

19 La Baume-Longue. Final transitional Montadian industry : proto-Castelnovian

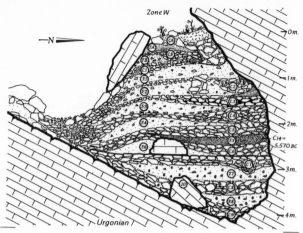

*20 Grand Abri de Châteauneuf : stratigraphic section. CA :
disturbed, Iron Age and Gallo-Roman (road). FA :
Chalcolithic. CB-FB : Epi-Cardial. 1-3 : Late Cardial.
4 : Middle Cardial. 5-6 : Lower Cardial (C14 date 5570
BC). 7-8 : Mesolithic Castelnovian*

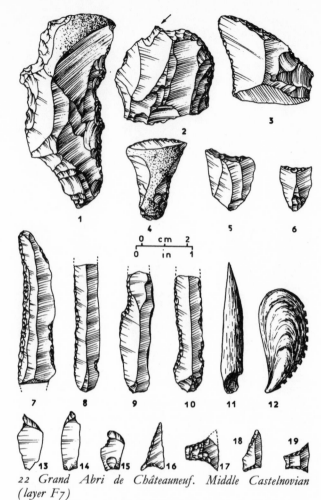

*22 Grand Abri de Châteauneuf. Middle Castelnovian
(layer F7)*

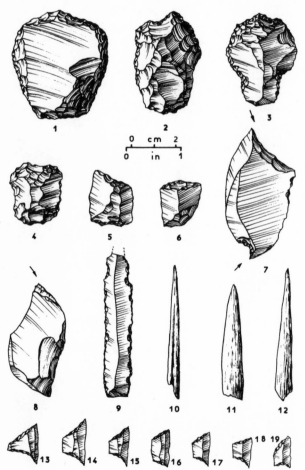

*21 Grand Abri de Châteauneuf. Early Castelnovian (layer
F8)*

*23 Grand Abri de Châteauneuf. Evolution of geometric
microliths* ▶

CHATEAUNEUF:	Evolution of Geometric Microliths						
Upper Cardial F3, C3, F2, C2, F1, C1.							
Middle Cardial F4, C4.							
Early Cardial F6, C6, F5, C5.							
Castelnovian C7							
Castelnovian F7							
Castelnovian C8							
Castelnovian F8							

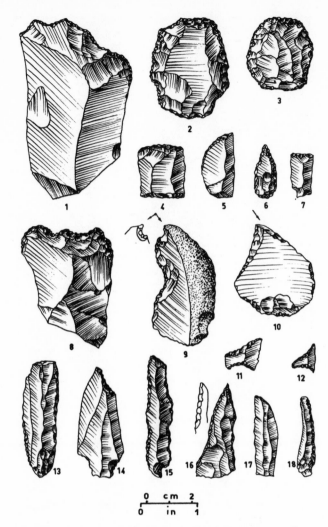

24 *Grand Abri de Châteauneuf. Final Castelnovian (layer C7)*

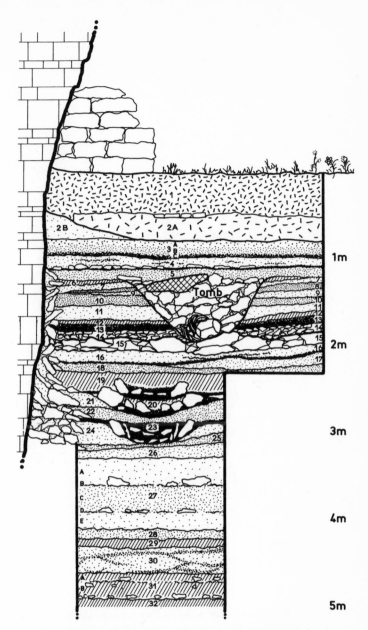

25 *La Baume de Montclus, Gard: section (unfinished exploratory excavation). Layers 32-18: final Sauveterrian (C14 date of layer 22: 6180 BC). Layers 16-15: Languedocian Tardenoisian I. Layers 14-9: Middle and Final Castelnovian. Layers 8-5: Epi-Castelnovian Proto-Neolithic. Layers 4-3: developed final Cardial. Layer 2B: Epi-Cardial. Layer 2A: Chalcolithic of Chassean tradition. The burial corresponds to layer 5. The built hearths, 19-20 and 23, are not cooking-places*

20
16 provides a fine stratigraphy complementary to that of Cornille, showing a superposition of early Castelnovian, final Castelnovian, Cardial Neolithic of Castelnovian tradition and an epi-Cardial Neolithic. Early Cardial pottery here is contemporary with the epi-Sauveterrian variant of the Tardenoisian of inland regions.

Montadian bone artifacts are extremely simple: awls and points with roughly rounded section. Few of these have been found. There was no art, as far as is known, though there may of course have been work in perishable materials which has not survived.

21-2, 24 From Boreal times, i.e. from about 6500 BC, the Montadian finally developed into Castelnovian. Basic equipment remained technically and typologically Montadian. Burins however became increasingly rare, before practically disappearing, and there was a regular

23 increase in the number of geometric microliths comprising triangles and trapezes obtained by 'micro-burin' fracture. These would seem to have been barbs for fish spears, to judge by the Châteauneuf shelter which yielded

quantities of fish remains, as well as aquatic mollusca, crustaceans, rabbit bones and snails.

Art had become of little importance. The Castelnovians had painted the whole wall of their shelter (at the name-site) a uniform red. They had also perforated sea shells, as in the Montadian. Middle Castelnovian 17

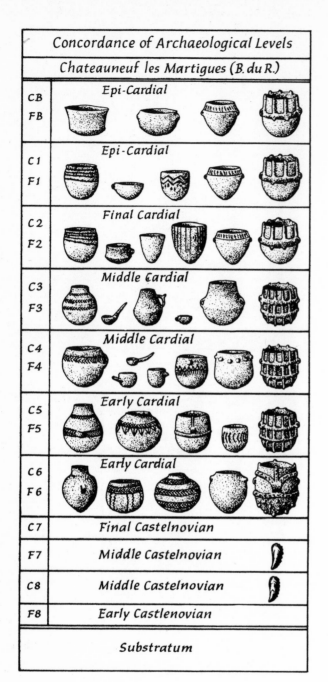

Concordance of Archaeological Levels			
Chateauneuf les Martigues (B. du R.)			
CB FB	Epi-Cardial		
C1 F1	Epi-Cardial		
C2 F2	Final Cardial		
C3 F3	Middle Cardial		
C4 F4	Middle Cardial		
C5 F5	Early Cardial		
C6 F6	Early Cardial		
C7	Final Castelnovian		
F7	Middle Castelnovian		
C8	Middle Castelnovian		
F8	Early Castlenovian		
Substratum			

Concordance of Archaeological Levels			
La Baume de Montclus (Gard)			
2B	Epi-Cardial		
3	Epi-Cardial		
4	Final Cardial		
5-6	Epi-Castelnovian Proto-Neolithic		
7	Epi-Castelnovian Proto-Neolithic		
8	Epi-Castelnovian Proto-Neolithic		
9 10	Final Castelnovian		
11 12 13	Middle Castelnovian		
14	Middle Castelnovian		
15 16	Tardenoisian of Languedoc		
17 to 22	Final Sauveterrian (C 14 = − 6·180)		

26 Comparative table of correlations between the sites of Châteauneuf and Montclus

yielded mussel shells which had been intentionally denticulated, but not perforated; their purpose, practical or artistic, is unknown. Some examples, however, seem altogether too fragile to have served as tools. Denti- 22 culated shells are found at Châteauneuf in the Castelnovian (layers C8 and F7). At Montclus they are present from the beginning of the Castelnovian (layers 13-14), as that Mediterranean industry migrated northwards and was superimposed on a Languedocian Tardenoisian of Sauveterrian affinities. There is no acculturation or influence at Montclus. It would clearly seem to be a replacement of the inland culture by a typically Mediterranean culture.

On the coast the Castelnovian, which had domesticated the native wild sheep by the start of the sixth millennium (Ducos 1958), had entered into a Neolithic phase by its end. There is evidence of fine flocks as early as the fourth millennium. This provides a probable origin of the pastoral civilisations found throughout the French Midi.

15 Grand Abri de Châteauneuf, Châteauneuf-lez-Martigues, Bouches-du-Rhône. General view before excavation, taken from the east. The rock gutter, which drains off any running water, can be seen forming the floor of the site.

16 Grand Abri de Châteauneuf. View during excavation. The large rock in the centre rests on the floor of the site; it had fallen during Dryas III. The Castelnovian layers are supported by it. The light-coloured rock to the right fell during Boreal times, on top of the Castelnovian. The rocks further away and to the left are lying on the ridged talus of early Chalcolithic deposits.

17 Grand Abri de Châteauneuf. Castelnovian bone industry and perforated shells.

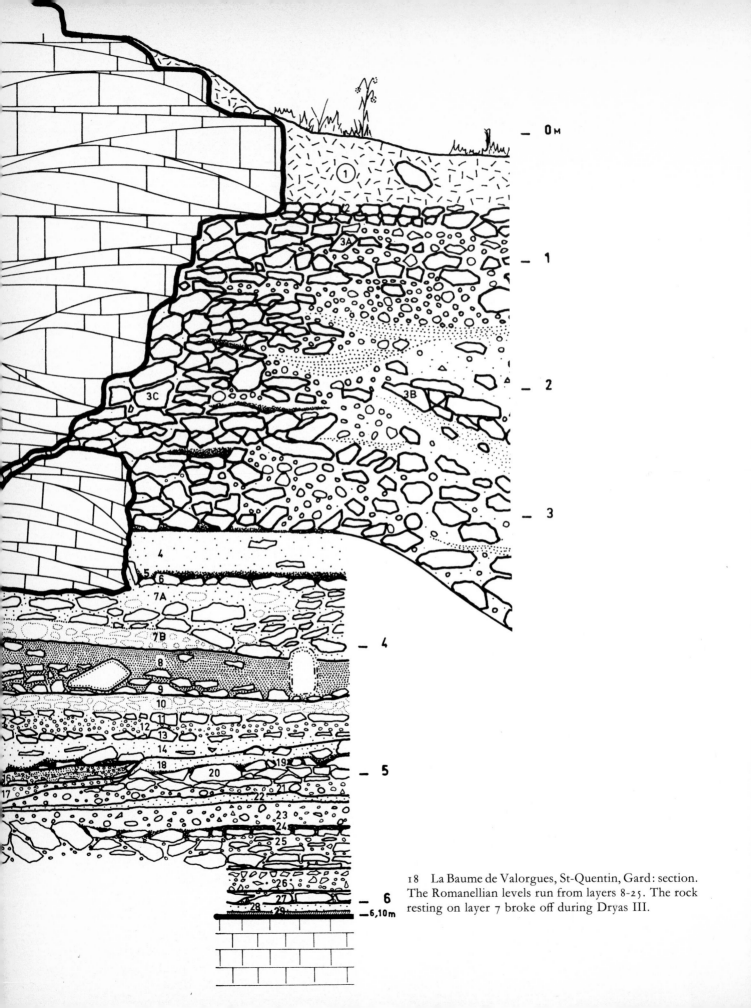

18 La Baume de Valorgues, St-Quentin, Gard: section. The Romanellian levels run from layers 8-25. The rock resting on layer 7 broke off during Dryas III.

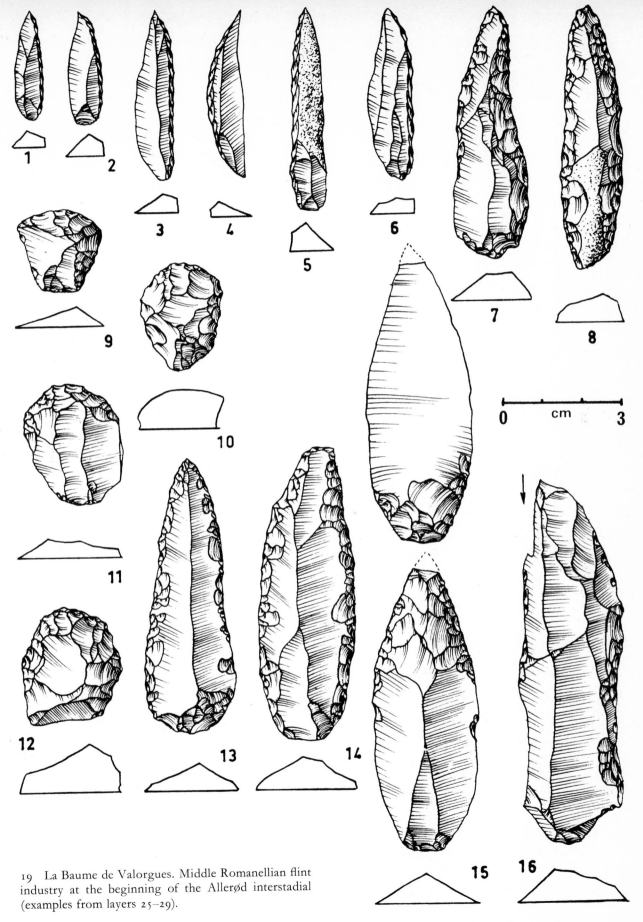

19 La Baume de Valorgues. Middle Romanellian flint industry at the beginning of the Allerød interstadial (examples from layers 25–29).

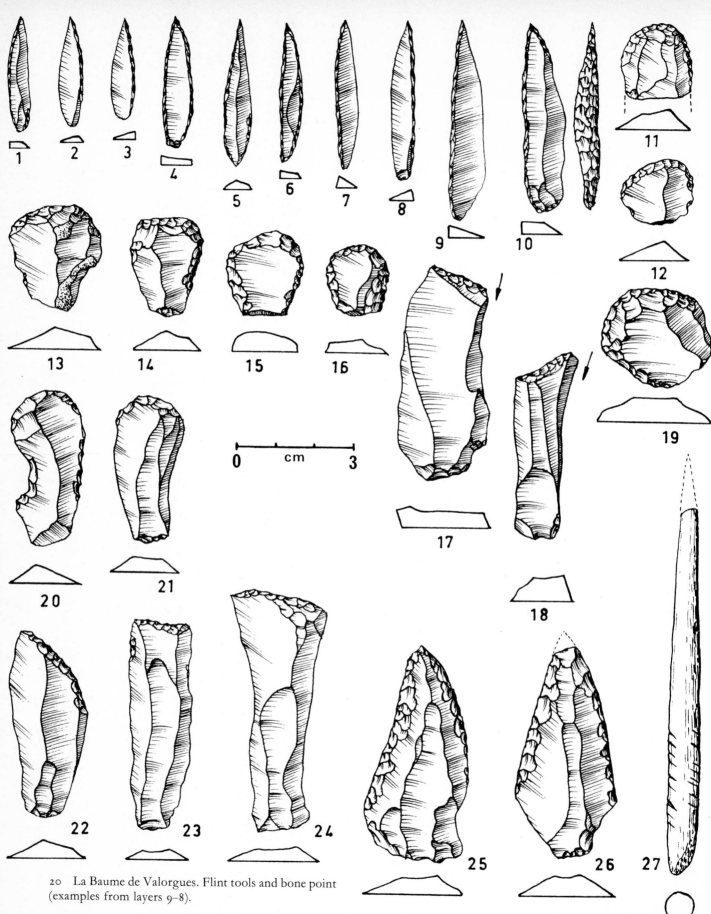

20   La Baume de Valorgues. Flint tools and bone point
(examples from layers 9–8).

21　La Baume de Montclus, Gard. General view taken from the west. The river is under the trees seen on the right. The site is at the foot of the cliff (40m. high).

22　La Baume de Montclus. Mesolithic skeleton from layer 5: Epi-Castelnovian Proto-Neolithic.

23　La Baume de Montclus. A partial view of the site: western zone.

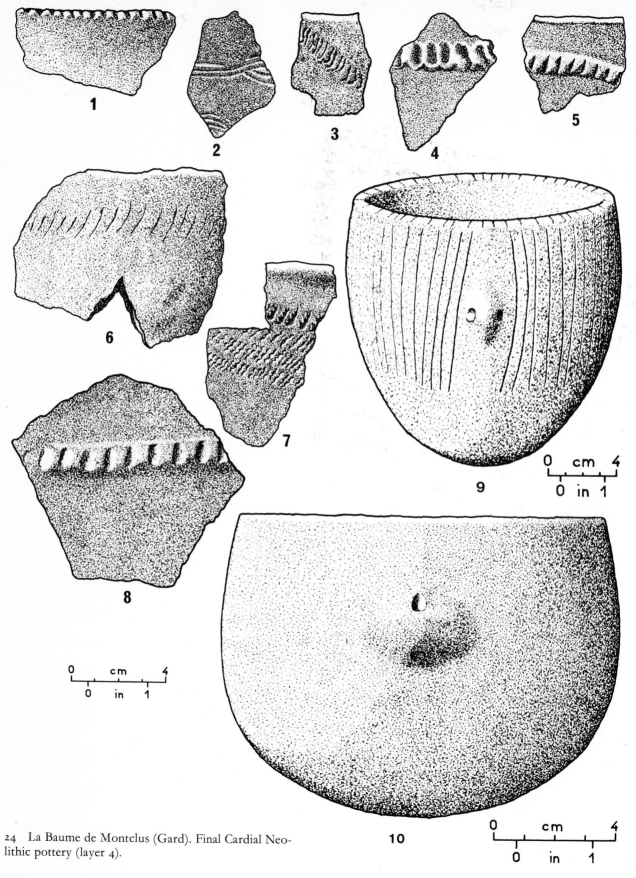

24 La Baume de Montclus (Gard). Final Cardial Neolithic pottery (layer 4).

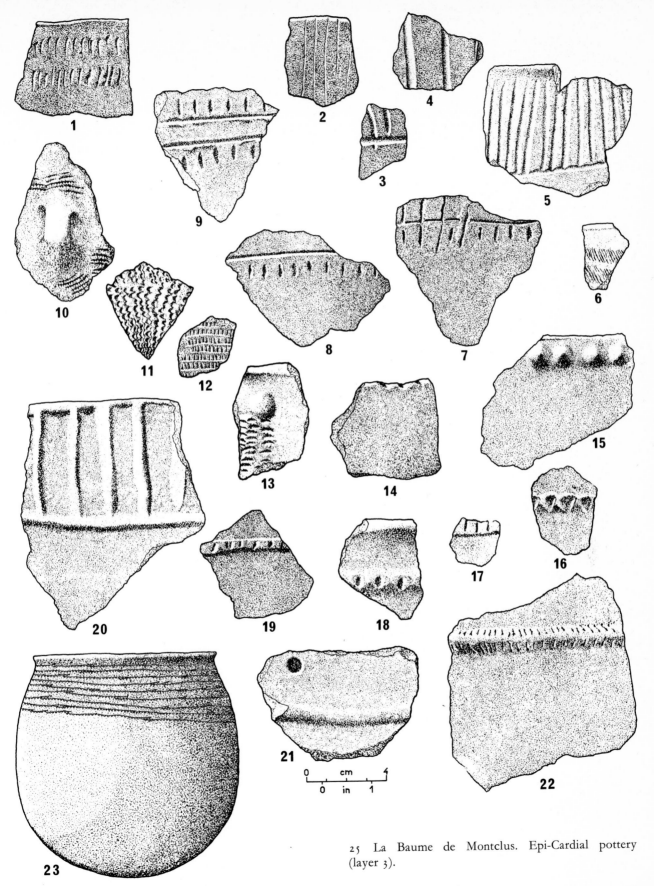

25 La Baume de Montclus. Epi-Cardial pottery (layer 3).

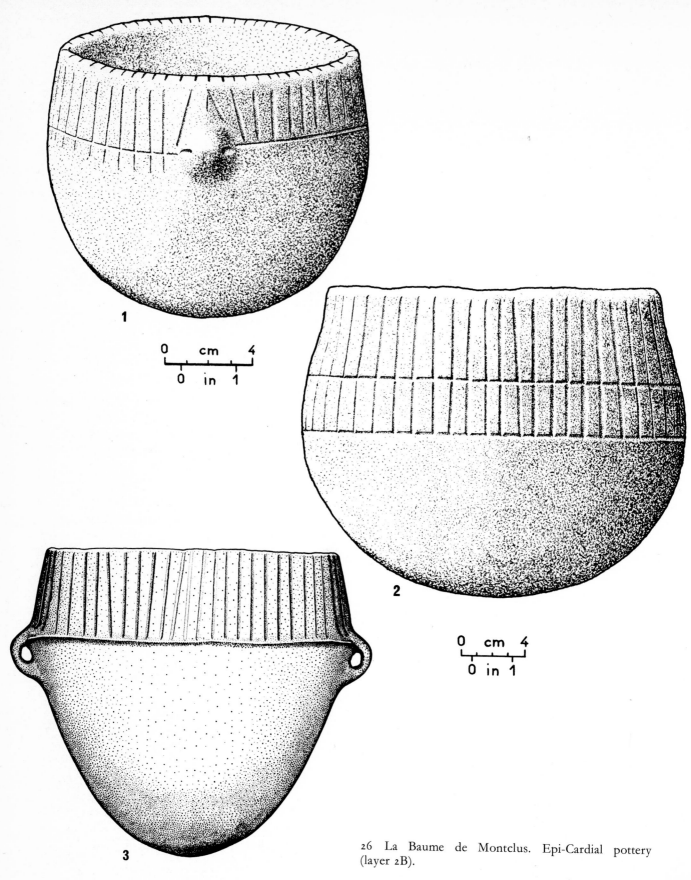

1

0   cm   4

0   in   1

2

0   cm 4

0   in 1

3

26 La Baume de Montclus. Epi-Cardial pottery
(layer 2B).

LA BAUME DE MONTCLUS

2	Chassean		
3 4	Evolved Cardial		
5 to 8	Late Mesolithic Proto-Neolithic		
9 to 14	Castelnovian		
15 16	Tardenoisian I of Languedoc Epi-Sauveterrian		
17 to 32	Sauveterrian		
	5m. trial trench incomplete–		

27 *La Baume de Montclus. Material from the archaeological levels in stratigraphic order*

Inland from the Mediterranean coastal zone and away from the main lines of communication the Castelnovian persisted as a 'proto-Neolithic' type of Mesolithic, contemporary with the middle phase of Cardial pottery-bearing cultures at Châteauneuf. The site of La Baume de Montclus is an example. There this proto-Neolithic of Castelnovian affinities (with trapezes worked with invasive retouch associated with others steeply trimmed) becomes Neolithic at a late phase, corresponding with the final Cardial Neolithic.

In regions far from the sea the process of development into a Neolithic was even more retarded, and ultimately acculturations or even colonisation may have taken its place.

Graves are still unknown in the Montadian and early Castelnovian. The proto-Neolithic Castelnovian at La Baume de Montclus contained a grave with a flexed and orientated skeleton. Above the tomb, which was an 22 irregular pit filled with large stones, had been placed a very large flat pebble, painted red. There were no grave goods.

The same type of dwelling characterises the Montadian and Castelnovian, namely huts below rock-over-hangs. Where the shelter was large enough there may be a group of huts, but this is very unusual at this period. Most often one large hut was built along the full extent of the natural shelter. There were no internal structures, apart from some vague settings of stones marking the edges of hearths. Wood must certainly have played an important part in the construction of these huts since, despite the frequently very precise limits to the occupation deposits, no stone structure or mounding of earth has ever been observed. The final, proto-Castelnovian stage of Montadian at Ponteau (Martigues, Bouches-du-Rhône) has revealed a round hut about 4 m. in diameter at the foot of a small natural rock-overhang.

Arudian (8500–6000 BC)
In the Atlantic zone of the Pyrenees the Azilian developed into a highland variant, without passing through either Sauveterrian or Tardenoisian phases. The Poeymaü cave produced a possible functional variant of an industry technically fairly close to Montadian in its final phase, though possibly a little later in date. The sequence is: epi-Magdalenian, highland Azilian, Arudian I, Arudian II, followed by layers with late Neolithic to metal-age pottery (Laplace-Jauretache 1953).

Arudian I, which represents a modified Azilian adapted to a different way of life, is composed principally of blades with trimmed truncations, serrated tools, indentations worked in blades and flakes, ogival scrapers which are often thick and heavy, and side-scrapers. There are some backed knives and burins.

In the following stage, Arudian II, the truncated blades become rare and there is a growing number of backed bladelets. Sauveterrian points also appear. Serrated tools and crude burins are still in evidence.

Arudian seems to be contemporary with the early Sauveterrian of southwestern France and the early Castelnovian of the Mediterranean coast.

Arisian (8500–7500 BC)
Above the Azilian deposit at Mas d'Azil (Piette 1892) there was a layer in which snail shells were extremely abundant. The industry was noticeably different from the Azilian. Unfortunately it was not preserved by the nineteenth-century excavators and new excavations have produced practically no new evidence (M. and St J. Pequart 1934) because several industries had been mixed together. However, by comparison with finds from other sites and by a process of elimination it is possible to assume that Arisian was a sort of epi-Azilian, or proto-Sauveterrian, like that, for example, 28 from the caves of La Crouzade and Roquefure (Paccard 1963).

Sauveterrian and Tardenoisian (7500–3000 BC)
It should be possible to find an epi-Azilian or an Azilio-Sauveterrian at the stage where industrial evolution or mutation took place in each region, but these transitional industries are rare and generally short-lived. Furthermore, since they were in process of active

81

adaptation to new ecological conditions, they are not very stable morphologically or typologically. Certain examples may be quoted, however, such as the Arisian just mentioned (discovered by Piette at Mas d'Azil) and the Azilio-Sauveterrian at La Crouzade and Roquefure layer 5 (Paccard 1963).

Azilio-Sauveterrian lithic industry is truly intermediate, in the sense that it preserves some Azilian-type tools (short and ogival scrapers, lunates, atypical Gravettian points, and micro-Gravette points and Azilian points) alongside novel forms (points on small blades blunted along both edges, triangles, microburins) which were to become increasingly numerous in the full Sauveterrian.

The Azilio-Sauveterrian developed during the eighth millennium, in the final cold (or cool) phase of Dryas III. It is contemporary with the Romanello-Montadian.

Early typical Sauveterrian next appeared in the pre-Boreal at the end of the eighth millennium, and solely, it would seem, in Provence and in south Aquitaine-Gascony. Local variation was by then pronounced (as at Le Martinet, Le Cuzoul, Rouffignac, Montclus, Roquefure).

Without entering into statistical detail it may be stated that the early Sauveterrian in Aquitaine was

30

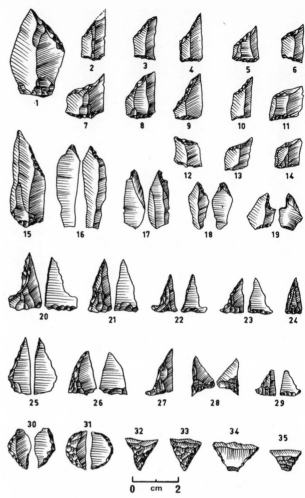

29 *Le Martinet de Sauveterre. 'Tardenoisian I-II' industry (after Coulonges)*

28 Cave of La Crouzade. Epi-Azilian proto-Sauveterrian industry

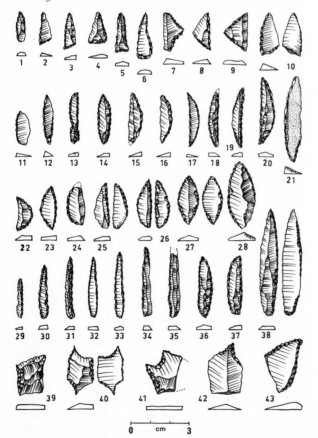

30 Typological table of the Mesolithic in Aquitaine

The Mesolithic of Aquitaine					
Sequence		Classification and Typological sequence of Principal Tools			
		Shared Types: Martinet and Cuzoul		Martinet	Cuzoul
Chalcolithic F	Martinet T. III Cuzoul VI VII	(Pottery)			
Tardenoisian E	Cuzoul V Martinet T. II				
Tardenoisian D	Cuzoul IV				
Tardenoisian C	Cuzoul III				
Tardenoisian B	Cuzoul II				
Tardenoisian A	Martinet T. I				
Sauveterrian	Martinet Sauvetr. Cuzoul I				
Break					
Magdalenian					

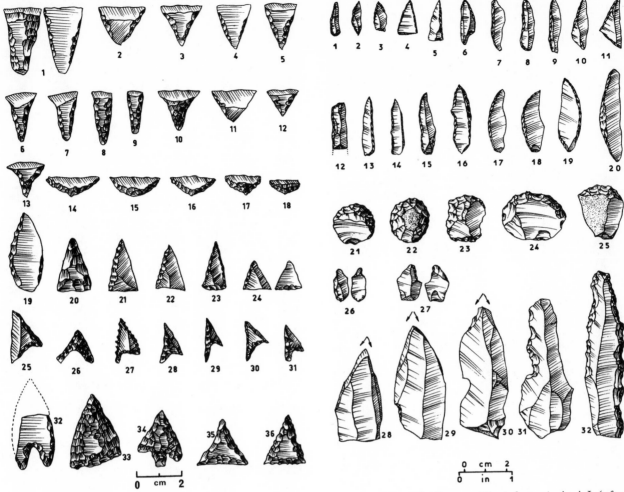

31 Le Martinet de Sauveterre. 'Tardenoisian III' industry (after Coulonges)

32 Le Cuzoul de Gramat. The industry in level I (after Lacam)

fairly homogeneous. The industry comprised ogival scrapers and their variants, truncated flints, Sauveterrian points and Tardenoisian points. The geometric microliths included triangles, which are always quite small, lunates and, especially at Le Cuzoul and Le Martinet, a sub-trapezoid form in which one of the steeply trimmed sides is slightly concave and the opposite edge convex. True trapezes appear in an early stage of the Tardenoisian. Tardenoisian points continue, but there are no more Sauveterrian triangles.

In the following stage, probably in the Boreal, the Sonchamp point appears in level II at Le Cuzoul. This form lasts right through the Atlantic period and beyond, as in levels IV-V at Le Cuzoul and at Le Martinet I-II.

In Languedoc early Sauveterrian is still imperfectly known. The middle and upper Sauveterrian are in effect composed of geometric microliths, all triangles. These are always small. There are long and short scalenes but also some very elongated and delicate triangles trimmed on all three sides (Montclus triangles).

In Provence, though the coast was occupied first by Montadian and then by Castelnovian, Sauveterrian and Tardenoisian are found in the interior.

The Roquefure shelter (Vaucluse) has yielded an important stratigraphy, entirely characteristic of the Mesolithic in the lower Rhône valley. Above the Azilian a transitional Azilio-Sauveterrian layer indicates the evolution of this industrial line. It contains Sauveterrian points, lunates, triangles (some of which are close to trapezes), truncated flints, backed knives and ogival scrapers. Above this there developed a Sauveterrian and a Tardenoisian level. The Sauveterrian included a Tardenoisian point in process of evolution towards a trapezoidal form, while the following stage saw the appearance of a broad triangle and a proto-trapeze which had derived by evolution from a considerably

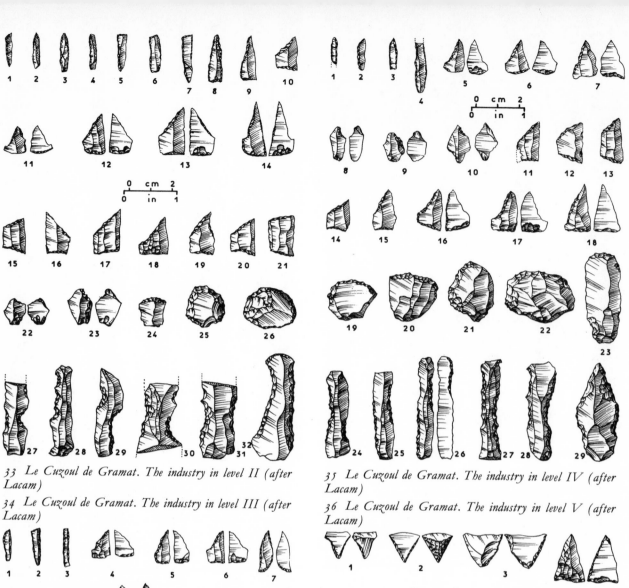

33 *Le Cuzoul de Gramat. The industry in level II (after Lacam)*

35 *Le Cuzoul de Gramat. The industry in level IV (after Lacam)*

34 *Le Cuzoul de Gramat. The industry in level III (after Lacam)*

36 *Le Cuzoul de Gramat. The industry in level V (after Lacam)*

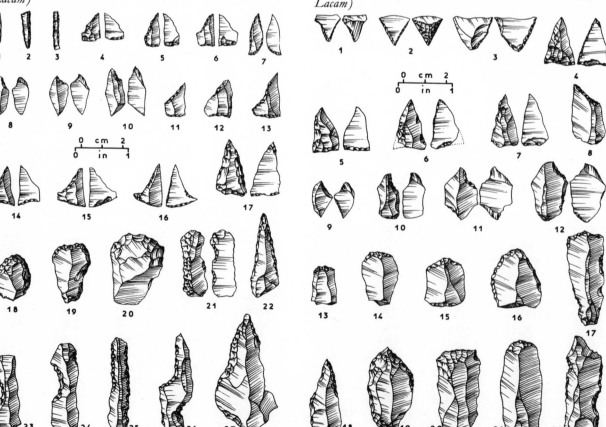

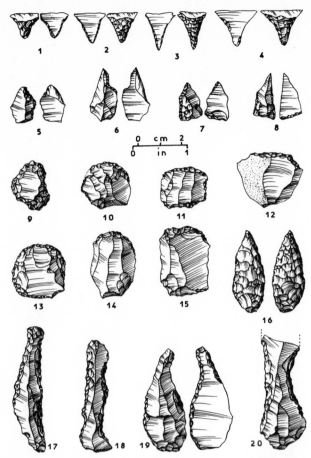

37 *Le Cuzoul de Gramat. The industry in level VI (after Lacam)*

38 *Typological table of the evolution of Tardenoisian and Sonchamp points shown in the chronological levels of principal Tardenoisian sites*

Climatic sequences	Strata	Typology
SUB-BOREAL	Le Martinet T. III (No. 1, 2)	
	Le Cuzoul VII (No. 3, 4, 5)	
	Le Cuzoul VI (No. 6, 7)	
ATLANTIC	Le Cuzoul V (No. 10, 11)	
	Le Martinet T. II (No. 8, 9)	
	Le Cuzoul IV (No. 12, 13, 14)	
BOREAL	Le Cuzoul III (No. 15, 16, 17)	
	Le Cuzoul II (No. 20, 21, 22)	
	Le Martinet T. I (No. 18) Roquefure 4 (No. 19)	
PRE-BOREAL	Roquefure 6 (No. 23, 24, 25) 23,Sous-Balme Abri (No. 26)	
	Le Martinet ; Sauv. (No. 27, 28, 29) Roquefure 7 (No. 30, 31)	

Abri de Roquefure (Vaucluse)	
Stratigraphy	Typological and Chronological sequence of Principal Tools
2 Lower Rhodanian Tardenoisian	
4 Lower Rhodanian Tardenoisian	
6 Lower Rhodanian Sauveterrian	
7 Lower Rhodanian Sauveterrian	
'5' Azilo-Sauveterrian	
9 Azilian	

39 *Abri de Roquefure (Vaucluse). Typological table showing the archaeological levels in their stratigraphic order (excavations by Paccard)*

broadened Tardenoisian point. This form shortly became a true trapeze, and the industry may then legitimately be termed a lower Rhodanian Tardenoisian. *40*

In the central and northern reaches of the Rhône *41-2* Sauveterrians developed only from the beginning of Boreal times, that is during the end of the seventh and the beginning of the sixth millennium. These people, who were in effect epi-Sauveterrians, were thus contemporary with the Castelnovian and with the early Tardenoisians of southern France.

The Mesolithic of the central and northern Rhône valley has in turn specific features, deriving from the industry of that region (Vilain 1966).

The interesting stratigraphy at Sous-Balme (Culoz, Ain) shows a Sauveterrian industry of the Boreal period *43* (Carrière zone) which includes a point with an untrimmed base. In layer F at the Abri des Layes No. 2 this form is absent, though it occurs above in layer B-C. This Sauveterrian includes Sauveterrian but not Tarde-

The Rhodanian Mesolithic		
Sequence	Classification and Typological sequence of Principal Tools	
Epi-Tardenoisian	Proto-Neolithic	
C Rhodanian Tardenoisian	Souhait Montagneu C.6	
B Rhodanian Tardenoisian	Abri Nº1 Sous-Vargonne	
A Rhodanian Tardenoisian	Sermoyer	
D Rhodanian Sauveterrian	Sous-Balme Abri	
C Rhodanian Sauveterrian	Abri Nº2 Les Layes B.C.	
B Rhodanian Sauveterrian	Sous-Balme Carrière I	
A Rhodanian Sauveterrian	Abri Nº2 Les Layes F	

40 *Typological table of the Rhodanian Mesolithic*

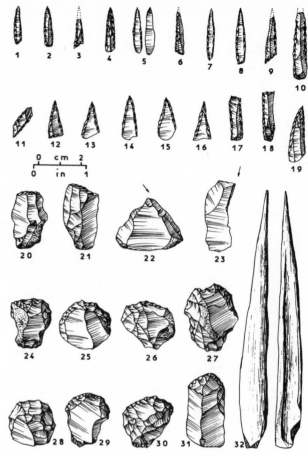

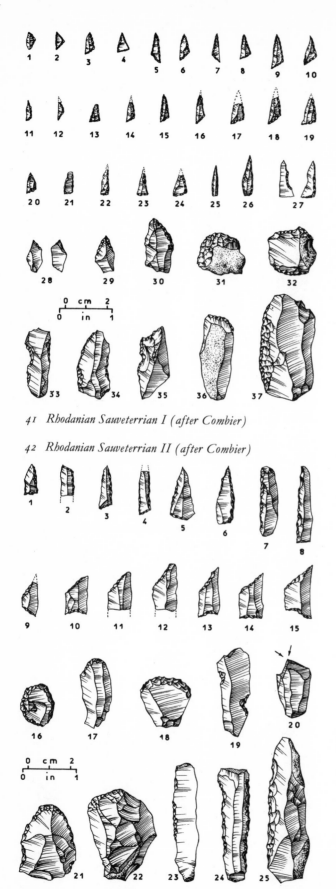

41 Rhodanian Sauveterrian I (after Combier)

42 Rhodanian Sauveterrian II (after Combier)

43 Site of Sous-Balme (Culoz-Ain) : the industry of La Carrière, level 1 (after Vilain)

noisian points. The Sauveterrian at Sous-Balme-Abri is dated to the Atlantic period; it still has Sauveterrian points, but there are Tardenoisian points and lunates in addition. Lunates were found in the B-C level at the Abri des Layes No. 2. There is also a proto-trapeze with concave trimming at Sous-Balme-Abri, which could *44* have evolved from the Tardenoisian point. But the point with an untrimmed base has disappeared and is replaced by the Tardenoisian point, which probably evolved from it.

Tardenoisian sites with trapezes are fairly numerous. *45* They are connected with the Sermoyer, Sous-Vargonne and Souhait-Montagneux types. This last site has yielded Sauveterrian points, but there are apparently no Tardenoisian points.

During the Atlantic period it seems that the epi-Sauveterrian of the Paris basin, after it had evolved into Tardenoisian I and II, was influenced in its evolution by the Tardenoisian of Aquitaine, along the Loire *46* valley, and possibly also by the Breton Tardenoisian. But at the same time it must be conceded that there were strong influences from the north, from the Tardenoisian in Belgium, and no doubt also movements of population.

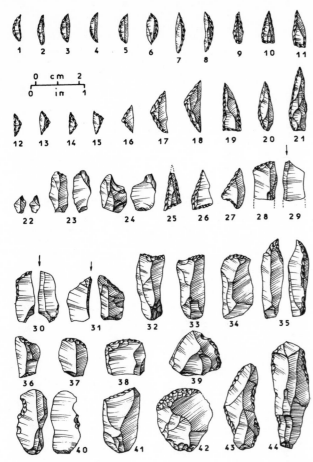

44 Site of Sous-Balme : the industry of l'Abri (after Vilain)

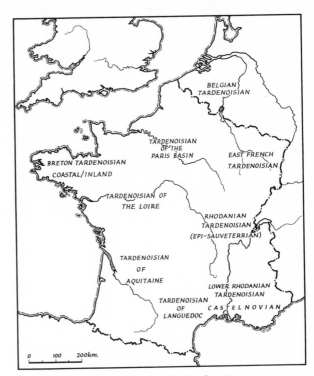

45 Map of regional groups in the Tardenoisian

Tardenoisian of the Paris Basin		
Subdivisions	Industries	Type Sites
Tardenosian III	Basis in Tardenoisian II with addition of: *Vielle Point* / *Trapezes* / *Rhomboids* — *Sauveterre Point rare or absent* — and Neolithic influences	Montbani — Les Rochers d'Auffargis Nº 2
	Basis in Tardenoisian I and Tardenoisian II with addition of Sonchamp Point	Sonchamp
Tardenoisian II	Basis of Tardenoisian I with addition of: *'Mistletoe' Point* / *Rare Trapezes* — Intrusion of Montmorencian Sandstone Tools: — Plane-Picks ; Crosier Picks	Le Désert d'Auffargis — La Sablonnière de Coincy — Piscop — La Chambre des Fées – Coincy
Tardenoisian I (Sauveterrian facies)	Tardenois Points / Triangles / Arc-Segments / Elongated Scalene Triangles / Sauveterre Points	Les Rochers d'Auffargis Nº 1

46 Classification of the Tardenoisian in the Paris Basin

The Mesolithic of the Paris basin has been repeatedly discussed elsewhere (Daniel 1932, 1946, 1949, 1954, 1965; Daniel and Rozoy 1966; Daniel and Vignard 1953, 1954; Hinout 1964; Parent 1962, 1967).

If an early stage exists, during the Boreal or perhaps even earlier, it is still ill-defined. A Sauveterrian variant is represented by a standard site, Les Rochers d'Auffargis No. 1. This Sauveterrian, which does not apparently belong to the earliest stage, comprises triangles, Tardenoisian and Sauveterrian points, lunates, a type of very fine and sharp backed blade, and elongated scalene triangles. These characterise what is called the Tardenoisian I of the Paris basin (Giraud and Vignard 1946).

Le Désert d'Auffargis and the shelters and open-air sites of Coincy and Piscop best represent the second stage, Tardenoisian II, which carries on the preceding industrial traditions while adopting in addition a point covered by invasive trimming (the mistletoe leaf point) and the trapeze. However, the trapeze is a rare form in the Paris basin throughout Tardenoisian II.

Tardenoisian III is well exemplified by Montbani and Les Rochers d'Auffargis No. 2, and by Sonchamp which shows a particular variant of it. In addition to what was inherited from the previous phase, Tardenoisian III includes a great number of trapezes, the Vielle point and rhomboids.

No Mediterranean influences can be detected in the Paris basin at any time during the Mesolithic, nor are there any signs of them in the valleys of the Saône or Rhine. Some objects from the Mediterranean, for example sea shells (*columbella*), managed to reach as far as the Ain (the Sous-Balme shelter, Culoz) along the Rhône

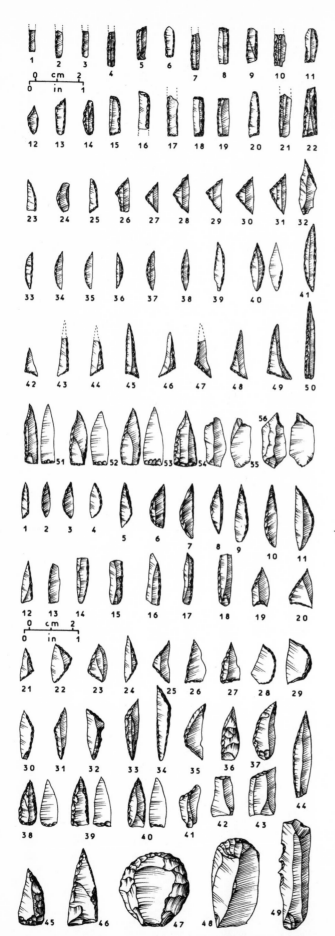

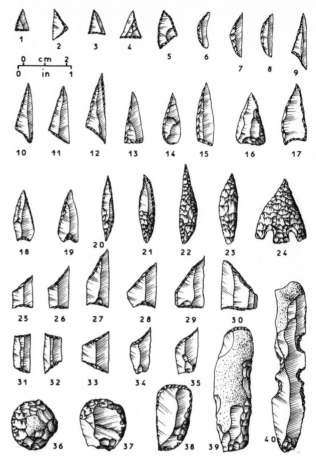

47 *Les Rochers d'Auffargis no. 1. Tardenoisian I of Sauveterrian variants (after Giraud-Vignard)*

◀ 48 *Le Desert d'Auffargis. Tardenoisian IIa (after R. Daniel)*

49 *Montbani. Tardenoisian III (after R. Daniel)*

valley. This route was closed towards the middle of the Atlantic period by the first arrivals of Danubian Neolithic communities from the east, with developed 'Linear' pottery. Its appearance, about 4000 BC, in the Paris basin set in train the proto-Neolithic acculturation of 'classical' Tardenoisian, which from this time on includes sporadic finds of Neolithic elements mixed with its traditional material.

From the beginning of the sub-Boreal these Neolithic influences become more noticeable in the Tardenoisian III of the Paris basin, which adopted an increasing number of borrowed forms. In the first stage of Tardenoisian III (Les Rochers d'Auffargis No. 2) the industry is unmixed, but in the following stage (Montbani) it includes Neolithic-type arrowheads. In its first stage the Paris basin Tardenoisian includes a further variant characterised by the Sonchamp point. It has been shown that Sonchamp points appeared in Aquitaine towards the end of the Boreal. If the point arrived later at

38

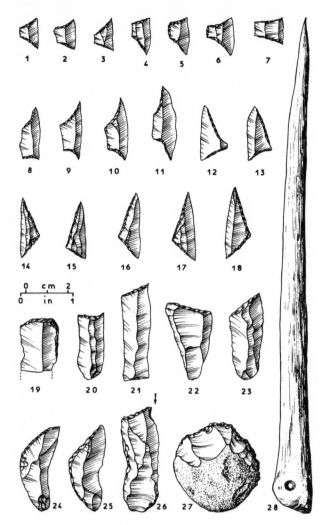

50 Téviec. Mesolithic in Brittany: coastal Tardenoisian industry (after Péquart)

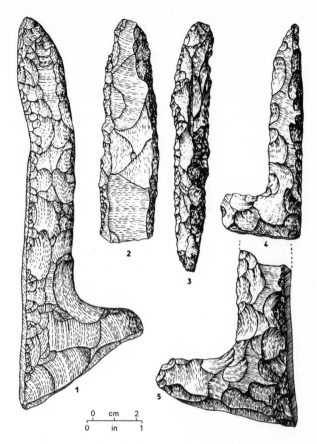

51 Montmorentian industry: 'crozier' picks and 'pics-planés' (after R. Daniel, Nouel, Vignard)

Sonchamp, which is in Seine-et-Oise, southwest of Paris, it may be an indication of influence from the Aquitaine Tardenoisian; this seems to have expanded first to the north and then eastwards by way of the Loire and its tributaries, which allow easy access into the Seine valley along the western tributaries of that river.

The coastal Tardenoisian of Brittany seems quite distinct. Like the Tardenoisian of the southwest and Aquitaine it became established at the end of the fifth millennium during the Atlantic period, but nevertheless it does not appear to derive directly from Aquitaine. It could be that it is the result of northward expansion by the Mugian of Arruda in Portugal, along the coasts of the Atlantic.

Forms closely comparable with certain of the geometric microliths from Muge-Arruda are found again at Téviec and Hoëdic (Brittany): short triangles, elongated *50* trapezes with concave trimming, truncated blades with

curved backs. The industry in bone and deer antler is also very similar. Again, the habitat is of the same type and so are the graves, wich lie actually in the shell mounds which grew up from the food refuse.

These similarities are all the more striking because there is other material in Brittany containing Tardenoisian points, small lunates and delicate triangles (deposits at La Pointe Saint-Gildas) which does seem related to the Tardenoisian of the Loire and Paris basin. At a later stage (the Préfaille site) there appear trapezes and tanged transverse arrowheads, then (at Sainte-Marie) shouldered truncated flints and pointed tanged arrowheads.

Montmorentian (4500–3000 BC)
This is a specialised industry containing a very high percentage of large heavy tools. The material used is sandstone (Montmorency *grès lustrê*) and finds include axes with transversely sharpened cutting-edge (*tranchets*), scrapers and above all adze-like picks (*pics-planés*) *51* which are of especial significance for two reasons. Those collected *in situ* (by Vignard) still show, on their flake scars, traces of tannin which came from the bark of trees. They were therefore wood-working tools and perhaps served, not only for preparing building timbers,

but it would seem especially for gathering bark to tan hides and skins.

Furthermore these picks, either broken or intact, are found on several Tardenoisian II and III sites in the Paris basin (M. and R. Daniel 1949, Daniel 1954) and round the Loire (Vignard and Nouel 1962).

Summary

The Mesolithic be an in the south of France about the end of the Allerød interstadial. It followed on directly from the parent Romanellian, in the case of the Mediterranean industries, or from the Azilian in other regions of France. In Brittany, in the upper valley of the Rhône and in the Paris basin the Mesolithic proper began a little later.

Each of the main ecological regions presents a different variant and its own industrial development. Everywhere, however, there is a notable tendency, increasing as Mesolithic industry developed, towards a growing percentage of geometric microliths at the expense of other tools.

At the end of the final Mesolithic the proto-Neolithic industries, probably under the influence of Neolithic archers, replaced their barbed spears[1] with arrows.

The Mesolithic peoples of the Mediterranean zone (Provence) succeeded in domesticating sheep. This may have triggered off the native pastoral cultures.

This native Mesolithic had passed into a Neolithic stage by the fifth millennium on the Mediterranean coast. Inland the Mesolithic lasted longer, conserving more or less its way of life and its traditional equipment.

The Early Neolithic (5600-4000 BC)

Origins

The earliest Neolithic in France is represented by only one culture, that characterised by the shell-impressed pottery known as Cardial ware.

Two contrasted cultural strands are perceptible from this time onwards. While the lithic industry maintains a traditional element which is indicative of the lineage of the groups just described, novel, or apparently novel, elements are introduced by the pottery and by the ground stone axes which generally coincide with its appearance.

Unquestionably the flint industry of the Cardial ware Neolithic is a local derivative from the Mesolithic Castelnovian. But how should the decorated pottery be interpreted? This appears suddenly (and there is nothing tentative in either the forms or the decoration) in the sixth millennium, on the coast of Provence at Châteauneuf-les-Martigues (Escalon de Fonton, 1956, 1967) among a population of shepherds. It cannot represent an eastern influence, since nowhere in the eastern Mediterranean or Near East are there precise analogues for either the pottery or the ornament. Furthermore, the antiquity of the Cardial pottery at Châteauneuf, confirmed geologically and by the C14 reading of 5570 BC (for level F5), puts the dated layer earlier than all other finds of the culture at present known on the coasts of the western Mediterranean. Furthermore,

the Early Cardial culture at Châteauneuf (levels F6, C6, *52* F5, C5) has not yet been found elsewhere. As might be expected, this phase of primary Neolithic is fairly rare, owing to its transitional nature. By contrast, Middle and Late Cardial pottery is known at several sites in France, Spain and Italy.

Cardial ware, Neolithic with shell-impressed pottery (5600-3000 BC)

In France distribution of the Cardial Neolithic is limited to those areas where a Mediterranean Mesolithic had spread, that is, to the Mediterranean regions of Provence and lower Languedoc.

Where could the idea of making pottery, and decorating it in this way, have come from? While pottery manufacture manifestly originated in the eastern Mediterranean, the decoration could have a different origin. It is in fact highly probable that Mesolithic Castelnovians made basketry containers, and possibly wooden and leather ones. These may very well have been decorated. When the Castelnovians developed a 'Neolithic' type of material culture, they could quite simply have transferred their traditional art on to pottery, without the stimulus of outside influence. This would explain the immediate appearance of elaborate ornament on the earliest pottery, and also account for the fact that this decoration is found nowhere else; it would further explain why the forms of the first pottery all appear to derive either from the egg, a natural vessel, or from *53-4* baskets.[2]

Flint industry remained traditionally Mesolithic until the Middle Cardial phase. The transverse arrowheads were in fact steeply trimmed trapezes.

With Late Cardial pottery the transverse arrowheads are trimmed with invasive flaking. It is in this phase *55* that the Neolithic reached Mediterranean regions away from the coast, for example Montclus (Gard). Contem- *24* porary with Early Cardial ware at Châteauneuf there had been, at Montclus, a proto-Neolithic Castelnovian, which is absent in the coastal regions of Provence. This Neolithic was established at Montclus at a stage comparable with level 1 at Châteauneuf, when shell-impressed decoration was becoming rare and clumsy and a furrowed ware was developing.

There is also an 'epi-Cardial', still not closely dated. This includes undecorated carinated pottery, which *25-6* resembles that of the earliest metal age and leaf-shaped arrowheads, together with a fairly degenerate shell-impressed ware (surface layers at Châteauneuf: Escalon de Fonton 1956; Abri de l'Eglise: Paccard 1957).

The earliest Cardial Neolithic is not strictly agricultural. Economically it continues the pastoral traditions of the Castelnovian, from which it derives. There is no trace of outside influence detectable in it.

---

[1] Alternatively the microliths may have formed barbs of a different design of arrow. – Ed.

[2] It should however be noted that impressed ware of various kinds is common elsewhere in the Mediterranean, notably in north Africa from 5000 BC onwards, as for example in Tripolitania (Mori 1965). – Ed.

Quern stones occur, but were used for grinding red ochre, as in the Mesolithic Castelnovian. And although the Châteauneuf site has yielded part of a sickle, gathering grass would be indispensable for successful maintenance of flocks. Rabbit, it is true, decreases appreciably in the food refuse associated with Cardial pottery at Châteauneuf, but there are still shell-fish, crustaceans and a great many fish remains.

Uninhabited caves close by Châteauneuf served as burial places. The skeletons were contracted and a few sherds of shell-impressed pottery beside them were the only grave-goods.

General

On the French Mediterranean coast the Cardial ware Neolithic appears as an episode in the expansion of broadly 'Neolithic' culture during the first third of the fifth millennium, that is to say, climatically at the beginning of the Atlantic period. It continued in traditional ways until the arrival in quantity of Chassey ware, in the sub-Boreal. Following upon this, it seems very likely that the latest material at Châteauneuf (level 1 and surface layers A and B) reflects acculturation from a Chassean source. However, although Cardial decoration ceases and the quality of the pottery deteriorates rapidly while adopting foreign forms (carination), the lithic industry retains its primitive types (denticulation), even if the blades and bladelets disappear. The explanation may be either that epi-Cardial culture became extinct about this time, or that the pastoralists, wishing to

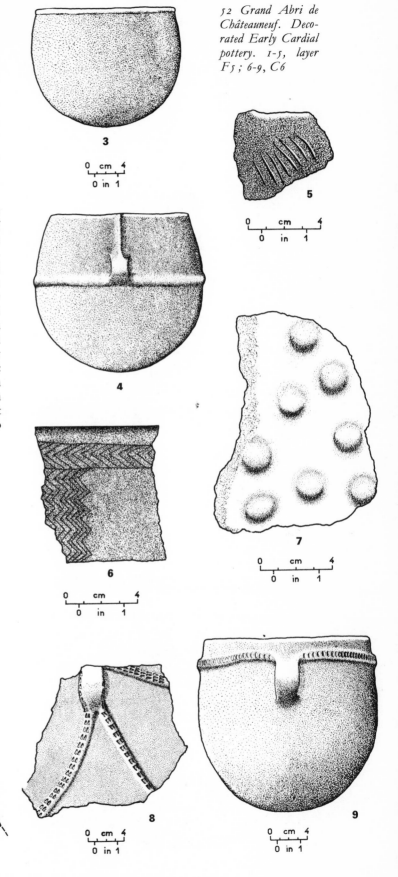

52 Grand Abri de Châteauneuf. Decorated Early Cardial pottery. 1-5, layer F5; 6-9, C6

91

53 Grand Abri de Châteauneuf. Middle Cardial pottery. 1-3, layer C4; 4-10, F4

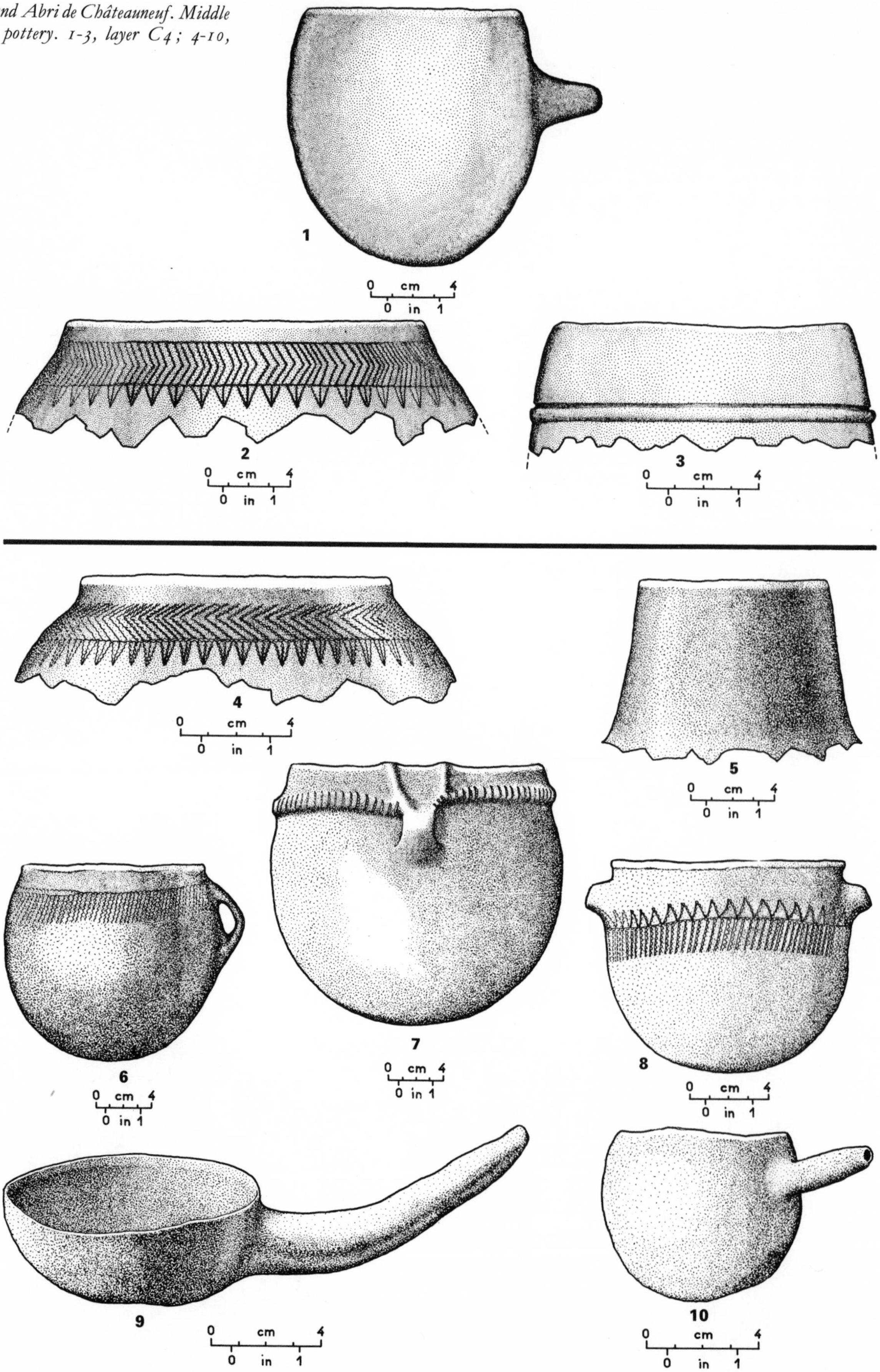

1

0 cm 4
0 in 1

2

0 cm 4
0 in 1

3

0 cm 4
0 in 1

4

0 cm 4
0 in 1

5

0 cm 4
0 in 1

6

0 cm 4
0 in 1

7

0 cm 4
0 in 1

8

0 cm 4
0 in 1

9

0 cm 4
0 in 1

10

0 cm 4
0 in 1

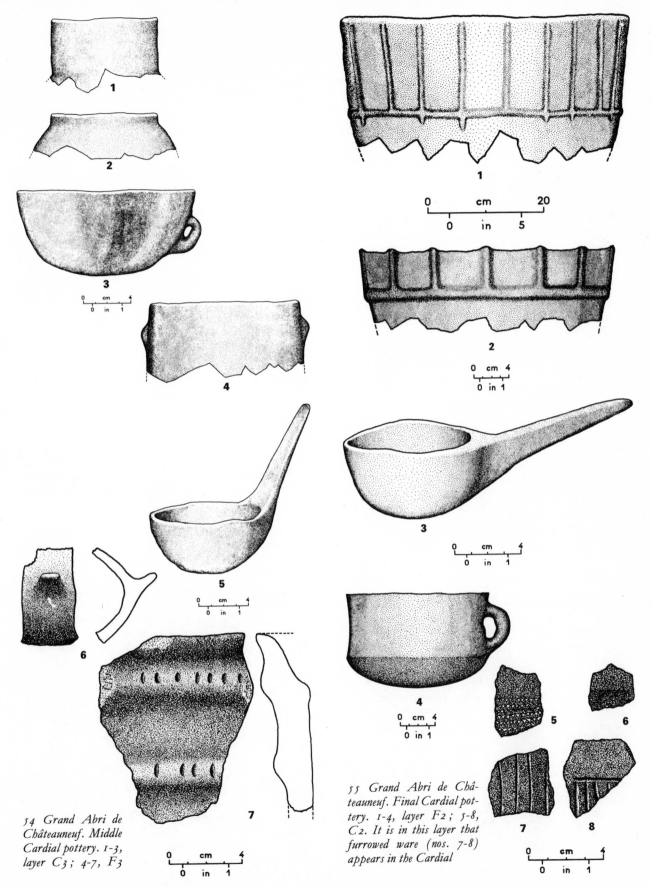

54 *Grand Abri de Châteauneuf. Middle Cardial pottery. 1-3, layer C3; 4-7, F3*

55 *Grand Abri de Châteauneuf. Final Cardial pottery. 1-4, layer F2; 5-8, C2. It is in this layer that furrowed ware (nos. 7-8) appears in the Cardial*

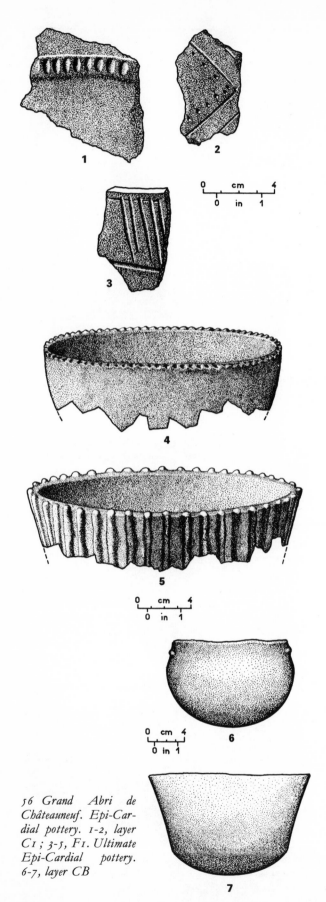

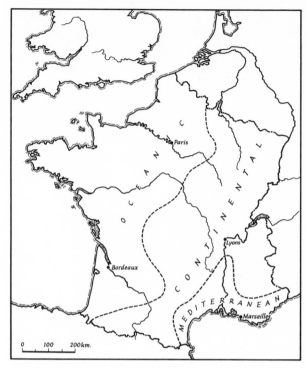

57 *Climatic regions in present-day France*

56 Grand Abri de Châteauneuf. Epi-Cardial pottery. 1-2, layer C1; 3-5, F1. Ultimate Epi-Cardial pottery. 6-7, layer CB

maintain their traditional way of life rather than become agricultural, took refuge in the upland country the agriculturists had disdained. Here, by mutation, they might have given rise to some differentiated groups among the local '*pasteurs des plateaux*'; but this is only a suggestion.

The relationship between the natural environment and the cultural succession

The Allerød interstadial (10,500-8500 BC)
In inland regions and in the north of France the Allerød 57 interstadial did not immediately make itself felt. Round the Mediterranean climatic amelioration began early, 58 though at first tempered by the presence of the final snows on nearby mountains. In the southwest, in the north and northeast, and in the upper Rhône valley reindeer were still present during the Azilian, although far rarer than in in the final Magdalenian.

In the south, and especially the southeast, reindeer disappeared early. The site of Valorgues (Gard) is a good source of information about the ecology of the early Allerød period in a region where the reindeer was regularly found with late Magdalenian, until the end of Dryas II. The first hearths lie directly on the bare rock floor, which had been washed clear by torrential streams at the beginning of the interstadial. The Valorgues valley at that time had been denuded of all earlier sediments by widespread erosion. The hearths contained charcoal from Scotch pine (*Pinus silvestris* L.) and bones of rabbit, a small species of wild horse and aurochs. The reindeer is absent from this initial industry which is Romanellian in type and has a C14 date of 10,390 BC. Subsequently a coarse gravel accumulated on the valley floor, brought down by a torrential river. This indicates that the sedimentary regime had changed and that vegetational cover had been re-established, reducing erosion by retaining part of the rainfall and impeding the too rapid run-off of water. A little later, towards the end of the Allerød interstadial (c. 8600 BC)[1] there was a marked resumption of torrential activity and the valley became almost filled with alluvial deposits. This can only have been caused by renewed precipitation of a force and frequency which could no longer be regulated by the natural forest cover, resulting in conditions of saturation. The increase in humidity appears to correspond also with a tendency to warmer temperatures, which reached a maximum towards c. 8500 BC.

It seems certain that in France every change towards warmer conditions began in the southeast and then spread to the rest of the country, initially leaving little islands of cold here and there on the mountain ranges and in their immediate vicinity. The view is widely held that cold climatic episodes set in from the north with a time lag further south so that the climate of the Mediterranean was not subjected to the same oscillations of advance and retreat of the cold.

Nevertheless, it is temperature variations that explain most effectively many industrial changes and so point to changing modes of life in prehistory. Each industrial succession is no more than the sum of adjustments aimed at a better adaptation to the environment. These adaptations come about in response to ecological changes, which necessitate such transformation of equipment to correspond with new requirements.

On the coastal strip of the Mediterranean, however, there had never been reindeer in the period we are dealing with. This animal had been consistently absent, at least from the middle of the Upper Palaeolithic, on account of the climate and, still more important, because the terrain was too broken and difficult. Provence is in effect a mountainous country, where wide plains are either absent or too marshy, so precluding 'Reindeer culture'. In its place we find the animal corresponding to reindeer elsewhere, namely ibex (*Capra ibex* L.). At first sight this may seem no more than an ecological detail of little importance, but on closer study it emerges as the dominant factor in the cultural sequence of southeastern France.

The epi-Gravettians never knew the reindeer, which meant that their descendants the Romanellians were not committed to the economy it demanded. It is for this reason that, already in the tenth millennium, Romanellian has the appearance of a precocious Azilian. It has, however, no other connection with the latter culture apart from a morphological resemblance which arose from an analogous context.

Some 1500 years later the warmer conditions of the Allerød interstadial had extended over the rest of the

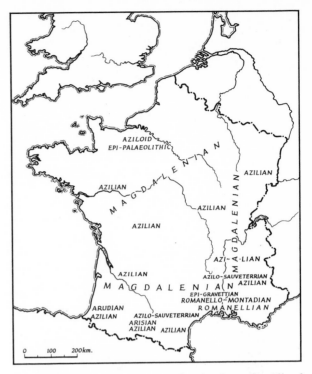

58 Distribution of prehistoric industries from the Allerød interstadial to Dryas III (10,500-7500 BC)

country. Gradually the cold receded, drawing the reindeer northward. It was only around 9000 BC that the final Magdalenian developed into Azilian, possibly under the influence of the Romanellian, which had already for a thousand years owned an industry adapted to the new conditions. The animals hunted were at this time, it may be supposed, a more immediate factor than temperature or humidity in conditioning men's lives.

At the end of the Allerød interstadial there was a further climatic change which stimulated new localised trends in industries across the length of France. While in the north the forest was spreading on to formations previously subject to glacial conditions (drifts, loesses and moraines), which favoured the establishment of Azilian and sub-Azilian cultures (in effect an epi-Magdalenian first with, and then without, reindeer), events were quite different in the southeast.

Towards the end of the Allerød interstadial in the French Midi a Mediterranean, maritime climate was re-established and began to expand over the territory where it now prevails. Thus, around 8500 BC, while the industries of northern France were taking on an Azilian aspect, those in Provence were leaving their Romanellian stage behind.

Dryas III (8500-7500 BC)

This period saw a progressive spread of the Mediterranean climate, although for about a thousand years some degree of continuing humidity is still apparent. While the forest persisted in alluvial valleys and fertile

---

1 Torrential activity was resumed after the end of the Allerød in more northerly latitudes. – Ed.

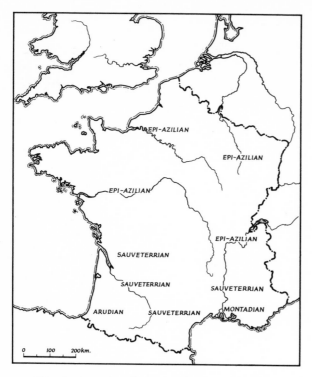

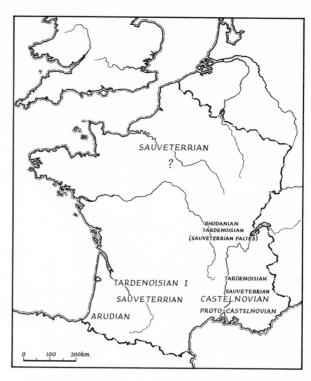

59 Distribution of prehistoric industries during the pre-Boreal (7500-6500 BC)

60 Distribution of prehistoric industries during the Boreal (6500-5800 BC)

basins in southeastern France, it began to retreat on the slopes and hills, which make up the major part of the region. Almost everywhere it was replaced by *garrigue* (scrub-covered) uplands, while the Crau plain and the developing Camargue were parkland, with more grass than forest.

The Romanellian of the region changed in response to the new ecological demands, giving rise to a Montadian lithic equipment. The cold however returned, beginning in the north, where rapid climatic fluctuation was unfavourable to settlement; prehistoric sites of this period are therefore rare and in some areas absent. Meanwhile, in the southeast, the Montadian devised, or revived, barbed missiles armed with geometric microliths (triangles and lunates). In the southwest the Azilian was transformed into Azilio-Sauveterrian and subsequently, a little later, into true Sauveterrian. In the northern inland regions conditions were temperate but cool, with slow forest expansion. The industries show various modes of adaptation, all classifiable as epi-Azilian or proto-Sauveterrian.

The pre-Boreal (7500-6500 BC)

59 The climate became progressively drier during this relatively short phase. In the south of France, following the disappearance of large game, the associated culture phase is notable for thick deposits of mixed snail shells and ashes. The Mediterranean zone added a new variant to the Montadian, characterised by geometric microliths. At first these took the form of triangles and

lunates, but towards the end of the pre-Boreal trapezes and rhomboids appeared. When the climate became less humid and while there was still forest, or at least heavy woodland along the watercourses, the streams in fact grew clear enough to allow fish to be harpooned. The Montadians increasingly abandoned their hunting, to rely primarily on fishing.

In the southwest Sauveterrian developed out of the local industries, in similar conditions. The hearths from this period still contain bones of deer, boar and rabbit, but there are also great quantities of snails, probably indicating a rise in temperature.

Owing no doubt to a parallel climatic change the north of France shows signs of the spread of an epi-Azilian culture, although the industry as yet remains somewhat ill-defined. It is possible however that lack of preservation may explain the relative scarcity of sites. Whatever the cause, there is once more a notable disparity in industrial development between the north and the south of France.

In the south the transformation of Epipalaeolithic into Mesolithic had occurred early. The first geometric microliths appear in the first half of the pre-Boreal in the form of the Provençal Montadian, and during the course of the period in the coastal and inland regions of the southwest. Elsewhere it is different.

Although there is a Rhodanian Sauveterrian in the lower Rhône valley and a Languedocian Sauveterrian, both contemporaries of Montadian with geometric microliths, the Sauveterrian in the upper Rhône valley appears only in the Boreal, when the general increase in dryness was especially marked in the Midi.

No Mesolithic Sauveterrian has yet been found in the northern half of France during the pre-Boreal. To know whether this implies that epi-Azilian continued unmodified in its traditional ways we need stratified sites, which unfortunately have yet to be discovered.

The Boreal (6500-5800 BC)

During this climatic period notably drier conditions prevailed. This is apparent throughout France, but much more marked in Mediterranean regions. Everywhere the forest retreated and soils were reduced; springs and streams dried up; men and animals concentrated around available water supplies.

In the Midi each variety of Sauveterrian changed into a distinct variant of Tardenoisian, further complicating the picture of the Tardenoisian in France. In Mediterranean Provence the Montadian, while preserving its traditionally crude tools, adopted the trapeze for its characteristic barbed missiles, as it developed into Castelnovian. On the Mediterranean coasts the forest retreated even more drastically than in other regions, as aridity grew increasingly severe. The countryside took on its present-day aspect, with low and thorny 'garrigue' vegetation spreading everywhere. Game tended to disappear; rabbit became the sole source of food, apart from fish.

The wild sheep which had always been present, though rare for several thousands of years, is an animal which adjusts well to a dry atmosphere, provided it can find sufficient food. It is adaptable in its diet and the food then available was sufficient for it. This was a favourable time to attempt its domestication and the Castelnovians undertook this during the sixth millennium, probably to preserve a source of game which was tending to disappear and which tolerated the proximity of men.

As the Mediterranean climate spread, so the Castelnovian expanded its territory. At Montclus (Gard), 100 km. from the coast, Castelnovian overlies a Languedocian Tardenoisian I of c. 6000-5500 BC. With a supply of fish in the river the Castelnovians were able to continue their traditional activities, substituting local fishing for seeking fish in the Mediterranean, and domesticating the sheep. The site serves to illustrate how local conditions bring about economic evolution and changes among an otherwise homogeneous population.

The Tardenoisian had still not penetrated farther up the Rhône valley at this time, though there was sporadic occupation by persistent Sauveterrian groups.

The same would seem to be true of the Paris basin, where we find a still uncertainly dated variant of Sauveterrian (Tardenoisian I of Sauveterrian facies). This cannot be put any earlier, however, and could even be later still, as it is north of the Loire in Brittany, Charente and in the centre and east of France. But one may wonder whether this seeming absence corresponds in fact to reality. All the Tardenoisian sites in the Paris basin have been dated to the Atlantic period by pollen analysis, recently confirmed by a C14 date of 3000 BC at Chambre des Fées, Coincy; but they lie in areas of sandy soil, and human and animal life requires water. Although today this region lacks water, as all streams are lost in the permeable sand, there were certainly adequate supplies when the Tardenoisians lived there during the damp Atlantic period – former stream beds, now empty, can be seen, or were until recently visible. Thus if Sauveterrians or Tardenoisians had lived in the Paris basin during the dry Boreal period they would have been obliged to settle elsewhere than on the permeable sands. They would have built their huts near to running water, in depressions, or on the banks of large streams and rivers. While it is very difficult to find any traces of these today, the fact is that in the south of France the Sauveterrian and early Tardenoisian of the pre-Boreal and Boreal are invariably found near running water or active springs.

The Atlantic (5800-3000 BC)

The moist conditions which set in with this phase in the climatic sequence (Roux and Leroi-Gourhan 1964) progressed by stages which extend beyond the truly prehistoric period. In the French Midi, after a sub-Boreal stage, a phase of maximum humidity seems to have occurred between the terminal Bronze Age and the Iron Age.

At the very beginning of the Atlantic the first increase in precipitation brought torrential conditions to the Midi, as there was no vegetation cover to modify the effects of the water. But gradually the forest regained its hold and the coastal plains became covered with natural grassland.

The sea-level had been low during the Upper Palaeolithic (down 30 m. during the Aurignacian) and then had gradually risen to establish itself at its present-day level by the end of the Boreal. Subterranean water dispersed less readily and numerous springs gushed forth all along the coast.

It grew progressively easier for the Castelnovians to breed their sheep, which had become domesticated. But an important fact was that they were not obliged to resort to nomadism in order to find pasture during dry seasons. They were now able to find abundant grass almost anywhere in the valleys and plains that had previously been arid and sterile. Thus they were able to adopt a relatively sedentary way of life, keeping their flocks near to their living sites.

In this way it was possible for the Castelnovians, under the stimulus of Mediterranean ideas, to pass into the Neolithic, about 5600 BC to judge from Châteauneuf-les-Martigues (Bouches-du-Rhône). This was the beginning of the Cardial Neolithic.

Once they became settled, these prehistoric people were able to make full use of pottery, which had already been current in other cultural traditions to the east. They did not however become agriculturists, but preferred to continue their pastoral tradition which, under the influence of a favourable climate, maintained an unbroken development. Progress was made, not in the sense of changing the economy, but along traditional lines.

In Atlantic and inland regions during this time forests covered the whole country, apart from a few habitable coastal areas. Tardenoisians continued their traditional

STRATIGRAPHY AND CHRONOLOGY OF FRENCH EPI-

DATE BC	CLIMATIC SEQUENCE	ATLANTIC ZONE		SOUTH-WEST				SOUTH		
		LA TORCHE (FINISTÈRE)	POEYMAÜ ARUDY (BASSES-PYRÉNÉES)	ROUFFIGNAC (DORDOGNE)	BORIE DEL REY (LOT-ET-GARONNE)	LE MARTINET (LOT-ET-GARONNE)	LE CUZOUL (LOT)	GROTTE DES SALZETS (AVEYRON)	PUECHMARGUES II (AVEYRON)	ABRI JEAN-CROS (AUDE)
0 / 1000 — SUB-ATLANTIC						Gallo-Roman / Iron Age	Gallo-Roman / VIIb Iron Age			
1000 / 3000 — SUB-BOREAL			Epi-Arudian			Tardenoisian III (pottery)	Bronze Age / VIIa Chalcolithic / VI Tardenoisian III			
3000 / 5800 — ATLANTIC		Coastal Tardenoisian 4020	Arudian			Tardenoisian II	V Tardenoisian II / IV Tardenoisian II		Tardenoisian 4470	Cardial 4590
5800 / 6500 — BOREAL			Arudian	Tardenoisian 5810 / Sauveterrian 6420	Tardenoisian	Tardenoisian I	III Tardenoisian I / II Tardenoisian I			
6500 / 7500 — PRE-BOREAL			Arudian	Sauveterrian 6640 / Sauveterrian 7045	Sauveterrian	Sauveterrian	Ib Sauveterrian	Sauveterrian 6820		
7500 / 8500 — DRYAS III			Arudian		Epi-Azilian					
8500 / 10,500 — ALLERØD					Azilian					
10,500 — DRYAS II						Magdalenian	Ia (reindeer)			

life of hunting and fishing, though like the Castelnovians and Cardial groups they added stock-raising to their economy. But they did not become fully Neolithic, being more firmly anchored in their traditions than were the coastal people who were less isolated and more exposed to influences from the Mediterranean.

Coastal and inland Tardenoisian in Brittany, the Tardenoisian of the Loire region, of the Paris basin and in eastern France are all dated, by various methods, to 5000-2800 B C.

From the arrival of communities practising evolved Linear-decorated Neolithic pottery (ultimately of

PALAEOLITHIC, MESOLITHIC AND EARLY NEOLITHIC SITES

SOUTH				SOUTH-EAST				RHONE VALLEY	PARIS BASIN	
LA CROUZADE (AUDE)	BIZE (AUDE)	VALORGUES ST-QUENTIN (GARD)	MONTCLUS (GARD)	CHÂTEAUNEUF-LES-MARTIGUES (B.-DU-R.)	ISTRES-CORNILLE (B.-DU-R.)	COMBE-BUISSON (VAUCLUSE)	ROQUEFURE (VAUCLUSE)	SOUS-BALME CULOZ (AIN)	PARIS BASIN (SITES)	CHAMBRE DES FÉES - COINCY (AISNE)
			1B Gallo-Roman	Gallo-Roman	1A Gallo-Roman					
				Iron Age			Iron Age			
			2A Chalcolithic 2B Chassey	A, B Chalcolithic 1, 2 Epi-Cardial	1B		Bronze Age 1 Neolithic		Tardenoisian III	
			3, 4 Late Cardial 5, 6 Epi-Castelnovian 7, 8 proto-Neolithic	3, 4 Late Cardial 5, 6 Early Cardial 5570				Sauveterrian (rock-shelter)	Tardenoisian II	Tardenoisian II 3079
			9, 14 Castelnovian 15, 16 Tardenoisian 17 to 23 Sauveterrian 6180	7 Castelnovian 8 Castelnovian	1C		2 to 4 Tardenoisian	Sauveterrian (quarry)	Tardenoisian I (Sauveterrian facies)	
			24 to 32 Sauveterrian		2 to 6 Montadian	1, 2 Montadian	6, 7 Sauveterrian			
Azilo-Sauve-terrian					7, 8 Romanello-Montadian	3 Romanello-Montadian	(5), 8 Azilo-Sauveterrian			
Azilian	Azilian	Romanellian 10,140 10,390			9 Romanellian	4 Romanellian	9 Azilian			
Magda-lenian	Magda-lenian						reindeer			

62 *Distribution of prehistoric industries during the Atlantic (5800–3000 BC)*

Chrono.	Sequence	Typological sequence of principal tools
3,000	ATLANTIC	Epi-Cardial
		Cardial
5,800	BOREAL	Castelnovian
		Proto-Castelnovian
6,500	PRE-BOREAL	Montadian
7,500	DRYAS III	Romanello-Montadian
8,000	ALLERÖD	Romanellian
10,500	DRYAS II	Romanellian
		Epi-Gravettian
11,000		

63 *Classification of the Epipalaeolithic, Mesolithic and Early Neolithic in coastal Provence. These industries follow each other in direct succession. The local tradition came to an end after the 'Cardial' Neolithic*

Danubian origin) about 4000 B C, the native Tardenoisian hunters and fishers became influenced and acculturated by these early farmers foreign to the region, who eventually colonised a large part of northern France.

Conclusions

63 The post-Glacial was a period of rapid ecological evolution and presents for study a wealth of new cultural departures. At the first sign that the cold was receding we already find attempts at adaptation by the Magdalenians, reflected in their lithic equipment by the development of geometric microliths: triangles, crescents, micro-lunates, rectangles, backed bladelets with double truncation, trapezes, Krukowsky micro-burins, etc. (Bordes and Fitte 1964).

The warmer conditions of the Allerød period came relatively early to the Mediterranean coast and the epi-Gravettian rapidly evolved into the Romanellian, the
61 prototype of the Azilian industries and probably indeed a factor in their formation. From the beginning of Allerød, Mediterranean climate and environment promoted adaptation and invention, and the flexible industry of the local population was able to change to meet new requirements.

In the Dryas III[1] phase this industry was quickly tranformed and split into two variants: Montadian

[1] The Younger Dryas of Scandinavian authors. – Ed.

without geometric microliths, the industry of exclusively hunting groups, and Montadian with geometric microliths, which was used by hunter-fishers. This distinction became pronounced in the pre-Boreal, when Montadian industry spread.

The Boreal climate occasioned a complete transformation of the latter group, through the stages hunter-fisher (proto-Castelnovian), hunter-fisher-herdsman (Castelnovian), fisher-herdsman (epi-Castelnovian). By the beginning of the Atlantic the Castelnovian (herdsmen) had become Neolithic, engendering locally the Cardial Neolithic. This was an exclusively pastoral culture, which was to vanish or be transformed on the arrival of the first agriculturists, the Chasseans.

On the Atlantic coast during the Allerød period there was an equally rapid evolution of the Azilian type of material culture resulting in two distinct variants: Arudian, an industry of the uplands, and early Sauveterrian, which quickly gave rise to a branch of coastal Tardenoisian, perhaps related to the Portuguese Mesolithic of the Atlantic phase.

In inland regions also the Azilian evolved to become Sauveterrian, and then Tardenoisian. This Tardenoisian comprised as many variants as there were regional parent industries. The form of the industry varies according to whether the Tardenoisians were hunters or fishers. A forest industry, the Montmorentian, impinges on the Tardenoisian II of the Paris basin during the Atlantic. In this region Neolithic infiltration (Late Linear pottery) produced acculturations, to increase the number of Tardenoisian variants from the beginning of the sub-Boreal, *c.* 4000 BC.

Thus by Atlantic times the Mediterranean region appears as a dynamic centre, while other areas displayed a certain conservatism. This conservatism, however, by no means reflects an inability to adapt, nor is it a sign of decadence. On the contrary, it merely indicates that there was no ecological transformation, such as had necessitated adaptation on the Mediterranean, and no reason for change. In other regions the environment did not alter appreciably and it is obvious that there was no call for any modification in man's way of life. The Rhône valley illustrates this point further. Whereas Mesolithic people on the Mediterranean were obliged to adapt when ecological conditions altered with the progressive humidity of the Atlantic period, those who had migrated up the Rhône abandoned traits which were specifically coastal while adapting to the 'archaic' environment, and this brought about a transformation in their industry until it became closer, morphologically, to inland Tardenoisian forms.

Tardenoisians, the pre-pottery proto-Neolithic groups of Atlantic times and the Cardial Neolithic people of the Mediterranean coast were all three well adapted to the environment in which they lived.

To transform an industry completely without adequate environmental reasons would be a strange aberration in cultural growth, scarcely progress.

4

The First Agriculturists:

4000-1800 BC

GERARD BAILLOUD

The two thousand years to be discussed in this chapter are of special significance for the historical evolution of western Europe. They witnessed in fact a complete transformation, effected progressively but inexorably, in man's mode of life, which until then had not altered in any fundamental way since Europe was first inhabited. Initially in a limited sector, and then over the whole area of present-day France, new methods of subsistence based on the domestication of animals and cultivation of edible plants took the place of hunting, fishing and gathering, which persisted only to supplement these new methods. Concurrently, technology underwent rapid and profound changes, enriched by entirely new techniques (pottery making, stone polishing, weaving of textiles, etc.), population increased significantly, becoming more sedentary, while cultural diversification progressively increased. The contrast to all that had gone before in man's cultural evolution is so marked that from the beginning of prehistoric research it has seemed appropriate to designate the final millennia of the Stone Age by a separate term, Neolithic, in distinction to the hundreds of thousand years of the foregoing Palaeolithic and Mesolithic.

These profound changes, however, took effect only gradually.

At the end of the Atlantic period (4000-3200 BC) the new economies and technology affected only limited areas of France, and they arrived by different routes to reach two separate regions, the Mediterranean coastlands and the plains of northeastern and northern France. In these regions we find an Early Neolithic, but in the vast area in between the population either continued in their Mesolithic mode of life, or made very limited changes borrowed from Neolithic techniques.

In the course of the transition from the Atlantic to the sub-Boreal period (3200-2500 BC) the new modes of life spread throughout France. The more accessible areas of the Jura, Alps and Pyrenees, the plains of the southwest and central western regions, the Massif Central, the Atlantic and Channel coastlands were affected in their turn. Settlement was however discontinuous, and some types of land remained unoccupied. This is the period known as Middle Neolithic.

During the first half of the sub-Boreal (2500-1800 BC) population density increased, and distribution tended to approximate to that which prevailed until urban development took place. Regional diversification very noticeably increased. Predominantly agricultural societies coexisted alongside pastoral, while some groups practised a rudimentary metallurgy in copper, gold and silver, which others either resisted or lacked the means to adopt. This we shall term either Chalcolithic or Late Neolithic, as seems appropriate.

The Early Neolithic

MEDITERRANEAN EARLY NEOLITHIC

The author of the previous chapter has shown that, if C14 dates are to be accepted, then from the beginning of the sixth millennium cultural evolution in the Mediterranean regions of France took a completely new turn. The appearance at Châteauneuf-les-Martigues of domesticated sheep, followed shortly afterwards by pottery, in a context which in other respects is closely comparable with what went before, shows that the French Midi participated far earlier than was realised before C14 datings were available, in the economic and technological mutations which had been operative for some thousands of years in southwestern Asia and the eastern Mediterranean. These changes are often termed the 'Neolithic Revolution', though in the Near and Middle East they did not assume the abrupt and catastrophic character this name implies. On the contrary, they appear as a phenomenon that came to pass relatively slowly and gradually during the course of the ninth-sixth millennia, with the adoption of sedentary life, progressive substitution of an economy based on herding and agriculture for hunting and gathering, modification of stone tools to the needs of agriculture and carpentry, and finally, somewhat later, the beginnings of pottery-making. The evidence shows that this evolutionary process proceeded more or less synchronously over a fairly wide area, involving several different groupings of people, who exchanged what each had learned by experiment. However, this 'nuclear' zone, where the new modes of life termed Neolithic were worked out, remains essentially Asiatic, with only limited extensions into southeastern Europe. In western Europe the evolutionary process seems quite distinct. By the time the first indications of new techniques for food-winning become perceptible in present-day France they had already been current for three or four thousand years in western Asia. Furthermore, in France they do not appear to be the result of a long and slow indigenous

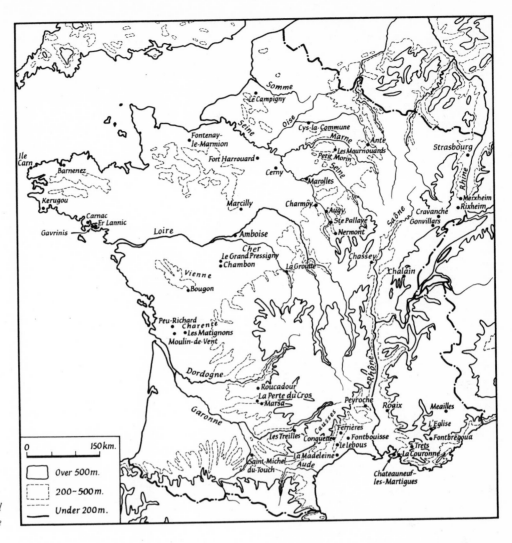

1 Map of principal Neolithic sites in France

evolution, running parallel with more or less related modifications in various other fields. They appear on the contrary rather abruptly and affect, selectively, only some of the cultural features incorporated in the Neolithic process in the Near East. Thus at Châteauneuf-les-Martigues (Bouches-du-Rhône) the transition from a food supply based essentially on the rabbit (hunted) to one based on the sheep (reared) was effected very rapidly, about 6000 BC, without any other perceptible modification. Shortly afterwards there appeared in turn a small breed of cattle, also apparently domesticated, and abundant pottery of excellent quality. From the start the pottery is fully developed, and it has not been possible to discover preliminary experimental phases, either at the site or elsewhere in the western Mediterranean. This Cardial pottery is so distinctive in its forms and decoration, which is often impressed with the edge of a *Cardium* shell, that it cannot be seen as the work of immigrants whose origin we are at a loss to find. None the less it is equally difficult to see the pottery as native invention, independent of external stimulus. It can hardly be simple convergence, when

c. 6000 BC we find pottery appearing all round the Mediterranean and Adriatic. We should rather suppose that from this time the first achievements of long-distance navigation brought about a rapid diffusion throughout the Mediterranean area of certain elements of the 'Neolithic Revolution', starting from the coasts of the Near East where they are longest attested. However rapid this diffusion – at least of the pottery – may have been, it does not present an assemblage of cultural traits grouped organically together to form a 'culture', and indicative of a particular people. On the contrary, domestication of certain animals, and subsequently pottery, appear in Provence in a cultural context where the majority of features – type of habitation, burial practice and stone industry – relate without perceptible break to native Mesolithic tradition. Though there are indications of outside contacts, nothing suggests immigration or any discontinuity of population. Caves and rock shelters are still the most frequent form of living site, and the few open-air sites known in the Var, Vaucluse and Gard are not numerous, nor do they appear to be earlier than Middle Cardial. The burials, which are flexed inhumations in caves or shelters, with few or no grave-goods, remain similar to those of preceding periods. The lithic industry associated with the Cardial Early Neolithic is a continuation of the Castelnovian which underlies it stratigraphically, differentiated only by the substitution of small trapezoidal arrowheads with transverse cutting-edge for asymmetric microliths, which disappear. It will be noticed that nothing, either in the type of site occupied or in the flint industry, supports the view that agriculture played a role of any importance. Positive indication that it did is at present confined to the evidence of Cardial sites in eastern Spain (charred grain from the Coveta de l'Or in the province of Valencia). Even the potentialities of stock-raising were not fully exploited, with the large preponderance of smaller livestock over cattle. Furthermore, the distribution age-wise and the high number of old animals in the flock is interpreted by P. Ducos (1957) as indicative of fairly rudimentary stock management, up to the end of the Cardial phase.

The precocious Neolithic established in the Mediterranean coastlands of France is thus an incomplete Neolithic, evidence of sea-borne contacts which were more sporadic than regular. These indeed enriched the cultural heritage of the native population, Mesolithic in origin, but not to the point of instilling any dynamic disequilibrium which would logically result in expansion. Density of population appears little greater than during the Mesolithic. If C14 dates are accepted, the Cardial phase will have lasted some three thousand years. This represents an exceptionally long span for a culture of Neolithic type, during which evolution seems to have affected only details of a secondary nature, such as pottery decoration (degeneration of impressed *Cardium* ornament and increasing preference for channelling) and the method of trimming flints (by a more invasive retouch). The fact that during this extensive period the Cardial, in so far as it constituted a culture, nowhere succeeded in spreading farther than 100 kilometres from the Mediterranean coast, but remained confined to the olive zone, points to a marked lack of dynamism indicative of a singularly well-adapted internal equilibrium. Its sources of subsistence were strongly diversified – hunting, fishing, collection of shell-fish, stock-raising and doubtless a little agriculture – a guarantee against temporary shortage in any one of these. Thus Cardial pottery folk had no need to hive off, even though their influence made itself felt peripherally, and to a limited extent, in parts of the southern half of France. Even within the territory occupied by the Cardial, the strong regional differentiation noticeable among Late Cardial or epi-Cardial groups at the end of the fourth millennium, which is reflected in the pottery, shows the groups were highly specific. For these reasons the Cardial is all the more likely to represent the end of an inward-looking world than the start of a new era.

EARLY NEOLITHIC
IN NORTHERN FRANCE (DANUBIAN)
It has been seen that the genesis of the Mediterranean

Early Neolithic in the sixth millennium did not involve any significant population movement, or the spread of a culture in all its elements, but solely diffusion of certain cultural traits of Neolithic type which were absorbed into a novel culture otherwise deriving from the native Mesolithic. It is easy to see that such diffusion can have been effected very quickly, thanks to the possibilities of sea travel. Quite different is the genesis of the Early Neolithic in the northern half of France, and this came about substantially later. Population movements were of far more significance here, being rather the result of gradual spreading from adjacent areas than of migration over great distances. It is to be expected that such a process required a longer time, on the other hand it allowed a far more complete transmission of the Neolithic cultural heritage. As the geographical area affected by the Neolithic spread increased, there must have been some mingling of cultural elements. Those from the native Mesolithic, however, were in this instance diluted and absorbed into the body of a Neolithic culture which was fully developed; and the diffusion of the latter can be traced from Anatolia and Greece in the sixth millennium to the Balkans and the Carpathian basin from the beginning, and to central Europe from the middle, of the fifth millennium. The role played by the Danube valley in this Neolithic expansion justifies the name 'Danubian' for the culture thus diffused. Even though in passing from the Balkans to central Europe it will have undergone marked cultural changes, genetic and no doubt ethnic ties between Anatolia, the Balkans and central Europe have to be allowed for. The history and internal evolution of the culture involved in the spread of the Neolithic into northern France are fairly well known, and in no event could it be thought to originate locally. The names *Bandkeramik*, or Linear, have been given to this culture, from the most prevalent ornament on its pottery, and it appears *c.* 4500 BC in the south of Czechoslovakia. The earliest phase, found both in Austria and Germany, does not however reach the Rhine. Colonisation of the Rhine valley, including Alsace, took place in the last centuries of the fifth millennium. After a halt imposed by the barriers of the Ardennes, Vosges and Jura the *Bandkeramik* complex appears in the north of France, in the Paris and Loire basins, in the first half of the fourth millennium, at a time when in central Europe it had reached the end of its evolution, if not been replaced by the stroke-ornamented (*Stichbandkeramik*) pottery. Typically the *Bandkeramik* complex shows a type of economy radically different not only from the Mesolithic which precedes it but equally from that of western Mediterranean Cardial. Hunting and fishing play an insignificant role. There was some stock-raising, and all the animals of the European Neolithic (dog, cattle, pig, goat and sheep) are represented. It was, however, quite subordinate to agriculture, which provided the bulk of the food supply, wheat and barley being predominant. The preponderance of agriculture is strikingly reflected in the culture's distribution, with selective occupation of light and fertile soils, in the main the loess plains, while vast regions in between remained empty. Agriculture however was relatively rudimentary, and without plough or manure it rapidly exhausted the soil and could not utilise the same fields continuously. Consequently, cultivated land and dwelling sites needed to be changed frequently, following a rotation cycle which left the soil to recover, and this involved frequent reoccupation of the same sites at regular intervals. The period of occupation was none the less sufficient to justify construction of substantial wooden buildings, some as houses and others for granaries or stabling, following a plan and construction techniques which were highly stereotyped. The large rectangular buildings were constructed on heavy posts, recognisable today only by their remaining post-holes. Six to eight metres wide and with a length which varied according to the number of families sheltered under one roof, these houses are surrounded by hollows dug primarily to obtain clay for plastering the walls, but with a secondary use as rubbish pits, which provide us with indispensable dating evidence. The buildings are grouped in small villages, with an estimated average population of 200, a figure which no Cardial site seems to have been able to attain. There are small cemeteries corresponding to the villages, with burials laid directly in the earth, without grave lining or superstructure. The positioning of the burials is somewhat haphazard. In the majority the corpse lies on its left side, flexed, with the legs bent and the hands drawn up to the face. Some burials have no grave-goods, but in others the body is accompanied by ornaments, a few stone tools and a pot. The lithic industry comprises two different elements: small flint tools and components and larger tools of hard stone. The flint industry was conditioned by the scarcity of material in the countries where it had developed. The flints are small and most frequently struck from a conical core. Blade fragments with little or no retouch were utilised as teeth in composite sickles, and could scarcely be identified as such were it not for signs of usage (silica sheen). Tools with secondary working comprise scrapers, on flakes or on short blades with steep, sub-rectangular working edge, awls, and, exceptionally, burins. Arrowheads, which are rare in central Europe, gain in importance in southern Germany, the Rhine and Meuse valleys and the Paris basin. These are small triangular flints, often asymmetrical, with little more than edge-trimming. Their affinities with the Tardenoisian are evident. The larger equipment, which is never made from flint, includes tools for agriculture (hoes), carpentry (adzes) and perforated 'maces', which could have served as tools or weapons. Querns are common, as are grooved polishing stones for finishing bone tools and beads. Pottery is always very abundant. Technically it is of high quality, though less well fired than Cardial ware. The forms are characteristically few and simple, with a predominance of rounded bases. Handles in threes or multiples of three are a feature, as is the rich decoration, which through the centuries shows a slow and continuous evolution. The basic motifs are spirals, meanders and chevrons,

2 : 1

2 : 3

2 : 8

2 : 4, 6

2, 5, 9-10

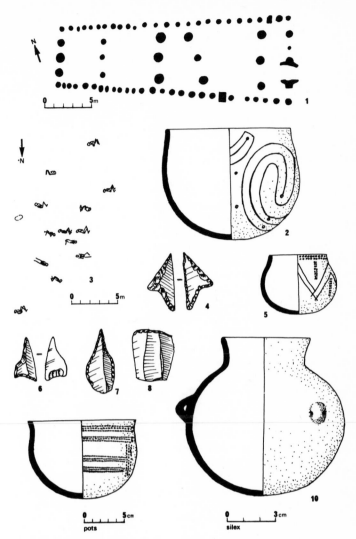

2 *Bandkeramik pottery culture: 1, house at Charmoy, Yonne; 2, early Alsatian Linear ware bowl from Schoenensteinbach, Haut-Rhin; 3, plan of the Hoenheim-Souffelweyersheim cemetery, Bas-Rhin; 4, flint arrowhead from Hoenheim-Souffelweyersheim; 5, Late Linear ware bowl from Merxheim-Zapfenloch, Haut-Rhin; 6-8, flints from the Late Bandkeramik culture: arrowhead, awl, scraper, from Armeau, Yonne; 9, Late Bandkeramik ware bowl from Hautes-Bruyères, Villejuif, Val-de-Marne; 10, flask from Menneville, Aisne (after Carré, Ruhlmann, Forrer, Sauer, Bonnet, Jehl, Bailloud)*

incised at first deeply, and later more lightly and with the patterns filled in with *pointillé*, strokes or hatching. Combed ornament marks the end of this evolution of Linear pottery in western areas. Large vessels often carry plastic decoration (finger impressions, rustication, knobs and cordons), which in early phases may cover the whole pot, as in Körös ware, but is later confined to the neck or runs in oblique bands connecting flanged handles, to stimulate suspension bindings. The ornaments initially included bracelets, beads and pendants made from *Spondylus* shell, deriving from the Mediterranean and the Aegean. The finds show that in the fourth and fifth millennia this shell was distributed fairly evenly from southeastern Europe to the Paris basin by way of the Danube lands.

The area of France reached by an Early Neolithic of *Bandkeramik* type falls into three zones of varying importance: the Rhine valley (Alsace), the Moselle valley (Lorraine), and the valleys of the Somme, Seine and middle Loire (the Paris basin). Of these Alsace, being the easternmost, was reached first, during the second Linear pottery phase (the first being unknown west of the Rhine). It would seem that, in the absence of any significant Mesolithic in Alsace, the substantial Linear occupation which appears abruptly in the course of the second half of the fifth millennium on the thick and fertile loess blanketing the Strasbourg region must represent colonisation from across the Rhine, or from areas farther downstream. A less dense scatter of sites also occurs in Haut-Rhin, lying north-south along the left bank of the Ill, where the soil is not always loess. Occupation sites and cemeteries are equally well represented in Alsace, and they conform entirely with the descriptions given above. Sites in the Strasbourg region, many of which were examined somewhat cursorily a long time ago, have produced little evidence of buildings. More recent excavations in the Haut-Rhin, at the Late Linear occupation site at Merxheim, have revealed rectangular buildings of modest size (12 m. × 6 m.), which are already closer to certain Middle Neolithic houses than to the classic Linear. A fine cemetery recently excavated at Rixheim, near Mulhouse, confirms that the Palaeolithic rite of ochre-covered inhumation was continued, with the bodies accompanied by a great quantity of *Spondylus* ornaments. The Linear lithic industry in Alsace shows a paucity of flint work, but has an abundance of larger tools in hard stone, imported from the Vosges. Successive phases can be distinguished in the pottery, and regional specialisation is more marked among the later than among the earlier phases. In Alsace comb-decorated ware, which plays an important role among other west European Late Linear groups, is absent. Funerary rites also show some evolution, and at a late stage extended inhumation appears, related to that associated with Middle Neolithic stabbed ware.

There is some slight indication that late Alsatian Linear, or influence from it, may have extended beyond the Belfort Gap towards northern Franche-Comté. By contrast, it does not seem that Late Linear sites recently found in Lorraine, on the alluvial plain of the Moselle, represent an extension of the Alsatian group beyond the Saverne corridor. The pottery shows connections, not with Alsace but with the later and final phases of the middle-Rhine Linear. Moreover, there is a scatter of sites linking the Rhine with Lorraine, right along the Moselle. Comb-decorated ware, absent in Alsace but well known on the middle Rhine, is fairly common in Lorraine.

Although the contrary has been argued, we find it more plausible to derive the substantial Paris basin *Bandkeramik* group from the Moselle rather than from the Maas group in the Dutch Limburg or Belgian Hesbaye. Despite its wide distribution, the Paris basin *Bandkeramik* culture is largely homogeneous and hardly allows of subdivision into distinct geographic groups. Finds are fairly dense in the east of the basin, though they become sparser in the western half and round the Loire. In these regions the Danubian colonists rarely found opportunity to exploit the preferred thick loess soils they had sought out in central Europe, and they are principally found along the main river valleys, on either alluvial plains or river terraces, with scarcely any trace of occupation on the plateaux. The economy of these colonies, which differs somewhat from that found in central Europe, was certainly in essence agricultural, as is shown by the number of sickle teeth; but stock-raising and no doubt also hunting must have played a more important role than was usual farther east. The presence of the large rectangular house, analogous to those of central Europe, has been demonstrated by recent finds in the Aisne (Cys-la-Commune) and Yonne (Char- 2 : 1 moy). Because it was easy to obtain flint and difficult to procure stone from the mountains, their proportions, compared with Alsace, are reversed to give an abundant flint industry and appreciably fewer large tools of polished stone. Even if certain flint forms do also occur in the local Tardenoisian, it does not necessarily mean that they were adopted locally, rather than in western Germany. At most, the microburin technique for dividing blades, which remains unknown on the right bank of the Rhine but occurs on a few French and Belgian sites, may indicate some local Tardenoisian influence. But in general the flint industry is so different from that of the Paris basin Mesolithic, that it would seem untenable to argue a derivation. In France, as in Belgium and round Cologne, there is some evidence of contact with the makers of macrolithic flint industries of Montmorency or pre-Campignian type. The evidence for this comes from rare finds of *tranchets* or trimmers (and not from the '*quartiers d'orange*' found in the Omalian group). The pottery gives every sign of being marginal to its main distribution, with marked impoverishment of forms and loss of much of the original decorative repertory (spirals and meanders). The predominant technique is a very fine comb ornament, whose origin can be sought in France itself, borrowed from Cardial techniques. Fine incision was also widely used. The chief motifs are chevrons, horizontal and vertical ribbons, triangles and semicircles. Form, technique and motifs in combination relate to the final phases of the Rhenish Linear group. There are better parallels for the ornament among central European stroke-ornamented pottery than among Linear ware, but the forms are exclusively Linear, and it is wiser to avoid these terms in classifying the *Bandkeramik* ware from the Paris basin. Carbon 14 datings are only too rare, and come from very late sites. They give dates in the middle of the fourth millennium, far later than those associated with early Linear and stroke-ornamented pottery in central Europe. The burials are inhumations, and the majority are flexed; use of red ochre is fairly common. Women's graves with very rich offerings of ornaments (stone bracelets, and a variety of forms in *Spondylus* shell) have been found at various sites in the eastern part of the Paris basin (Cys-la-Commune, Aisne; Frignicourt and Vert-La-Gravelle, Marne).

All the groups with *Bandkeramik* pottery in northern France relate back in the general ensemble of their cultural traits to the *Bandkeramik* cultures of central Europe. Admittedly they are marginal, impoverished, and late; but there is no geographical or chronological break in the series. It would seem that, unlike the Cardial, there can be no question here of a selective acquisition of certain Neolithic features by a native Mesolithic population. On the contrary the evidence shows abrupt and complete discontinuity, with a fully developed Neolithic culture succeeding to – or at most juxtaposed alongside – a Mesolithic, with only a few flint types in common. This must be interpreted as immigration, rather than native evolution or acculturation. These events occurred far later than the start of the Mediterranean Neolithic – at the end of the fifth millennium in Alsace and the beginning of the fourth in the Paris basin. However, the Early Danubian spread far more rapidly than the Mediterranean Neolithic. This expansion should doubtless be ascribed to internal tendencies within Early Danubian Neolithic economies, which were less balanced than the Cardial, rather than to absence of external constraints. The predominance of an agriculture based on rudimentary techniques necessitated continual exploitation of fresh lands. Population density also, though this is less significant, was no doubt higher than among the Cardial, and thus a factor of more importance.

Marginal *Bandkeramik* ware groups lasted a long time in and around the Paris basin, while in the Rhineland significant cultural changes were beginning in the first centuries of the fourth millennium, with the replacement of Linear by the Rössen culture. This brought changes among various geographically and chronologically determined groups, whose interconnections, in the absence of stratigraphical data, remain largely conjectural. There are indications that the group with stab-decorated pottery, found thickly distributed in sites and cemeteries in the Strasbourg area, may well belong to an early phase of Rössen, although for the last thirty years it has been called Late Rössen in the literature. There are no C14 dates at present, but affinities of the pottery suggest a probable date in the first half of the fourth millennium. This group is distinct from the Linear complex in both its pottery and its burial rites. There is great variety in pottery forms, which include 3:2-3 novel types such as hollow-footed vases and quadri-lobate bowls. The decoration is exuberant, consisting 3:1, 5-6, of heavy stab marks and wide incisions, enhanced with 8-9 coloured inlay. The stabbed ware could have evolved in southwestern Germany from the impact of stroke-ornamented influences on local epi-*Linearbandkeramik* groups (Hinkelstein). The role played by local Mesolithic influences in this development, which is sometimes

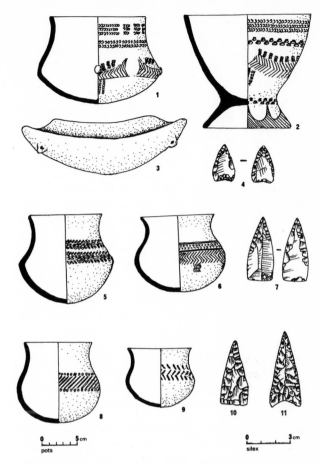

3 *Rössen culture: 1-4, pottery and arrowhead from the Lingolsheim cemetery, Bas-Rhin; 5-7, pottery and arrowhead from the Cravanche burial cave, Belfort; 8, bowl from the Roche-Chèvre cave, Barbirey-sur-Ouche, Côte-d'Or; 9-11, bowl and arrowhead from the Gonvillars cave, Haute-Saône (after Schaeffer, Vernet, Petrequin)*

stressed, does not appear significant if one takes account of the lithic industry, house types, and settlement 3:4, 7, patterns or economy, all of which are rooted in Linear 10-11 ware tradition. Only the cemeteries, with their tightly-packed groups of extended burials, all strictly oriented in the same direction (NW-SE), betray a social organisation which is more rigid, and an undoubtedly higher density of population.

In Alsace, and probably at a later date, a Rössen which is termed 'early' occurs far more sporadically. It did however infiltrate through the Belfort Gap (Cra- 3:5-7 vanche) into the north of Franche-Comté (Gonvillars), 3:9-11 if not into Burgundy. Carbon 14, alike at Gonvillars and elsewhere, indicates a date around 3400 BC. From this time marked changes begin in house types, burial rite, settlement patterns, economy and equipment, as becomes evident in a series of fairly distinctive regional groups which are a feature of the final Rössen phase, and which are described below.

Between and to the west of the zones occupied by Cardial and *Bandkeramik* groups a large area of France remained unaffected by the Early Neolithic. It is certain that in the fourth millennium these regions were not unpopulated; but they were occupied by peoples who continued in a way of life handed down from the Palaeolithic, based essentially on hunting and fishing. These groups are generally termed Tardenoisian, though the unity of such a culture is becoming increasingly open to doubt. We may need to take account of other groups in northern France, such as the Montmorency-Campignian, though its relative and absolute chronology alike are far from clear. It can also be shown that there were similar survivals even amid the Neolithic areas. Pollen analysis recently undertaken for several Tardenoisian sites, which lie on sandy soil in the Paris basin unsuited to cultivation, in fact shows that they all date to the end of the Atlantic period, which is when the valleys were being colonised by Danubian folk. Typological analysis of stone industries in turn indicates that various final Tardenoisian and Early Neolithic groups made common use of certain types of flint arrowhead: small transverse ones, with invasive trimming in southern France, and pointed, often asymmetric examples, in the north. While it is difficult to determine in which direction an exchange could have operated, it is at least evident that there were contacts. In numerous instances, these appear to have gone much further than a simple exchange of flint types, suggesting that the Tardenoisian received rather than gave. There are indications that certain Tardenoisian groups in southwestern and western France possessed some domestic animals, principally sheep or goats. It therefore seems probable that, in imitation of the Cardial, they began on a more modest scale to keep stock, though without changing their essential dependence on hunting and fishing. The practice does however appear to have been sufficiently widespread to warrant a beginning to the destruction (no doubt by fire) of the forests which covered a large area of France during the Atlantic period, in order to encourage the substitution of vegetation more suitable for pasture. Pollen analysis suggests that such practices had become an important factor in western France in the fourth millennium, long before any indication of agriculture is evident in these regions. The developed Tardenoisians who already possessed small flocks may be called proto-Neolithic. Certain groups took the evolution still further, a typical, although up till now fairly rare, instance being that of layer C at Roucadour in the Lot, carbon-dated to the beginning of the fourth millennium. Though the site remains Mesolithic in type, with only slight evidence of stockkeeping (which was at all events insignificant compared with hunting), cereals were not unknown and potterymaking, novel in technique, shapes and ornament is attested. Technique had been very incompletely mastered and the forms (large jars with a conical base) must partly derive from basketry. The decoration could be a clumsy imitation of the final Cardial in the Aude. Rou-

cadour C seems to represent a renewal of the cultural process seen two thousand years earlier on the French Mediterranean coasts: incomplete adoption of Neolithic ways by a native Mesolithic group under outside stimulus (here Cardial in origin), with no population movements involved.

ORIGINS OF THE ATLANTIC NEOLITHIC

The cultural position along the French Atlantic coast, and part of the Channel coasts, during the fourth millennium presents a problem which is still being worked out. On the Atlantic side between Médoc and Finistère a distinctive Mesolithic group is known, which would not be especially remarkable apart from discoveries in the Téviec and Hoëdic cemeteries in Morbihan. These cemeteries, probably fifth millennium in date, include some fairly elaborate burial structures, which in some instances have been used for several successive burials. Now it is precisely in the spectacular development of funerary monuments, usually designed to house collective burials, that the Atlantic Neolithic from the start shows its essential originality. The lithic industries of the earliest groups are by no means typical, though it can well be argued that arrowheads with transverse cutting edge originated in the local Mesolithic. The pottery is so characterless in form and poor in decoration that its origin must remain largely conjectural. What now tends to be distinguished by the name Carn pottery, like that at Roucadour C, may well represent a local ware set in train by external stimulus, either from Paris basin Danubian ware or from maritime contacts. It would be difficult on the other hand to represent the tomb types as a local development. Two basic types can be distinguished: circular chambers built of drystone walling or slabs, with an access corridor (*dolmens à couloir*, or passage graves) and covered by a circular rubble cairn; and fairly low, rectangular mounds containing cists and hearths ringed with stones. Both types are represented in a pure form on the south coast of Brittany, and a few rectangular mounds at least in Morbihan have produced pottery with Danubian affinities. On the north Breton coast as far as Calvados one finds close fusion between the two traditions, producing large quadrangular cairns of rubble which contain several passage graves. These tombs have minimal, or indeed non-existent, deposits, as for example in the primary cairn at Barnenez (Finistère). In Calvados the Hoguette tumulus at Fontenay-le-Marmion did however produce decorated ware of Danubian type. Sparse as they are, the oldest of these funerary deposits are not inconsistent with the C14 dates of about 3800–3600 BC lately obtained from both Finistère (Barnenez, Ile Gaignog III) and Calvados (La Hoguette). It should however be stressed that no comparably early date has yet been obtained either for the most likely forerunners of the rectangular mounds, which are very numerous in the north of Poland and Germany, or for the passage graves, which proliferate in the Iberian peninsula. Whatever the dating problems, the appearance of tomb forms identical with those of far-off lands in northern

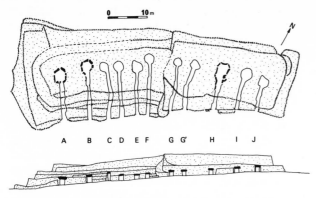

4 *Barnenez cairn, Plouezoc'h, Finistère (after Giot)*

and western Europe bears witness to a first systematic development of coastal navigation in the North Sea, the Channel and the Atlantic during the fourth millennium. From its central position, Brittany was particularly well placed to effect new syntheses between very different ideas.

The Middle Neolithic

The cultural pattern during the Middle Neolithic in France is noticeably more complex than during the Early Neolithic. Thus in order to present a clear picture it will be necessary to clarify the main outlines, rather than give all the details. In the north of France, late Danubian groups moved progressively farther from the cultural model represented by the Linear *Bandkeramik* culture. In the south the brilliant and dynamic Chassean culture cut across the Cardial, and its influence made itself felt throughout almost all the country. In the west a vigorous and novel Neolithic developed, either megalithic in aspect – and this was especially brilliant in Brittany – or in an entirely different form, such as occurs in the Charente basin in the cultures of Les Matignons and Peu-Richard.

LATE DANUBIAN GROUPS

The close of the Atlantic period and the coming of the sub-Boreal saw internal dislocation in the Danubian Neolithic of the form known in the Linear pottery group, or with stab-decorated pottery in southwestern Germany and Alsace. Groups still related to Danubian in part at least of their equipment can yet be identified throughout northern France; but the type of their economies and houses, their adjustment to environment, their stone and bone industries, and probably also their ethnic composition, are very markedly different from those of the preceding phase. It is possible that climatic modification, associated with the advent of the sub-Boreal, played a part in these changes. Doubtless, too, they reflect absorption and acculturation of native population, or indeed fusion with it. Concurrently, regional differentiation becomes much stronger than during the Early Neolithic. The immigration phase had come to an end, and each local group continued for several centuries to evolve, if not quite in isolation,

then at least along its own original lines. In the Rhineland and on the Saône local groups of Rössen origin grew progressively more individualistic. Round the Seine and the Loire, and as far as the Armorican massif, faint Rössen influence affected groups which appear to result from a mixture, in varying proportions, of descendants of the *Bandkeramik* colonists and the native populations they encountered. We shall give a brief account of the principal groups which have been identified during the last fifteen years.

In the Rhineland, the end of the Rössen culture was marked by the formation of regional groups, such as the Bischheim on the Middle Rhine, the Schwieberdingen in the Neckar valley, Bischoffingen in Baden and northern Alsace, and the Wauwil on the upper Rhine, in northern Switzerland and in Franche-Comté. The two first, not being represented in France, will not detain us. The Bischoffingen group is in fact known only from a few isolated finds, and cannot pretend to any great duration or significance. It is really only its pottery which can be recognised, represented by globular pots with clearly offset neck, generally carrying a ring of applied dots at the base. The belly may be decorated with stabbed or incised motifs derived from the Rössen repertory. From the Strasbourg region, this pottery appears to have spread west of the Saverne corridor as far as the valley of the Aisne, where a related collection has been found at Menneville. The Wauwil group is represented by more numerous and substantial assemblages, and seems to have lasted longer than other epi-Rössen groups, which gave way more or less quickly to the Michelsberg and Schussenried cultures. Recent excavation of the Gonvillars cave (Haute-Saône) has produced an excellent example of Wauwil, stratified above an older Rössen layer. It has also provided a C14 date of 3050 BC, and this crosschecks with what could be inferred from pottery imported from various Swiss lakeside sites, which probably lasted at least until about 2800. The Wauwil group is clearly distinguished from classical Rössen in various ways: by its occupation of limestone plateaux and mountainous country more suited to stock-raising than to agriculture, by occupation of caves at high altitudes, cave burial, a strongly developed antler industry with novel types (curved objects, picks, sleeve hafts) and novel ornaments, such as irregular disc-rings made from the fine stone available in Alsace and Franche-Comté. The flint industry is predominantly Rössen (pointed, triangular arrowheads and numerous knives) as is the pottery, with a fairly restrained stabbed ornament. By contrast the larger stone tools, basically aphanite axes of square section from the Vosges, are a novelty. The Wauwil group is fairly well represented in northern Franche-Comté and seems to have extended its influence as far as Burgundy (Côte-d'Or and Yonne).

Equally prevalent in Burgundy and the Yonne is another late Danubian group, whose origin cannot be sought in Rössen contexts. This is the Augy-Sainte-Pallaye group, which probably derives by local evolution from the *Bandkeramik* groups which were thickly settled in the Yonne. The only sites so far examined carefully – notably the village of Sainte-Pallaye – lie in the Yonne, but fairly typical finds and assemblages occur equally in the Saône-et-Loire, Côte-d'Or and Aube. Sainte-Pallaye, a village deep in a valley, has furnished a trapezoidal house plan with post-holes, unmatched in the Middle Neolithic of central Europe. There was also a good series of hearths. Little is known of the stone industry, in which a transverse arrowhead replaces the pointed flints of the Early Danubian complex. Best known is the pottery. The forms seem to show the same lack of variety as among Linear ware. Plastic ornament predominates, with small, pushed-up knobs, applied large knobs and cordons, and bosses on the pot rims. The Nermont cave in southern Yonne produced early Chassean, late Rössen sherds and Augy-Sainte-Pallaye pottery in conjunction.

The Cerny group is far more widely distributed, covering the *Bandkeramik* ware area of the Paris basin and also reaching farther into northern France and on to part of the Armorican massif (Morbihan, Jersey). Most known sites are settlements and their distribution is far more varied than among Early Danubian sites. There are still settlements deep in the valleys, but others in country not suitable for Neolithic agriculture on the edge of plateaux or on spurs, which may be fortified, grow more numerous and come to predominate. The one site to furnish house plans is Gours-aux-Lions (Seine-et-Marne), where a rectangular building 30 m. long, containing five rows of posts, has been completely uncovered. This is analogous to finds in *Bandkeramik* contexts. The same site contained a series of graves, all single inhumations (except for one double), in which neither the orientation nor the position of the bodies was constant. Grave-goods, where present, were sparse. The Linear element is preponderant in the pottery, evident alike in the small variety of forms and in the decoration. The two techniques most utilised are comb-impression and heavy stabs, similar to those on Rössen ware. Pushed-up knobs likewise occur, as well as incised 'sun rays' round a boss. By contrast, the stone industry differs radically from the *Bandkeramik* industry. Tools made on flakes practically exclude the blade type, and include flint axes, heavy scrapers, planes and side-scrapers, numerous tranchets and chisels, small picks or trimmers, and small polyhedric objects which may be throwing-stones. All the arrowheads have a transverse cutting edge, and sickle teeth have completely disappeared. Thus, overall, the lithic industry resembles what is termed Campignian, and in this region it lasts until the Bronze Age. This transformation of the stone artifacts alongside unquestionable continuity in pottery development, based on local *Bandkeramik* ware can be variously interpreted. The origin of the Cerny group could as reasonably be read as an acculturation of the descendants of the Montmorencian or pre-Campignian population, through their borrowing of Early Danubian Neolithic techniques, as an adaptation of equipment to new needs by descendants of the first Danubian colonists, faced with clearing the thickly wooded plateaux. Both processes may have gone on together. Whatever its origin, the Cerny economy is very different from that of the Linear pottery folk. Agriculture is far less prevalent (cf. the disappearance of sickle flints), and at the one site where fauna has been analysed there is a slight preponderance of hunted over domestic animals. Chronologically Cerny should straddle the turn of the fourth and third millennia (Videlles: *c.* 2800 BC).

In the Loire basin the Middle Neolithic is known only from a restricted number of excavations, too few for us to say that we are yet familiar with all its cultural aspects. Various recent discoveries lead us to suppose there are several groups in the area, generally or partially related to the Danubian. In the Loir-et-Cher some unexcavated sites, the most important at Les Marais, Marcilly, have produced interesting lithic and pottery assemblages which could represent an independent late Danubian, tending in the main to relate to the Augy-Sainte-Pallaye group. South of the Loire, two largely unpublished recent excavations, in the south of Indre-et-Loire (Chambon) and the north of Vienne (St-Martin-La Rivière), have revealed a highly novel Neolithic, which can be seen as a final echo of the Danubian, doubtless mixed with other elements.

Before turning to developments in the south and in the Atlantic zone, we should revert to the Rhineland to mention a culture which must fall within the chronological limits of this section – the end of the fourth and beginning of the third millennium. This is the Michelsberg culture which, since it was first recognised, has been subject to a variety of interpretations, being related by different writers either to the west European Neolithic (especially to Chassean), to the central European, or to the north and east European Neolithic. Most recent work inclines to see it as an autochthonous evolution deriving from the late Rössen Bischheim group, with a gradual extension throughout the Rhine basin concurrent with evolution of regional variations in southwestern Germany (Münsingen) and round Lake Constance. The culture is abundantly represented in Alsace, notably in the Strasbourg region. Although no homogeneous assemblages characteristic of Michelsberg have yet been found west of the Vosges, it is most probable that some degree of influence from the culture was felt in Lorraine, Franche-Comté, Burgundy, and as far as the southeast of the Paris basin. The variety in sites chosen (on the plain, as in Alsace, or upland sites, which are often fortified) and in burial practice, where there is little standardisation, reveals a society in process of rapid evolution. In the economy, cattle seem to play an important role alongside agriculture. Although the lithic industry is hardly abundant or typical, pointed triangular arrowheads preserve the Rössen tradition. Belgian mines seem to have contributed largely to the flint supply. Pottery is characterised by a multiplicity of forms, and by the virtual disappearance of ornament. Many of the shapes are entirely new in western Europe: flat- or conical-based jars, tulip-shaped beakers, amphorae, bowls and flat-based carinated dishes, ladles and discs of baked clay. Evolution in forms supports a division into chronological phases, almost all of which are represented in the Strasbourg region.

CHASSEAN

The term Chassean is traditionally applied to various Middle Neolithic groups which cover almost all of France, as well as part of Italy (where recent work has emphasized how misleading is the frequent use of the term 'Lagozza' to describe them). A basic unity of pottery types tells us that these various groups are related, although the lithic industries show strong variation, determined at least in part by their ecological contexts. In the south of France a highly homogeneous group, with a flint industry of small blades and using axes of green stone, occupied the Mediterranean Midi, some areas of the Alps and Pyrenees, the south of the Massif Central and a part at least of the Garonne lands. This is the southern version of Chassean. In Burgundy, Franche-Comté, the north of the Massif Central and the Loire country the Chassean spread, with progressive modifications resulting either from adaptation to different circumstances or from contact with different earlier inhabitants (final Tardenoisian, Rössen, and then Michelsberg). In the Paris basin and the north of France heavy stone tools in Campignian style and flint axes consistently replaced the lighter equipment and green stone axes of the Midi, to form the Chassean of the north. The west of France (Charente, Poitou, Brittany) in its turn experienced a Chassean, which intruded into the megalithic context absent in other areas. However differentiated these groups become, there are no distinct divisions between them, but rather gradual modification as one moves from the south towards the north or west. Traditionally, the southern group has been regarded as the earliest and the progenitor of the others; but the firm evidence of C14 gives very comparable dates for all the facies, ranging from 3200 for the earliest to 2500-2400 BC for the latest.

Southern Chassean is known from a group of densely distributed finds, the number of sites being far higher than among the Cardial. Allowing for the far shorter duration of Chassean, this is evidence of a marked and rapid increase in population in the French Midi during the Middle Neolithic. Occupation is divided between caves and open-air sites, with strong regional differences attributable to local geography. Thus the Causses plateaux contain almost exclusively cave sites, while from their nature the Garonne plains are given up to open-air sites. There were considerable settlements in these regions, spectacularly illustrated by the excavation in progress at Saint-Michel-du-Touch near Toulouse. The site here is a spur defended by two palisades of timber set two metres into the ground. The houses covered some twenty hectares, and more than two hundred of them have already been explored. The buildings take two forms, circular and rectangular; the former are about 1.80 m. in diameter, the latter – in all probability the actual dwellings – are up to 12 m. in length. Enclosures for stock are also known. The ground beneath the buildings was scrupulously prepared; a clay foundation was baked (leaving a layer of charcoal) and finally paved with pebbles. The walls were certainly of wood, but far lighter and less robust than in the timber houses of the Danubians. Other settlements of this type are known in the region of Toulouse and Montauban. The open-air village sites which have been excavated in the Mediterranean regions of Languedoc (Montbeyre in the Hérault, for example) also suggest rectangular houses in perishable materials, and the dry-stone building usual in the following period is unknown in the Chassean culture. The search for fertile land seems far more evident among the Chassey than among the Cardial folk. On the Causses and among the *garrigue* healths the population pushed up the valleys and hardly left their vicinity. Even in what seem most unpropitious circumstances (the gorges of the Verdon and Gardon) sickle blades and carbonised grain show that cultivation was practised, and that agriculture was everywhere predominant in the economy. It was associated with well advanced animal husbandry, which was more specialised than in the Cardial, with cattle equalling or surpassing the number of sheep and goats. Hunting on the other hand played an insignificant role, except in the Lot, where it provided half the meat consumed. The lithic industry is very different from the Cardial, and has, curiously, a more Epipalaeolithic aspect. It is based on bladelets (*lamelles*) or small blades, often used without secondary trimming as knives or sickles. Flints with retouch include terminal scrapers, numerous awls and 5:14-15 burins, and there are occasional microliths. The arrowheads are of two types: triangular with transverse cut-5:11-13 ting edge, covered with retouch, which can be related to those of the final Cardial, and pointed leaf- or lozenge-5:16-17 shaped, not without analogues in Italy. The first alone are found in the southwest, the second predominate in eastern Provence, while elsewhere the types are mixed. Axes were fashioned from river stones. Pottery, too, is totally different from the Cardial. As in the corresponding period in the Rhineland, we find pronounced differentiation of forms coupled with remarkably little decoration. The technique is excellent, and demonstrates the strong homogeneity of the Chassean. Forms include large jars, conical-necked flasks, cooking pots and bowls with the neck separated from the body by a ridge, numerous carinated bowls, globular bowls, plates, ladles 5:1-2, 4, 7 and spoons, beakers and stoppers for small vases. There is great variety in the devices for handling, including types hitherto unknown in the French Neolithic: cordons and lugs with multiple perforations, single or 5:5-6, 10 adjacent tubular handles, terminating in the '*flûte de Pan*' type. The rare ornament was finely incised before or after firing, with a limited repertory of simple geometric motifs. There can be no doubt that it originated in Italy, where it is more richly represented in several different cultures. Throughout much of France this decoration is especially associated with one novel form, the *vase-support*, which is probably a ritual object. Al-5:18; 6 though not absent, it is rare in the Midi. Evidence of burial practices, which seem fairly diverse, is somewhat

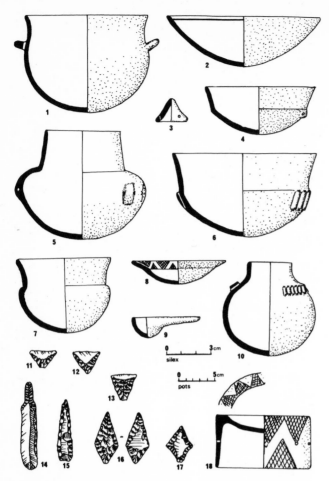

5 *Southern Chassean: 1-17, pottery, awls and arrowheads from the cave and occupation site of La Madeleine, Villeneuve-les-Maguelonne, Hérault; 18, 'vase-support' from the Camp de Chassey, Saône-et-Loire (after Arnal, Boudon, Vidal, Roudil, Thévenot)*

scanty. They include flexed inhumations, with or without a cist, cave burial, and inhumation, at times partial and secondary, in pit graves. Grave offerings are generally modest (pottery, arrowheads, callaïs beads). Saint-Michel-du-Touch produced a pit measuring 8 m. × 4 m. which contained two incomplete, secondary burials, with rich grave offerings, and was filled in with 25 cubic metres of pebbles. Any attribution of the earliest megalithic tombs to the Chassean rests so far on evidence too indecisive for definite acceptance.

The southern Chassean cannot be interpreted as simply a local evolution based on the Cardial, with which it contrasts in all its aspects. Neither can it represent total substitution of one population by another, since in some degree it possesses local roots, either in the final Tardenoisian or in the Cardial. These are most evident in the flint work (transverse arrowheads, microliths, etc.). But the complete transformation of this native element, economically and technologically, would seem to indicate a contribution from outside, which is un-

likely to have been brought in without some incursion of people. Pointed arrowheads, the presence at numerous sites of tiny obsidian blades obtained from the Lipari islands, and forms and decorative techniques among the pottery, all relate specifically to Italy. Purely Chassean sites there, however, have not yet provided dates as early as those from France, and it is probable that the culture did not arrive from Italy completely developed. We would rather suggest that it evolved locally in the French Midi, and reflects reaction of the local population to small groups of immigrants arriving from widely diverse regions of Italy, and doubtless also from other regions of the Mediterranean. The Aegean in fact provides better prototypes for the tubular and *flûte de Pan* handles than does Italy. Whatever its origin, from its first appearance the Chassean shows very strongly expansive tendencies, which must have had both economic and demographic grounds. In the French Midi there is one rather distinctive group, standing somewhat apart, and this is the Trets (or Lagozza) type in Provence. Its pottery is indistinguishable from the Chassean, the only slight difference being in the stone industry, which indicates either an unusual Mesolithic substratum or adaptation to a special biotope (in this instance, swamp). The most interesting feature of this cultural facies lies in its small, anthropomorphic stelae with highly schematised ornament. These are apparently associated with cremation graves, the oldest of a series which developed in the following phase.

Starting from the Midi the Chassean went on to spread towards the centre and north of France, apparently very quickly but not without subjection to a variety of influences *en route*. The Rhône-Saône corridor seems to have been used by a quite considerable group of migrants, who established in Burgundy, around the famous and badly excavated site of Chassey itself, a Chassean which is very close to that in the Midi, though far richer in *vases-supports*. In the north of Burgundy 5:18; 6 and in Franche-Comté there are numerous sites with a pottery which, basically, certainly belongs with Chassean, though *vases-supports* and decorated ware are either rare or absent, and some forms have been lost. Very many elements here relate to other cultural currents. The flint industry, a blade industry but without the smaller *lamelles*, characterised by its robust knives with convex cutting edge and pointed triangular arrowheads, is reminiscent rather of the Wauwil group than of the Chassean of the Midi. The same may be said of the frequent choice of upland sites, fortified by a dry-stone wall, and the growth of antler work. A little later, influence from the Michelsberg culture can be seen in the appearance of flat-based vases, tulip-shaped beakers and discs of baked clay. In this area it is not yet possible to distinguish cultural groups precisely, and the facies of the Salins region of Piroutet only serves to conceal the rarity of utilisable excavations. The well known Cortaillod group farther to the southeast, centred on the Swiss plateau but well represented in France in the southern Jura, we should interpret as a close fusion of Rhenish and Mediterranean cultural elements, rather

27 The giant tumulus of Saint-Michel, Carnac, Morbihan.

28 Middle Neolithic of the Paris basin, Cerny culture: decorated sherds from layer E of the Les Roches occupation site, Videlles, Essonne.

29 Tombs of the Atlantic Middle Neolithic: one of the passage graves in the La Hogue tumulus, with circular chamber in drystone walling, Fontenay-le-Marmion, Calvados.

121

30 Megalithic art in the Atlantic Middle Neolithic: Tossen-Keler tumulus, Penvenan, Côtes-du-Nord.

31 Megalithic art: Gavrinis passage grave, Morbihan.

32

33

32 Middle Neolithic of west-central France, Peu-Richard culture: decorated sherd from Chaillot de La Jard, Charente-Maritime.

33 Head of a statuette in baked clay from Roanne, Villegouge, Gironde.

34 Neolithic dwellings: Middle Neolithic house (Cerny culture) at Les Gours-aux-Lions, Marolles-sur-Seine, Seine-et-Marne.

35 Stumps of house posts from the Neolithic at Chalain, Jura.

36 Late Neolithic of the Paris basin, Seine-Oise-Marne
culture: gallery grave of Blanc-Val, Presles, Val-d'Oise.

37 Sculptured slab from the vestibule of the Damp-mesnil gallery grave, Eure.

38 *Statue-menhir* at Puech-Réal, Saint-Salvi-de-Carcaves, Tarn.

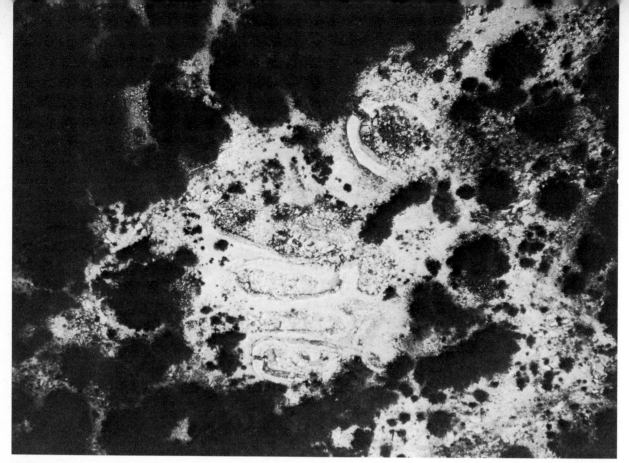

39 Village of Conquette, Saint-Martin-de-Londres, Hérault.

40 Chalcolithic of Langudeoc, Fontbouïsse culture: fortified enclosure at Lébous, Saint-Martin-de-Tréviers, Hérault.

than a late descendant of the Mediterranean Neolithic alone. The inventiveness and originality of the group, on the other hand, should not be undererestimated.

In the Massif Central and the Loire lands Chassean spread continuously, alongside, it would seem, assimilation or acculturation of the Tardenoisian groups who previously had occupied most of the region. Two different movements appear to cross, the first bringing a southern Chassean northwards and the second, which was possibly a little later and from east to west, bringing a version mixed with Rhenish and Jurassic elements from east-central France. Excavated sites are only too rare but, for example at La Groutte (Cher) or Amboise (Indre-et-Loire), they illustrate a rich profusion of *vases-supports*. At the first site the classic incised decoration is replaced on half the examples by geometric patterns against a *pointillé* background, a style which becomes preponderant in the west of France and which is known as the Bougon or Luxé style. It always occurs in a Chassey context. This Chassean in the west of France is *8:3-7* known almost exclusively from funerary deposits, for the most part from megalithic monuments. We shall return to the subject in the next section.

The heavy flint equipment known as Campignian rapidly increases in importance among the Chassean of central France. There is a modest amount at La Groutte, a better representation at Amboise in the Loire valley, while its prevalence in the Paris basin and the north of France is a characteristic of the Chassean of those regions. This northern Chassean occurs parallel with, or superimposed on, final Danubian of Cerny type, with which it has numerous traits in common. Their settlement patterns are very similar, though there was more extensive Chassey occupation on the heavy soils of the plateaus, which the heavy Campignian flint industry was doubtless designed to claim for cultivation, by clearing the forest. To obtain the flint it required, an increasing number of extraction shafts were dug to uncover deposits yielding large nodules. These were certainly the work of specialists, the first to appear in France. The flint industry is difficult to distinguish from the Cerny, except in the increased number of backed knives and the occurrence, in company with transverse arrowheads, of triangular or almond-shaped forms, spreading from east-central France (these show a proportional decrease between the southeast and northeast of the country). Only part of the Chassean range of forms is preserved among the pottery, and *vases-supports* are practically the sole decorated type. However, the abundance of baked clay discs, like the pointed arrowheads and rare antler objects, are evidence of influence from east-central France. The continuity, especially in flint work, between Cerny and the northern Chassean disproves any total replacement of one population by another. Rather the cultural changes perceptible at the start of the third millennium may be taken to indicate immigration by small groups originating in central and east-central France, which could easily be absorbed in a region still largely underdeveloped. This would have led to fusion, and the emergence in each area of the

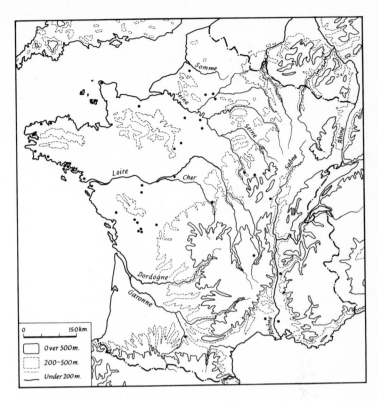

6 *Distribution of Chassean 'vases-supports'*

more progressive or better-adapted elements – the heavy Cerny flint equipment on the one hand, the more varied Chassean weapons and pottery on the other.

ATLANTIC MIDDLE NEOLITHIC

We have already noticed that the origins of the Atlantic Neolithic appear to date from the end of the Atlantic period, and have outlined its possible initial components. Over most of its area it is characterised by an exuberant development of funerary and cult monu- III ments, of architecturally complex and often grandiose form. Very different, but no less novel, aspects are also found in west-central France, seen here more in occupation sites than in tombs.

As mentioned earlier, at the start of the Atlantic Neolithic two types of tomb were prevalent, contrasting both in type and in their geographical connections. The low, rectangular mounds over cists and hearths, with analogues in northern Europe, may date back to fairly early times, to judge from pottery with Danubian affinities from certain tombs in the Carnac region (Morbihan). In the same region other mounds of the same type, though sometimes larger in size (35 m. long at Le Manio, 100 m. at Kerlescan) and marked by menhirs, *7:1* could be a little later, on the evidence of the typical Chassey ware found at Le Manio. Survival of this tomb type into the Late Neolithic, on the evidence of a single C14 date from a mound at St-Just (Ille-et-Vilaine), does not seem convincing. Certain gigantic tumuli, which 27 are unparalleled outside France, may be related in origin

121

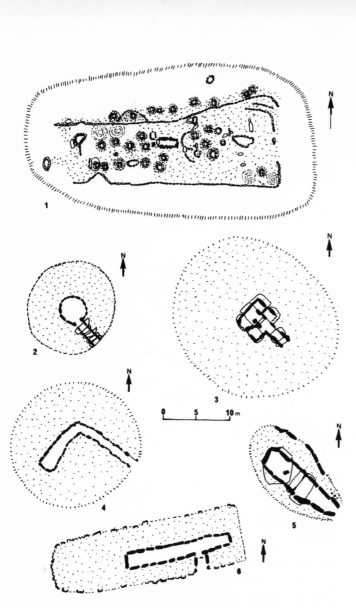

7 *Various tomb types in the Atlantic Neolithic: 1, the Le Manio quadrangular mound, Carnac, Morbihan; 2, passage grave of Kermaric, Languidic, Morbihan; 3, the Mané-Bras passage grave with subdivided chamber, Erdeven, Morbihan; 4, 'angled' dolmen of Le Rocher, Le Bono, Plougoumelen; 5, V-shaped grave of Ty-ar-Boudiquet, Brennilis, Finistère; 6, Crec'h-Quillé grave with lateral entrance, St-Quay-Perros, Côtes-du-Nord (after Le Rouzic, Martin, L'Helgouach)*

to this series of mounds. They are found in Brittany, concentrated in the Carnac region, and in west-central France, where they are widely distributed in Charente, Charente-Maritime, Vienne and Deux-Sèvres. These imposing monuments used to be dated right at the end of the Neolithic, but they are now more generally attributed to an early phase of the Atlantic Neolithic, about 3000 BC. Usually oblong but, exceptionally, circular in plan, they are extremely large: from 80 m. to 160 m. long, 30 m. to 60 m. wide and up to 10 m. high. Obviously their construction required a lengthy collective effort, which presupposes a fairly well organised

society. They contain several sub-megalithic cists, either closed or open along one side, but with no approach passage. In Brittany, the grave-goods are richer than in the rectangular mounds. A special feature is the extensive series of ceremonial objects – large axes of fine stone (jadeite, fibrolite), and disc-rings, beads and pendants of callaïs – for which all the material is probably exotic. By contrast, there is an almost total absence of pottery. The passage graves occasionally included in these tumuli appear to be secondary. Such graves are 7:2-3 the second basic type of tomb, with affinities in Iberia. Their evolution continued locally throughout the greater part of the Neolithic. The oldest types make IV great use of dry-stone work, with false-corbelled chambers which may be faced along the base of the walls with small slabs. This early type, in which the chamber is almost always circular and the open passage in the eastern quadrant, occurs in highly stereotyped form from the Charente as far as Calvados. Grouping of several passage graves under a single tumulus, unknown in west-central France, is not exceptional on the south coast of Brittany, and there are spectacular examples along the Channel coasts (eleven graves under the same tumulus at Barnenez, Finistère, and at Fontenay-le- 29 Marmion, Calvados). At some sites in the same region anthropomorphic stelae were set up in the chamber. Elsewhere the walls were adorned with pecked designs of a symbolic nature. The primary grave deposits are of 8:1-2 the Carn type already mentioned. Passage graves show development during the first half of the third millennium, with the employment of larger slabs, which tended to exclude dry-stone work and modify the circular plan of the chamber. This resulted in the classical type of tomb with slab-covered, quadrangular chamber, set either alone under a circular mound or grouped 7:3 with one or two others in a round or oval one. The chambers are sometimes subdivided internally, or the chamber and passage may be provided with annex cells, as in the Iberian peninsula. Engraving of symbolic art 30 became widespread in these tombs, culminating in the magnificent array at Gavrinis (Morbihan), where all the slabs are entirely covered with patterns which develop 31 a limited number of themes. In Brittany and west-central France alike the primary tomb deposits include a strong Chassean component, alongside forms of pos- 8:3-7 sibly Iberian inspiration (bowls of Le Souc'h type). 8:8 Deposits at the ritual hearths associated with the stone circle of Er Lannic (Morbihan) suggest that the stone circles and megalithic alignments specific to Brittany, and especially spectacular in Morbihan, probably belong to this phase. Towards the middle of the third millennium a tendency to elongate the chambers, common to a large part of Europe, led to the evolution of several distinct megalithic types which were certainly local in origin: in Brittany, V-shaped dolmens, in which the 7:5 distinction between passage and chamber had become obliterated, angled dolmens, and those with a lateral 7:4, 6 entrance. Primary deposits belong to the Kerugou type, equally local in origin, in which the pottery, rich in carinated forms and with flat or rounded bases, is 8:9

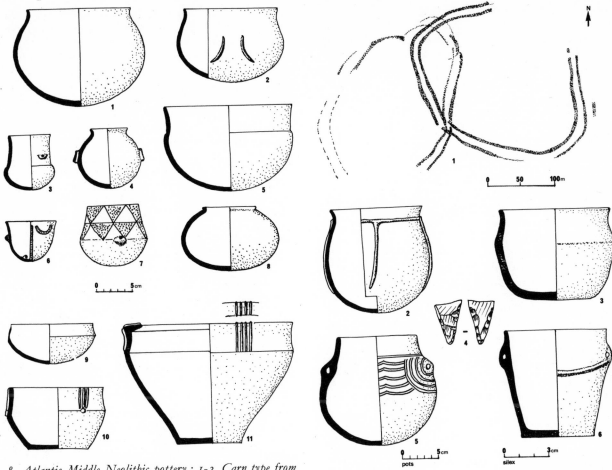

8 Atlantic Middle Neolithic pottery : *1-2, Carn type from L'Ile Carn, Ploudalmézeau, Finistère ; 3, Chassey ware from the Sournan dolmen, Saint-Guyomard, Morbihan ; 4-6, Chassey ware from the Parc-Nehué dolmen, Riantec, Morbihan ; 7, Chassean bowl from the Roh-en-Tallec dolmen, Carnac, Morbihan ; 8, vase of Le Souc'h type from the Bonne-Nouvelle dolmen, Plogoff, Finistère ; 9-10, Kerugou type pottery from Renongar, Plovan, Finistère ; 11, Kerugou type pottery from Roh-Vihan, L'Ile-aux-Moines, Morbihan (1, 2, 6-8 after L'Helgouach)*

9 Middle Neolithic of west-central France : *1, Camp des Matignons, Juillac-le-Coq, Charente ; 2-4, pottery and arrowhead of the Les Matignons culture, Les Matignons, Juillac-le-Coq, Charente ; 5, Peu-Richard ware vase from Mourez, Berneuil, Charente-Maritime ; 6, Peu-Richard ware vase from Peu-Richard, Thenac, Charente-Maritime (after Burnez, Case and Morel)*

8 : 10-11 decorated with groups of small vertical ribs. In the Loire valley development of what is termed the Angevin form of megalith, in which a simple portico replaces the passage, should be contemporary or a little earlier; but the absence of known deposits makes precise dating difficult. With the scarcity of occupation sites corresponding to the megalithic aspect of the Atlantic Neolithic we cannot know how the people lived, but there must have been agriculture and stock-keeping. In certain areas, like the coasts of Brittany, population was dense; but it was unevenly distributed, with some areas of the interior, apparently, hardly occupied at all.

33 The valleys of the Charente and Gironde during the Atlantic Middle Neolithic present a very different picture. While no specific tomb type has been identified, occupation sites seem to be extremely numerous, indi-

cating a dense and evenly distributed population. These sites are most often in the plains or on low hills, and are surrounded by several circular ditches, strengthened by stone walls. This feature, which is unknown elsewhere in France, has no close analogies except in Italy. In the west of France it is found in association with two cultures quite strongly contrasted in pottery, but identical in their economies and choice of sites and with closely related flint industries. These are the Les Matignons and Peu-Richard cultures, both carbon-dated to the first half of the third millennium, though at several stratified sites the first is seen to be earlier than the second. An abundance of sickle teeth and querns show the importance of agriculture, though stock-keeping is no less well represented: it supplied three-quarters of the meat consumed, with cattle clearly more

9 : 1

important than smaller stock. The flint industry is fairly sturdy, worked mostly on flakes, and with flint axes. The principal types are flake side-scrapers, flakes and blades with small serrations, used as sickle teeth, large
9:4 transverse arrowheads on flakes with heavy secondary work, a few trimmers and awls. The pottery, which is technically of good quality, is distinctive in its high proportion of flat or flattened bases, which do not otherwise occur so early in France, except in the Michelsberg of Alsace. Forms and decoration differ greatly in the cultural groups recognised. Les Mati-
9:2-3 gnons pottery is only rarely ornamented, and then with a few vertical cordons. Peu-Richard ware on the other hand is higly decorated, with horizontal cordons, inci-
32 sion, channelled strokes and lines, forming a variety of patterns: eye motifs set around tunnel handles, sun
9:5-6 motifs, wave patterns, rectangular motifs, etc. Having no roots in the local Mesolithic, the Les Matignons and Peu-Richard cultures abruptly introduce a developed Neolithic into west-central France. Nonetheless, neither within nor outside France is it possible to detect convincing forerunners for the two groups, and only a few isolated elements relate to Portugal or the Mediterranean. The problem posed by the origin of these cultures therefore remains. From its centre in Charente, the influence of the Peu-Richard group extended as far as the Loire valley, with characteristic pots in the Chacé dolmen (Maine-et-Loire) and typical flint types in the Chassean site of Amboise (Indre-et-Loire).

As a whole, the French Middle Neolithic, whose components we have now analysed, saw the extension of a Neolithic mode of life to all parts of the country, though not without many blanks on the map. Progress however was not uniform, and while the Midi experienced a great increase in agriculture compared with the Early Neolithic, in the northern half of France agriculture declined in comparison with stock-keeping, sickle blades disappearing in all groups. The climate may possibly be a factor in these differences. The sub-Boreal is in fact held to be cooler and drier than the Atlantic in the north of France and more humid, by contrast, in the Midi, which could possibly resolve the apparent anomalies.

The Late Neolithic and the Chalcolithic

During the Middle Neolithic, as has been seen, the southern half of France presents a fairly uniform picture by virtue of the southern Chassean, while the north of the country at the same period shows the formation of numerous and differing cultural groups. At the end of the Neolithic the opposite is true. The northern part of France is largely unified under the banner of the Seine-Oise-Marne culture and the closely related culture of the Armorican gallery graves, both of which lack local metal work, and are thus Late Neolithic in type. In the south, on the other hand, cultural specialisation becomes more marked and gives rise to a multitude of clearly distinguishable small groups, often covering no more than a modern *département*. To study each separately is out of the question here, and we shall have to content

ourselves with drawing the outlines of this period of thriving life and diversity, which saw the first native copper metallurgy established in Languedoc and on the Causses and thus justifies the term Chalcolithic. The one factor common, not only to all regions of France, but to the larger part of western Europe, is the intrusion of the Beaker culture, whose numerous local groups date round the turn of the third and second millennia.

THE LATE NEOLITHIC IN NORTHERN FRANCE
During the Late Neolithic the north of France, Belgium and the Paris basin were occupied by a culture whose duration was to be as extensive as the geographical area it covered. This is the culture termed Seine-Oise-Marne, which according to C14 dating lasted from *c.* 2500 BC until after 1700 BC, a prolonged period in which cultural evolution seems to have been minimal. During this time occupation of the heavy soils of the plains and the plateaux, begun at the start of the Middle Neolithic, was completed, and a Neolithic economy extended on to less fertile soils, hitherto occupied by the Tardenoisians. Land occupation apparently came to approximate to that of the present day. This is indicated by both collective tombs and occupation sites. While the tombs contain a considerable number and variety of grave-goods, living sites (almost always situated on cultivated ground disturbed by ploughing) provide almost nothing but stone tools. They have only rarely been excavated methodically, and their contribution to our knowledge of the Seine-Oise-Marne remains slight. The sole site where the economy could be studied showed a rather feeble development of agriculture, with hunting strongly outweighing stock-keeping. The situation here, however, was rather specialised (on Etampes sandstone), and this may give a somewhat distorted view of the basic economy. No trace has been found of houses, which must have been built of far lighter materials than in the Danubian. The stone industry, which had to serve the same requirements as during the Middle Neolithic, remains in the Campignian tradition already illustrated by Cerny and the northern Chassean. *Tranchets* however are rarer, and heavy saws with side notches for hafting replace backed knives. The most noticeable modifications are among weapons, with the appearance of large daggers, often made in flint imported from the Grand-Pressigny floors of the Touraine, and in new types of arrowhead: leaf- and lozenge-shaped, and tanged. 10:11-13 Transverse arrowheads remain the most numerous, but 10:8-10 they differ in type from those of the Middle Neolithic. Bone and antler industries developed actively, producing new types of hafts for small tools and axes, pendants, picks, hammers and battle-axes. The pottery by contrast is miserable, in technique, form and decoration 10:5-7, 14 alike. There is only one basic shape (a handleless, flat-based mug) and no more than isolated cases of decoration (finger-tip, or fine-awl impressions). Ornaments are very abundant in the tombs, with several characteristic types, such as perforated axe-amulets, crescent-shaped pendants of schist, double-bored buttons in mother-of-pearl, and skittle-shaped antler pendants.

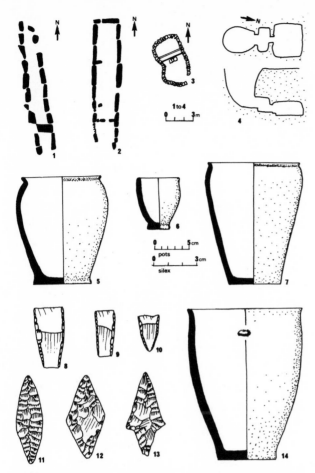

10 *Late Neolithic in the north of France: 1, Armorican gallery grave, Mougau-Bihan, Commana, Finistère; 2, SOM gallery grave at Chamant, Oise; 3, SOM trench grave at Crécy-en-Brie, Seine-et-Marne; 4, SOM underground chamber, Les Ronces 22, Villevenard, Marne; 5-7, 11-13, SOM pottery and pointed arrowheads from the underground chambers of Le Petit-Morin, Marne; 8-10, SOM transverse arrowheads from Congy, Marne; 14, pottery from the Armorican gallery grave of Kermeur-Bihan, Moëlan, Finistère (after L'Helgouach and Bailloud)*

The very rare beads of sheet copper imported from Germany are slight justification for calling this group Chalcolithic. The practice of collective burial, which we have seen was general in northwestern France during the Middle Neolithic, spread during the Late Neolithic to the whole Paris basin. The type of tomb varies widely according to the subsoil, with rectangular chambers cut in the rock in Champagne, underground mega- *10:4* lithic galleries, with extended rectangular chamber *36* separated from a short vestibule by a perforated (porthole) slab, in the northwest and in the centre of the *10:3* Paris basin, and trenches arranged beneath natural stone blocks, with dry-stone walling, in intermediate areas. Inhumation was practised everywhere, either as primary or secondary burial. Trepanation was not unusual. Certain tombs are decorated with sculpture, representing

either hafted axes or a feminine figure often reduced to breasts and necklace. There is an obvious discontinuity between the Seine-Oise-Marne and the culture which had occupied the same regions during the Middle Neolithic. The new cultural features which appear from the middle of the third millennium in northern France, however, are nowhere else known in association; it seems probable that the Seine-Oise-Marne originated locally, as a result of reactions on the part of the previous, already fully Neolithic population to a variety of outside influences. The pottery finds its closest parallels on the Upper Rhine (Horgen), whence some immigrants must have come. The perforated axe hafts and new type of transverse arrowheads are best matched in the Netherlands area, the pointed arrowheads in eastern France and the Midi, the rock-cut tombs in Sardinia, the megalithic galleries in southern Spain, and the axe-amulets in Brittany and the Mediterranean. The more distant of these parallels could scarcely be held to denote population movements, and are likely to reflect diffusion of methods and religious beliefs by no more than a few travellers.

In the east of France, it is possible that the Seine-Oise-Marne is represented in Lorraine, but not it seems in Alsace, where apart from a few graves with Corded ware it is difficult to know what culture to ascribe to the Late Neolithic, except for late derivatives of Michelsberg, which survived a long time. Similarly in Franche-Comté, the sole group to be identified clearly is at the lakeside site of Chalain in the Jura. In northern *35* Franche-Comté, as in Burgundy, there could have been widespread survival of cultures descended from the Middle Neolithic. The practice of collective burial appears here equally, in cists or simple dolmens, which are no more than a translation into megalithic terms of the cists of the Middle Neolithic.

In the valley of the Loire the Angevin dolmens, which probably began in the Middle Neolithic, developed during the Late Neolithic into more elongated and monumental forms, known by the name of Loire-type galleries. Their grave-goods are unknown, and the cultural affinities of the region can be judged only from material found in a small series of pit graves, related to those in the east of the Paris basin; this indicates a local variation of Seine-Oise-Marne culture.

In the Armorican massif, the Late, like the Middle Neolithic, is known primarily from tombs. Their distribution shows the population more evenly spread than in the previous period. Gallery graves and coarse pottery appear in association, as in the Paris region, but the passage from Middle to Late Neolithic in northwestern France is effected without a break. The megalithic tombs had long been in use, and the tendency to elongate the chambers, probably resulting from modified funerary practices, had progressed continuously from the end of the Middle Neolithic. Galleries with side entrance form a transition between Middle Neolithic T-shaped dolmens and the gallery graves of the Late Neolithic. The Armorican gallery graves are com- *10:1* posed of a long chamber and a very short antechamber on the same axial line, like galleries in the Paris and Loire basins, but there are certain features which distinguish them: the absence of port-hole slabs, and the frequent addition of a small, closed compartment behind the terminal slab of the chamber. The tombs were built at ground level, and no doubt they were covered by an oval barrow, which is less well preserved than the rubble cairns of the passage graves. Very rarely, gallery graves have decoration on the walls, most frequently the breast and necklace motif, which is sometimes repeated many times. Pecked shapes are derived from passage-grave art, with the addition of new signs, for example one depicting copper daggers of Cypriote type. There is little variety in the stone industry, which includes greenstone axes, flint daggers and barbed-and-tanged arrowheads. Coarse, flat-bottomed vessels of Seine-Oise-Marne type are an important element among the pottery, associated with degenerate derivatives of Kerugou ware, and a few collared flasks which probably derived their inspiration from the Netherlands. Although it shows evidence of numerous external contacts with a great diversity of regions, there is no doubt that the culture of the Armorican gallery graves represents only the local evolution of the native megalithic population.

10:14

8:9-11

In west-central France, the valley of the Charente preserved its cultural individuality. The Moulin-de-Vent group carried Peu-Richard tradition into the second half of the third millennium. Neither the economy nor the upland sites, surrounded by circular ditches, show fundamental change from the Middle Neolithic of the region, and furthermore the same sites were often re-utilised. A special feature in the stone industry is the proliferation of small, short and thick awls, which must betoken a particular type of wood- or leather-working. Pottery shows a fusion of Les Matignons and Peu-Richard traditions. Peu-Richard tunnel-handles have disappeared, and the decoration makes more use of small relief ribs than of incision or channelling. Cordons and raised dots are also found, with 'dimples' and a rudimentary use of painting. Patterns in the main derive from Peu-Richard pottery.

The remainder of west-central France was occupied by a culture which shows a close fusion of elements from the Moulin-de-Vent and Seine-Oise-Marne groups. This is the Vienne-Charente group, which like the Seine-Oise-Marne is known almost entirely from its tombs and their contents. Specifically attributable to this group are some pit graves, which we have already noticed extending into the Loire valley, and modestly-sized chamber tombs under circular barrows, built of slabs and dry-stone work, but without any clear entrance structure. Elsewhere megalithic tombs were re-utilised. The stone industry, with its daggers, transverse, lozenge-shaped and tanged arrowheads, the antler work (perforated hafts) and the ornaments (crescent-shaped pendants) indicate close contact with the Seine-Oise-Marne; but the pottery, with its mixture of round- and flat-bottomed forms and abundant handles, relates essentially to the Moulin-de-Vent group (as does its rare decoration). A facies hardly distinguishable from the Vienne-Charente is well represented in the Dordogne, where large flint-working floors, similar to the 'Campignian' workshops of the Paris basin, are found in the neighbourhood of Bergerac. By contrast, Level A1 in the Roucadour cave (Lot), which contains coarse, handless, flat-bottomed pots with finger-tip and finger-nail impressions, or with a clay slip applied in semi-liquid form, presents a distinct cultural group.

LATE NEOLITHIC AND CHALCOLITHIC IN THE FRENCH MIDI

As on the plains of northern France, the Late Neolithic in the Midi saw peasant cultivators and herdsmen adapting to all types of usable land. The *garrigue* uplands and the Causses, which were hardly occupied during the Middle Neolithic, became covered with megalithic tombs, which indicate at least some use of the land for pastoralism. But the large and permanent villages, with stone-built houses, on the *garrigues* in Languedoc betoken something quite different from the semi-nomadic pastoral economy suggested by the bucolic label '*pasteurs des plateaux*'. This exploitation of lands previously disdained was perhaps assisted by the advent of a more humid climate during the first part of the sub-Boreal, a change occasionally attested locally by sedimentology and palaeobotany. Occupation of areas of different potential will obviously have led to economic specialisation. Sickle teeth, which are abundant in favourable areas, grow noticeably scarcer on the limestone plateaux. Here flocks of sheep or goats assumed importance, always in association with a small breed of cattle and pigs. The increase in population density compared with preceding periods was very marked, and this, combined with the close geographical confinement of the region, led to far greater cultural diversification than on the north French plains at this time. Numerous cultural groups are clearly identifiable by variations in their choice of sites, their pottery, ornaments and burial monuments. The distributions of the groups, however, are extremely limited, and the list of them is far from complete (especially in Provence). It would be impossible to describe them one by one within the limits of this chapter, and we shall do no more than outline the cultural modifications affecting southern France at the end of the third millennium. Recent excavations allow two chronological levels to be detected as a rule among those groups usually attributed to the Late Neolithic and the Chalcolithic. The first corresponds to the second half of the third millennium: finds of metal being unknown or inconsiderable, it is termed Late Neolithic, or initial Chalcolithic. The second corresponds to the turn of the third millennium, including the first centuries of the second. A copper industry is well established among sites in the Cévennes, both on the Grands Causses and in eastern Languedoc, whence there was fairly extensive export of its products between Charente and Provence. This was a truly Chalcolithic stage, broadly contemporary with the Bronze A1 of central Europe. The intrusion of Beaker ware occurred at the

39-40

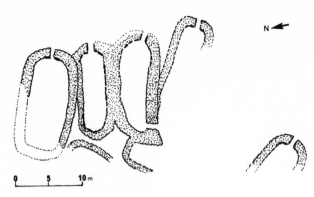

11 Village of the Fontbouïsse culture at Conquette, Saint-Martin-de-Londres, Hérault

Our knowledge of the sites is very uneven, and depends on what materials were utilised. Although still used, cave sites give way to village sites in the open. The best preserved are the groups of dry-stone houses of the Fontbouïsse culture in Languedoc. Excavation at the Conquette village (Hérault) revealed roughly oval *11* houses built up against each other; on average they were 12 m. long and from 3 m. to 5 m. wide. The dry-stone walls, some faced with slabs inside, are more than a metre thick, and must have supported a roof of perishable materials. The settlements were often extensive: for example, Cambous (Hérault) comprised some forty houses. At Lébous (Hérault) the site was sur- *12* rounded by a rectangular stone enclosure, with round towers set at regular intervals. Most sites, however, were not defended. In Provence, the village of Collet-Redon at La Couronne (Bouches-du-Rhône) is of very different construction: the large, rectangular buildings stand on marl-coated ground, with foundations of marl-jointed stones, and walls of cob.

The tombs used include a great variety of types and, as over most of France at the time, collective burial was the custom. Use of caves for burial purposes, already known previously, was much developed. In western Provence and eastern Languedoc burial chambers are hollowed out of the soft rock, and their circular plans recall those of the Iberian peninsula rather than those of *13:9* Sardinia or the Paris basin. The spectacular galleries of Arles, while dug out in the manner of the burial chambers, are elongated in plan and covered by slabs, like *13:7* gallery graves; they recall in particular the large gallery graves of Andalucia. The extended chamber dolmens of western Provence and the Aude are typologically related *13:5-6* to them. The passage graves of eastern Provence and the Hérault, set under a round tumulus, with a rectan- *13:1-4* gular chamber and walls of slabs or dry-stone work, have a south-west orientation which is quite different from Atlantic passage graves. The hundreds of simple dolmens on the Causses and to the west of the Massif Central probably represent a degeneration of Languedocian chamber tombs. Oval, circular or sub-rectangular chambers are built in dry-stone work, or in a mixture of this with small slabs, under a round barrow. More often than the other types they contain cremations. At Canteperdrix (Gard) these graves opened directly into the large rectangular stone buildings, and from their contents they seem to be dwellings, rather *13:8* than funerary structures. Several tombs of this type, as well as the rock-cut chambers, have been found to contain sculptured slabs, anthropomorphic in representation, and with more complex subjects than the Trets stelae. It is difficult to determine whether these stelae are primary, or re-used; but none is known in a Middle Neolithic context. Menhirs are not unusual on the limestone plateaus, and in Aveyron and Tarn a considerable series of statue-menhirs remain poorly dated, for want *38* of context. These however show forms closely comparable with the stelae of the Gard, which cannot be later than Chalcolithic. The statue-menhirs of Aveyron are found in newly occupied regions, which lack collec-

demarcation line between these two phases; and they are seen in stratigraphical succession at the cave of Marsa (Lot), at the Les Treilles and Les Cascades caves (Aveyron), at the sites of Conquette (Hérault) and Chauzon (Ardèche), at the cave of Peyroche II (Ardèche), in the La Couronne village (Bouches-du-Rhône) and in the underground tomb of Roaix (Vaucluse). Included in the first phase are the Crosian of the Lot, which is related to both the Vienne-Charente group and the Mediterranean Midi; the early phase of the megalithic culture of the Grands Causses and of the Aude-*14:2-3* Roussillon group; the Ferrières group of eastern Languedoc; and the La Couronne group of western Provence. The second phase took in the Artenac culture, which extended over the Lot, the west of the Massif Central and west-central France; the Rodezian on the *14:4-7* Grands Causses; the culture of Fontbouïsse of eastern Languedoc; as well as late regional groups of Beaker culture in Aude and Provence.

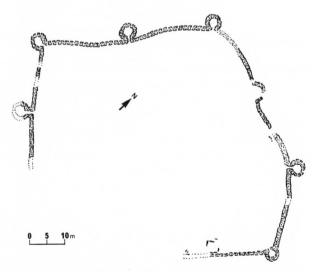

12 Fortified enclosure of the Fontbouïsse culture at Lébous, Saint-Mathieu-de-Tréviers, Hérault (after Arnal and Sangmeister)

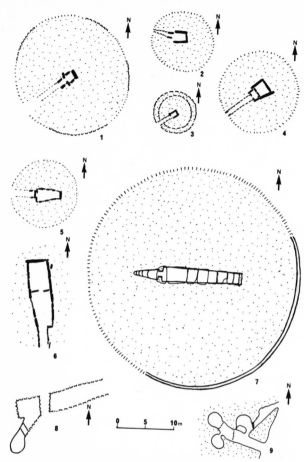

13 *Various tomb types in the Late Neolithic and Chalcolithic of Languedoc and Provence: 1, the Les Peyraoutes passage grave, Roquefort-les-Pins, Alpes-Maritimes; 2, the Grand Juyan de la Figarède passage grave, Les Matelles, Hérault; 3, the La Liquisse passage grave, Rouet, Hérault; 4, the Capucin 1 passage grave, Claret, Hérault; 5, Maurely dolmen, Saint-Antonin-sur-Bayon, Bouches-du-Rhône; 6, Saint-Eugène dolmen, Laure-Minervois, Aude; 7, Bounias underground chamber, Fontvielle, Bouches-du-Rhône; 8, chamber hollowed from the rock with corbelled roofing, and opening onto a quadrangular construction in drystone walling, at Canteperdrix, Gard; 9, underground chamber at Pié-Miéjan, Vers, Gard (after Courtin, Arnal, Guilaine, Vallon, Audibert)*

tive tombs; but a funerary purpose is likely. Still within the realm of religious practices would come the high number of trepanations found on the Grands Causses.

Clearing the limestone plateaux of the Midi needed far more robust equipment than the Chassean possessed and, as in the rest of France, this gave rise to specialised extraction and working of flint. In western Provence huge open-cast workings were exploited, using quartzite mauls with a median groove for hafting. In the Gard and in Aveyron shaft-mining of flint has been recognised. The most important site is at Salinelles (Gard), where seams of tabular flint were exploited industrially.

Long, broad knives were made from it, and these were widely exported in Languedoc. The Chassean industry on tiny blades tended to disappear, except in peripheral regions, like the Alps. Long flint blades were often used without further trimming; they were also made into various types of dagger, certain of which, with oblique retouch and partial polishing, show work of very high quality. The majority of tools were on flakes, with a great abundance of foliate forms with bifacial working, which had no doubt a variety of uses. Certain pieces have a sheen, from use as sickle blades. Scrapers and awls were made on massive flakes. Arrowheads are abundant and varied; transverse forms become very *14:9* rare, while there is an increase in leaf- and lozenge-shaped, tanged and barbed-and-tanged forms. Arrows *14:10-13,* with serrated edges are a speciality of the Rodez region *16-17* on the Causses. Those with a long tang are generally linked with late Beaker groups.

The bone industry shows little originality, and owing to an apparent lack of raw material deer antler is generally not used. A few antler sheaths are however found on the Causses, with a small spread in a very limited zone of northwest Hérault.

Pottery is almost exclusively round-bottomed (except *14:8* in the Lot), the range of forms and handle types being far more limited than in the Chassean. Practically no novel features are encountered, but we may note the half-spool handles at La Couronne for their possible affinities with Italy. Great use was made of plastic decoration: relief cordons and pushed-up knobs are *14:1, 14-* found in almost every group, and in some of them this is the only ornament known. Applied dots are less frequent. Channelled decoration is fairly common and is especially prevalent in the Fontbouïsse group, with *14:4-7* semicircular and metope patterns. Fine incision in the Chassean style has practically disappeared, but chevrons, *14:2-3* incised before firing, are the most characteristic ornament of the Ferrières group. In many of the Provençal groups, as in Dauphiné, decoration is almost absent.

Ornaments are extremely numerous and show great invention. From among a far larger repertory, we may cite winged beads, pointed beads, claw-shaped and hooked pendants, cylindrical, barrel-shaped and biconical beads, the triangular pendants of the Causses and V-perforated buttons. Many of the forms are good type fossils for distinguishing local groups or chronological phases. Some types were translated into copper, and in fact this metal was primarily used for the manufacture of small ornaments. Metal weapons are represented only by daggers, metal tools by awls and flat axes.

The cultural groups which followed the Chassean culture in the French Midi are often formulated in terms of population change. Nowhere in Europe, however, does one find cultures which could have been transported, fully formed, into southern France by invaders. It is true that a number of the cultural elements which appear in the Midi can be paralleled outside France, where their distribution may be widespread or localised. But we never find the association of traits necessary to support the notion of migration. There are

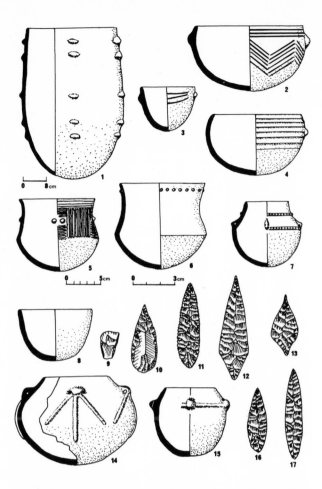

14 Late Neolithic and Chalcolithic in Languedoc and Provence: 1, vase from the occupation site of Saint-Jean-de-Cas, Mailhac, Aude; 2-3, pottery of Ferrières type from Ferrières-les-Verreries, Hérault; 4-7, pottery of Fontbouïsse type from Fontbouïsse, Gard; 8-17, pottery and arrowheads from the bottom layer (8-13) and the top layer (14-17) in the Roaix underground chamber, Vaucluse (after Taffanal, Arnal, Courtin)

plenty of parallels, for example, for the use of tabular flint in the Swiss Horgen and Bavarian Altheim cultures, for certain of the tomb forms in the Iberian peninsula, for Fontbouïsse stone building in Mediterranean islands, for the Lébous 'château' in southern Iberia, and for several of the dagger forms in Italy; but it is always a case of isolated elements in highly disparate contexts. No parallels for the pottery can be found outside France, save perhaps for vague resemblances to the La Couronne group in Italy (Diana). Pottery shapes are not fundamentally different from those of the Middle Neolithic, and characteristic features in the ornament (cordons, repoussé knobs, channelling and even chevrons) already existed, discretely, among Chassey ware. In our view the unity of the southern Chassean broke down as the result primarily of internal dislocation, and the profound changes in its flint work were a response to economic necessity. The other changes which came

about would then reflect a sudden intensification of contacts with the outside world, especially sea-borne contacts. These may have brought a few colonists, but they certainly did not introduce whole populations, except in the one case which remains to be examined.

THE BEAKER CULTURE

For more than half a century the Beaker culture has been known to prehistorians in all parts of Europe, and they have devoted much time to studying and writing about it. This culture is dated to the turn of the third millennium, when the change from Neolithic to Bronze Age took place. Its geographical distribution is enormous, and its origin remains uncertain. In various aspects, it is represented throughout France, sometimes as isolated finds, but elsewhere in compact assemblages. It is equally widespread in all neighbouring countries, to the north, south or east. There is a standard association of certain elements, to which are added other features borrowed from local cultures. The only possible explanation seems to be that there was a single point of origin, and very rapid diffusion, by both land and sea. Where the centre was, however, has still not been determined, and both central Europe and the Iberian peninsula remain possibilities. Certain writers combine the two in a theory of flux and reflux, which we mention only in the absence of a better solution. We shall not discuss the problem further here, since it can be answered only in a European context, and not that of France alone.

The basic features of the Beaker culture are its high mobility and adaptive faculty, the practice of copper and gold metallurgy, a special type of tanged copper *15:2, 7* dagger, the novel pottery, an object with terminal perforations often identified as an archer's wrist-guard, *15:6* use of V-perforated buttons and crescent-shaped ornaments. The stone industry, pottery and burial practices associated with different local groups all show a wide variety, and almost nothing is known about the occupation sites.

The pottery which gives its name to the culture, and is present in all groups, consists of a bell-shaped vase of a fine bright red or black colour, with flat or omphalos *15:3-4* base. The technical quality is high, and the vessel is decorated with fine combing or parallel horizontal lines, or equidistant, alternating bands of short oblique lines. *15:1, 5* This type is found over almost all of France, and generally it appears as intrusive in collective tombs, or less often on sites belonging to different native cultures. Numerous variants developed from this primary type, through an enrichment of decorative techniques and motifs to include incision or heavy, deep impressions, *15:9* chevron, horizontal, and 'zip-fastener' patterns, simple or overlapping triangles, checker-board, etc. The form with horizontal bands continued unaffected. Other forms found with Beaker ware vary from region to region. There are carinated bowls in the west, and single-handled cups, flat-based or polypod bowls, and jugs in Alsace. In the Midi there are omphalos-based *15:8, 10* bowls, conical bowls, jars, some handled pots and hollow-footed cups, and large flat-bottomed vessels with a horizontal cordon at the rim. Arrowheads are numerous and always of barb-and-tang type in France. The only type of burial proper to the Beaker folk is single inhumation, with or without a tumulus, and examples are found only in regions lacking native collective tombs. Everywhere else these tombs were systematically utilised.

Over much of France Beaker ware appears as intrusive among local populations, with whom its makers lived in symbiosis, having no territory specifically their own. They must have had some specialised role, as potters, or in metallurgy, which now appears for the first time in France, indicating the beginnings of a metal age. There was no development beyond this

15 Beaker culture: 1, beaker from Rosmeur, Penmarc'h, Finistère; 2, copper dagger from Lesconil, Plobannalec, Finistère; 3-4, beakers from Crugou, Plovan, Finistère; beaker from Keriaval, Carnac, Morbihan; 6, wrist-guard from Plédéliac, Côtes-du-Nord; 7, copper dagger from Soyons, Ardèche; 8, 10, bowl and jar from the Murée cave, Montpezat, Basses-Alpes; 9, beaker from the Capitaine shelter, Sainte-Croix-de-Verdon, Basses-Alpes (after Tréinen, Courtin)

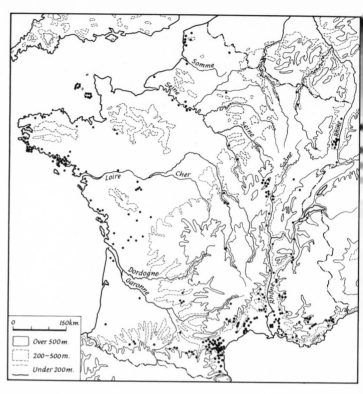

16 Distribution of Beaker ware in France

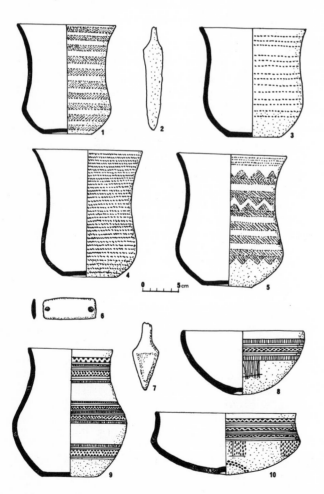

stage anywhere in western France, or over the greater part of the north, east or centre of the country. Certain indigenous local groups, by contrast, seem to have formed derivatively in defined areas: on the coast near Boulogne, on the upper Rhine, in Provence and in the Aude. In the south it has recently been possible to study what are specifically Beaker dwelling-sites, which are unknown over much of Europe. Some of them have produced remains of horses, which could have been used as traction animals; and possibly this may not be unrelated to the great mobility shown by Beaker folk. These people had no roots in France, and must have been immigrants there. In a country which at the end of the Neolithic was highly fragmented culturally they were a unifying factor, and contributed to technical progress since, except probably in the Midi, they were the first to introduce metallurgy. Beaker folk already foreshadowed the Bronze Age, and made an essential contribution to the formation of certain cultures at its beginning.

Bronze Age Cultures: 1800-600 BC

JACQUES BRIARD

The sequence of events from the beginning of the second millennium until about 600 BC is principally characterised by the appearance of a bronze industry, which superseded the often local and scattered centres of copper production.

Development of this industry, in quality as in quantity, had led to the accumulation of enormous stocks of metal shortly before its rather abrupt decline in face of early iron-working.

A consequence was that the social and religious structures of the Neolithic population were disrupted by the quest for copper and tin ores, often from widely separated sources; by the new technical specialisations, bringing new castes of prospectors and smiths; and by the resultant need for communications, serving both the search for raw materials and the circulation of an increasing number of finished products. In addition, new ethnic elements appeared. Not only was domestic life affected by these changes, but the modification of the basic economy meant an upheaval in social relationships and religious ideology.

Cults of fecundity and fertility, symbolised among Neolithic cultures by more or less stylised mother-goddess figures, gave way to mythological portrayals, which are far more difficult to interpret. Some early elements, like the clay horns found among footings of a hut in Alsace (Zumstein 1964), may represent the persistence of a pastoral cult. But new symbols, wheels, discs, waggons and horses, relate to a cult of the sun, or of the fire required in metallurgy.

By studying funerary customs we can learn much about the evolution of social structure in a society. The collective character of Neolithic tombs, megalithic monuments and ossuaries in caves and underground chambers, very often becomes blurred, and individual burial is preferred, perhaps introduced by Corded-ware peoples from northern Europe.

At times social differentiation is maintained beyond the grave and veritable princely tombs, belonging to local rulers or warrior chieftains, are found alongside far more modest burials. The rite of cremation advanced to the point of becoming standard among some groups, like the Urnfield peoples.

Apart from the large tumuli raised to the memory of the divine princes, few monuments of any size were constructed by the metallurgists and pastoralists of the second millennium; although it is probable that the latest large Breton menhirs (Kerloas en Plouarzel, Finistère) were contemporary with the beginnings of bronze-working (Briard 1965). In some regions this absence of monuments presents an increasing challenge to posterity. In the Atlantic zone, for example, it is very difficult to discover the tombs or religious monuments relating to those peoples who have left tangible evidence of their existence in their immense output of bronzes.

The introduction of metallurgy

It is difficult to determine the routes by which metallurgy was introduced into France. About 2000 BC, or even earlier, Chalcolithic groups, including the Beaker people discussed in the previous chapter, brought a knowledge of metals to the Midi, the Rhône valley and the Atlantic coasts, which manifested itself in the form of small tanged daggers of copper and little gold ornaments. In the Midi this knowledge stimulated the first exploitation of local mineral resources and gave rise to a brilliant Chalcolithic civilisation, though other influences certainly played a part. According to S. Piggott (1965) knowledge of metals in southwestern Europe may derive from trading-posts, with seafarers, prospectors and merchants from the Aegean. There is evidence for this interpretation in the bastioned dry-stone fortifications found in the Iberian peninsula (Los Millares) which reproduce east Mediterranean prototypes (Chalandriani). An analogous type of fortification recently discovered at Lébous, near Montpellier (Arnal and Martin-Granel 1961), may possibly belong to the same group. Representation on certain Breton gallery graves of weapons which recall the Cypriote daggers in use in the Near East (L'Helgouach 1965) relates to the presence of a few such daggers in the south of France. Finally, influence from Corded ware groups from northwestern Europe, who have been seen as the first Indo-Europeans, may have played a part, as is suggested by certain burials in Alsace or by battle-axes of arsenical copper from Kersoufflet and Trévé in Brittany.

Copper-producing centres very soon developed. A considerable number of flat axes were made as early as this, for example in the Vendée, though unfortunately their archaeological contexts are difficult to determine since often they are single finds and furthermore of a simple form which persisted for a long period.

However, if Beaker elements and, to a lesser degree, Corded-ware elements did play a role in establishing metallurgy, alongside the various Mediterranean impulses, it seems that they were operative only locally, and few regions would justify the term 'epi-Beaker bronze', in contrast to events in other European countries, like the British Isles. The real impetus towards bronze metallurgy in France resulted from new impulses from the east. S. Piggott (1965) has shown how a terminal phase in the acquisition of a metal technology developed in the south of central Europe, leading to the manufacture of weapons and ornaments of new types. Its triangular daggers equipped with rivets, an important technical advance, came increasingly to supplant those weapons, popular with Beaker people, hafted by means of a tang. Among ornaments, spiral forms developed alongside types imported from the Levant, such as the famous torcs with reverted ends deriving from prototypes in Syria. C. F. A. Schaeffer (1926) long ago proposed the idea that their presence indicated Syrian 'torc bearers', exploring in barbarian Europe for outlets for their new products and for new sources of metal, since primitive methods of exploitation, often superficial, quickly exhausted deposits. Following these arrivals, of men and imports, schools of metallurgy were set up and developed through a continuous succession of novel techniques and forms, utilising local materials, to establish a European 'Bronze Age'. Its originality and strength underlie the earliest civilisations of western history, Celtic and otherwise. Most important initially were the centres of Únětice in Bohemia and its German derivatives, Straubing and Leubingen. But their techniques and products soon reached France, and metal cultures developed in the east, especially in the Rhône valley, where distinctive workshops came into existence.

Two metal-using cultures were established in the west of Europe as the result of contacts and trading along the Channel coasts: the Wessex culture of southern England and the Armorican Tumulus culture in the far reaches of Brittany. Their undoubted relationship derives from a similarity in origin: the quest for new sources of tin and gold and possibly, too, a traffic in amber. The long-distance and sometimes astonishing contacts they maintained with the Aegean world were another reason for their prosperity.

These initial metal-using cultures in France appear only well into the second millennium, when metal-using had become firmly established in central Europe. On the other hand there were more archaic cultures, in which metal was merely a curiosity reserved for ornaments or, rarely, for weapons of very limited size. On occasion metal is depicted in engravings, like the disc-headed pins in the underground chambers in the Midi (Arles) and in Champagne (Epernay). Bone imitations of metal daggers and pins are also known.

It is not our intention to describe the megalithic and Neolithic groups which persisted into the second millennium. No doubt they scarcely differed culturally from those discussed in the previous chapter. None the less, it should not be forgotten that there was this juxtaposition of older and newer, and that around 2000 BC France must have appeared as quite a mosaic of cultures. These disparities would be lessened somewhat after the important movements which were to affect this region with the far-reaching phenomena of, successively, Tumulus and to a greater degree Urnfield expansion. These frequently resulted in an impression of greater homogeneity, and their importance was such that a good many authors have often seen in them the first indications of a nascent Celtic civilisation. But even at this stage numerous regional variations are still discernible. The migrations originated for the most part north of the Alps and eastern France was the first to be affected. Subsequently there was some slowing-down, which was sometimes considerable, and certain regions, particularly in the Atlantic zone, were not penetrated. An area like Britanny exhibited a traditional 'peninsularism' and often inclined towards the British Isles, while the south of France was continuously reconciling cultural impulses from the east with those which arrived, as might be expected, from other Mediterranean countries.

The birth of Bronze Age cultures (1800-1500 BC)

THE POOR RELATION:

ARTENACIAN AND ITS VARIANTS

Initially bronze was a luxury reserved for those who were fortunate in their commercial relations or in having a knowledge of mineral deposits. In some regions Neolithic tribes were succeeded by new cultural groups which are difficult to distinguish because of their poverty in metals. A typical example of this series is the Artenacian, defined by Bailloud and Burnez in 1962. Its eponymous site is the Artenac burial cave at Saint-Mary, Charente, which was discovered by chance during the working of a quarry and excavated in 1960. It contained some hundred disturbed inhumations, the sole intact burial being a contracted skeleton. Numerous flint objects, daggers with polished backs and barbed- *1:3-4* and-tanged arrowheads had been deposited as funerary offerings. Pottery was abundant and included flat-based conical vases, dishes and round-bottomed bowls, some- *1:1-2* times carinated. Among the numerous sherds was a very fine handle with an extension of the 'nosed' or 'beaked' type, which will be found again among groups *1:7, 10* related to the Artenacian. Another device for handling is a single lug on the bowls. Decoration consists of little knobs or more rarely of incised lines.

These associated finds from Artenac are highly characteristic of a group which is well represented in Charente-Maritime, Charente, Vienne, Haute-Vienne and Deux-Sèvres. The material comes from natural burial caves (Artenac and Vilhonneur in Charente), graves and small barrows (Fleuré, Vienne), from various re-utilised megaliths or from promontory forts, where for the most part it has not been possible to determine the age of the bank. Artenacian seems to follow a local Neolithic of Vienne-Charente type at the Chenon dolmen (Charente) and of Peu-Richard type at the Biard camp at Segonzac (Charente). Metal finds are very rare: some copper beads at Artenac and a crutch-headed pin from the Cordie dolmen, Mérignac.

1 : 5-6

Certain features found scattered in northwestern France relate to the Artenacian. In Brittany 'beaked' handles have been recorded in the Carnac region, but the most typical group is a surface find reported in 1966 by Dr Lejards at Len-Vihan en Arzon, Morbihan. A round-bottomed bowl among the pottery collected carries a vertical handle with lateral appendages of a form closely related to 'nosed' handles.

In the Paris basin two sites are relevant. The first is the celebrated Camp de Fort-Harrouard at Sorel-Moussel (Eure-et-Loir) excavated by the Abbé J. Philippe (1927-37). G. Bailloud (1962) regards beaked handles as typical of its second occupation level, together with some novel forms including internally decorated bowls. Metal was very rare and had not yet displaced the flint represented by Grand-Pressigny daggers, barbed arrowheads and notched saws.

1 : 8-9

The occupation site of Les Roches at Videlles (Seine-et-Oise) has fortunately complemented the evidence from Fort-Harrouard (Bailloud 1958). Significant material, some stratified, was obtained from hollows beneath boulders on the rocky site. The level of interest to us here is that intercalated between a Seine-Oise-Marne (SOM) occupation and one with excised pottery of Haguenau type, as in locus No. 2, to use the excavator's terminology. The pottery, which includes flower-pot shapes, distinguished from the SOM by their lugs, spooms and ladles and biconical cups, is reminiscent of level II at Fort-Harrouard. Flint is still abundant and metal exceedingly rare (one flanged axe). Videlles and Fort-Harrouard clearly demonstrate the presence in the Paris basin of new groups which follow the SOM culture, whose late survival has perhaps been exaggerated by some writers.

Similar material has been recognised in the southwest of France and in the Midi. 'Nosed' handles are reported by J. Roussot-Larroque from the Roquefort camp at Lugasson (Gironde), a link perhaps with the Pyrenees where J. Guilaine has recorded beaked handles at Le Petit Caougne de Niaux and at Las-Morts in Ariège. It is however the Marsa cave at Beauregard (Lot) which has produced the principal stratigraphic evidence for dating 'nosed' handles. Here A. Galan (1961) has distinguished three levels:

1 : 11-13

Level I – Chalcolithic layer with Fontbouïsse pottery
Level II – 'nosed' handles and bone crutch-headed pins
Level III – large jars, bowls and a bone pin of 'Middle Bronze' type.

The position of 'nosed' handles later than the Chalcolithic is very clear, since levels I and II are actually separated by a sterile layer. It is of interest to find, associated with them, bone pins coming to replace the metal, which is very scarce (some copper beads). Other variants are known in the Midi (the Mazuc cave, at

1 : 14-18

1 : 19

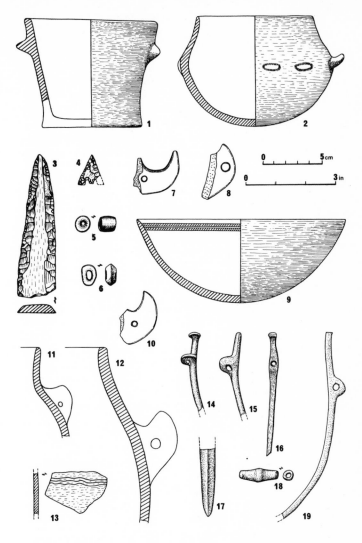

1 1-7, Artenac, flints, copper beads, 'beaked' handle; 8-9, Fort-Harrouard, 'beaked' handle and bowl; 10, Cordie, 'beaked' handle; 11-18, Marsa, 'beaked' handles, bone pins, copper beads and point; 19, Penne, Tarn, bone pin (1-10, after Bailloud; 11-19, after Galan)

Penne, Tarn) though the prototypes are possibly Swiss (Locras). Level II at Marsa produced another pin form, this time with bulging head and perforated neck, of a late type for which the metal prototypes may belong already at the beginning of 'Middle Bronze' Tumulus culture.

From Artenac to Marsa all the sites which have been considered, both burial places and occupation sites, attest the existence of small cultural groups, stratigraphically later than the Neolithic but still rather impoverished and not yet caught up in the cycle of true metal cultures. The Artenacian problem is one that continues to engage the attention of archaeologists. Radiocarbon dates obtained by Mme Roussot-Larroque at Lugasson, Gironde, indicate that this culture began before 2000 B C.

The first metal objects in the east of France, found either in burial deposits or as hoards of finished goods, originated across the Rhine, coming principally from the Straubing group in Bavaria, or as derivatives of already evolved forms from the potent metal-working centres of Únětice culture in central Europe.

The burials of this series are fairly scattered and metal grave-goods seem to be reserved for the ruling élite. One of the oldest burials is the inhumation at Riedisheim (Haut-Rhin) which contained products of the newly-established European metal industry: two neck-plate pins of poor bronze and spirals in copper and silver (Zumstein 1964).

Torcs appear at a later stage, sometimes with rolled-back terminals. It is known that such ornaments were in use in the eastern Mediterranean around 2100-1900 BC in the middle Ugarit phase at Ras Shamra in Syria, and from this we may assume they were current somewhat later in Europe, about 1800 BC. One such torc was associated with a knot-headed pin, a triangular dagger with grooved decoration parallel to the edges, and spiral bracelets in one of the oldest tumuli, Donauberg 12, in the Forêt de Haguenau, Bas-Rhin (Schaeffer 46:1 1926). Another torc burial, the Eguisheim cist (Haut-46:2 Rhin), contained two skeletons, a flint arrowhead, a 46:1 metal neck-plate pin with rolled terminal and a triangular dagger decorated with hatched triangles, a mode which was to become prevalent in the Rhône valley. The Eguisheim torc, with slightly thickened ends, has been variously interpreted as a Únětice import (Zumstein 1964) or a product of the Straubing group (Millotte 1963). The export of these ornaments farther west (Jaulny, Meurthe-et-Moselle; Epernay, Marne) remains questionable. The torcs not only served as ornaments but were also used for trading raw metal.

Trade in shaped ingots, most frequently of copper, is known from the beginnings of bronze metallurgy. The oldest form, along with the torcs, is the double-axe with a small hafting hole, the 'votive double-axes' of earlier writers. The prototypes are Mediterranean, if not Cretan, but production centres are known in Germany (in the Mainz region), whence they were exported to France, as shown by the finds of Nohan (Indre), Citeaux (Côte-d'Or), Saran (Marne) and possibly Jaulny (Meurthe-et-Moselle).

Also imported from Germany were bar-shaped ingots (*Rippenbarren*, *Spangenbarren*) (Kleeman 1954). They reached not only Alsace (a hoard of fourteen at Widensolen and one example from Eguisheim) but also central 44 France: a hoard of seven at Fonds-Gaidons near Bourges and one recovered from a large late hoard at Azay-le-Rideau.

Hoards and burials are however sporadic. In central France a few tumuli are known here and there. In one at Saint-Menoux (Allier) a Únětice-type pin was associated with triangular daggers, and in the poorer grave at Lair (Cantal), with a dagger with two rivets. Hoards of bronzes are exceedingly rare. In central France they consist of imports from Rhône valley workshops: daggers at Corent, Puy-de-Dôme, and axes with wide cutting-edge at Bègues, Allier.

Developed flanged axes from hoards in Alsace, like those of Bonhomme or Habsheim in the Haut-Rhin, are still modelled on Germano-Swiss forms (Langquaid type); these appear fairly late, in about the sixteenth century BC (Zumstein 1964). There was no flourishing metal industry in Alsace until the time of the Haguenau tumuli.

Elsewhere, however, new groups were already prospering and these gave rise to native workshops.

THE RHÔNE CULTURE AND THE MIDI

The Rhône culture was identified gradually as the result of work by Swiss and German archaeologists. G. Kraft in 1927 defined a Valais group in western Switzerland. Subsequently E. Vogt expanded this idea and postulated a Rhône-Straubing-Kisapostag grouping, relating Rhodanian culture to its contemporaries in Bavaria and Hungary. O. Uenze (1938) particularised the Rhodanian dagger, and more recently N. K. Sandars (1957) and J. P. Millotte (1963) have analysed the pottery. Finally, the existence of Rhodanian in the Midi was established by G. Bailloud (1966).

Closely connected with the Swiss group, the French Rhodanian covers a wide area extending from the Jura to Provence and Languedoc through the Rhône valley, with some extension into the Alps. Within such an area local variants are numerous but they are still not completely elucidated. The Rhodanian culture is characterised less by a homogeneous population than by the adoption or manufacture of certain bronze types, the presence of common pottery and a community of commercial relationships. The Rhône corridor is its main axis for the diffusion of new techniques. It was linked via the Saône valley, the Jura and the Belfort Gap with the Rhine circuit, and there was increasing exchange along the length of the route between Germany and the Mediterranean. Únětice products reached the axial Rhône valley and connected regions. These included pins, of which the most spectacular is the gold example 46:3 from Serrigny (Côte-d'Or), which was unfortunately acquired without note of its context (Déchelette 1910). This find, which may be dated to the end of the sixteenth century BC, is reminiscent of gold ornaments from the well-known princely tomb of Leubingen in Saxony. Pottery of Únětice inspiration was traded towards the south, for example the sharply carinated little cups from the La Bergère tumulus at Verzé (Saône-et-Loire) and from the Greux de Miège cave in Hérault.

A reciprocal north-bound trade grew up in shells from the Mediterranean, which were sought as ornaments. The best known form is the *Columbella rustica*, exported as far as Germany, Switzerland, Austria and even Hungary. It is well represented among the German Adlerberg group, and there are some indications of its route between the Midi and Germany, for example in the inhumations at Bouze in the Côte-d'Or. Less well known types, particularly molluscs (lamellibranchs), were also exported and have been noted (Bailloud 1966) as far away as Switzerland (the Champlan cist, Valais) and Burgundy (Les Bourroches at Dijon). These were one form of currency with which the Mediterranean people paid, in part, for their new metal and ceramic products.

Alongside these imports and various exchanges, the Rhône culture's own products spread between the Jura and the Mediterranean. One of its most distinctive group was that which developed in the Jura. Its most distinctive grave-groups are from the Bois de Parançot, the Forêt des Moidons at Mesnay, and the Bois de Séry at Salins. Racquet and more especially trefoil pins, sometimes decorated with a St Andrew's cross, are associated with lozenge-shaped awls and small, rather crude, triangular daggers with two or three rivet-holes. Pottery is rare, but should include some handled cups (Piroutet 1913; Sandars 1957; Millotte 1963).

Less is known of habitation sites, but camps (Saint-André at Salins), rare caves and some littoral sites, like those on the Lac de Chalain and Clairvaux, have been recorded. Pottery includes large cordoned pots, whose Swiss prototypes are well represented at Les Roseaux at Morges. This type of Rhodanian pottery recurs at the Camp de Chassey in the Saône-et-Loire, and extends throughout the Rhône valley as far as the Midi.

The novel forms from Rhodanian workshops derive from Swiss models. In the early phase they include low-flanged axes (Neyruz). Later the axes acquired more distinctive shapes, some having very wide, semicircular cutting-edges (Morges type), others taking the form of elongated spatula-axes. Some single finds are known in the Jura, but it is predominantly along the Rhône and in the Alps that the Rhodanian culture is attested by hoards and single bronzes. The earliest instance of a stock of finished bronzes is the hoard of 58 Neyruz axes at Ternay in the Isère (Bocquet 1968).

The finest product of the Rhodanian workshops is the well-known triangular dagger with metal hilt (Jully and Rappaz 1960; Courtois 1960). Often the blade is ornamented with grooves running parallel to the edges and the semicircular indentation below the guard is decorated with geometric motifs in the form of a cross or with incised chevrons, as is sometimes the hilt or pommel. This weapon has been found in the Rhône valley at Lyons, Mirabel and Loriol in the Drôme and also in the Alps at Saint-Laurent-du-Pont (Isère) and Les Taburles at Avançon (Hautes-Alpes). It was exported as far as Provence and Languedoc, as shown by finds at Nîmes (Gard), Saint-Nazaire-de-Ladarez (Hérault) or Solliès-Pont (Var). In its production the Rhodanian metallurgists gave proof of their great technical skill.

Though burials are rare in the Alpine zone there is nonetheless a cist burial at Rame (Hautes-Alpes) from which there survive a triangular dagger, a spatula-axe and a headband with incised decoration, a form exceptional in this area but with well-known analogues in Switzerland.

In the Midi, Rhodanian influence can be recognised

2:6, 12-13
2:4-5, 7
2:1-3

3:1

4:2

46:4

4:1

4:3-5

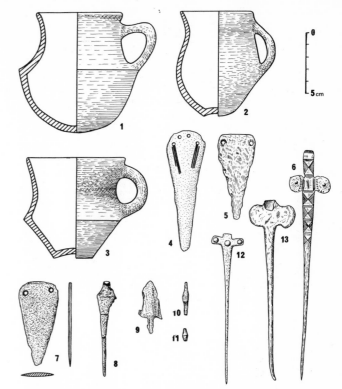

2 1, Sainte-Anastasie, Gard, handled cup; 2-3, Mireval, Hérault, handled cup; 4, Grotte de Pâques, Collies, Gard, dagger; 5-6, Bois de Parançot, Jura, dagger and pin; 7-11, La Montade, daggers and pins; 12, Tumulus des Gardes, pin; 13, Bois de Séry, pin (1-3, after Bailloud; 4 and 12, after Audibert; 7-11, after Courtin; 5-6 and 13, after Piroutet)

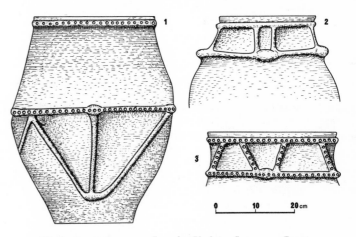

3 Rhodanian pottery: 1, Lac de Chalain, Jura; 2, Grotte Nicolas, Sainte-Anastasie, Gard; 3, Saint-Gervais-les-Bagnols, Gard (after Bailloud)

not only in flanged axes and triangular daggers, sometimes with massive hilts, but frequently also in the presence of Rhodanian pottery – large flat-bottomed jars decorated with cordons. G. Bailloud, J. Guilaine and J. Arnal have listed a number of examples: Saint-

5

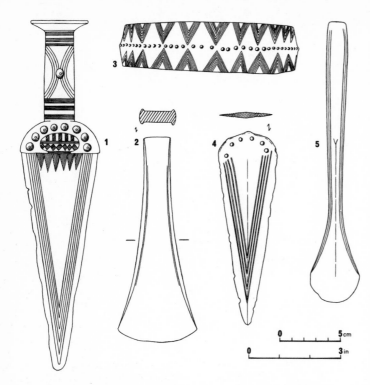

4 *1, Loriol, Drôme, dagger; 2, Sinard, Isère, flanged axe;
3-5, Rame, Hautes-Alpes, diadem, dagger and spatula-axe
(1-3 and 5, after Courtois; 2, after Bocquet)*

Anastasie (Gard), Le Lébous and Saint-Jean-de-Cuculles (Hérault), Grotte du Baou (Bouches-du-Rhône), etc. In lower Provence the burial cave of La Carrière at La Montade (Bouches-du-Rhône) likewise demonstrates the arrival of metal from the north, with a racquet pin *2:7-11* with rolled head, a little triangular dagger and awls (Courtin and Puech 1963). But in Provence other influences are encountered. The pottery from Aven de Gage at Allauch (Bouches-du-Rhône) includes a little cup with a decoration derived from Beaker motifs and in particular an Italian-type handle with extensions, which Courtin and Puech compare with analogues in Sardinia or northern Italy (early Polada).

Graves and mounds with single burials are rare and use of burial caves and even dolmens persisted, as is shown by certain grave-groups, of which the best known is from La Liquisse at Nant (Aveyron). The trefoil pins here are from the Jura. At times local forms, such as the curious 'cabochon' pins, are preferred. It is true there are some of these in the Jura and in northern Italy, but they come principally from the Midi, from the dolmens of Les Lacs at Minerve (Hérault), La Macelle at Saint-Hypolithe-du-Fort (Gard) and Les *2:12* Pounches at Mons (Var), and from the Gardes tumulus at Concoules (Aveyron). Weapons consist of small riveted triangular daggers, often in copper. Small *2:1-3* handled cups were used as grave deposits.

The Rhône culture was a complex ensemble which in the Midi mixed with diverse influences deriving from the Chalcolithic or from Italy. Its early forms were current about 1800-1600 BC, but some types, like the developed Morges or spatula-axes and the large cordoned jars, enjoyed a widespread survival into the middle of the second millennium.

THE PRINCELINGS OF ARMORICA

A region which was particularly alive during the first quarter of the second millennium was that along the Channel coasts. There was intense commercial activity, involving Nordic, British and even Aegean peoples engaged in a search for new sources of metal: copper and tin from Cornwall, tin from Brittany and gold from the 'Garden of the Hesperides' revealed in Ireland, with its famous lunulae. Trade in Nordic amber was equally brisk.

Two cultures were to emerge from this activity: the Wessex culture of southern England and the Armorican Tumulus culture in the west of Brittany. Their most spectacular features were the, at times imposing, barrows rich in metal grave-goods. These reveal the existence of a warrior aristocracy, which probably monopolised commerce and enriched itself from dues levied on merchants and sea-traders. We know nothing of its relations with descendants of the Neolithic population, but it is probable that they were subjected to its rule. What is certain is that, in Brittany at least, the building of tumuli each incorporating three to four thousand cubic metres of material must have required the voluntary or enforced support of local manpower.

The Armorican Tumulus culture is relatively well known and fairly homogeneous. The first barrows were excavated and studied from the end of the nineteenth century, notably by P. du Chatellier in Finistère. Two phases have been distinguished (Giot and Cogné 1951), a first series with rich metal goods and arrowheads, and a second, later, series with pottery. Some overlap between them is probable. It is the first series which interests us here: it is found in some thirty tumuli, often of considerable size and in the main concentrated along the Channel and Atlantic coasts of Finistère. Occasionally these people penetrated to the interior of Brittany along the rivers (Plouyé, Finistère; Elven, Morbihan).

Among the grave-goods, what is immediately arresting is the size of the new weapons, the richness and variety of the amber, or even gold, ornaments and the technical supremacy shown in the flint arrowheads. A fine example is the Kernonen, Plouvorn tumulus (Finistère) excavated by the author in 1966. This is a huge tumulus, some 50 m. in diameter and 6 m. high, over a burial vault 4 m. long by 2 m. wide and 2 m. deep, with paving covered by a wooden floor. It was closed by a block of granite, with two small slabs at each end. The grave-goods were lying among oak débris, the remains V from crude wooden boxes. The first, to the west, contained three low-flanged axes. Farther away a dozen flint arrowheads had been laid in a line. A second box in the centre of the tomb contained three bronze daggers with the remains of wooden hilts decorated with microscopic VI

41 Plouhinec tumulus, Finistère.

42 Vault of the Plouhinec grave, Finistère.

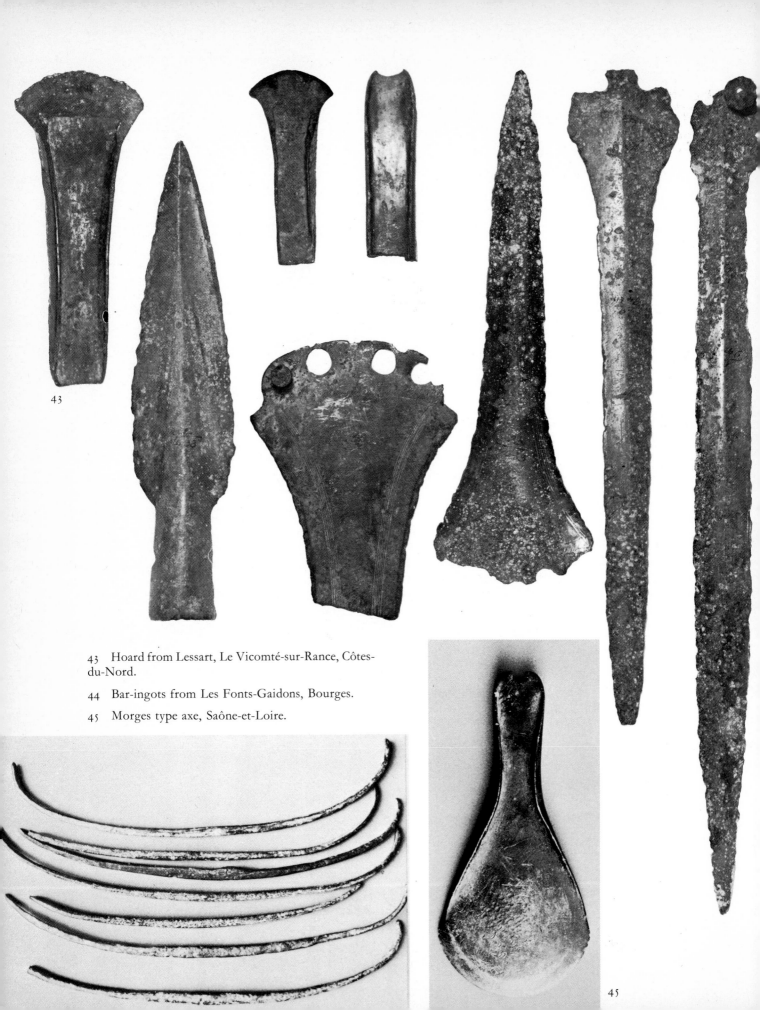

43 Hoard from Lessart, Le Vicomté-sur-Rance, Côtes-du-Nord.

44 Bar-ingots from Les Fonts-Gaidons, Bourges.

45 Morges type axe, Saône-et-Loire.

45

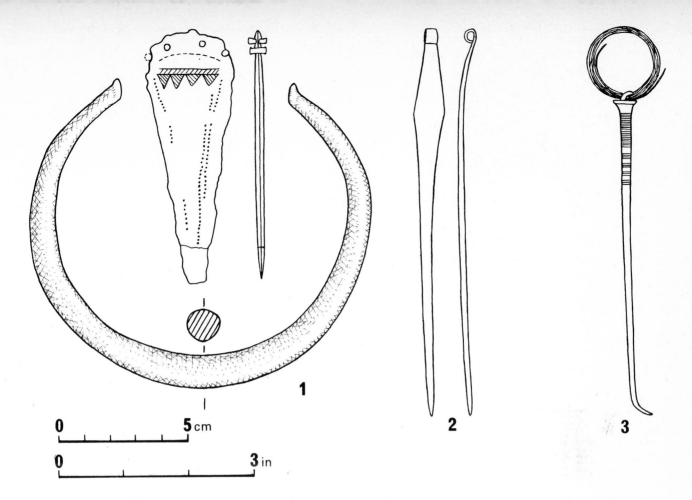

46 1–2, Eguisheim, torc, dagger and roll-headed pin; 3, Serrigny, Côte-d'Or, gold pin; 4, Cessieu, Isère, Morges type axe; 5–6, Donauberg, pin, torc, bracelet and dagger.

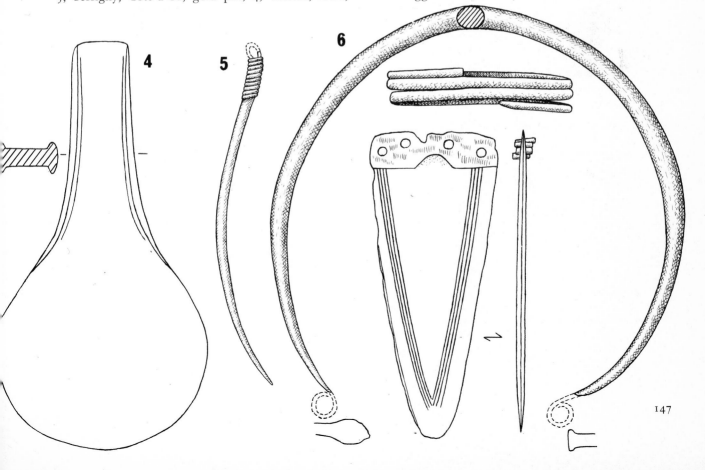

47

49

48

50

51

47 Excised pottery, Videlles 12.

48 Pottery with cordons and finger impressions, La Rousselerie, Loire-Atlantique.

49 Vase with imitation basketry decoration, Lesneven, Finistère.

50 Gold torc of Yeovil type, Cesson, Ille-et-Vilaine.

51 Polypod vase, Lombrives, Ussat, Ariège. Hgt 8·6 cm.

52 Handled jug, Milhes, Clermont-sur-Lanquet, Aude. Hgt 8·4 cm.

53 Jar, Milhes, Clermont-sur-Lanquet, Aude. Hgt 23 cm.

52

53

54 *Statue-menhir*, Filitosa V, Corsica. Hgt 2·95 m.

55 Vase from the Chissay urnfield, Loir et Cher.

56 Knives from Mehun and Vasselay.

57 Antennae sword, Lyons.

58 Pendants, La Prairie de Mauves, Nantes, Loire-Atlantique.

59 Swords from Bellevue, Loire-Atlantique.

60 Armorican socketed axe, Le Trehou, Finistère.

55

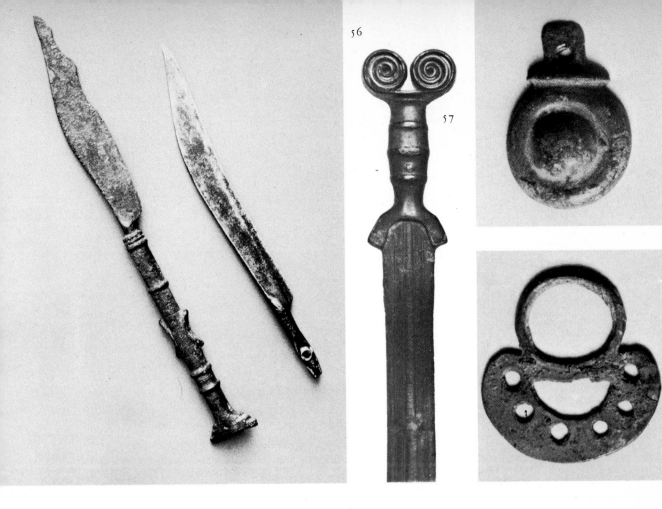

56 57 58

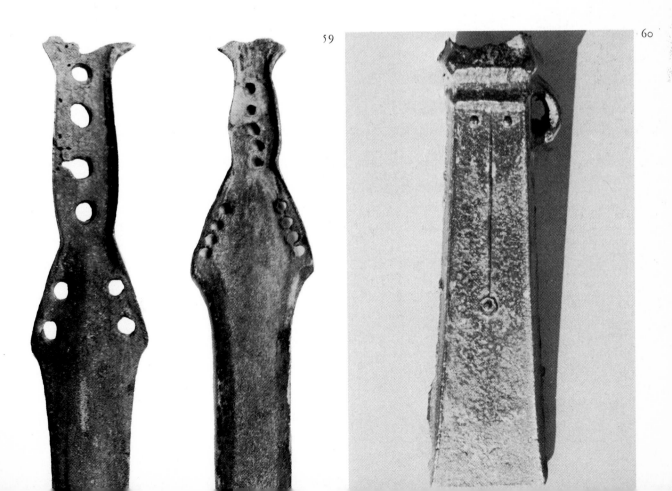

59 60

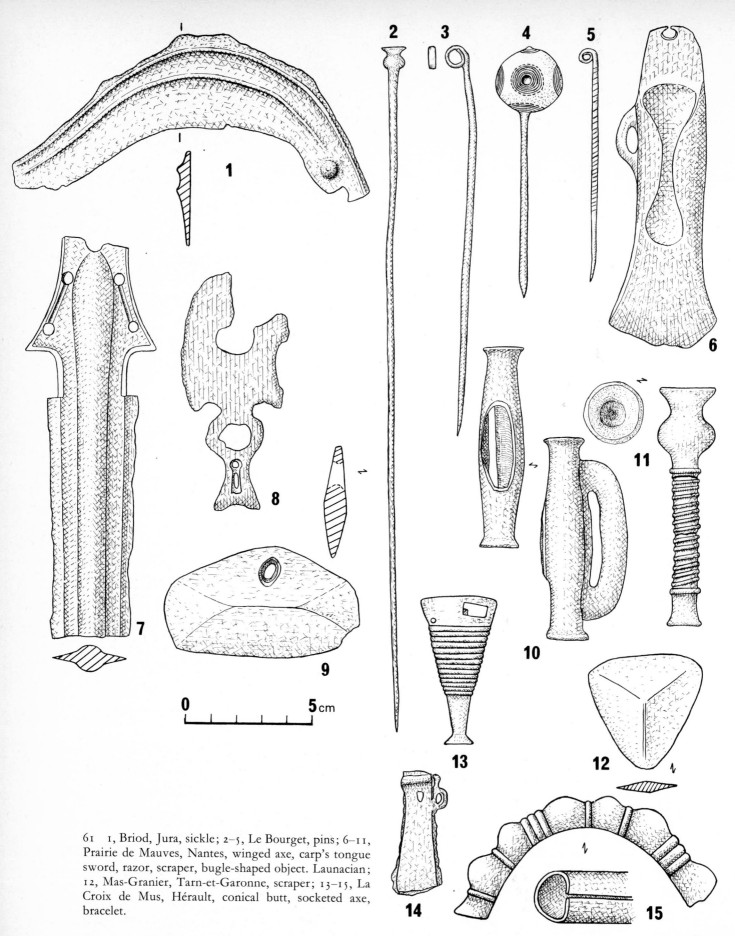

61 1, Briod, Jura, sickle; 2–5, Le Bourget, pins; 6–11, Prairie de Mauves, Nantes, winged axe, carp's tongue sword, razor, scraper, bugle-shaped object. Launacian; 12, Mas-Granier, Tarn-et-Garonne, scraper; 13–15, La Croix de Mus, Hérault, conical butt, socketed axe, bracelet.

gold nails (one thousand of them weigh 1.7 gr.) set in geometric patterns. The daggers were decorated on each face with three large gold studs with wide, flat heads. Curiously, two bronze pins, one ring-headed and the other with a cruciform head, had been arranged between the blade of one dagger and its wooden sheath. Beside this central box lay the remains of an amber necklace, made from large disc beads and smaller trapezoidal ones. Finally, a third box contained a dagger with a bone pommel, arrowheads and an archer's wrist-guard in amber. In all some sixty flint arrowheads of the ogival Breton type were recovered.

Plouvorn is a masterpiece among a fairly rich series of graves which have yielded numerous weapons in poor bronze or arsenical copper, in association with flint arrowheads. Occasionally spacer beads in jet or lignite are found, imitating the famous amber ones known in the Midi, in Germany, and again in Greece (Kakovatos), from which an interesting correlation has been established, about 1500 BC. Polished stone sceptres, similar to the regalia of Wessex princes, confirm a relationship demonstrated by S. Piggott (1938) and P. R. Giot (1951). Across the Channel amber and arrowheads, though less elegant, recur, as well as the famous little gold nails (Bush Barrow, Normanton). Long-distance connections link Wessex and Armorica with the Mycenaean world. Some of the Breton vaults recall in their rectangular form the famous shaft graves in the agora at Mycenae. The wealth of weapons and gold in Wessex and Breton burials is also a pale reflection of Mycenaean opulence. Finally, a few imported objects, like the Rillaton gold cup from Cornwall or the little carinated vessel from Ploumilliau, Finistère, could be taken to confirm these connections, and may be related to the Fritzdorf find in Germany. Other connections with the east are discernible. Ring-headed pins have counterparts in Switzerland, and the form of the flanged axes is reminiscent of the Rhodanian Neyruz type. Similarly, a little spiral bracelet from Carnoet is probably a Straubing import.

Some burials in Normandy relate to the Armorican group: Longues (Calvados) and especially Loucé in the Orne with a fine series of Breton type arrowheads, studied by G. Verron. The dagger from Hervelinghem (Pas-de-Calais) on the other hand has a distinct pointillé decoration on the blade and is more likely Germanic in inspiration.

The Tumulus culture in Armorica reflects a brilliant society of metallurgists, merchants and stock-raisers. The princely tombs are the graves of an aristocracy, where warrior-priests were buried with ceremony. As S. Piggott has suggested for Wessex and Mycenae, it is perhaps not excessive to call to mind the heroes of Homeric tradition. However, chronological systems are not yet definitive. Some authors, among them Colin Renfrew, note that corrections of C14 dates by dendrochronology may add so much to the age of the Wessex culture that relations with Mycenae would have been impossible. This approach indicates that the 'western barbarians' were not the servile imitators suggested by

those who regard the orient as the source of all culture, but creators of original civilisations.

The culmination of Bronze Age cultures (1500-1200 BC)

TUMULUS CULTURE

The Tumulus culture (*Hügelgräberkultur*) flourished from about 1500 BC. Its various groups covered an area stretching from the Alps to northern Germany and from eastern France to Czechoslovakia. It was so considerable that often it is interpreted as a preliminary stage in the formulation of Celtic civilisation, and the term 'proto-Celtic' has, perhaps prematurely, been applied to it. The standard rite of inhumation under a tumulus was increasingly displaced by cremation. Grave-goods show regional variation and illustrate the evolution of metallurgical techniques. The excised *Kerbschnitt* style appeared on the pottery, in which 47 motifs, here invariably geometric, are left in relief.

The most distinctive group in France is in the Forêt de Haguenau in Alsace. Other groups encountered in the Paris basin and Rhône valley, as well as outposts to the south and west, are less easily defined in terms of pottery, hoards and exported objects.

Six hundred tumuli were excavated in the Forêt de Haguenau by X. L. Nessel, and from their material two hundred of these may be attributed to the 'Middle Bronze Age'. They were first studied by A. W. Naue, but the significance of the Haguenau group was demonstrated primarily in a celebrated monograph by C. F. A. Schaeffer (1926). Various phases in its evolution have been distinguished (Hatt 1955). In the earliest phase the pins have a thickened head and the swollen neck is perforated transversely; bracelets are simple with incised decoration. Pottery comprises small handled cups 5:4-5 and amphorae decorated with incision. The first anklets were simple windings of wire with spiral ends, a heritage from the Straubing style.

In the second period (Bronze C of German archaeologists) pins with splayed ('trumpet') or wheel heads were in use, sometimes decorated with incision or ringed with light ribbing. Grave goods now included jugs, amphorae and cups with excised ornament. Anklets were elaborated, with a wide ribbon of bronze to encircle the leg. Weapons were daggers or short rapiers with two or four rivets and wooden or horn hilts.

In a final phase there is an admixture of new elements with the Tumulus culture's most accomplished metalwork, notably fine ribbon and wire anklets with re- 6 poussé or engraved ornament. Pottery and bronzes were decorated in an abstract geometric style, using 5 chevrons, triangles, dot-and-circle or multiple circles, etc. Representation of men or beasts is unknown. The general impression is of a period of stability and calm, with life devoted to metallurgy, stock-raising (especially pigs) and agriculture. A non-sepulchral bronze form was a thick-bodied palstave (Haguenau type), similar to its German congeners. Some amber beads, of the Kakovatos type known in Mycenaean contexts, allow the early phase to be dated 1500-1400 BC.

In the Haut-Rhin, Tumulus culture is represented by club-headed pins with perforated neck (Horbourg) and some jugs, including one with wart decoration which was possibly brought from the Swabian Jura (Zumstein 1964). Single finds are limited to a few axes and fragments of swords. The position is similar to that in Lorraine, with a few single metal finds (Millotte 1965).

In the Jura and the Rhône valley the situation shows no great change. Rhodanian culture continued and the addition of Tumulus culture probably denotes commercial exchanges rather than a change in population. Millotte (1963) has defined a 'Middle Bronze Rhodanian-Jurassic' group, a fairly loose ensemble of hoards, finds and scattered burials. The finds are primarily

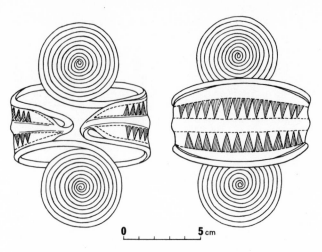

6 *Spiral anklet, Mägstub, Forêt de Haguenau, Alsace (after Naue)*

evolved flanged axes, with an incipient stop or a wide, bell-shaped cutting-edge, and massive Haguenau-type palstaves, with the occasional addition of bronzes from Atlantic workshops. The weapons are riveted rapiers but there are also fine swords with bronze hilts and grooved ornament in the centre of the blade (Reugnay, Doubs; Le Cheylounet, Haute-Loire; Jugnes, Aude). The richness of this ornament below the shoulders is not unlike the type of decoration on Rhodanian daggers. A few tumuli are known here and there. R. Joffroy and P. Mouton have excavated a little barrow fashioned from a natural sandy mound at Orgelet, Jura. A skeleton covered by stones was accompanied by a large pin with a central perforation in the bulging neck and a decoration of alternate vertical and horizontal incisions, quite like that current in the Hesse Tumulus group (German Bronze C).

Further south in the Isère the cemetery of Saint-Paul-de-Varces (Bocquet 1968) shows influence from Tumulus culture. The skeletons had been deposited in the débris at the foot of a slope in three groups. The second group lay at two levels, the lower with Beaker pottery and the upper dated to a late 'Middle Bronze' phase, about 1200 BC, with massive, incised bronze bracelets, a large cone-headed pin with spindle-shaped swelling, also decorated by incision, amber beads, spiral rings and tubes and two small cups, one with excised chequered ornament at the level of the carination and possibly, according to Bocquet, Rhenish in origin. Other burials with pins are known in Isère, at Cessieu and Parmilieu; here the bodies had been inserted into crevices between rocks, following local usage. A local product is a flanged axe with bell-shaped cutting-edge. The most typical examples come from the well-known hoard of Porcieu-Amblagnieu (Isère), in association with, among other things, daggers with two rivets, pins with incised decoration, and the earliest sickles, evidence of the importance of agriculture in the area.

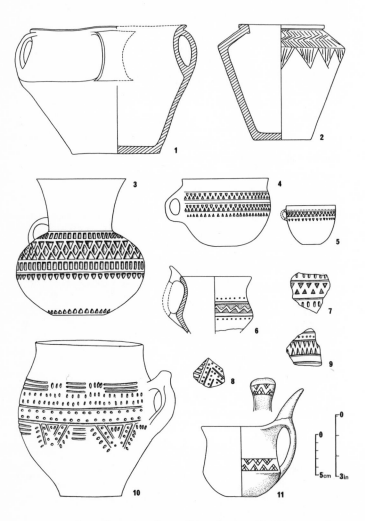

5 *Armorican tumuli : 1, Plouneventer, Finistère ; 2, Cruguel, Morbihan. Haguenau 'Kerbschnitt' ; 3, Kurzgeland ; 4-5, Harthausen. Mediterranean pottery ; 6, Eyguières, Bouches-du-Rhône ; 7, Grotte de Seynes, Gard ; 8-9, Tharaux, Gard ; 10, Labeil, Hérault ; 11, Grotte-Murée, Basses-Alpes (1-2, after Briard ; 3-5, after Naue ; 6-11, after Courtin ; 8-10, after Audibert and Bousquet)*

The Hautes-Alpes department has also produced some Tumulus daggers and pins (Courtois 1960). By contrast, excised pottery seems exceedingly rare.

In the south of the Paris basin several habitation sites have stratified deposits with Tumulus-related pottery. At Marion des Roches near Montigny-sur-Loing, Seine-et-Marne (Bailloud 1961) there were some small two-riveted daggers and pottery stamped with a triangular tool, in particular a fine handled jug which would be quite appropriate among tumulus deposits in the Forêt de Haguenau. Other goblets and comb-decorated pots recall forms from contemporary levels at Fort-Har-rouard (Eure-et-Loir). At Les Roches, Videlles (Seine-et-Oise) stamped pottery is associated with pots with finger impressions, either on cordons or covering the belly. Metal is rather scarce on these habitation sites and by contrast there is plenty of evidence that flint was utilised (scrapers, axes, etc.). A study of the fauna from Videlles by Th. Poulain-Josien shows that domestic animals were slightly more numerous than wild ones. Pig predominates, with some cattle and sheep. Pollen analysis shows the progressive retreat of the forest. Tumulus influence was felt only later among groups, in the Paris basin (Yonne) and the Midi.

ATLANTIC SMITHS

Where the position was favourable to commerce, both maritime and inland following the rivers, metal-working centres grew up all round the Channel and Atlantic coasts. The new groups are fairly clearly differentiated and in the main they were situated (Savory 1948) at the mouth of the great estuaries of the Seine, Loire and Gironde.

The oldest, the Médoc group, developed about 1500 BC. It has been known since early work by Berchon and Daleau (among others) and recently has been studied afresh (R. Riquet 1959; Riquet and Coffyn 1964). In origin the group is complex. It is possible there were Rhodanian influences at the beginning and R. Riquet has not hesitated to call daggers from Singleyrac and Cissac 'incontestably' Rhodanian. Subsequently, however, the Médoc group was to turn towards the Atlantic and increase its connections with Brittany and Normandy. Its best-known bronze is an elongated flanged axe with straight sides and barely splayed blade. Forty-three hoards, from Pauillac, Saint-Laurent, Saint-Estèphe, Saint-Julien, Vensac, etc., which together have produced over a thousand examplars, attest to the vitality of the Médoc workshops. Gradually the flanged axes were replaced by palstaves, and some of these, decorated with a midrib, are very similar to Breton examples. Bracelets are rare (Le Pouyalet at Pauillac) but their incised, geometric ornament recalls a type which is equally well known in Armorica (Bignan) and in the Rhône valley (Vernaison).

Apart from bronze hoards Riquet has noted the sporadic occurrence of excised pottery on sites round the edges of the Médoc area, at Vilhonneur and Chenon in Charente and La Roque-Saint-Christophe in the Dordogne. But it is pottery with plastic or cordon orna-mentation that is found on habitation sites. Finally, a new type, a small handled jug with incised chevron decoration from around Sauveterre-la-Guyenne, Gironde (Sireix and Larroque 1967) is reminiscent of Armorican forms from the second Tumulus series.

After the brilliant first phase of the Armorican Tumuli, Brittany reverted to a less luxurious, and doubtless more democratic, way of life. Graves in rectangular cists or vaults, with or without barrows, become far more numerous, though poorer. Metal offerings are reduced to a few triangular daggers, but pottery reappears again. Best known are the biconical urns with four strap-handles. But there is also a great variety of pottery with incised decoration, of chevrons, hatched triangles, zigzags, etc. Even imitation of basketry is found (Lesneven, Finistère). East French excised or 49 stamped ware is unknown.

The earliest of the great Breton hoards, the Tréboul group (Briard 1965) includes flanged axes and unlooped palstaves, together with new forms like the fine bronze-hilted rapiers of Saint-Brandan type. Subsequently production became specialised for the output of palstaves and there are some sixty hoards composed of these alone (Briard 1966). Decoration often consists of a simple midrib. The high tin content of these bronzes may be the result of local exploitation of the tin deposits of the lower Loire, Morbihan and north Finistère. Towards the end of the period, round 1200 BC, massive bronze bracelets were made, with incised geometric decoration (Bignan, Morbihan), a form found in Normandy and equally in the Rhône valley. Habitation sites corresponding to the metallurgists of this phase remain sparse. Defended promontory sites (Trémargat, Ploubazlanec, Côtes-du-Nord) were occupied and Atlantic coastal sites near the Loire, discovered by Dr Tessier, contain abundant finger-impressed pottery (La Rous- 48 sellerie). Recent works on coastal peat-bogs (Plouescat, Finistère) show that sheep was domesticated.

A centre for palstave production grew up round the mouth of the Seine; its material has been published by Coutil, Dubus and Doranlo and more recently by, among others, Edeine and Verron. These palstaves have a wide cutting-edge and decoration is more varied than in Brittany, incorporating chevrons, semicircles and trident patterns. Here again, the hoards often contain as many as a hundred implements. Tumulus influence is indicated by occasional finds of incised or ribbed pins, primarily from dredgings in the Seine. Finds which are quite similar to the Breton and Norman bronzes occur in northern France (Amiens, Abbeville, Bernay).

Manufacture of palstaves spread widely in central France; inventories recently drawn up by Nouel, Cordier and Abauzit show a development of local workshops as far away as the Allier department. The Loire valley was of paramount importance in spreading the knowledge of metal. Regions which previously had known only sporadic imports were drawn into an active participation in bronze culture. From this period hoards in central France become composite, consisting of Atlantic alongside eastern forms.

This development of regional industries did nothing to impede long-distance trade. On the contrary, British products were welcomed, especially in northwestern France where trapeze-butted rapiers and basal-looped spearheads are found. Gold was another object of trade 50 and the famous Tara-Yeovil type torcs, made from a twisted flanged rod often more than a metre long, were despatched from Ireland and England to the Continent, where there are finds at Cesson (Ille-et-Vilaine), Fresné-la-Mer (Calvados), Jaligny-sur-Besbre (Allier) and possibly even at Carcassonne. Not all gold came from the west; the celebrated gold cone from Avanton, Vienne, prompts us to look rather to the east. This embellishment for a shrine, or priestly head-dress, is a distant derivative from certain Phoenician diadems of the early second millennium. It is decorated with concentric circles in repoussé, in a style known elsewhere only in two German analogues, from Franconia and the Palatinate. A bronze palstave associated with the latter (Schifferstadt) seems to indicate a date at the end of the 'Middle Bronze Age', around 1200-1000 BC. There can be only subjective interpretation of the exact purpose of these finds, but there is a suggestion of religious practices utilising costly and sumptuous ornaments.

SOUTH FRENCH CULTURES

The Midi lagged in its use of metal. Sporadic bronze finds are more often imports than local products. Use of flint and bone persisted, as is indicated by a Tumulus-type pin from level III in the Marsa cave (Lot). Modern research has modified the long-postulated idea of a 'retarded Chalcolithic'. The presence of agricultural and pastoral groups has been revealed by a variety of pottery from re-utilised dolmens, barrows and habitation sites and from stratified deposits in caves. Local forms are mixed with Rhône culture and Tumulus elements and more especially with Mediterranean types. Polada ware (named from a north Italian peat-bog) has recently been the subject of various summaries (Arnal and Audibert 1956; Audibert 1957; Guilaine and Abélanet 1966; Courtin 1963). Its Italian origin is no longer in doubt, since the work of Laviosa Zambotti. Its southward expansion has been studied by Maluquer de Motes, and Bernabò Brea has recorded forms in Sicily and the Lipari Islands.

Polada-ware handles carry an appendage or thumb-grip to assist the hold. Early forms are hardly distinguishable from 'beaked' handles, unlike the evolved types with a tongue or knob. More elaborate axe (ad ascia), bifid or even anthropomorphic forms are found in late contexts, contemporary with Urnfield culture. This pottery has a wide chronological, as well as geographic, spread. The Polada ware which occurs in France between Provence and the Pyrenees confirms ethnic exchanges with Spain and Italy. Some associated finds are known. In the Murée cave at Montpezat, Basses-Alpes (Courtin 1963) a Polada cup is associated with a double-riveted dagger and the excised pottery which is common in Midi contexts. Some pots were imported from Tumulus centres (Le Salpêtre, Gard; La

Couronne, Bouches-du-Rhône) and others were made locally. The Labeil cave, Hérault (Bousquet 1965) has 5:10 yielded a fine series of them with Polada handles, from a post-Chalcolithic level, and associated with a bronze arrowhead, a bone pin, shell ornaments and basalt querns. The cave of Saint-Vérédème at Sanhilac (Gard) has given its name to a local pottery style in which excised motifs are surrounded by punch-decorated bands (Déchelette 1910). Numerous variants are found in Languedoc and Provence (Tharaux, Gard; Deffends, 5:6-9 Bouches-du-Rhône).

In the southwest there are novel polypod vases, the feet formed by little protuberances. They have been 51 related to central European analogues, and an association with Beaker ware is made even more probable by a polypod Beaker find from the gallery grave of La Halliade (Hautes-Pyrénées). J. Guilaine (1962) has shown that this pottery is of a later date and its presence in some megaliths is due only to re-use. Moreover at Puyo-Hourmanio a polypod vase has a Polada handle. This new-type pottery is the work of a local group whose economy remains at present unknown.

A study of south French pottery reveals complexity in the population living between Provence and the Pyrenees. Polada influence was strong, but even though some classic coffee-pot forms are known, Polada handles are often found on local types of pottery, polypod or Saint-Vérédème, and at times on *Kerbschnitt* ware.

Other archaeological evidence, metal goods or sites, is often disappointing, apart from a few exceptions like the Collier cave near Lestours, Aude (Charles and Guilaine 1963). Associated with bronzes – a rapier point, bracelets and spiral or tubular beads – are blue and green glass beads of Egyptian type and amber beads, including one spacer of the Greek Kakovatos type, an indication of connections with Mycenaean and Egyptian centres, of about 1500 BC.

To the south, the island of Corsica provides illustration of the many particular insular cultures found in the Mediterranean. The Sardinian Nuraghic culture and the *talayots* of the Balearics have long been known; but it is only in recent years that, thanks to the great efforts of R. Grosjean, the tower structures (*torri*) and 'statue-menhirs' of Corsica have been revealed. Filitosa is one 7 of the principal sites of this culture (Grosjean 1961). It is a defended promontory, discovered in 1954, fortified by a surrounding wall of stout splendour, which includes a fine series of re-used Corsican 'statue-menhirs'. 54 These are decorated with weapons, long swords or short daggers with T-shaped pommel, a mode current in the Mediterranean since the days of Crete and Mycenae. These statues derive from earlier menhirs, which gradually evolved towards anthropomorphic forms and became increasingly elaborate. According to Grosjean (1966) they represent hostile warriors killed by the megalithic people of Corsica, who set them up round their tombs as a memento of their victory. Who were these warriors? The strange kinship of the 'statue-menhirs' with some Egyptian bas-reliefs (Medinet-Habu) leads Grosjean to recognise them as Shardana,

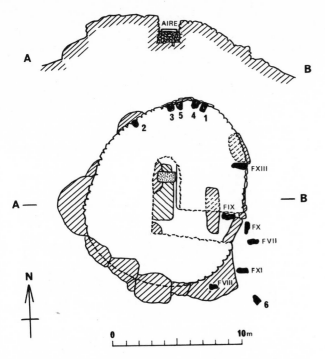

7 Plan of the central monument at Filitosa, Corsica (after Grosjean)

the Sea-People who terrorised Egypt about 1190 BC. Identification of the 'statue-menhirs' as Shardana warriors is suggested by a common use of a horned helmet with neck-guard, strip corselets and fairly similar weapons. The megalithic civilisation of Corsica succumbed to the attacks of these enemies, who had the advantage of metal equipment. The civilisation of the *torri* then took root, destroying the famous 'statue-menhirs' and using them as building material. The *torri* were constructed on elevated sites, hill-tops or promontories, and sometimes dominated a village of circular huts (Filitosa). They are built with a narrow corridor leading to a central corbelled chamber, either simple or with crescent-shaped annexes. Outside, the tower is surrounded by a circular berm, 2-3 m. in diameter (Foce). The smallness of the chambers forbids an interpretation of them as refuges or lordly castles. A cult function is probable, and inside the towers there are querns, traces of fire, bones of cattle and even humans, the remains of sacrificial burials. While pottery recalls certain pre-Nuraghic forms, metal is rare.

Archaeological correlations and radiocarbon readings date the apogee of *torri* culture around 1400-1200 BC.

Transition and change (1200-1000 BC)

Between 1500 and 1200 BC France gives the impression of a certain stability which favoured the flourishing of regional cultures and the development of a thriving industry. Tumulus culture prospered in eastern France and the products of Atlantic workshops for flanged axes and palstaves were widely exported, giving rise to secondary workshops in central France. The Midi was less forward in developing metallurgy and remained in a pastoral or agricultural phase, although there were some advances in pottery. About 1200 BC this relative stability was disturbed, as is indicated by new weapons and pottery which appear among the traditional forms. Their incidence may be ascribed to fresh migrations which are related more or less directly to events of serious import taking place around this time in the eastern Mediterranean, namely the activity of the 'Sea-Peoples' in Egypt, the end of Mycenaean civilisation and the fall of the Hittite Empire. These complex phenomena caused a wave of unrest to sweep through Europe, leading to the rise of what is termed Urnfield culture. This was long neglected by French prehistorians, but the considerable research progress of recent years has brought us far from the Lausitz label applied to its pottery since the time of Déchelette (1910).

TRANSITIONAL GROUPS

The most significant group grew up in the upper Seine valley (Courtois' Aube-Seine-Yonne group).

A variety of graves has been found: a large tumulus over a central vault at La Combe-Bernard at Magny-Lambert (Côte-d'Or); inhumation cemeteries at Veuxhaulles, Vinets or La Colombine (Côte-d'Or); urn cremations at Saint-Gervais, Auxerre, and at Monéteau (Yonne).

The material is best illustrated from La Colombine cemetery at Champlay (Yonne), which has been excellently published, from the excavation notes of G. Bolnet, by A. Lacroix (1957). Some hundred flat graves, oriented east-west, were either dug or destroyed by vandals. The finest burial was of a woman, a princess of high rank, showing there was no prejudice against women in this regard. She was wearing ornaments of bronze: earrings, necklace, bracelets and magnificent spiral anklets. The bronze tubes, buttons and glass beads no doubt decorated her dress. By one of her femurs had been laid a boar's tusk in a bronze mount with repoussé decora- *8* tion and encircled with spiral wire. The anklets and the decoration of the mount are typically Tumulus. A similar boar's tusk in a bronze mount has been recently described by R. Joffroy (1970) at Barbuise-Courtavant, Aube. Joffroy does not regard it as a diadem, the usual interpretation for La Colombine, but, in view of its position, as a breast or belt ornament. Other graves at La Colombine reveal foreign influences. Among the new bronze types are ribbon bracelets decorated with the St Andrew cross, a very long trumpet-headed pin *9 : 1* (50.7 cm.) with transverse ribbing and daggers which differ from the classic trapeze-butted Tumulus blades in their triangular hafting-plate. There is also a change in the pottery: bowls and jugs are decorated with knobs *9 : 2-3* and wide rilling. A possible influence would be the Bavarian Riegsee group, itself a transitional group (among the *Fremdkulturen* of Holste).

In the Vinets cemetery (Yonne) Tumulus anklets are associated with ribbed pins and triangular-plated daggers. The same pin form occurs in graves at Champs, *9 : 8*

Yonne (Hesse 1962). Occasionally excised *Kerbschnitt* pottery is found with the new types (Guerchy, Yonne; Courtavant, Aube). This increasing mixture of old and new suggests fresh commercial activities, perhaps with some migration, rather than serious invasions.

THE FIRST URNFIELDS

Alongside these mixed graves, in which new influences have been assimilated by the old Tumulus population, some more novel burials correspond to incursions of the 'preliminary Urnfield phase' distinguished by Kimmig (1951).

One of the 'preliminary' groups, which was identified by Kraft and Kimmig, is characterised by a poppy-head pin and is found in Württemberg, in the Rhine valley and in Switzerland. Some of its elements reached eastern *9:4-6* France: Audincourt (Doubs), Royaumeix (Meurthe-et-Moselle) (Millotte 1963). In Alsace there are single finds from Rouffach, Wolfgantzen and from the cremation graves at Bennwihr, where the pin was associated with ribbed bracelets, amber beads and a humped-back knife. This knife, of which the Mels-Rixheim type with a socketed handle is one variant, introduced a form which was to be widely used in Urnfield contexts. Poppy-head pins come from women's graves, while the contemporary men's graves include a new weapon, the Rixheim sword, in which the narrow blade terminates in a triangular hafting-plate: Rixheim, Haut-Rhin; Prépoux,

Yonne; Courtavant, Aube (Sandars 1957). These swords accompany either inhumations or urn cremations. Under an urn holding cremated bones at Wittelsheim, Haut-Rhin, the two pieces of a broken sword had been arranged in a cross. Variants of this rite occur in which weapons or ornaments of the deceased are broken or burned.

Another initial Urnfield group is characterised by a collared pin (Kimmig 1951; Millotte 1963). Possibly the *9:13* form originated in Bavaria, but it spread rapidly in the east and southeast of France. It reached not only the Midi but also central France, as is shown by a recent discovery at Chéry, Cher, where a collared pin appears in a mixed hoard with Atlantic palstaves and eastern sickles. These trading and metalworking peoples give evidence of a certain well-being. Gold ornaments were current, like the little repoussé plaques from Courtavant.

Among new types of tools was a massive form of winged axe. While mainly confined to eastern France it sporadically reached the Atlantic regions, as far as Finistère.

In Brittany a distant reaction to events in eastern France is perceptible in the appearance of hoards, which contain the first razors and hilt-plate rapiers (Rosnoën, *9:9-12* Finistère). But such imports were restricted and Atlantic workshops continued to make an abundance of palstaves.

8   *The La Colombine diadem, Yonne (after Lacroix)*

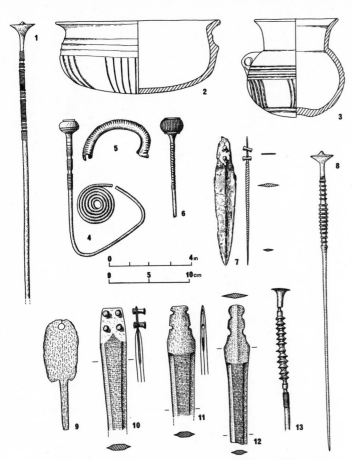

9 *1-3, La Colombine, Yonne, pin and channelled pottery; 4-6, Audincourt, Doubs, pins and bracelet; 7-8, Champs, Yonne, dagger and pin; 9-12, Rosnoën, Finistère, razors and swords; 13, La Salette, Isère, collared pin (1-3, after Lacroix; 4-6, after Kimmig; 7-8, after Hesse; 9-12, after Briard; 13, after Courtois)*

Urnfields and the Atlantic Bronze Age (1100-800 BC)

THE CLASSIC URNFIELDS

By the first millennium Urnfield culture had reached Alsace, Champagne, the Ile-de-France and the Midi, and later it established itself in the south-west. Only Atlantic regions were resistant, despite some reciprocal exchanges.

The ritual practice among the newcomers was individual cremation. The ashes of the dead, burnt on a funeral pyre, were placed in an urn which was buried in an 'Urnfield' cemetery. Details vary from region to region. Sometimes there is inhumation, or a barrow was erected, a heritage from Tumulus culture, making the ceremony more complex. Finally, in a late phase, some groups surrounded the grave with a ditched enclosure. Urnfield origin and chronology remain disputed, and the numerous studies which are in hand show an increasing variety of regional types. W. Kimmig in 1951 proposed a chronology with four divisions, Champs d'Urnes I-IV (CU I-IV). The first (CU I) phase

corresponds to the 'preliminary' groups already mentioned. Phases II and III are the classic Urnfields, and a final phase (CU IV) comprises late groups contemporary with the first iron-using cultures. Kimmig demonstrated the connection of French groups with those across the Rhine. His Swiss-Rhenish group is characterised by globular, biconical urns and conical, sometimes footed, dishes with internal decoration in geometric motifs: festoons, chevrons, arcs and dog-tooth. At a late phase, use of haematite and white encrustation result in polychrome patterns. Kimmig's Main-Swabian group manufactured more elaborate pottery, including two-handled amphorae, biconical or straight-necked urns, deeper or carinated dishes. Decoration is more restrained, with external bosses or fluting in swag pattern. Mixed forms combining the two styles occur on the middle Rhine. Both these and the pure styles recur in France.

In 1957 N. K. Sandars gave an account of French Urnfields and laid stress on pottery with light rilled ornaments. J. P. Millotte (1963) described the diversity of this style, with its first examples as current among German transitional groups (Riegsee) as among French (La Combe-Bernard). At all events this pottery appeared early in the urnfields of central France (Pougues-les- *10:1-3* Eaux) as well as in occupied caves in the Jura (Courchapon).

10 *Urnfields: 1-3, Courchapon, Doubs; 4-6, Dompierre-sur-Besbre, Allier; 7-8, Orval (Cher) (1-3, after Kimmig; 4-8, after Abauzit)*

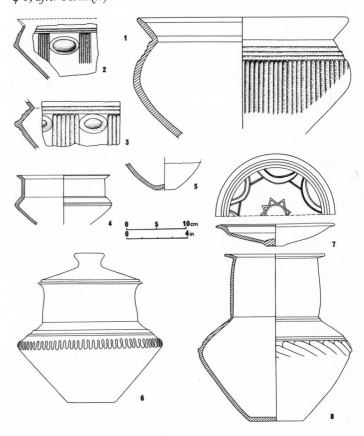

Urnfield elements were occasionally mixed with Tumulus elements. At Oberfeld in Alsace rilled ware was associated in a grave-group with small Haguenau-type jugs. But the first urnfields are already evidence of the arrival of new people. A new group in central France was summarised by Abauzit in 1962 and recently there have been further discoveries (Abauzit and Vannier 1966). The cemeteries are composed either of cremations (Dompierre-sur-Besbre, Allier; Orval, Cher) or of combined cremations and inhumations (La Ferté-Hauterive, Allier; Pougues-les-Eaux, Nièvre). At Orval the burial urns were accompanied by small pots with offerings. There had been analogous forms to the upright necks in eastern France (Sassenay). As covers for the urns there were dishes of a distinctive form (Dompierre) or in Rheno-Swiss style with swag ornament (Orval). Judging from the fluted decoration and bosses, the central French group began in an early phase (CU II), though more evolved forms (Orval) are dated by Abauzit to the beginning of the eleventh century. The cemeteries of central France illustrate the progress of invasion westwards. The Loire and its tributaries played an important part in this penetration, as witnessed by urns in the Loiret and Touraine, at Aulnay-la-Rivière, Martroy-de-Feyrolles or Chissay in the Touraine (Cordier 1961). Possibly it was by this route that west-central France was reached (Rancogne, Bois-du-Roc en Vilhonneur, Charente). Among early urnfields Miss Sandars (1957) draws attention to burials in Alsace (Achenheim and Lingolsheim) which are very similar to finds across the Rhine, and she identifies two distinctive French groups, the Sassenay and the Chambertrand. The Sassenay group is characterised by large biconical urns with carinated body and straight, cylindrical neck, decorated with marked horizontal fluting. It is represented in the urnfields of Granges and Sassenay (Saône-et-Loire) and among the tumuli of Saint-Bernard (Ain). Possibly it originated in migration from southern Baden. The presence of similar pottery in central French urnfields (Pougues) could be attributable to peaceful commercial relations (Millotte 1963).

Miss Sandar's Champbertrand group is concentrated in the cemeteries of Champagne, Burgundy and lower Lorraine; it is closely related to Rhenish material. On the Plaine de Champbertrand (Yonne) a carinated dish of Main-Swabian type is decorated in the Rhine-Swiss festoon style. Associated bronzes include the 'Urnfield' pin with large globular head with stem ribbing below, arched-back knives and heavy palstaves of Rhenish form. But the group's best known and most striking cemeteries are at Aulnay-aux-Planches, Marne (Brisson and Hatt 1953), which run from the earliest Urnfield to Iron Age times. The oldest burials (tombs A-Z) are a series of flat-grave cremations, with urns or pits which are sometimes lined with small stones. Nearby, there is suggested evidence of sacrifice in hearths containing animal bones, hollowed out of the chalk. Grave-goods include tanged knives with geometric decoration on the back, biconical urns with upright or inverted neck, incised or fluted, and carinated dishes decorated in

Rhenish style with concentric arcs. Adjacent to the burials Brisson and Hatt (1967) have excavated some hut-footings or cavities hollowed out of the chalk, with oblique post-holes for a sloping roof. Most of the huts belong in a latter period. J.-J. Hatt considers that the initial phase at Aulnay corresponds to the arrival, c. 1000 BC, of a limited number of people still practising transhumance. True settlement, which corresponds to the main concentration of huts, followed c. 750 BC, with the arrival of newcomers, who merged with the local population.

Other settlement sites in the Paris basin show new populations becoming established, notably at Fort-Harrouard and Videlles (Bailloud 1958).

The later Urnfield phase (CU III) saw developments in the old cemeteries of central and eastern France (Aulnay-aux-Planches). There was evolution in pottery forms: a narrowing of the urn-necks, and hollow-footed dishes. Polychrome decoration appears. Fluting persists in its various forms, at times to outline the handle. The number of decorative motifs increases: dot-and-circle, angular and complex patterns, and, at the very end of the period, Greek designs and sometimes excision, under Hallstatt influence. In the latest phase in Champagne the urn is protected by a funerary enclosure. Brisson and Hatt (1953) have excavated many examples of this in the Aulnay-aux-Planches cemeteries and it is a practice found in variant forms in Belgian urnfields. At Courtavant, R. Joffroy discovered adjacent, double enclosures, one encircling the urn and the other empty, in accordance with a rite it is difficult to interpret. In Champagne, further excavations are being undertaken (B. Chertier) which will furnish additional material for the Urnfield studies.

New Urnfield groups grew up in the Alpine lake areas. Miss Sandars (1957) noted connections between French sites (Lac du Bourget) and the material at

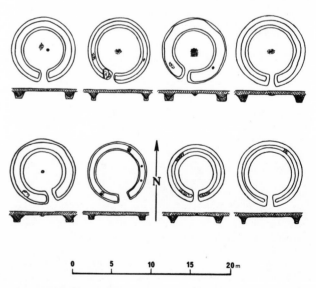

11 *Aulnay-aux-Planches, Marne. Ring-ditch graves (after Brisson and Hatt)*

Singen, near Constance, or from Gündlingen in Baden. Pottery includes bowls, jars and cups, often with a narrowed neck. Decoration is in a late style: concentric circles, stamping, chequering or even Greek motifs, in addition to fluting.

In these and in higher Alpine regions (Courtois 1960) there was intense metallurgical activity, producing the finest of Urnfield bronzes. Bronze-hilted (Auvernier or Mörigen), as well as antennae, swords replaced the tanged (Rixheim) or hook-tang (Pépinville) types still in use during CU II. Pins are very common, and show a predilection for vase-headed or crooked forms, or for a hollow globular head, sometimes inlaid with stone or amber. Winged axes were made in quantity, and sickles (Briod, Jura) reflect the agricultural activity of Urnfield folk. There are numerous pendants, belts and harness-pieces. Armour was improved, with helmets and cuirasses for the warrior. The first cult-waggons came into use and the most famous, from Côte-Saint-André (Isère), has four wheels carrying a bronze situla and bowl (Chapotat 1962). The situla is possibly Hallstattian, but the casting of bronze wheels is established as an Urnfield invention. A further discovery in the Midi, although unassociated, expands the evidence for the beliefs and practices of the time. A slab, or funerary stele, from Substantion (Hérault) shows a warrior surrounded by his accoutrements: chariot wheels, notched shield, spearhead and possibly swan protomes, symbolising the soul (Soutou 1962). This stele belongs in the Iberian group (Gerona).

There was early Urnfield penetration into the Midi where numerous caves have their 'Late Bronze' layers with fluted or bossed pottery and sometimes dishes in pure Rhenish style (Grotte des Chats at Saint-Martin, Ardèche; Grotte de Clapade at Millau, Aveyron). Italian influence is still strong (with *ad ascia* or bifid handles: Châteauneuf-de-Grasse, Alpes-Maritimes).

57

61:2-5

61:1

58

12

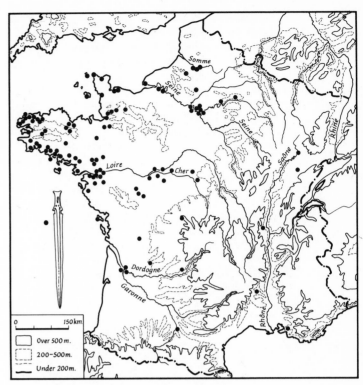

13 Distribution map of carp's-tongue swords

THE ATLANTIC BRONZE AGE

The idea of an Atlantic Bronze Age, popular wth Spanish authors (Almagro, Santa-Olalla) was taken up by H. N. Savory (1948). Kimmig (1951) demonstrated the existence of Urnfield hoards, other 'Atlantic' ones, and a mixed group combining the two series geographically between them. Riquet (1959) emphasised the local variations throughout the Atlantic zone. N. K. Sandars (1957) sought to examine Urnfield influence in the west. It is attested in Charente, Dordogne (Roque-Saint-Christophe) and even in Normandy, but Brittany was more resistant.

The Atlantic Bronze Age is known from its large hoards, some of which are contemporary with early iron-using cultures (Vénat). The beginning of the first millennium saw the manufacture of the first swords with the blade widened (leaf-shaped) for slashing. They were inspired by Rhenish prototypes (Erbenheim), some examples of which have been dredged from the Loire at Nantes. Soon, however, the Atlantic bronzesmiths were making a series of distinctive swords with a flat tang which required organic hilt-plates (the Loire type or Saint-Brieuc-des-Iffs in Brittany, Saint-Denis-de-Pile in Gironde). The 'ricasso' became progressively marked, to protect the grip from a sword cut, and this led to the 'carp's-tongue' sword, so called because of its tapering *61:7* point. The 'carp's-tongue complex' has been well *13* known since the work of E. Evans (Savory 1948; Briard 1965). Typically it includes 'hog-backed' razors, 'bugle-shaped objects' or horse-bits, bifid razors, etc. *61:8-11* These types are found again, in variant forms, in south-

12 Engraved stele from Substantion (Hérault) (after Soutou)

eastern England (Beachy Head) and in Spain (Huelva). In France the complex is well represented between the Somme and the Vendée (Challans), though in Gironde the archaic types of Saint-Denis-de-Pile persisted. The Atlantic community revealed in the hoards was the result of common commercial contacts (Burgess 1969), population exchange and exploitation in this period of tin and lead resources in Cornwall and Brittany. It is in fact from this time that alloys are found to contain increasingly more lead, which facilitated metal-casting and perhaps supplemented supplies of tin and copper, which were quickly used up.

Influence from the east is evident in the change-over to winged axes and in the occasional use of vase-headed pins (Morbihan) or bronze-hilted swords (Déville-lès-Rouen). Mixed hoards are well represented in north-eastern France and in the Loire valley (Azay-le-Rideau).

Into a fresh era: the change from bronze to iron (800-600 BC)

LATE BRONZE-WORKING

From the eighth century Europe once again experienced incursions of new peoples, with the birth of Hallstatt culture following the movements of more remote mounted horsemen. But the greatest innovation was technical, the development of a new metallurgy. This proved a godsend to those who made use of the new products and to those who controlled the superior ores; but it spelled economic catastrophe for those whose prosperity had been centred on commerce in copper, tin and manufactured bronze. Trade routes were gravely disrupted and the Atlantic world was hard hit by the change.

60 In Brittany and the Channel regions an excessive specialisation resulted in the mass production of thousands of square-socketed axes (Armorican type: Briard 1965). At the start, commerce in them was remarkably successful and, in spite of some dubious specimens, it is certain that the traffic reached Great Britain, Germany and possibly even Poland. Some have interpreted them as a primitive sort of money, but use as simple metal ingots is equally possible. The quality of the alloys became more and more indifferent, which possibly explains the enormous stocks of thousands of axes still discovered today (Loudéac, Côtes-du-Nord; Le Tréhou, Finistère). Radiocarbon dates (550 BC) and associations (embossed bracelets) alike show that socketed axes were still used in Brittany at the time when late Hallstatt tombs of Boquidet type were being built. These small tumuli, ringed round with dry-stone walling, cover burial pottery of metallic form or even actual situlae, which according to W. Kimmig are Rhenish in origin.

61:13-15 A further late complex is the well-known 'Launacian' of the Midi. It was Déchelette who first defined this bronze industry, contemporary with iron-using cultures. The group of hoards in Hérault (La-Croix-de-Mus, Launac), Aude (Carcassonne, Durban) and Tarn (Briatexte, Vielmur) has outliers towards the Massif Central (Saint-Pierre-Eynac) and the Pyrenees (Le Peyré,

Ariège) (Soutou and Arnal 1963; Millotte 1963). Typical forms are conical spear butts, unperforated triangular razors and various types of socketed axe, in association with objects of Hallstattian inspiration: semicircular razors, earrings, incised or embossed bracelets. The 'Launacian' is often dated to the earlier Hallstatt period (seventh century) but Soutou does not hesitate to put it later, at the beginning of La Tène.

THE LATE URNFIELD OF LANGUEDOC
AND ROUSSILLON

Many of the previous period's urnfields remained in use in the lake regions (Le Bourget) and in the north-east (Aulnay-aux-Planches). In the eighth century Languedoc and Roussillon were reached and the movement crossed the Pyrenees into Catalonia.

One of the main sites is at Mailhac (Aude). The urnfields, patiently excavated by O. and J. Taffanel (Louis and Taffanel 1960), are situated at a short distance from the Le Cayla *oppidum*, which was occupied during this period. The oldest cemetery (750-700 BC) is Le Moulin (Mailhac I). Comparable material is known at Las Fados at Pépieux (Aude) and Las Canals at Millas (Pyrénées-Orientales: Sandars 1957). At Le Moulin shallow pits contained the urn and offerings: pots, ornaments, toilet articles and joints of meat. The pit was closed by a flat stone, with small stones heaped on it. The pottery recalls Bourget forms, though urn 104 is a distant derivative from the straight-necked Sassenay style. There is great variety in the bronzes. The pins (vase-, crook- and wheel-headed) can be matched in the east French lakes. Rectangular razors and a double-spring fibula are Italian. Lunate and perforated razors derive by exchange from the Hallstattian peoples who were occupying the *garrigue* to the north. Decoration on the pottery from Le Moulin, Le Cayla and Millas I is based on the meander and on highly stylised anthropomorphic or animal (horse) representations. The habitation site of Le Cayla 1 shows a large village with wooden houses. Agriculture and stock-raising (pig, sheep, cattle and horse) were practised, and wolf, boar and deer were hunted. Later, the Grand Bassin I (Mailhac II) cemetery saw the evolution of pottery with a developed foot, carinated dishes, two-handled amphorae and a greater abundance of iron, which came into common use. Soon afterwards the first imports of Phocean or Iberian ware provide valuable synchronisms. Near Le Grand Bassin the grave of a cavalier chieftain at La Redorte contained 58 accessory vases with the urn, together with damaged bronze and iron ferrules from a chariot or cart and parts of harness for two horses. Thraco-Cimmerian bit-pieces indicate a central European origin, and the nearest analogues are probably in Baden (Sandars 1957). Part of the urnfield at Arcachon dates from this period, corresponding to phases 2 and 3 of Taffanel, as do the first cemeteries of the Tarbes region studies recently by J. P. Mahon.

THE FIRST HALLSTATT CULTURE
The Hallstatt herdsmen and warriors from north of the

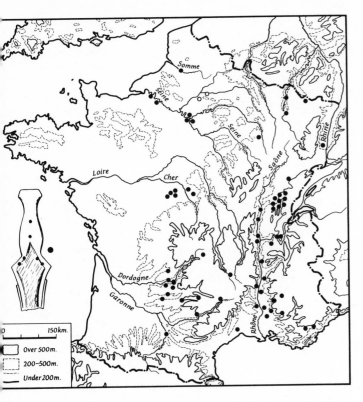

14 *Distribution map of bronze Hallstatt swords (after Déchelette, Cowen and Soutou)*

Alps introduced into France a knowledge of iron-working. The rite of inhumation under a barrow which had earlier been prevalent in the Tumulus culture was resuscitated, and an excised pottery style recalls *Kerbschnitt*. These reversions are associated with imports of pottery and new metal types (iron fibulae, situlae, etc.).

New settlement in different regions resulted in locally divergent groups, though in each the same rites and common material are found. In the early phase (800-700 BC) swords are of bronze, with a flat tang and a trapezoidal pommel-piece (the Gündlingen type: Cowen 1967). These are abundant in France, in the Jura, the Rhône valley, the Massif Central and in central France. Western examples are often questionable. The sword is already associated with classic Hallstattian types: excised pottery and lunate or perforated razors. The large winged chapes have been interpreted as part of a horseman's equipment, to facilitate drawing the sword. There are no known French examples of the very long bronze sword (Cowen's Mindelheim type), though its iron counterpart is the classic *'grande épée de fer'* of French archaeologists (Millotte 1963).

Some regions were rapidly and thoroughly occupied, with numerous Hallstattian tumuli and utilisation of old barrows. In the Jura large numbers of tumuli were hurriedly examined during the last century. J. P. Millotte (1963) has described some grave-groups which

include a long iron sword, from La Combe d'Ain, Barésia and Bucey-lès-Gy. Some massive rings ornamented with incision or grooving, alternating with plain zones, could have come from Bavaria. Lunate razors (Gevingey) and typical chapes are rare.

Finds from Lorraine belong to various groups, which differ in origin. In the Argonne spherical pots suggest a relationship with Belgium (Court-Saint-Etienne), while in the Meurthe-et-Moselle the Clayeures mounds contain iron swords and ribbed bracelets of Bavarian type (Millotte 1963).

The classic Burgundian group was the most thriving (Henry 1933). Some thirty tumuli have been excavated in the Côte-d'Or. One of the finest is the Magny-Lambert barrow (Joffroy 1954), 40 m. in diameter and

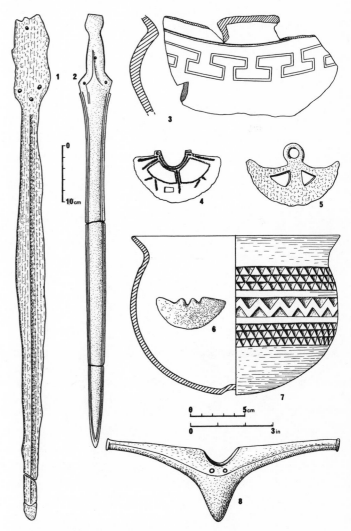

15 *Hallstatt culture : 1, 3-4, Prusly-sur-Ource, Côte-d'Or, iron sword, pottery and razor ; 2, 8, Cazevielle, Hérault, bronze sword and chape ; 5, Monceau-Laurent, Côte-d'Or, bronze razor ; 6-7, Ravin-des-Arcs, Notre-Dame-de-Londres, Hérault, razor and excised pottery (1-5, after Joffroy ; 2, 6-8, after Audibert)*

155

5.90 m. high. It is made of corbelled stones enclosed in a layer of clay which was then covered by an arrangement of stones. It contains secondary burials and a central Hallstattian inhumation. This warrior had been provided with a service of bronze vessels, including a ribbed *cista* which can match the finest examples at Hallstatt itself. To his right had been laid a metre-long sword with bronze rivets. On the other side of the head lay a classic razor of perforated bronze. In other Burgundian tumuli a lunate or circular razor is almost always associated with a long iron sword. Pottery is represented by burnished black bowls, sometimes deco- *15:3* rated with Greek motifs (Bois de Langres at Prusly-sur-Ource, Côte-d'Or).

Bronze Hallstatt swords are known throughout the Rhône valley, but primarily they are indications of a route through it, as Hallstatt settlement sites show a preference for the upland *garrigues* of Languedoc or the edges of the Massif Central. There are great differences in the richness of the graves. In one of the barrows at Cazevielle (Hérault) a warrior buried in a flexed position was equipped with a classic bronze sword and chape, *15:2, 8* together with flaring cups of local style. Lunate razors are common, as is excised or stamped pottery (Ravin *15:6-7* des Arcs at Notre-Dame-de-Londres). Local daggers with three rivets are known from Saint-Jean-de-la-Blaquière and from Argelliers, a re-utilised dolmen which also yielded a clay nozzle, evidence for local metallurgy (Audibert 1963).

Although it covered two-thirds of France, the spread of Hallstatt culture was blocked by certain groups, namely the Languedocian urnfield people and the bronze-workers of Brittany. The richness of the earliest iron-using cultures varied from region to region; but the well known prosperity of some groups, like that in Burgundy, already anticipates the magnificent princely tombs which were to monopolise trade in the finest products from Greek workshops.

6

From 600 BC to the
Roman Conquest

F. R. HODSON
R. M. ROWLETT

'In the times of Tarquin the king, youthful Phocaeans from Asia reached the mouth of the Tiber and made friendly alliance with the Romans; then, leaving with their vessels for most distant shores of Gaul, they founded Massalia among the Ligurian and savage Gallic tribes' (Justinus 43, 3).

For the sixth century BC onwards, literary accounts, like this, provide a new dimension to the study of pre-Roman France. Peoples and personalities start to be named and precise dates are sometimes given. However, at first this historical account is scanty, sometimes contradictory and is specific only for the civilised Mediterranean powers. Native peoples, Ligurians and Celts are named, but not seriously distinguished. Until the Roman conquest, the prime evidence for these 'barbarians' remains archaeological and their grouping and development has still to be discussed in archaeological terms.

The evidence on which this archaeological reconstruction must be based is at present very one-sided. The European Iron Age was a time of outstanding craftsmanship, and until recently Iron Age studies have concentrated on the *objets d'art* that this skill produced, with the result that cemeteries and settlements have tended to be investigated mainly as a source for fine objects. The information that may be extracted through a careful study of the nature, distribution and associations of these *objets d'art* must not be underestimated: they can provide an essential framework of reference both chronological and 'cultural' within which the period as a whole may be studied; they also point to the major centres of wealth, industry and art, and to influences and contact between these centres. Much of this chapter will inevitably be concerned with inferences of this kind. Other more basic kinds of information about

1 Sites mentioned in the text

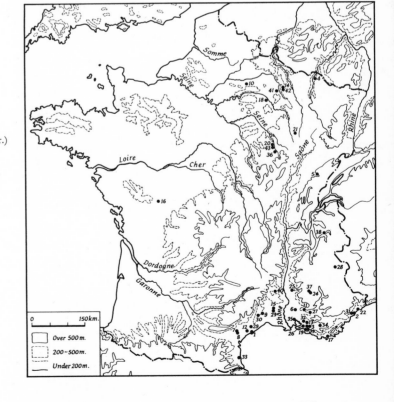

1	Agde (Hérault)
2	Antibes, *Antipolis* (Alpes-Mar.)
3	Baou-Roux (Bouches-du-Rhône)
4	Basse-Yutz (Moselle)
5	Camp de Château (Jura)
6	Cavaillon (Vaucluse)
7	Cayla du Frouzet (Hérault)
8	Cayla de Mailhac (Aude)
9	Cazevieille (Hérault)
10	Chassemy (Aisne)
11	Cucuron (Vaucluse)
12	Ensérune (Hérault)
13	Entremont (Bouches-du-Rhône)
14	La Gorge-Meillet (Marne)
15	Grézan (Gard)
16	Gros-Guignon (Vienne)
17	Hyères, *Olbia* (Var)
18	Les Jogasses (Marne)
19	Marseilles *Massalia* (Bouches-du-Rhône)
20	Mont Lassois (Côte-d'Or)
21	La Motte-St-Valentin (Haute-Marne)
22	Nice, *Nicaea* (Alpes-Mar.)
23	Nîmes (Gard)
24	Orpière (Hautes-Alpes)
25	Le Pègue (Drôme)
26	Les Pennes (Bouches-du-Rhône)
27	Pertuis (Vaucluse)
28	Peyre-Haute (Hautes-Alpes)
29	Pézenas (Hérault)
30	La Roque (Hérault)
31	Roquefort (Alpes-Mar.)
32	Roquepertuse (Bouches-du-Rhône)
33	Ruscino (Pyr.-Or.)
34	Sainte-Baume (Bouches-du-Rhône)
35	Saint-Blaise (Bouches-du-Rhône)
36	Sainte-Colombe (Côte-d'Or)
37	Sainte-Colombe (Hautes-Alpes)
38	Saint-Jean-de-Belleville (Savoie)
39	Saint-Marcel (Bouches-du-Rhône)
40	Saint-Remèze (Ardèche)
41	Sept-Saulx (Marne)
42	Somme-Bionne (Marne)
43	Vix (Côte-d'Or)

general subsistence and social organisation can only be obtained by the detailed investigation of the layout of sites and their content, organic and inorganic. Such evidence is being actively sought, but is not yet available for much of Europe, and these major aspects can scarcely be touched on in the following account.

In a well-known passage, Justinus (43, 4) referred to the effects of the Greek colonisation of southern France in euphoric terms: to judge by appearances, Gaul had not so much been colonised as transported to Greece! This may seem to us a romantic exaggeration written long after the event (in the third century A D), and yet any discussion of the later Iron Age in France must start with the Greek colony of Massalia (Latin *Massilia*). It will also be convenient to discuss native cultures of Gaul in two main groups that to a certain extent reflect their involvement with the colonists: first, groups along the Mediterranean coast that felt the full impact of the Greek presence (typified for the sixth century B C by sites like Cayla de Mailhac near Narbonne and, later, by Ensérune and Entremont to the west and east of the Rhône respectively); second, groups farther inland, economically involved with the Mediterranean but following a more Alpine, continental sequence of development, first 'Hallstatt' and subsequently 'La Tène'.

Massalia:
the literary and archaeological evidence

Literary accounts relate how Greek adventurers from the Ionian cities of Asia Minor had explored the western limits of the Mediterranean by the late seventh century B C. About 600 B C, one of these city states, Phocaea, actually founded a colony of citizens, Massalia, on the site of present-day Marseilles (Clerc 1927; Villard 1960; Morel 1966). Although in regular conflict with Carthage at this time, Massalia held her own, and her early prosperity is reflected by the rich votive treasury she dedicated in 525 B C at the Greek Sanctuary of Delphi. Historians were silent about Massalia's fortunes during the fifth century B C, but it is generally assumed that the settlement became less prosperous and lost ground in the west to Carthage.

Although apparently friendly at first, natives of the hinterland soon became a constant threat. At the time that Rome fell to Celtic marauders in 390 B C, Massalia was also beleaguered, but seems to have come to some more sensible – though no doubt costly – arrangement with them. The traditional, classical account claims that the Celtic leader, Catumandus, was pacified at the critical moment by the vision of a Greek goddess. At all events, by the end of the fourth century B C Massalia was again in a strong economic position, and was able to establish a chain of sub-colonies along the coast towards Italy. Her seafarers were legendary at this time, and Pytheas, one of them, is reported to have circumnavigated Britain.

Massalia supported Rome against Carthage in the Second Punic War and, as Rome's power increased, gradually came to rely upon the latter as an ally. In the second century B C, she was forced to appeal to Rome to protect her against 'Celto-Ligurians' who seemed likely to destroy her. The Romans arrived in force, defeated the native tribes near Aix in 123 B C and annexed the coastal strip of southern France with the lower Rhône valley to form a new province. Massalia remained an autonomous Greek city, but real political and economic control in the area now passed to Rome.

The recorded history leaves many important questions about Massalia to be answered by supplementary archaeological evidence. The nature of the trade which was her real reason for existence and its success at different periods; the extent, if any, of her inland territory at different times; the status of other colonies like Agde at the other side of the delta: about these subjects the writers say virtually nothing.

Archaeological finds from Marseilles itself have been rather disappointing so far, although recent large-scale excavations on the site of the Bourse could remedy this. Virtually the only architectural evidence from the earliest Greek city is an Ionic capital found re-used in a Roman structure. But this is at least enough to attest monumental architecture at Massalia before the end of the sixth century B C. Architectural remains *in situ* (of a theatre, dock and walls) seem to date from the Hellenistic and Roman periods (Euzennat and Salviat 1968).

Occupation debris of the early colony has been found from time to time during building operations near the Vieux-Port, and the fine pottery from these deposits has been studied in detail by Villard (1960) and Benoît (1965a). This is made up of imports from Greece and from Greek and Etruscan workshops in Italy, imports from Ionian Greece (Asia Minor) and wares made locally by Ionian techniques. The finest and most exactly datable of these are imported Attic Black Figure (mainly sixth century) and Red Figure (mainly fifth to fourth century) vases. Villard's count of datable Attic sherds, from a number of scattered deposits, shows a remarkable peak towards the end of the sixth century and a sudden drop in the fifth. Although not so clearly documented, a similar sudden drop in Attic wares seems to occur at other trading sites near the Rhône delta, but not in other west Mediterranean ports in Spain and Italy. Villard suggests that this index of finest Attic imports may be taken as an indication of general trading prosperity in the western Mediterranean at the time, and he deduces a sudden eclipse of Massalian economic fortunes *c.* 500 B C. He adds that the diffusion of Massalian coins for the same period shows a similar rise and fall.

Other categories of imported pottery in the Marseilles deposits cannot be dated as accurately as Attic wares. However, they demonstrate that Etruscan as well as Greek pottery changed hands at Massalia in the early sixth century B C. (An ancient wreck discovered off Antibes has proved to be an Etruscan merchantman of this period.)

Pottery imported from the Greek cities of Asia Minor was made in two main techniques: brownish patterns or zones painted on a cream ground ('Ionian wares') and plain, grey wares with comb-incised, straight or wavy lines (often referred to as 'Phocaean' ware, although the technique was not as localised as this name implies). The techniques for producing Ionian and Phocaean-type wares were introduced into Massalia and the western Mediterranean in general by Greeks and it is often

7:2, 11 difficult to distinguish imported from locally imitated pottery. However, 'Phocaean' seems less widespread than the dark-on-light 'Ionian' and seems confined to workshops along the south French coast, perhaps reaching into northeastern Spain. Another kind of pottery produced locally by generalised east-Mediterranean techniques was a type of large, plain wine amphora with pointed base and large handles at the neck. The local Massalian amphorae of this kind are remarkable for the quantity of mica flakes included in their clay before firing.

The careful study of scattered finds of pottery from early Marseilles is thus most instructive. It shows trade with Italy and the east Mediterranean, intense in the sixth century BC, perhaps less so in the fifth; it indicates that Ionian ceramic technology was transferred to the area, and some of the resulting pottery has been recognised to have a localised Massalian stamp (mica-tempered amphorae, and 'Phocaean' wares). This is in itself of some importance since the diffusion of these wares inland, as far as the Alps and beyond, gives specific evidence of Massalia's special trading role with the north.

The extent of Massalian territory outside the city limits at various periods is a subject of controversy. Coastal sub-colonies were certainly founded in periods of prosperity: Emporion (Ampurias) soon after 600 BC, Olbia (near Hyères), Antipolis (Antibes) and Nicaea (Nice) later, perhaps in the fourth century BC; but the status of some other sites closer to Marseilles is not so definite and it is not certain that Massalia controlled any inland territory at all. This point is of considerable interest for understanding Massalia's economic position: if she owned extensive vineyards and agricultural land she could consume and trade with her own produce. If not, she was uncomfortably dependent on her trading partners. Several near-coastal and inland sites have produced quantities of Greek pottery (Reim 1968). At Saint-Blaise, 40 kilometres northwest of Marseilles, there is even evidence for an active trade in Etruscan and, to a lesser extent, Greek goods in the late seventh century BC before Massalia herself was founded (Rolland 1964). However, imports do not mean that sites were permanently occupied by Greeks (or Etruscans) or that they formed part of a Greek *territory*. Much depends on the relative quantity of Greek versus native material belonging to different periods, but non-Greek material from most relevant sites has not yet been examined and published in detail. Quantities of hand-made pottery and La Tène metalwork from Les Pennes in the outer suburbs of present-day Marseilles show that this strategic site, only about five kilometres from the sea and about fifteen from the main Greek harbour, was a native village (Chaillan 1917). Had there been a Greek territory, it could hardly have extended

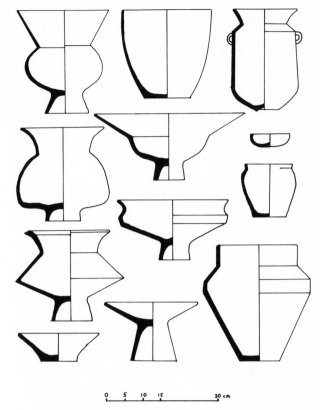

2 *Cayla de Mailhac, Aude: pottery from the Grand Bassin I cemetery. Musée Taffanel, Cayla de Mailhac (after Taffanel and Kimmig)*

this far. For a detailed sequence of 'native' material in southern France contemporary with early Massalia, however, it is necessary to turn to Languedoc and the site of Cayla de Mailhac near Narbonne.

The sixth century BC

NATIVE DEVELOPMENTS IN THE SOUTH
Languedoc
At Cayla, as described in the last chapter, a continuous sequence of development for the Late Bronze Age and Early Iron Age has been worked out from two adjacent sites, an occupied hill-fort and a large cemetery of cremation burials in the plain below it. To recapitulate, the first stage of development, Mailhac I in the useful terminology of Kimmig (1954), is documented by the lowest levels of hill-fort occupation (*Cayla 1*) and by the first nucleus of the cemetery (*Le Moulin*). The culture represented is of Urnfield type with strong west Alpine connections and it had become established at Cayla before the seventh century BC.

A second stage of development, Mailhac II, may be seen from graves radiating outwards at each side of the Moulin nucleus. The Taffanels have named this stage of the cemetery *Grand Bassin I*. So far, no corresponding level of occupation has been found at the Cayla hill-

159

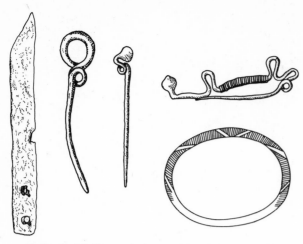

3 Cayla de Mailhac, Aude: metalwork from the Grand Bassin I cemetery. Iron knife; bronze pins, fibula and bracelet. Length of knife 12 cm., the rest to scale. Musée Taffanel, Cayla de Mailhac (after Taffanel and Kimmig)

fort (Louis *et al.* 1958; Taffanel 1962; Taffanel and Taffanel 1962).

Burials of this second stage are still exclusively post-cremation, but they tend to have more offerings than before. Pottery takes a great variety of florid shapes, but it has relatively little decoration, and so is difficult to identify from sherds at settlements. The finest vases are not decorated as previously with scratched or fluted decoration, but with bold, excised and encrusted motifs – a clear borrowing from the seventh-century Hallstatt C tumulus groups established farther inland. More regular ceramic features are wide, flaring mouths, high pedestal feet and an angular, facetted profile to the body – a simplified version of earlier fluting. The most regular shape is a florid cylinder-neck urn, quite close to Mailhac I prototypes, but having a marked similarity with the range of vases found in the near-by Hallstatt C tumuli.

Mailhac II metal objects regularly placed in tombs are simple iron knives and curious serpentiform fibulae of bronze or iron. More exceptional metal finds of this stage are sets of horse trappings (graves 68 and 99), a dipper (grave 68), and a fragmentary antennae dagger (grave 55). The latter and some fibulae with symmetrical springs and raised, button feet are possible prototypes for forms standardised in the next stage (Schüle 1960a, 1961). These metal objects seem to represent a local development of Spanish, Italian and Alpine prototypes. Not even the richest Mailhac II burials include imported pottery and it seems most unlikely that this stage at Cayla extends far, if at all into the sixth century B C.

The next topographical and chronological series of graves, Grand Bassin II, spreads outwards from the existing cemetery. These finds correspond with a second main phase of occupation at the hill-fort, Cayla 2, and define the Mailhac III stage of development (Louis *et al.* 1955, 1960; Taffanel 1962). The burial rite is still inurned cremation and some metal types also show a certain degree of continuity with the previous phase.

Nevertheless, contact with Greeks and Etruscans is clearly documented, and this contact changes a great deal of the material culture of these natives. An imported wine amphora, Greek or Etruscan, is often used as an ossuary, and fine imported cups are placed in graves (Attic Black Figure, Etruscan black bucchero, and 'Phocaean' ware). These firmly date this series of tombs at Cayla to the decades before and after the mid-sixth century B C. So far the beginnings of this phase are not particularly well documented at Cayla, though a rich Urnfield under study at Saint-Julien (near Pézenas) should fully document the transition (Giry 1965). As well as imported, wheel-made pottery, it is clear that a native 'pseudo-Ionian' ceramic industry was producing quantities of 'ochre painted' and grey bucchero wares 5:1-3 by Ionian techniques.

COLOUR PLATES

I The 'Venus' with horn, Laussel.

II Grotte de Cougnac, Lot. Style III. Ibex painted in ochre.

III Ménec alignments, Carnac, Morbihan.

IV Mané-Kerioned passage graves, Carnac, Morbihan.

V Kernonen barrow, Plouvorn, Finistère. Wooden coffin with bronze dagger and flint arrowheads.

VI Kernonen barrow, Plouvorn, Finistère. Bronze dagger decorated with minute gold nails.

VII Basse-Yutz, Lorraine: Early La Tène wine flagon. One of a pair found with two imported bronze wine 'stamnoi'. Bronze with coral and enamel inlay. Maximum height 38.7 cm.

VIII Portrait of Vercingetorix, from the obverse of a gold stater.

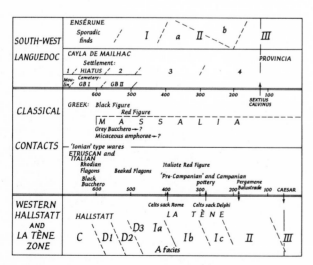

4 Relative and absolute chronology of the Iron Age in France

III

◀ II

IV

V

VIII

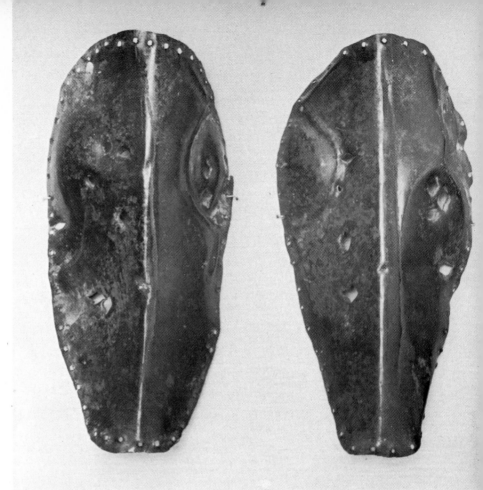

62 Roquefort, Alpes-Maritimes: bronze greaves found with a bronze bracelet and a corroded iron spearhead: perhaps from a cremation burial. Length 31·5 cm.

63 Three-hooked belt buckle in bronze of Mailhac III type. Possibly found near Cannes. Length 9·9 cm.

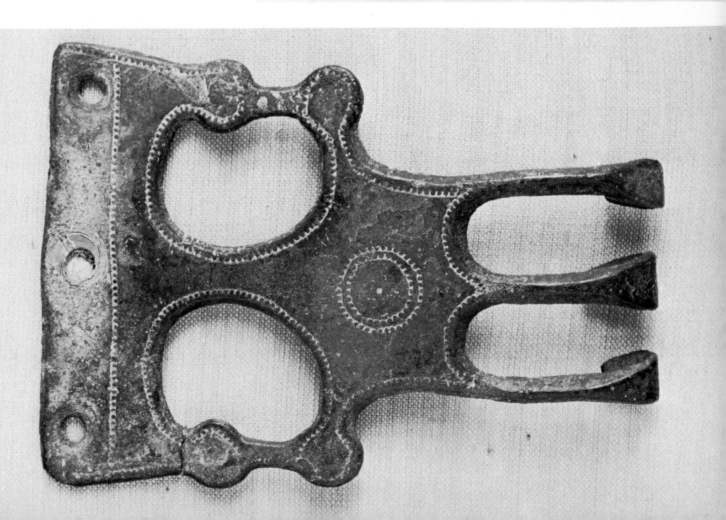

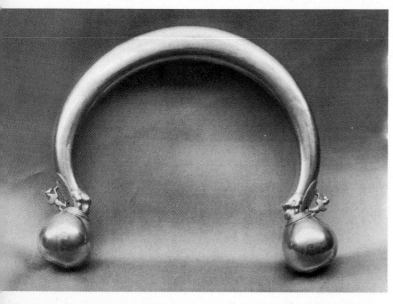

64 The burial at Vix, Côte-d'Or: imported gold collar. Place of manufacture uncertain. Maximum exterior dimension 23 cm.

65 The Vix burial: imported wine flagon of 'beaked' type. Probably made in Etruria in the second half of the sixth century BC. Maximum height, 27·5 cm.

66 Wine flagon of so-called 'Rhodian' type, probably made in Etruria about 600 BC. From a cremation burial beneath a tumulus at Pertuis, Vaucluse.

67 The Vix burial: imported bronze krater of Greek workmanship. Maximum height 164 cm.

67

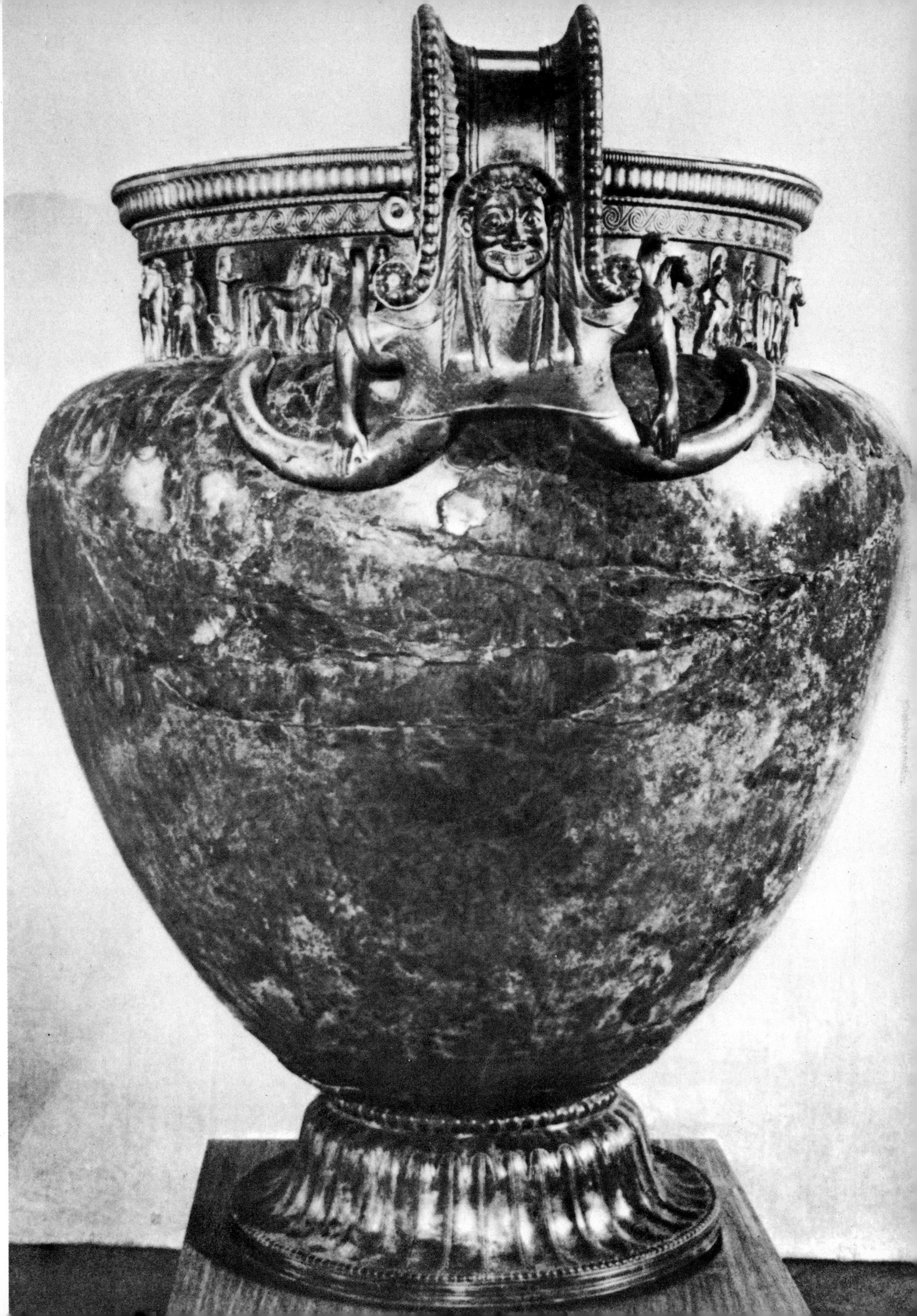

68 The Vix burial: imported Attic cup decorated in the Black Figure style by the 'Wraith Painter' *c*. 525 BC. Diameter 18 cm.

69 Somme-Bionne, Marne: imported Attic cup from a chariot burial; decorated in the Red Figure style, *c*. 415 BC. Diameter 13·2 cm.

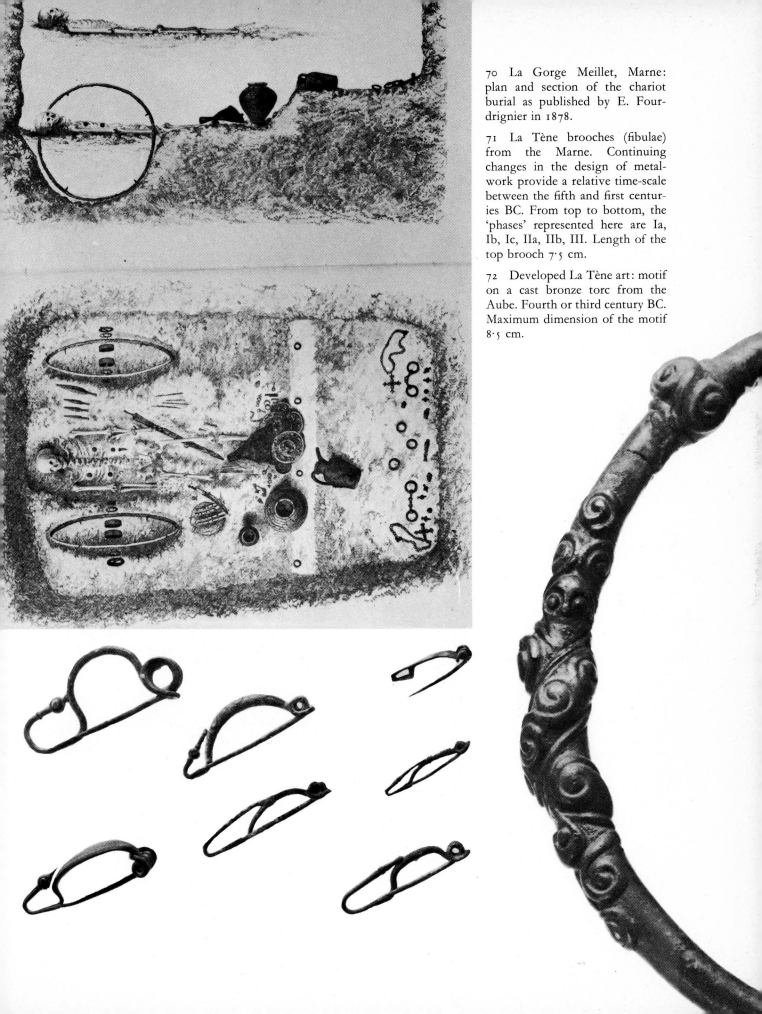

70 La Gorge Meillet, Marne: plan and section of the chariot burial as published by E. Fourdrignier in 1878.

71 La Tène brooches (fibulae) from the Marne. Continuing changes in the design of metalwork provide a relative time-scale between the fifth and first centuries BC. From top to bottom, the 'phases' represented here are Ia, Ib, Ic, IIa, IIb, III. Length of the top brooch 7·5 cm.

72 Developed La Tène art: motif on a cast bronze torc from the Aube. Fourth or third century BC. Maximum dimension of the motif 8·5 cm.

73 Ensérune, Hérault: view of the *oppidum* from the southeast.

74 Marnian pottery: dish from Bergères-les-Vertus with dark grey burnished finish. Rim diameter 170 mm. Vase from Marson; black, burnished finish, with traces of red filling the incisions. Height 15·5 cm.

75 Marnian pottery: pedestal urn (left) from Prosne with black, burnished finish. Height 250 mm. Vase (right) from Bergères-les-Vertus with light red barbotine decoration on a burnished, black ground. Height 12·4 cm.

76 'Combed urn' from Les Pennes (Marseilles): views of side and base. Height 15 cm.

77 Roquepertuse, Bouches-du-Rhône: portico of a sanctuary with 'têtes coupées' pillars and sculpture.

78 Grézan, Nimes, Gard: torso in stone of a warrior with cowl-like helmet, torc, breastplate and belt with hooked buckle. Perhaps fourth century BC. Nimes. Height 70 cm.

77

78

79 Roquepertuse: double head in stone. Height 20 cm.

80 Entremont, Aix-en-Provence, Bouches-du-Rhône: hand with 'tête coupée'. Height 23 cm.

81 Celtic coins. Four gold coins from Gaul imitating staters of Philip II of Macedonia. The Greek inscription, ΦΙΛΙΠΠΟΣ, copied closely on the first and third coins, has disintegrated on the other two. Diameter of top coin 1·9 cm.

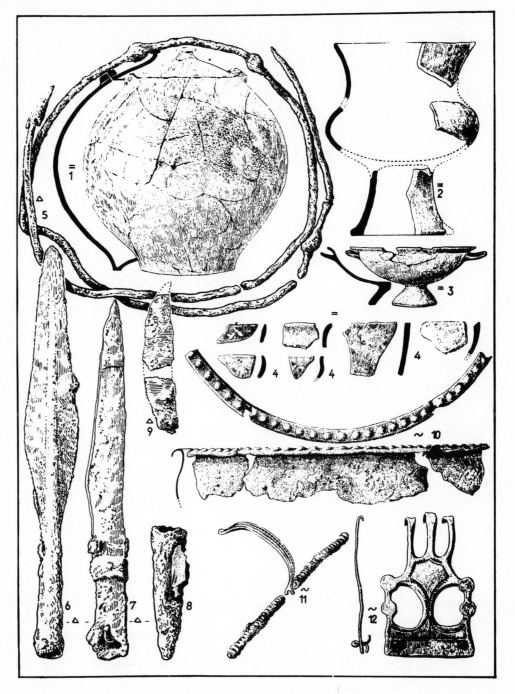

5 Cayla de Mailhac, Aude : cremation grave 14 from the Grand Bassin II cemetery. 1-3, local, wheel-made pottery; 5, iron shafted spearhead bent to encircle the ossuary; 4, sherds of Attic black glazed ware; 6 and 8, iron spearhead and butt; 7 and 9, iron knives; 10, fragments of bronze bowl with beaded rim; 11, fragments of bronze fibula of cross-bow form; 12, bronze three-hooked belt-buckle. Drawn to two scales: the ossuary and its lid (1) 18.4 cm. high; 2-3 and 5 to the same scale; the buckle (12) 9.4 cm. long; 4, 6-11 to the same scale. Musée Taffanel, Cayla de Mailhac (after Taffanel and Schüle)

The most regular and characteristic bronze objects of this Mailhac III phase are belt-hooks with a distinctive waisted shape and one to three hooks, and cross-bow fibulae with extremely long springs and with raised, button feet. Iron weapons are now regular: antennae daggers, and spearheads that are sometimes iron-shafted. This assemblage of metalwork is found in northeastern Spain as well as the Cayla area at this time (Schüle 1961; Vilaseca 1963), and in both areas it seems to be an integral part of Urnfield development on an ultimately Mailhac I type of background.

The most informative burial of this phase at Cayla was not found in the main cemetery but at Corno-Lauzo near by (Taffanel and Taffanel 1960). Alongside regular grave goods like those just mentioned, this burial produced sheet metalwork badly damaged by the pyre but probably including a bucket and pieces of armour. An imported Attic Black Figure cup dates from about 540 BC.

This series of finds from Cayla and near-by sites provides a detailed material sequence for the area, but its interpretation is not entirely straightforward. Taking

63
5 : 12
5 : 11

5 : 5

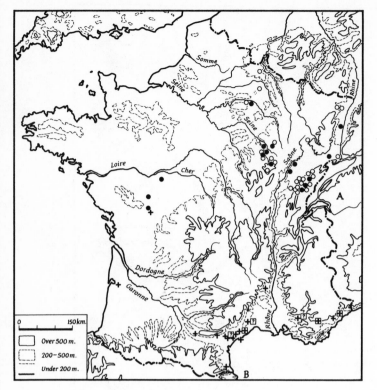

- ● Burials with vehicles

- ○ Double-bossed brooches (see fig. 8:2)

- + Hooked belt-fasteners of constricted form, with one to three hooks (see pl. 63)

- ⊞ Bronze greaves (see pl. 62)

- ⍰ Possible remains of bronze armour from cremation burials

6 Some native features of the sixth century BC

into account contemporary evidence from Catalonia such as that from Urnfield burials near the colonial site of Emporion (Almagro 1955), the simplest hypothesis is probably to see one basic Urnfield culture developing in the coastal zone between the rivers Ebro and Hérault. During the Mailhac I and III phases, the whole of this zone shows roughly the same material features. However, during an intermediate stage (roughly the second half of the seventh century BC) the northern part of this territory is influenced by the Hallstatt C developments which overtook Urnfield cultures more closely in touch with the original Alpine centres. On this view, Mailhac II could be seen as a temporary, local reaction to Hallstatt C influence or infiltration from the Garrigues and Causses; but before the whole of this coastal zone could be affected, suddenly increased contact with Greek and Etruscan traders led to invigoration of the coastal Urnfield groups, and allowed them to halt the process of cultural domination from the north.

Finds from the tumulus cemeteries of Languedoc, like Cazevieille, suggest that this flow was not only halted but reversed. Relatively few tumulus burials in these groups seem to date from the Mailhac III phase, but the richest (Frouzet, Saint-Remèze) have imported pottery, cross-bow fibulae and belt-hooks of Mailhac III type (Louis *et al.* 1960). By the end of the sixth century BC, were it not for their geographical location and their occurrence in tumuli, it would be difficult to separate these few burials culturally from the Mailhac III coastal complex.

Similar Mailhac III metalwork is found to the west in continuing cremation cemeteries in Aquitaine (Fabre 1952; Kimmig 1954).

Native developments in Provence
East of the Rhône, there is no site like Cayla to act as a key to the native groups around Marseilles at the time that the colony was founded. Many near-by hill-fort *oppida* are known to have been occupied in this period, but cemeteries belonging to them (which would give the best basis for a material sequence) have not yet been found, and as a whole the native material is not yet understood in any detail.

Farther inland, some of the seventh-century Hallstatt C tumulus cemeteries seem to continue into the sixth, but little is known of their contents. The most famous late-seventh or early-sixth-century tumulus of this group is the 'Oenochoe Tumulus' at Pertuis on the Durance. It takes its name from the Etruscan ('Rho- 66 dian') flagon found there with less exotic native material (Cotte 1909; Frey 1963). This evidently included three-and-a-half kilogrammes of bronze fragments damaged by the funeral pyre but thought by Cotte, the excavator, to be from body armour, a suggestion that more recent finds in southern France have made quite feasible. *6, 62*

Other poorer, badly documented tumulus groups were closer to Marseilles but still in fairly mountainous country around and in the Sainte-Baume massif (Lagrand 1959a). It is possible that the natives encountered by the early Greek colonists were of this tumulus group. However, finds of Urnfield pottery from *oppida* in the suburbs of Marseilles like Baou Roux and Saint-Marcel, and from many other near-delta sites make it possible that a distinct Urnfield population survived along this coastline, as it did farther west at Cayla. Most of these finds are preserved in the Musée Borély at Marseilles.

It is interesting that the earliest literary references to Massalia consistently speak of two native groups in the hinterland, Ligurian and Celtic. These terms are not defined but could perhaps reflect this Urnfield/Tumulus dichotomy, the former Ligurian, the latter Celtic.

Farther north, on the confines of the Rhône delta and on into the Rhône valley, native *oppida* continue to produce evidence for contact with Greeks and Etruscans in the form of Black Figure pottery, 'Phocaean' bucchero and wine amphorae. Another feature of these Rhône valley *oppida* is a local wheel-made ware in the Ionian dark-on-light technique (Lagrand 1963). This local version is best known from the *oppidum* of Le *7:2*

Pègue (Drôme), where it is dated by associated Black Figure fragments to the second half of the sixth century BC. Preliminary accounts of excavations at this site show that more traditional types of hand-made pottery remained in fashion as well, characterised in 7:1 particular by the use of lightly incised, linear motifs. A marked level of burning at Le Pègue terminates this stage of development there (Lagrand 1963; Leglay 1968, 589).

Farther north and into the Alps, native sites continue to produce similar Greek imports. At Sainte-Colombe in the Hautes-Alpes, coastal imports are found in a sixth-century village that was also destroyed by fire (Courtois 1966). A wide variety of hand-made wares include some with lightly incised motifs on a burnished ground, as at Le Pègue, but others have encrusted white linear decoration. Although occasional sherds of this distinctive ware are known as far south as Marseilles, the style is really more at home in the richer centres of native development farther north at sites like Mont Lassois. Further, there is no evidence for a local imitation of Ionian pottery, as at Le Pègue.

We seem to have reached the divide between two related but contrasting zones of development: the first focussing on the immediate hinterland of Massalia, the second flourishing to the north and west of the Alps at the upper reaches of the Rhine, Danube, Rhône and Saône. The next famous *oppidum* farther north, at Château-sur-Salins, Jura, already belongs firmly with the more northerly complex.

The western Hallstatt D groups and Vix

For the Late Bronze Age and on into the Early Iron Age, it is possible to discuss a basic material complex on the northern periphery of the Alps centering on the upper valleys of the Rhine and Danube, but including much of northeastern France as well. Despite local differences, especially in pottery styles, this complex was united by common trade, burial rites and a shared metal industry. Linked changes in metal types allow a general relative chronology of the area to be established:

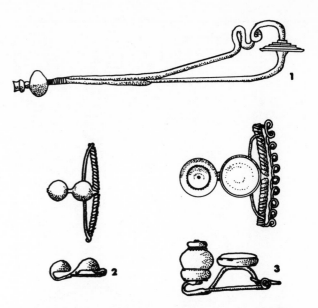

8 *Bronze fibulae of Hallstatt D types: 1, of serpentiform type from Saraz, Doubs, Musée de Besançon (after Dunning); 2 and 3, from the Vix burial: 2, double-bossed type, 3, with coral on the foot, amber on the bow and a non-functional auxiliary spring; Musée de Châtillon-sur-Seine (after Joffroy). 1, 10.2 cm. long, 2 and 3, to scale*

stages in this sequence have been labelled conventionally, and approximate absolute dates have been derived 4 from contacts with the Mediterranean world. The conventional labels used in this chapter – Hallstatt (or Ha) D1 and D2, La Tène Ia, Ib, Ic, II and III – are those most precisely defined in recent chronological studies of the northwest Alpine zone (Dehn and Frey 1962; Hodson 1968).

As this complex developed, its centre, or centres, of inspiration tended to drift, and its outer boundaries were fluid. As described in the last chapter, these boundaries for the Ha C stage (roughly the seventh century BC) could be defined by the distribution of burials with long Ha C swords of bronze and iron: much of France away from the south and west coasts was clearly involved. However, the main centres of inspiration at that time, as indicated by burials with elaborate hearses and horse trappings, lay outside France in Bohemia, Bavaria and Belgium.

The next stage of development within this complex, Ha D, is defined by a material assemblage with new weapon types (antennae daggers or short swords rather than the long Ha C swords), a new range of personal ornaments, fibulae, bracelets, anklets and so forth, and new regional pottery styles. These Ha D types were current broadly in the sixth century BC. The practice of burying the most prominent members of society with a hearse continued, but if the distribution of this rite is taken, as before, to indicate the main centres of development, northeastern France is now seen not as an off- 6 shoot, but as a cultural nucleus (Schiek 1954; Joffroy 1957; Drack 1958; Cordier 1968). The same conclusion

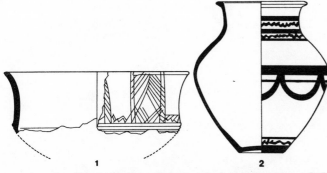

7 *Le Pègue, Drôme. Pottery of the sixth century BC. 1, Hand-made cup with lightly incised decoration on a burnished ground. Diameter 22 cm. 2, Wheel-made ochre-painted vase with brown motifs on a pale slip, imitating Ionian technique. Height 19.4 cm. (after Lagrand)*

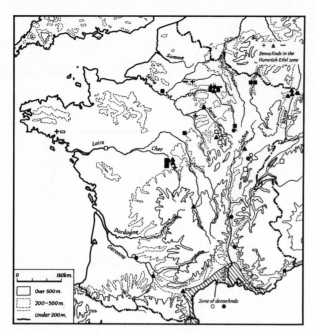

Bronze vessels, Greek and Etruscan, of the late seventh and sixth centuries BC (excluding basins and 'beaked' flagons)

Greek or Etruscan bronze basins with scroll decoration on the rim (late seventh to sixth century BC)

o Attic Black Figure pottery of the sixth century BC

+ Bronze situlae of north Italian type

▲ Etruscan beaked flagons of the late sixth and fifth centuries BC

■ Etruscan bronze stamnoi and stamnos-situlae of the fifth century BC

– Etruscan bronze basins of the fifth century BC

• Attic Red Figure pottery of the fifth century BC

9 Major categories of datable imports from the Mediterranean and north Italy (late seventh to late fifth century BC)

is drawn from studying the distribution of other obvious signs of wealth, like gold objects and imports from the Mediterranean. The distribution of these imports may well hold the clue to understanding the sudden cultural importance of Burgundy and the Jura, for they *9* demonstrate that the Rhône-Saône corridor did then effectively link this zone with Massalia and Mediterranean civilisation.

· Within Ha D as a whole, there was clearly a good deal of stylistic development that should help to define precise chronological stages, but this typological sequence has still to be discovered in detail for most regions, especially for the end of the phase and the beginnings of the La Tène phase that succeeded it.

Pirouet's excavations before the Second World War at Château-sur-Salins are directly relevant to this problem. He put forward a detailed interpretation of the site's stratigraphy, but post-war explorations have failed to locate equivalent deposits, and there are still reservations about some of his conclusions (Pirouet

1937; Dayet 1967). One of Pirouet's suggestions was that 'serpentiform' fibulae occurred before 'cross-bow' *8:1-3; 11* fibulae and before the importation of Black Figure and 'Phocaean' pottery. This typological distinction has *10* been confirmed elsewhere and helps to separate an early Ha D (D1, in the early sixth century BC) from a later Ha (D2, in the later sixth and, perhaps, early fifth century).

The most instructive Ha D finds in France are from the Vix burial in Burgundy and its adjacent hill-fort, Mont Lassois (Joffroy 1954, 1957, 1960). This site dominates the upper Seine valley at roughly the point where the river ceases to be navigable. Eastwards, the Rhône-Saône corridor is within easy reach, while westwards the Seine leads directly to the Atlantic coasts. That some Rhône valley trade reached Mont Lassois at this time is immediately shown by fragments of mica-tempered 'Massalian' amphorae found there.

Although little of this hill-fort has so far been excavated and little is known of its internal character, small finds of Ha D2 type testify to a short-lived but exceptionally active occupation in the second half of the sixth century BC. At least three hundred sherds of Greek pottery dating from this period have been found, largely Attic Black Figure.

The native finds, mainly pottery and brooches, are of great interest. As well as coarse wares, a number of distinct styles of fine pottery have been found. Some of

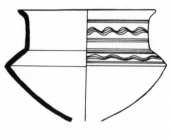

10 Camp-de-Château, Salins, Jura. Large fragment of grey bucchero vase ('Phocaean ware') with decoration incised by a comb. Brown polished surface over fine grey paste. Musée des Antiquités Nationales (after Dunning). Height 8.3 cm.

11 Mont Lassois, Côte-d'Or: bronze fibula of cross-bow form with simple, button foot. Châtillon-sur-Seine Museum. Length 5 cm. (after Joffroy)

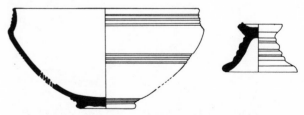

12 Mont Lassois, Côte-d'Or: wheel-turned pottery with black translucent finish. Probably made locally. Bowl with low foot-ring (rim diameter 29 cm.) and fragment (pedestal foot). Musée de Châtillon-sur-Seine (after Joffroy)

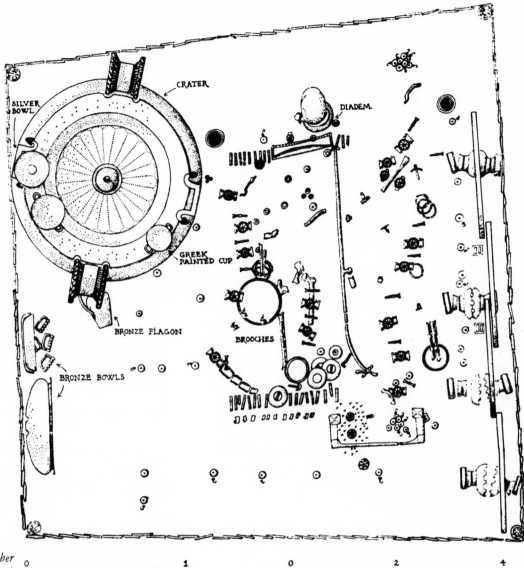

this is wheel-made in a technique rather like that of the coastal 'Phocaean' wares, but it is clear that the technique of manufacture itself and not simply imports had been introduced to the area – the first sign of wheel-turned technology north of the Alps. At the same time much hand-made ware is extremely fine, with dot or line decoration in pale clay on a dark burnished ground, so-called barbotine wares. Here we have a likely source of inspiration for the barbotine ware found farther south at Château-sur-Salins, Sainte-Colombe and Marseilles. Other decorative techniques at Mont Lassois are the use of a comb to roughen the surface in vertical strips or all over, and impressions made by a finger nail, hollow tube or other instrument. Shapes are varied but high pedestal-feet are especially favoured. These, and some neat, stamped cruciform motifs could well be inspired through contact with Iron Age groups on the south face of the Alps in Italy (the Golasecca group).

About three hundred bronze fibulae have so far been found at Mont Lassois, including some types mentioned at Château-sur-Salins (e.g. like those in fig. 8 : 1-2). However, a favourite new variety has a non-functional, auxiliary spring, as shown in fig. 8 : 3. Simple cross-bow fibulae with raised, button feet, like that in fig. 11, are very similar to forms that had developed in the Cayla zone, and it is likely that the whole vogue for fibulae with cross-bow construction was inspired from the south. However, these are developed in Burgundy into extremely elaborate varieties, like that in fig. 8 : 3.

The famous Vix tomb was discovered in 1953 by René Joffroy at the foot of this hill-fort. A woman of about thirty years of age had been buried with treasures of immense value. The grave itself was a wooden mortuary chamber under a tumulus and it included a dismantled vehicle relating it to the general series of Hallstatt cart or hearse burials.

Among the native objects, as well as the hearse with its fittings, are fibulae of the general types described for the hill-fort, and bracelets and anklets that fit the burial into its native late Hallstatt context. But the find is really remarkable for its wealth of imports. The most
67 outstanding of these, the immense bronze krater and its lid have been and no doubt will continue to be the centre of controversy. The most closely argued view of its exact origin and date (Gjødesen 1963) attributes the krater, its lid and its statuette to a Corinthian workshop of about 575 BC. How and when it came to Vix it is impossible to determine, but at some stage the frieze was dismounted and labelled with Greek letters to ensure correct reassembly.

The second finest, and perhaps even more enigmatic,
64 object from the burial is the gold collar or diadem. No really close parallels are known, but Schüle (1960b) has pointed out detailed links with goldwork of the Spanish peninsula, and a craftsman from this gold-producing area could conceivably have made this exceptional piece. Less spectacular gold bracelets and ear-rings from the near-by hearse burial of La Butte and a bracelet from the Frouzet burial of Languedoc provide more obvious links at this period with goldworking in the Iberian peninsula. However, a Black Sea origin and transport via the Danube are also conceivable for this Vix piece.

65 The bronze beaked flagon is certainly Etruscan, as are possibly three bronze basins found leaning against the side of the burial chamber.

68 The Attic Black Figure cup provides a fairly close absolute date of about 525 BC, and the tomb as a whole cannot be dated before the last quarter of the sixth century BC – a useful fixed point for the associated native metalwork.

It would seem that this Ha D culture in Burgundy developed out of the preceding Ha C complex as part of a continuing circum-Alpine cultural process. Direct contacts with the Mediterranean and perhaps north Italy led to a sudden enrichment of the northwest Alpine branch of this culture, which is seen at its richest at sites like Heuneburg-Hohmichele on the upper Danube and Mont Lassois-Vix in Burgundy.

The main centres of the Ha D culture in France are
6 indicated by concentration of imports and hearse-burials of the period. These include Burgundy, the Jura and southern Alsace. Related but less spectacular groups are known from the Hautes-Alpes (Courtois 1964) and from much of northern France.

THE JOGASSIAN GROUP

In the north, in generally lower and flatter areas, the Hallstatt people were outside the main sphere of Graeco-Etruscan trade, although finds of coral, glass beads and amber show that they had access to the major trading routes of the time.

During the D1 phase (roughly the first half of the sixth century BC) concentrations of settlement are very rare and, to judge by the number of finds from the north, population itself was thin. Already, however, the main regional subdivisions of the northern French Hall-

statt were established, with tumulus burial occurring in the eastern half (the Ardennes, Alsace, Lorraine, and southern Champagne), while in the rest of Champagne, the Ile-de-France, Picardy and Normandy there is a thin scatter of small, flat-grave cemeteries. Cremations and inhumations occur together in both areas, though the latter predominate in the flat-grave zone.

A great many of these Hallstatt sites continue to be used during the succeeding Ha D2 phase in the latter half of the sixth century. At this time, a considerable increase in population seems to occur, although the numbers involved are still quite low by later, La Tène standards. This increase in population seems partly linked with increasing rainfall at the height of the sub-Atlantic climate (of the latter part of the sixth and on into the fifth century BC). This increased precipitation would help to make the relatively arid chalk plains of Champagne and Picardy, and to a lesser extent the calcareous Ile-de-France, more productive for vegetation and crops. At the same time, the water-absorbent chalk would provide a traversable route in bad weather, and quantities of amber in Jogassian graves show that this area was actively trading in this material.

This Jogassian culture is the leading Ha D2 manifestation in the north (Favret 1936). Taking its name from the cemetery of Les Jogasses near Epernay (Marne), it is characterised by a specific series of burial rites and grave-goods and is, strictly speaking, a phenomenon of central Champagne. Although cremations are known, the burial rite is predominantly inhumation in trench graves, often with slab linings and covers. The fairly distinctive funerary pottery tends to be moderately burnished and warm pinkish-grey in colour. It may be decorated occasionally with geometric incisions, a pale thick barbotine, or a carmine slip. Vases tend to be small; most have extremely low carinated shoulders that sometimes merge with the vessel's feet, and wide, 14 flaring necks. From the few scant settlements which have been reported, it appears that for everyday purposes a wider variety of wares were made, some reflecting more closely earlier ceramic traditions of the area.

14 Les Jogasses, Marne : small vase from inhumation grave 89 in the late Hallstatt cemetery. Grey, burnished finish. Height 7.2 cm. Musée d'Epernay (after Dunning)

Only a few settlements and cemeteries, such as Aulnay-aux-Planches, near the Marais de Saint-Gond, continue from Urnfield to Iron Age times, and even these are discontinued during Ha C or D (Brisson and Hatt 1953, 1967). Nevertheless, many ceramic features clearly hark back to local Urnfield antecedents, and an

Urnfield base is generally thought to underlie Jogassian and later developments in most of the north.

Jogassian metal artifacts are less regionally specific, many being shared with Burgundy and the rest of the Hallstatt world. 'Vixian' artifacts such as the double-bossed fibula, hollow tubular torcs, bracelets, anklets and fragile bronze bangles (used in sets of as many as sixty per arm) are regular grave-offerings for women, while both sexes wore rectangular-plaque belt-hooks. The men were armed chiefly with quite large spears, but sometimes also with short, narrow daggers and bows-and-arrows. These metal types are diffused westwards in northern France, but the rare pottery from farther west seems to differ from the Jogassian. It is perhaps more reminiscent of 'Vixian', although easily distinguishable from it.

A four-wheel wagon burial from eponymous Les Jogasses is the northernmost in France in Hallstatt times. An interesting detail is that four holes were cut in the chalk at the corners of the grave to take the wheels. The accompanying inhumation seems to be that of a woman, as at Vix. This frequency of wagon burials with females shows that women played a significant role in these societies.

Oppida do not seem to occur in this Jogassian area: perhaps the secondary nature of trade made their formation unnecessary. Settlements generally remained small villages, lightly fortified, if at all.

The Haulzy group of the Argonne forest stands in marked contrast to the rest of northern France so far described (Goury 1911). In this region, where easily-worked limonite iron-ores were available, several cemeteries of inurned cremations beneath tumuli have been found. One in the Haulzy Woods is associated with an '*éperon barré*' hill-fort (dating originally from Ha C); both cemetery and settlement last into La Tène Ib times. At Haulzy, ceramic traditions point towards the Low Countries, not back to local Urnfield cultures as in much of the rest of northern France. The Argonne is by nature colder than its surrounding territories and the wetter phases of the sub-Atlantic must have discouraged settlement there.

SUMMARY FOR THE SIXTH CENTURY BC

To summarise the main lines of development in France in the sixth century BC: three main cultural foci have been suggested with attendant, overlapping zones of influence: Greek colonists at Massalia, the Cayla Mailhac III complex, and the Vix complex. Although in detail much still remains obscure, one basic factor seems to lie behind each of the three main groups as we see them: a suddenly revived interest in western Europe displayed by the civilised Mediterranean powers. Southern Iberia tended to remain a preserve of Phoenicians and later, Carthaginians, but, after preliminary explorations, Massalia was successfully established as a link between Greek and barbarian in France. From this contact sprang first the Mailhac III version of Cayla's Urnfield culture (originally of circum-Alpine descent but long since following its own, Mediterranean course)

and second, the enriched version of basic circum-Alpine Hallstatt culture seen at princely sites like Vix and the Heuneburg.

The reason behind this 'civilised' participation in barbarian affairs must have been economic, and the flow of trade north from the Mediterranean coasts is clearly documented by the distribution of prestige objects concerned with wine drinking and less bulky trinkets like coral. But there is no specific evidence from classical authors or from archaeology for what was traded in return during the sixth century BC, and scholars are left to guess at likely kinds of raw material that would appeal to the Greeks at this period. Iron ores and the wood to reduce them are abundantly available in the Vix region and must surely have played some part in her prosperity. Salt from the Jura and amber passed on from farther north are other likely commodities. However, the most favoured theory is of an overland tin-trade described for a later period and hypothetically linking the Atlantic and the Mediterranean in the sixth century BC via the Seine and then the Rhône-Saône corridor. Evidence for direct contact between the tin-producing area of Britain and the continent is extremely tenuous for this period, but Brittany was in touch with Hallstatt centres and could have traded tin to them (Schwappach 1969).

Perhaps a stronger cultural and commercial link may be suspected between the Atlantic coasts of Aquitaine and Languedoc during the sixth century BC. The Urnfield or mixed Urnfield/Tumulus cemeteries of Aquitaine have metalwork in the Mailhac III tradition (cf. the distribution of belt-hooks), and at the moment it is possibly simpler to think of connections between the Atlantic and Mediterranean via the Carcassonne gap than through Burgundy. A few of the 'Launac hoards' (it is not clear how many) date from the sixth century BC, as fibulae and belt-hooks in them show. These hoards from the Languedoc coastal area are largely made up of archaic bronzes, many of Atlantic type, but they also include copper and tin ingots (Soutou and Arnal 1963; Bouscaras 1964). Here, perhaps, we do have some of the material collected from a wide area to pay for Greek and Etruscan wine.

The fifth century BC and after

THE LA TÈNE CULTURE IN FRANCE

The fifth century

During the first half of the fifth century BC, profound changes took place among the groups north and west of the Alps. These changes are most obvious in the typology of material remains: by the mid-fifth century a completely new range of pottery, weapons and jewellery had appeared, most of it strikingly different from anything seen before. This new range of styles and traits defines the material side of the La Tène complex. One of the most remarkable innovations, and one that to some extent summarises the general revolutionary spirit of the times, is the sudden appearance of a new, original La Tène art style generally referred to as 'Early Celtic Art' (Jacobsthal 1944; Frey 1955). This new style, or rather series of styles, borrows heavily from designs that were already current on native and imported metalwork: classical lotus, palmette, spiral and mask motifs make an especially strong contribution, as do animalising 'steppe' motifs (perhaps seen on imported textiles). However, in borrowing these designs, the La Tène artist changed and combined them into an extremely VII, 72 characteristic and original range of decoration for fine metalwork and, to a much lesser extent, pottery.

The material changes that characterise the new La Tène culture were accompanied by just as violent changes in the centres of industry, trade and wealth. The most direct indication of this upheaval is the distribution of fifth-century hearse burials (now two-wheeled-cart, perhaps war-chariot burials). Their main concentrations are now right outside the rich Ha D areas, on the middle Rhine (associated with the Hunsrück-Eifel 15 branch of Early La Tène culture) and in the Jogassian area of Champagne (associated with the Marnian La Tène branch). Furthermore, these are now the two areas with the greatest concentrations of prestige imports from the Mediterranean. The distribution of these imports and other southern influences strongly suggests a route of diffusion via north Italy and the eastern Alps rather than the Rhône corridor, although fifth-century Attic pottery at the Château-sur-Salins *oppidum* implies that the latter route was not completely abandoned. Areas like Burgundy and the Jura that had been so rich in Ha D times take over many of the new La Tène styles, but their ascendant, innovating role is eclipsed.

Once established, the La Tène complex survives until Caesar's conquest of Gaul. Stages in its development 71 are marked by typological changes in material remains, especially in brooches and other jewellery, since these generally conformed to the whims of widespread and rapidly changing fashions. These stages have been defined most precisely in Switzerland, but to a certain extent it is possible to follow them over much of the rest of the La Tène world. The Swiss terminology generally used for these relative phases defines Early, Middle and Late stages (or La Tène I, II and III, the first stage subdivided into Ia, b and c). Absolute dates for these relative stages cannot yet be given with any accuracy, but those suggested on the chronological table should not be too misleading (Hodson 1964, 1968).

The Marne culture

At the time that the La Tène 'revolution' was taking place in the fifth century, there seems to have been a further marked increase in population in northern France; at least the finds from this stage are much more plentiful than in the previous Late Hallstatt phases. Nowhere is this great increase more pronounced than in northern Champagne (in the northern Marne, southern Aisne and Ardennes), but there are significant increases also in some surrounding areas (the southern Marne, northern Haute-Marne, Aube and eastern Seine-et-Marne). The cultural manifestation of this population in northern Champagne is that of the celebrated Marne

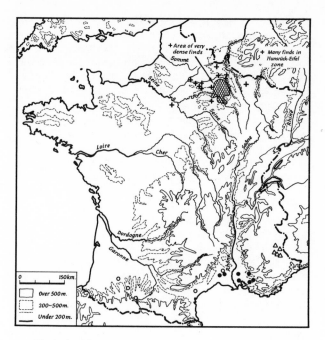

+ Chariot burials

o Hooked belt-fasteners with more than three hooks

● Architectural fragments with niches to display *têtes coupées* or with sculpted *têtes coupées*

△ Brooches of Jausiers type (see fig. 19)

15 Some regional features during the Early and Middle La Tène phases

culture (Déchelette 1927). This is characterised by many distinctive traits and objects even if most of these merely reflect local variations on more general La Tène themes.

Archaeologically, the Marne culture is distinguished above all by its burial practices which contrast sharply with those of its neighbours. The frequency of chariot 15 burials is most striking. This rite becomes more widespread later (although not so frequent), but nearly all the fifth-century chariot burials in France belong to the Marne culture (Joffroy and Bretz-Mahler 1959). The burial rite itself, whether accompanied by a chariot or not, is almost exclusively extended inhumation, the head to the west, in a trench grave filled with a black, 16 humic forest soil. A few graves are surrounded by a ditch which may be circular or, more significantly, square in plan. Vases were regularly placed in graves along with a carving knife and food offerings (animal bones are regularly associated). Most graves contain jewellery for the women – torcs, bracelets, fibulae, earrings; and for the men some ornaments and weapons – swords, daggers, long knives and spears.

One of the most diagnostic Marnian traits is the characteristic funerary pottery (Dehn 1950). The ware 74-5 is thin, moderately well baked and burnished; it is often lustrous black or dark grey, but in the southeastern Marne area it is frequently of a light ochre colour painted with broad, red bands. Decoration on the dark pottery is by incision, combing, punching or painting with a thick barbotine. While a great variety of shapes are regularly found, the most indicative is the angular, carinated vase. Pottery was now made on the wheel for the first time north of Burgundy, usually in the shape of tall pedestal urns which may be red-slipped on an ochre ground or simply black. Some smaller 'compressed' vases of basically the same form were also wheel-made. Other kinds of wares harking back to Urnfield times and beyond have been found at settlements.

74

Marnian metal types, generally less heavily made than in the Rhineland or Switzerland include a high frequency of twisted torcs, disc-fibulae often incorporating coral and/or amber, and a fairly high frequency of bronze sword scabbards. Horse and vehicle trappings are exceptionally rich and varied, and include a series of specialised bits with small, central links.

La Tène art appears richly on Marnian objects and curvilinear motifs are developed early from classical prototypes. One special style of art singled out for emphasis by Jacobsthal (1944) but without stressing its early concentration in the Marne culture is a 'multiple-choice' version of these motifs where two, three or even more renderings may be made of the same design. By contrast, animalising 'steppe' motifs are rare in Marnian La Tène art.

70

The richest intact Marnian chariot burial, and one of the best reported, was found at 'La Gorge-Meillet', a hilltop of Somme-Tourbe (Marne), where many other chariot burials have been found (Fourdrignier 1878). The burial contained two simultaneous inhumations with typical Marnian orientation and grave-filling: the upper one, a fully-mature male, was accompanied only by a sword and iron suspension ring, while the lower, a youth who had not yet cut his wisdom teeth, lay on the two-wheeled chariot. He wore two La Tène Ia fibulae, a golden bracelet on the left arm, and on his breast four decorated bronze buttons, the corrosion salts of which had preserved a scrap of his thickly-woven, woollen tunic. He was armed with a long sword and four spearheads equipped with iron shaft-butts; a toilet set contained tweezers, ear scoop, and forked scratcher or nail-cleaner. At his feet were a paring knife and food remains (joints of pork, fowl, small game and eggs in a black hand-made bowl); these were accompanied by another black vessel, a more sumptuous red slipped, wheel-made pedestal urn and an imported Etruscan bronze beaked flagon. Beside these vessels were a tall conical bronze helmet engraved with a net-and-swastika design, and six iron *phalerae* with curvilinear, open-work S scrolls. Horse harness in the grave was heavily studded with bronze and coral ornamental buttons and was decorated with cast palmette and S designs. There was a pair of rather unusual bronze bits which had a central link connecting the side links. The iron tyres of the chariot, 96 cm. in diameter, stood in specially scooped-out pits about 130 cm. apart. Most of the other chariot components were strictly utilitarian iron pieces, but the bronze hub-caps for the wheel naves were

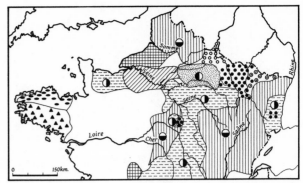

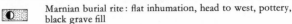

	Marnian burial rite: flat inhumation, head to west, pottery, black grave fill
	Multiple inhumation without pottery under tumulus
	Flat inhumation without pottery; variable orientation
	Single inhumation with pottery under tumulus
	Elliptical tumulus with sunken grave rite
	Single cremation under tumulus
	Armorican single cremation under tumulus
	Multiple cremation under tumulus
	Flat inhumation cemetery in dunefield
	Flat cremation
	Flat inhumation with non-Marnian pottery; variable orientation

16 Predominant burial forms in northern France during the Early and Middle La Tène phases. Some areas (e.g. northern Champagne) had more uniform rites than others (e.g. Lorraine and Alsace) where departures from the predominant rite often occur

decorated both in the new curvilinear La Tène style and with rectilinear motifs derived from Hallstatt tradition.

Mediterranean 'prestige' imports in northern France are at this time almost confined to the Marne area, with a lesser scatter at the bend of the Loire near Orléans. As at La Gorge-Meillet, they are usually found in rich chariot burials associated with a variety of native objects, for which they suggest approximate absolute dates. Some of the earliest of these imports during La Tène times must be the Etruscan 'beaked' flagons from La Gorge-Meillet already described, and from Sept-Sault; both these are of the early type known from Hallstatt contexts like Vix. The Somme-Bionne burial, located within sight of La Gorge-Meillet, contained a different kind of beaked flagon with spirals on the handle attachment. North of the Alps, this type is exclusively found in La Tène contexts. It was accompanied by a Red Figure kylix dating from about 420-400 BC. In the main, the native Somme-Bionne grave-goods are closer to La Tène Ib styles than are those of

9

65

69

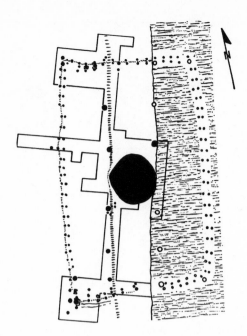

17 Chassemy, Aisne: reconstructed plan of Marnian house. Shaded area destroyed before the rescue excavation; limits of the excavation trenches are indicated. Large fire pit in centre; large and smaller post holes indicate structural details. Length of house 9.75 m. (after Rowlett et al.)

La Gorge-Meillet and Sept-Sault. Although found with a cremation beneath a tumulus and outside the Marne culture proper, a 'scale-kantharos' from La Motte Saint-Valentin (Haute-Marne) is relevant here: it was associated with La Tène material and, again, suggests that these styles were established by the middle of the fifth century.

Little is known of the settlements that must have accompanied Marnian cemeteries, but a house-plan has recently been published from a riverside settlement at Chassemy (Rowlett *et al.* 1969). Although partly bulldozed, the main features of the layout could be recov-
17 ered: a roughly rectangular, timber-framed structure about 10 m. long, with a large, deep fire pit in the centre.

Superficially, the La Tène Ia culture on the Marne represents such a break with previous developments there that an alien population is thought by many to have been responsible. Nevertheless, most archaeological evidence emphasises direct continuity with the preceding Jogassian groups and suggests an economic and commercial rather than an ethnic revolution. Most known Jogassian cemeteries and settlements contain La Tène graves and houses as well, in most cases the latter remains outnumbering the former, and many Jogassian artifacts and burial practices are clearly antecedent to local La Tène forms. For example, at Les Jogasses itself, the Jogassian cemetery was extended and used in Marnian times; the burial rite was basically the same for

both and vehicle burials of both phases are represented with detailed similarities (notably the separate wheel-holes cut into the chalk). One of the clearest typological sequences between Hallstatt and La Tène styles may be seen in the evolution of daggers and swords at this cemetery. In fact, at Les Jogasses and related sites, there seems to be no obvious *break* between Hallstatt graves of about 500 BC (datable by analogy with the Vix association) and La Tène Ia forms of about 450 BC (datable by analogy with La Gorge-Meillet and other burials with imports).

Admittedly, the Marnians were in contact with the Hunsrück-Eifel culture of the Moselle-Rhine confluence, which has long been recognised as having played a leading part in the development of the earliest La Tène styles, but the Marne culture was in no sense an offshoot. Marnian objects are known from Hunsrück-Eifel contexts (triconic carinated vases, pedestal urns and tulip-shaped cups) and balance Hunsrück-Eifel features in Marnian pottery, such as rusticated 'Kalenderberg' decoration (Dehn 1950). Like the Hunsrück-Eifel group, the Marnians also show influence from south-Alpine peoples, but in different ways. The Marnians did not adopt any of the pattern-burnished ('*stralucido*') pottery of the Tessin valley as did the contemporary Rhinelanders, but the Marnian red-banded situla-shaped urns recall those of the Atestine and Golaseccan cultures, and carinated cups, cylindrical cists and other metallic forms are common to both areas.

What the material evidence does seem to indicate for the Marne area (and the other rich Early La Tène centres like the Hunsrück-Eifel) is an amazing increase in wealth with a consequent increase in population and the standard of living, especially for the ruling class. The basis for this wealth is not clear. For the Hunsrück-Eifel group, Driehaus (1965) has noted the close relationship between the richest iron deposits and the richest burials, but the native mineral resources of the two areas do not bear comparison and Marnian wealth must have had some basis other than the direct production of metals. Perhaps the Marne was at this time the collecting point for goods from the Atlantic coasts (especially tin, but perhaps other raw metals, salt and hides), since Marnian contacts with Brittany and the British Isles are now documented: to judge from finds like Pexton Moor in Yorkshire (Stead 1959), there may even have been Marnian outposts in the west. Another factor in the Marnians' prosperity could be the wet sub-Atlantic climate, as the soils of Champagne, so water-pervious as to be excessively arid today, would have provided a good passageway for trade and a good basis for agriculture.

The Marne culture clearly influenced much of contemporary development elsewhere in France. In south- *16* ern Champagne, Early La Tène is very close to the true Marne culture just described: even the characteristic dark grave filling is found, but pottery is not placed in graves – a marked departure in burial rite. To the east and southeast in Lorraine, Alsace and Jura, the existing population with its tumulus cemeteries was open to La

Tène influences from many centres including the mid-Rhine as well as the Marne (Schaeffer 1930). However, north and west of Champagne, specifically Marnian influence is soon apparent. West of the Ardennes in southern Belgium, Marnian pottery styles (if defined in general terms) appear with cremations in the flat and tumulus graves of an ostensibly sparse population. The Marnian rite of flat grave inhumation with ceramic offerings extends west of the Ile-de-France, but although Marnian pottery is in evidence, the typical dark grave filling is not.

Strong Marnian influence is seen in tin-producing southeastern Armorica and also at the big bend of the Loire, but in both areas the general rite of multiple burial in tumuli implies different tribes from those on the Marne. The Armorican ceramic parallels are so strong that Favret (1936), who worked in both areas, postulated an actual migration from Champagne to Brittany at about the time that La Tène styles appeared. Few would accept this interpretation today, since burial patterns and most non-metallic artifacts in the two areas are clearly different (although fragments of chariots have been found with Armorican burials). However, Marnian influence in this more western pottery could reflect active trade in tin and Atlantic products. The Marnian connections with the big bend of the Loire could likewise be linked with a suggested Loire tin route across France (Hencken 1934; Schwappach 1969).

Farther north than the tin region, on the northern slope of Armorica and in Normandy, Early La Tène exists but with much less that is specifically 'Marnian'. Possible Marnian links with Yorkshire have already been mentioned.

Later La Tène developments in northern France
During La Tène Ib, Ic and II, the features established in La Tène Ia continued to develop through much of temperate Europe. One marked occurrence was the spread of flat-grave, inhumation cemeteries (like those of Les Jogasses and the Marne) to areas where tumulus burial had previously held sway. This development had already taken place in Switzerland in La Tène Ia, but the large La Tène flat cemeteries of southern Germany, Czechoslovakia and Hungary started mainly in La Tène Ib or later. This wide-spread conformity to a standard burial rite was accompanied by more material conformity as well: although local metal and pottery types appear throughout this flat-grave zone, a great number of inter-regional forms occur as well. Dux 71 fibulae, for example, named from the site of Duchcov in Bohemia, are found throughout the zone, as are the features of the 'Waldalgesheim' and later 'Plastic' art styles described by Jacobsthal (1944). A marked social change is the general disappearance of an outstandingly rich aristocracy with access to Mediterranean imports.

By La Tène Ib times, the density of finds implies that most of northern France was quite thickly populated, and with the wider distribution of standardised La Tène styles the Marne culture as such now appears less paramount: other groups are likewise well-provided with jewellery, weapons and La Tène art. Chariot burials continue in the Marne culture, but are somewhat rarer and less spectacular than before. Part of this apparent deceleration may be owing to a more general diffusion of the beneficial Iron Age innovations early taken up by the Marnians, but it could also have been caused in part by the disruption of trade routes at the time of the main Gallic invasions of northern Italy. For these a date of about 390 B C (the date when the Gauls took Rome) still seems most likely: finds of La Tène material in a genuine La Tène cultural context in Italy seem to be mainly of La Tène Ib or later character, while the sporadic Ia types, sometimes ascribed to earlier invasions, could result from trade of the kind already discussed.

Among the Celtic peoples who invaded the classical world at this time, the Gallic Senones may actually have come from southwestern Champagne, since in Caesar's day a tribe of similar name was centred there around present-day Sens. The cis-Alpine Senones were reputed to have migrated because of over-population. In the possible Senonic homeland around Sens, La Tène Ia graves are rare but many date from Ib. If this is the origin of the Italian Senones and if their exodus was due to over-population, the rapid growth must have come late in La Tène Ia, perhaps within a generation.

To judge from grave-finds, La Tène Ib was perhaps the time of greatest population in northern Gaul; a subsequent decline in La Tène Ic could be due to losses affected by migration. There is a slight resurgence of finds for La Tène II, but this apparent increase could simply mean that La Tène II types were current longer than those of Ic. Lacking imports from the south, both of these phases have to be dated absolutely by rather circumstantial evidence from the Mediterranean.

A noteworthy economic development in the La Tène world was the appearance of a native coinage, perhaps during the third century B C. Designs were at first copied fairly exactly from different Greek prototypes, especially from the 'Philippics' of Macedonia, but 81 gradually the design, the weight and the purity of the metal were all debased. The gradual breaking-up of the head and chariot motifs of the original 'Philippics' represents one of the best-known and most striking typologies in European archaeology. However, the chronology of these developments and their interpretation in economic and political terms present a great many unsolved problems and one of the richest fields for future research (Colbert dè Beaulieu 1966; Scheers 1968; Soutou 1966; Allen 1969).

Despite the migrations and apparent disturbances in the La Tène world between the fifth and the last century B C, defensive architecture in northern France seems little developed, and settlements seem generally to have been small, open affairs. In contrast to the south with its well-built stone houses, the northern dwellings that have been recovered so far, as at Chassemy, were lightly built, sub-rectangular wattle-and-daub buildings, which leave scant traces in the ground.

With the Late La Tène stage of development (La Tène III), this pattern is radically changed. Throughout the La Tène world, there was a marked concentration of population into large, defended *oppida*. Often the defences were formed by a specialised type of rampart with a framework of nailed, horizontal timbers, a type clearly described by Caesar (Cotton 1957). The industrial production of pottery, metalwork and glass, and the minting of coins was concentrated in these *oppida*, and the resulting material cultures were remarkably uniform throughout the La Tène world. Burial by cremation became an equally diffused, standardised practice. The date and mechanism of these developments are obscure, but the whole process seems to be closely linked with the intrusion of Roman power into Gaul and beyond the Alps. It will be dealt with as such in the next chapter.

SOUTHERN FRANCE FROM THE FIFTH CENTURY BC

While in northeastern France the fifth century BC is documented by a wealth of material, in the south it is relatively obscure. The dearth of fifth-century Attic Red Figure at Massilia and Villard's interpretation of this have already been mentioned. Contemporary native material is also meagre. This apparent lack of native evidence might be to some extent illusory: given the scarcity in the region of datable Attic imports, it is difficult to see how native material would be assigned to this period. It is just possible that levels attributed to the sixth century and no later because of their Attic imports in fact represent fifth-century occupation as well. However, it is clear that many settlements with Attic Black Figure in the Rhône valley and along the coast were destroyed by fire, among them Cayla, Ruscino II, Le Pègue E, Sainte-Colombe and Lattes (Arnal *et al.* 1969), and it seems reasonable to interpret this as a horizon of disturbance linked somehow with the politico-economic changes that marked the transition from Hallstatt to La Tène farther north.

From the fourth century onwards, Massalia herself was again flourishing and further sub-colonies were founded along the coast towards Italy. A massive Greek wall at Saint-Blaise may date from this century and represent part of this Massalian revival and expansion (Rolland 1951, 1956, 1964).

At native *oppida*, occupation from the fourth century onwards is again well documented. West of the Hérault, the native sequence may be followed through further levels at the Cayla hill-fort (Cayla III-IV) and at Ruscino (level III), but the most complete record is available at Ensérune just west of Béziers (Jannoray 1955; Gallet de Santerre 1968). Here, around the beginning of the fourth century BC, a carefully ordered town of stone buildings (Ensérune II) was evidently built over a more straggling and primitive settlement of the sixth century BC (Ensérune I). A network of roadways with its attendant buildings now filled an area of the hill-top that was delimited by a massive stone rampart. Huge storage jars (*dolia*) were sunk into house-floors, and larger pits, or 'silos', were dug into the soft tufa for additional storage (perhaps of water). The western part of the enclosed area was given over to a cemetery, and it is finds from these graves that provide the richest evidence for the material culture of southern France during the fourth and third centuries BC.

This Ensérune cemetery was again an urnfield with pits dug into the ground to contain the ossuary, cremated bones and grave-goods from the pyre. In some areas, successive burial pits were so crowded together that existing graves were disturbed, and the structure and contents of many are consequently not clear.

The graves seem to represent a continuous sequence, but two series may be distinguished by the typology of their ossuaries and contents. The first (Ensérune IIA) is characterised by ossuaries in 'ochre-painted' ware with lids improvised from suitable amphora fragments. Fibulae are most regularly of developed cross-bow type (local, south French versions), but annular and Early La Tène forms have also been found. Hooked belt-buckles may be of La Tène type but a few resemble Mailhac III prototypes (like fig. 5:12). Weapons include iron spearheads and 'soliferrea' spears (again with Mailhac III antecedents (e.g. fig. 5:5)) but also Early La Tène swords in their scabbards. Some fine cups in Red Figure or black 'glazed' techniques were imported from Attica and Italy.

The second main series of tombs at Ensérune (IIB) has imported ossuaries – black 'glazed' Italian canthari (or, once, an Attic Kertch krater) of the third century BC, La Tène fibulae (Late La Tène I and local types), swords (La Tène I and II types) and shield bosses (Late La Tène I and La Tène II types). Similar metal types are also found with simpler ossuaries in a grey wheel-turned ware, sometimes decorated with burnished lines.

As a whole, the graves of this second series are clearly related to the first by their burial rite and contents, and indeed there is no very clear boundary between the two.

The cemetery was built over at the time of a major reconstruction of the town, presumably at about 200 BC (Ensérune III). The cemetery for this phase has not yet been discovered. This third town seems to carry on most features of the second and to survive right through the period of Roman conquest; it was abandoned only in the first century AD. Imports in Ensérune III show increasing contact with Italy, but connections with Spain are still marked.

A most important feature of both Ensérune II and III are short inscriptions, usually graffiti scratched on pottery. The language of the inscriptions is completely unknown but the script seems to be inspired from Ampurias, with its ultimately Ionian traditions. For this feature at Ensérune, the links are clearly with the Catalan coast, emphasising once more the strong cultural uniformity during the Iron Age of the zone between the Ebro and the Hérault.

Although apparently separated by a century or so from the latest burials of GB II at Cayla, the graves of Ensérune II are clearly related to them in their burial rite, pottery and some metalwork. It seems very unlikely that the population of Languedoc had changed very much between the sixth and fourth centuries B C, whatever disturbances may have occurred during the fifth. The location of the Ensérune cemetery within the city defences is a departure, but this could simply be a result of disturbed conditions. The one major new element at Ensérune is La Tène metalwork – swords, shields, belt-buckles and fibulae. However, the impression given by the Ensérune graves is that these types infiltrated, without fundamentally changing, a local Urnfield culture whose traditions may be followed back, without any major cultural break, to the urnfields in Languedoc and Catalonia of Mailhac I times.

As for the sixth century B C, so for succeeding centuries, native development is less well documented to the east of the Hérault than it is to the west. No large cemetery of the period, like Ensérune, has been found and few comprehensive groups of material from the many known oppida have yet been published. However, there are hints that the lower Rhône area was culturally distinct from the Ensérune/Cayla zone just described (Robert 1965).

One marked feature of settlements in this more easterly zone is the regular appearance in houses of decorated hearths with accessory clay fire-dogs and vases with pierced bases. A series of three such superposed hearths has been found at the oppidum of La Roque, near Montpellier (Larderet 1957): the first was a simple cobble hearth attributed to about 425-400 B C, the second was of clay, decorated with simple geometric motifs (about 400-325 B C), the latest, also of clay, had elaborate triskele and key patterns (about 325-250 B C). Horse-headed fire-dogs were associated with the latest hearth. Fire-dogs of this kind have been found in many sites in the Nîmes area, and now similar hearths are starting to be recognised. Whatever the origins of this domestic hearth assemblage, it is a marked feature of the lower Rhône sites but is poorly represented west of the Hérault.

Another contemporary feature of this area is the great quantity of native coarse pottery produced with a characteristic 'combed' roughening of the surface. This roughening regularly extends over the base as well as the sides of urns but their necks are usually left smooth or burnished. Large series of these urns have been 76 found at oppida near Nîmes and Marseilles – at Les Pennes, for example (Chaillan 1917). This pottery type is not confined to the lower Rhône area: in the west, an early example has been found in a sixth-century native grave at Ampurias (from Muralla N.E. No. 2), and farther east, sherds have been found in the Hautes-Alpes (at Sainte-Colombe and Orpière) and even in Piedmont at Guardamonte (Lo Porto 1954). But the greatest concentrations occur close to the Rhône delta, and this seems to be the centre for the type. Even after the Roman conquest, local pottery is produced to the same specification, with combed sides and plain necks but use of the wheel then leads to a more regular, globular profile. Another regular and distinctive type

of native pottery from these sites is a rather crude, straight-sided and flat-based bowl with notching on top of the rim.

Perhaps the most instructive associations of this material for the fourth and third centuries have been published from sites in the Durance valley by Dumoulin (1965). At the oppidum site of Cavaillon a series of deep shafts have been discovered in the course of gravel digging. The reason for such deep pits is not clear: they could be unfinished or filled-in wells, or ritual shafts of the kind later known from Toulouse and at some La Tène sites north of the Alps (Schwartz 1962). At all events, two of these shafts at Cavaillon, numbers 1 and 13, provide interesting groups of coarse pottery dated to the fourth and third centuries by imports. Pit 13, the earlier of the two, produced four La Tène fibulae, amphora fragments and 'Phocaean' ware as well as a wide range of coarse wares. Pit 1 is dated to the third century by small fragments of Red Figure and black- 'glazed' wares.

A few contemporary burials from the Durance valley have been discovered at Cucuron, near Apt (Dumoulin 1962). Burial was post-cremation, but in the best-preserved grave it was clear that the cremated remains were not inurned. Grave-goods include 'combed urns' and La Tène fibulae. Very few other burials in this lower Rhône area may be dated before the Roman conquest, but another series of cremation burials near Nîmes seem to start as early as the third century B C, even if the best documented of the series are of the first. In these, too, cremation was the exclusive rite. Complete amphorae appear to have served as ossuaries.

From these finds it seems that although this material culture of the lower Rhône valley was in some respects similar to that at Ensérune, it differed sufficiently to be regarded as a distinct, local facies. This interpretation is reinforced by the most spectacular archaeological finds from this zone, not so far mentioned: religious sanctuaries with attendant sculptures, from sites like Roquepertuse and Entremont (Benoît 1955, 1965b). The recurring features of these sanctuaries are a portico with head-trophies on the pillars (either real or carved) and sculpted figures, most characteristically squatting cross-legged in a Buddha-like attitude. The distribution of these sanctuaries is shown in fig. 15.   15

The most impressive remains of such a sanctuary, from Roquepertuse, may be seen reconstructed in the 77 annex of the Musée Borély at Marseilles. Roquepertuse occupies a small rocky outcrop just west of Aix-en-Provence, too small for a settlement, but evidently favoured as a religious centre. As well as the regular features of these sanctuaries, Roquepertuse produced a fine double head and a bird carved in the round. 79 The date of this particular sanctuary is difficult to fix exactly. It was almost certainly desecrated at the time of the Roman conquest (ballista balls have been found at the site), as was the Entremont sanctuary near by, but the sculptures are quite different from those at Entremont and could well have originated a century or two earlier.

A date well before 123 BC for some features of this general assemblage is suggested at Saint-Blaise, where a head-trophy pillar was found built into the Greek rampart. If a fourth-century origin for this rampart is accepted, this gives a terminal date before which the native pillar was in use. A similar date is suggested for a typologically early group of sculptures from the Nîmes area; the most complete of these is the 'warrior of Grézan', with a curious, cowl-like helmet, a torc, a breast-plate and a belt fastened by a four-hooked belt-buckle, derived typologically from the Mailhac III three-hooked series. This belt-hook seems the only specific means for dating this sculpture, and for it a fifth- or fourth-century date seems most reasonable.

Until better associations are known from these sanctuary sites it seems reasonable to consider them an integral part of the fourth- to third-century *oppidum* complex that has just been discussed at sites like La Roque, Cavaillon and Les Pennes. That this complex flourished until the Roman conquest in 123 BC is clear at many sites, but most notably at Entremont, an *oppidum* just north of Aix and the native precursor of Aquae Sextiae. The site may be taken to typify a native town in Provence at the time of the Roman conquest (Benoît 1968).

The conquest itself is documented at the site by stone ballista balls weighing between three-and-a-half and eight-and-a-half kilograms and found scattered among the remains of occupation. The *oppidum* was defended naturally to the south by rocky precipices; to the north, two parallel lines of defence were built, the outer perhaps later than the inner and reflecting an extension of the fortress. Each was a massive stone rampart with towers at intervals of about 20 metres. The *oppidum* proper enclosed three and a half hectares, but dwellings have been found clustering outside as well. Signs of occupation after the Roman conquest are claimed to be slight, and the majority of finds may be taken to antedate 123 BC.

Buildings so far excavated were single-room affairs facing directly on to streets. Small finds include large quantities of coarse hand-made pottery, especially 'combed urns' of the basic type described. As well as native coarse wares, imported coarse and fine wares have been found in quantity including wine amphorae from the Aegean and Italy, and Italian 'black-glazed' table ware. Many of these imports are exact replicas of pottery found stacked in a sunken wreck just outside Marseilles harbour – the famous Grand Congloué wreck (Benoît 1961). The date of the wreck is controversial, but Benoît is likely to be right in suggesting the early second century BC.

The most remarkable and famous finds from Entremont are the sculptures. They probably belonged to a portico of Roquepertuse type, but have been found dispersed on the site. The head-trophy (*tête coupée*) rite is prominent: actual skulls pierced for hanging or with long iron nails still through them have been found, as well as simple outlines and bas-reliefs of cut heads on stone pillars and other architectural fragments. The

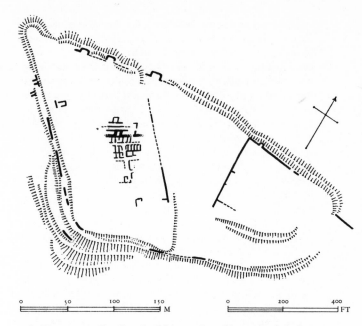

18 Entremont, Bouches-du-Rhône : plan of 'oppidum' (after Benoît and Piggott)

most remarkable sculptures, however, are fragmentary figures in the round : several seem to represent squatting warriors with one hand resting on a *tête coupée*, but at least one horseman and a female head have been reported. These figures are represented with clothing or equipment of various kinds : breast-plates with heraldic emblems and chain-mail are not known from this area, though some carved features correspond with archaeological finds. For example, two of the figures have bracelets with rather crude spiral decoration just like bronze bracelets of a type discovered in Provence. Another upper arm has bracelets that resemble glass exemplars of the kind known at Entremont and many other sites farther north. The sculptors at Entremont seem to have attempted a truly realistic representation of detail, with varying success. It is impossible to discuss them adequately in a few words, and the most generalised comments must suffice.

Some natives in the area must have been familiar with Greek sculpture and architecture from the sixth century BC onwards, and it is not surprising that they themselves attempted monumental architecture and sculpture for their sanctuaries. Yet, from the early Grézan warrior to the heads and warriors of Entremont there is nothing Greek in these sculptures either in style, content or spirit.

The main concentration of the Entremont complex may be seen from the distributions just mentioned. The coastal zone as far as Toulon was clearly involved. Farther east, large numbers of *oppida* are known but not much associated material from this period. Judging by the finds of 'combed' urns from the Hautes-Alpes and Piedmont already mentioned, a wide area could have been involved in, or at least influenced by, developments near the Rhône delta.

However, some inhumations on the high Alps near Barcelonnette suggest at least one contrasting group (Courtois 1961). Its special hall-mark is a type of large fibula evidently worn on the head, and conserving archaic Hallstatt D features (especially the disc at the top of the pin). The one clear association, at Peynier, included La Tène II material. Other less remote Alpine cemeteries in Savoy, for example at Saint-Jean-de-Belleville, seem to show more direct influence from main Hallstatt and La Tène centres than the Ensérune and Entremont groups nearer the coast, and must be considered as part of the basic Alpine Hallstatt-La Tène complex.

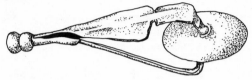

19 Bronze fibula of Jausiers type from Saint-Pons, Hautes-Alpes. Length 13.1 cm. (after Chantre)

Conclusions

An attempt has been made in the preceding sections to distinguish the main archaeological groups in evidence just before and at the time of the Roman conquest of Provence. The following grouping has been outlined: first, a La Tène group in northeastern France forming one branch of the central La Tène culture, which also includes Switzerland, southern Germany and Czechoslovakia, and which represents the persistence from Urnfield and Hallstatt times of a cultural force on the northern periphery of the Alps. The second main group is centred on the Mediterranean seaboard and has two facies, typified by Ensérune and Entremont. Both show influence in metalwork from the central La Tène culture, but this element is only one, perhaps a relatively

minor one, that was added to a local Urnfield/Hallstatt tradition, the whole overlaid by Mediterranean, 'civilised' influences. The Ensérune facies has closest links with Catalonia and the Iberian peninsula and is better documented than its eastern neighbour. The latter has some weak links with, or influence over Liguria and Piedmont, but seems to represent a genuinely local phenomenon of the lower Rhône valley combining, like Ensérune, existing Urnfield and Hallstatt traditions with Mediterranean and La Tène elements.

Outside these two main centres of development, the northeast and the Mediterranean seaboard, the picture is one of influence from these zones on existing groups. In Aquitaine, Urnfield and Urnfield/Tumulus cemeteries survive with extremely archaic features (bossing on pottery, for example), but have metalwork inspired from the main centres. In Brittany, there seems to be a complex mixture of La Tène influences (especially in art style and metalwork) acting on an already mixed Atlantic/Urnfield basis. In the French Alps the position is again complex, but La Tène influence seems to blanket what has gone before.

Despite all these local differences in France of the latter centuries BC, there seems to be one ultimate background that is important for most of them: in one way or another they all stem largely from the Urnfield complex that was developing around the northwestern Alps at the end of the second millennium BC.

This common Urnfield background could be the major element that is reflected in the term 'Celtic' which in the second century BC Polybius applied in a general way to the different tribal groups in southern France. However, it is probably unwise to claim too close a correlation between known archaeological groups at this period and undefined names like Celtic and Ligurian, that may have had all manner of meanings – ethnic, linguistic, political, purely geographical or even semi-mythical – to the early writers, or later scholiasts, who recorded them.

7
The Coming of Rome and the Establishment of Roman Gaul
OLWEN BROGAN

Gallia Transalpina

As proto-history passes into history we become familiar with many Gallic tribes, and 'cultures' begin to give way to known, named communities. Before tracing the process which made Gaul into a group of Roman provinces, it may be well to look at the Celts as the Romans saw them.

The transalpine society which welcomed luxury imports from the lands to the south was an aristocratic one. The grave-goods of the Hallstatt and La Tène chieftains of the sixth to the third century BC are the kind of thing that goes with the concept of the Heroic Society as we see it in Homer, and that is also to be found in early Irish literature with its heroes like Cuchulainn and his peers. Something of this is also mirrored in classical literature of the last centuries BC where we read of champions parading in front of the battle-order, challenging their opponents to come forward and engage in single combat (Diodorus Siculus v, 29). Before battle joined there was a mighty din of war-cries and of the famous Gallic trumpets. Polybius, describing the battle of Telamon (225 BC; ii, 29,5-7), writes of 'such a tumult of sound that it seemed that not only the trumpets and the soldiers but all the country round had got a voice and caught up the cry'. Their weapons and shields, often finely decorated, are known from archaeological finds of various periods. The Celtic physical type according to ancient writers is the tall muscular blond whom we see in the statues of the school of Pergamon. This was the type the Celts themselves admired and they are said to have treated their hair with a wash of lime to make it more blond (Diod. Sic. v, 28). This, however, underlines the fact that in a country so long settled as Gaul, and with so many strains in its population, there must have been many Gauls, probably a majority, who were not as blond as they would have liked to be.

Chiefs had their bands of personal followers, called clients by the Romans, who were bound to their leader by ties of service in return for his protection. Below them were the artisans, peasants and herdsmen. Except along the Mediterranean seaboard most of the population lived scattered about the countryside in small villages or farmsteads which were often isolated, using hill-top refuges in case of need. Near the Mediterranean there were already agglomerations of a more permanent nature, as at Ensérune in the fourth century (Chapter 6, p. 188). By the mid-first century there are indications of the beginnings of some degree of urban life in central Gaul (p. 201-3).

It was a vivacious, quarrelsome society, and the headstrong Gallic nature is stressed again and again by classical authors. Valour was prized, but so also was the wisdom of the religious leaders, the Druids. The bards, the poet-musicians, were highly regarded by a poetry-loving people. The Celts had great talents and had produced a splendid art (Jacobsthal 1944; Megaw 1970) inspired by classical, Etruscan, Scythian and Iranian models, but manifestly creative in its own right. Finds of the late second and the first century BC in Gaul cannot be compared in richness with those of the earlier period, an impoverishment ascribed frequently to the devastating effects of the Cimbric invasions and the unrest of the succeeding years. The finest late Pagan Celtic art has been found in Britain and in Ireland. We may however remind ourselves of the enormous booty gathered by Caesar and his soldiers during the Gallic War. Caesar, according to Suetonius (*Div. Iul.* liv, 2) did not hesitate to rob the holy places of Gaul and he brought so much gold back to Rome that the price of the metal fell heavily. In such circumstances many fine examples of Celtic metalwork must have disappeared for ever. An echo of the antique Gallic wealth is found in the tale of the treasure deposited in a sacred lake at Tolosa (Strabo iv, 1, 13) and in the chance preservation of the gold torcs of Frasnes-lez-Buissenal, Belgium (Piggott 1970, 129) and of Mailly-le-Camp, Aube (Joffroy 1969), both ascribed to the first century BC.

The Gauls excelled in the techniques of mining and metalworking but above all they were highly skilled farmers and stock-raisers, as the Romans quickly appreciated. The widespreading ramifications of La Tène culture and trade have already been noticed (Chapter 6). We have seen how numerous were the contacts between the peoples of Gaul, as we may now begin to call it, and the classical world, how Massilia (Greek Massalia) had for generations been trading with the people to the north, how *oppida* in Languedoc (p. 160) showed a brisk demand for Greek and, later, Italian goods. From the late third century the Gauls issued coins.

It was not the Gauls who brought the first Roman army to Languedoc, but the passage of Hannibal in

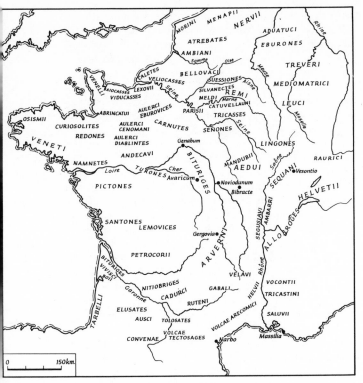

1 *Gallic tribes in the time of Caesar*

218 BC. The Gallic chiefs for the most part let Hannibal pass without hindrance and were paid handsomely (Livy xxi, 20; Polyb. iii, 41, 7). The Massalians viewed his arrival with natural dismay and welcomed the Romans. The outcome of the Second Punic War, however, with Rome's acquisition of two provinces in Spain, inevitably affected southern Gaul, which was an essential link in communications between Rome and Spain.

Massalia, in the second century, came to look to Rome for help against the tribes of the hinterland (Jullian i, 519-22) and it was Rome's defeat of the Saluvii of Entremont in two successive campaigns (125 and 124) that prepared the way for the Roman province. Meanwhile, the Arverni of the Massif Central, who had for some time been the dominant Gallic tribe, were attempting to extend their hegemony at the expense of their rivals, the Aedui of the Morvan, another major group, and formed alliances with the Allobroges of the Rhône valley and with the Sequani to the northeast of the Aedui. The Aedui answered this threat by the fateful step of appealing to Rome; and Rome, with an eye to future advantage as was her habit, agreed to befriend them, so that from about 125 BC the Aedui enjoyed the title of Friend and Ally of the Roman people (Livy, *Ep.* 61; Jullian iii, 14 and 28).

In 124-123 Saluvian fugitives took refuge with the Allobroges who prepared to make war on their behalf. Rome answered with an army sent to Gaul in 122, led by the consul Cn. Domitius Ahenobarbus. Behind the Allobroges were their allies the Arverni, now beginning to take alarm. The splendour of the Arvernian kings had fired the imagination of the Celts. There had been Luern with his sumptuous feasts for all comers, and his silver-plated chariot in which he drove forth scattering gold and silver coins among the people (Jullian ii, 548-50). Now there was his son Bituitus who, says Appian (*Celtica* XII), sent an ambassador to meet Domitius, 'arrayed magnificently and followed by attendants also adorned, and by dogs; for the barbarians of this region use dogs also as bodyguards. A musician too was in the train who sang in barbarous fashion the praises of king Bituitus.' Domitius paid no attention to the ambassador or his dogs or his bard, and pushed forward. He defeated the Allobroges and when in 121 Bituitus at last came down from his mountains and crossed the Rhône it was to fall an easy prey to Quintus Fabius Maximus who had been sent north with a fresh army.

The last struggle of the Saluvii has left traces in their *oppidum* Entremont (Benoît 1968) on the hill to the northwest of Aix-en-Provence, where many Roman ballista balls and *pila* have been found by the excavators. Sextius, the Roman commander, auctioned off most of the inhabitants into slavery and then built a military post, the *castellum* of Aquae Sextiae,[1] below, but still on ground high enough to dominate the important lines of communication which had been one of the factors in the rise of Entremont.

Domitius attended to the pacification of the land between Rhône and Pyrenees. He is justly regarded as the founder of the province of Gallia Transalpina. Two vital steps followed, the laying out of the *Via Domitia* and, a few years later, the foundation of the colony of Narbo Martius (Narbonne). A milestone bearing the name of Domitius was found twenty Roman miles south of Narbonne in 1949 (Duval 1949). The colony was founded by his son and M. Licinius Crassus (the later Triumvir) about 118 BC. It was not a virgin site. It lay in the territory of a tribe called the Elisyci and an *oppidum* Naro (= Narbo) had long existed here (Jannoray 1955; Benedict 1942; *Carte Arch.* fasc. 12) and had issued bronze coins before the arrival of the Romans. Tribal land of the defeated natives was automatically impounded for the settlement of the new colonists. Narbo, the first successful Roman colony outside Italy, had become an exceedingly prosperous port within a generation, but in recognising its commercial importance we must not forget its strategic function as the western counterpart of Aquae Sextiae.

Before the young colony was ten years old Gaul suffered invasion by wandering tribes, the Cimbri from Jutland and their following, who entered Gaul in 109 BC seeking booty and land. Crossing the Rhine with them were many adventurers they had picked up en

[1] The early *castrum* of Aquae Sextiae must lie under the old town; parts of the wall of its successor, the Augustan colony, have been found. The *Via Aurelia* passed near the present Hôtel de Ville. (*Gallia* XI, 1953, 107; XIII, 1954, 294; Grenier *Manuel*, I, 296f.; II, 670f.)

route, the Teutones of uncertain origin, the Celtic Tigurini (a part of the Helvetii) and the German Aduatuci. The difference between German and Celt is at this stage far from clear-cut and is probably more a degree of civilisation than any ethnic distinction. Nevertheless Gauls and Romans now made acquaintance in dramatic fashion with a danger which later became one of the chief cements between them. The Gauls re-fortified their old *oppida* (Hubert 1932, 133). Roman armies were hastily brought north of the Alps to cope with the danger. There followed three total Roman defeats, culminating in the destruction of two consular armies at Arausio (Orange) in 105. In the spring of 104 Marius arrived in Gaul with a new army which he proceeded to train. At last came the famous defeats of the Teutoni and Ambrones near Aquae Sextiae in 102 and of the Cimbri at Vercellae in northern Italy the following spring; this saved Gaul as well as Italy.

Gallia Transalpina was destined for a brilliant future, but it could not escape the misfortunes and malpractices of the last uneasy years of Republican rule. Here, as in other provinces, the population was squeezed for money by agencies both public and private. The native inhabitants had to pay their *tributum* (the tax levied on a conquered population) and to endure the various official exactions, such as the upkeep of roads, requisitions for the subsistence of armies, and the provision of lodgings for soldiers in winter quarters. Narbo drew to itself increasing numbers of Roman and Italian *negotiatores*, merchants and financiers who were often rapacious money-lenders. Here was a new area to exploit, and how eagerly and successfully this was done is to be seen in Cicero's *Pro Fonteio* (Jullian iii, 98-100, 119-20 for this and other references); it is not surprising that there was unrest. Fonteius, governor from 76 to 74 BC, had to suppress a rising that threatened Narbo. The burning of the *oppidum* of Cayla at this time may well have been a case of punitive action on the part of the Romans (Taffanel 1967).

Roman armies in the field (like other armies) were accompanied by traders profiting by supplying the troops and also prompt to deal in such matters as booty – this in particular in its most plentiful form, slaves. Such traders had gathered round the Roman camp when the prisoners of Entremont were put up for auction, and there will have been the same hard-headed men with the armies that defeated the Allobroges and the Arverni. They looked with sharp eyes for any opportunities of further profit that might accrue in Gallia Transalpina, and the long-familiar demand of the Celtic people for wine found ever more and more willing suppliers. A corollary to this was the well-established trade in south Italian pottery, chiefly wine cups, which continued to expand. Ancient wrecks examined off the south French coast are nearly always found to have carried cargoes of wine.[1] Wine jars and cups of the period occur on numerous sites all over Gaul (see p. 208).

A more pleasing side of the picture can be seen in the links which some of the leading Roman families forged with the Gauls. It was traditional that a commander to whom a people had surrendered should feel responsible for their subsequent well-being, and on the Gallic side there was the long-established relationship of patron and client which was transferred to the new conditions of life. Accordingly the Domitii are found as patrons of the Allobroges and Vocontii. They and other high officers used the old right of conferring Roman citizenship on native notables, who took the gentile name of their patron. It was thus that the many Domitii, Valerii, Cornelii and Pompeii of the Province originated. The presence of Pompey in 72 left an important mark in the Pyrenean foot-hills, in the establishment of the city of Lugdunum Convenarum (Saint-Bertrand-de-Comminges) at the foot of an older *oppidum*, where he settled some of the followers of the Roman rebel Sertorius.

The Via Domitia has left many traces between Nîmes and Roussillon (Grenier *Manuel* II; *Carte Arch.* fasc. 8, 10, 12). Its causeway persists as field boundaries, paths and minor tracks, and in places it is still the line taken by the modern highway. It followed the ancient route said to have been taken by Hercules on his way back from the Hesperides. It crosses numerous streams and several sizeable rivers like the Aude, Hérault, Vidourle, and for a road of this importance bridges were a necessity. Narbonne must have had one from the first. The remains of several are known along the road, but their dating has not been ascertained. From the Antonine Itinerary we know that a small trading post on the road between St Thibéry and Nîmes bore the name of Forum Domitii.

Other public monuments of the age have disappeared. Such were the trophies of Pompey, on the frontier between Gaul and Spain (Cass. Dio xli, 24) and those set up by Domitius Ahenobarbus and Fabius near the Rhône (Florus iii, 2; Strabo iv, 1). The *Fossae Marianae*, a canal dug by the troops of Marius to facilitate navigation through the Rhône delta, was handed over to the city of Massilia.[2] It reached the sea at Fos (*Fossae Marianae*) and is believed to be the Bras-Mort running from the Rhône at Le Grand-Passou to the Etang de Galejou (Grenier *Manuel* II, 493, 501-6). Glanum is the only site that has produced Italian-type houses of the pre-Caesarian period (Rolland 1946, 38, 77ff.). The old *oppida* of the southwest, however, were not abandoned at the conquest, for example Montlaurès close to Narbonne, and Ensérune, where settlement continues into the early first century AD.

---

[1] *Gallia* XVI, 1958, 5; XX, 1962, 147-76; XXVII, 1969, 465: a wreck near Porquerolles with a cargo of metal is an interesting exception; *Gallia* suppl. XIV, 1961.

[2] Greek Massalia has been covered by later buildings through 2000 years. The Quartier de la Bourse was badly damaged during the Second World War and excavation has revealed remains of the Hellenistic period, including 150 m. of town wall (M. Euzennat, *Gallia* XXVII, 1969, 423-8).

The campaigns of Caesar

CAESAR

By their defeat of the Arverni in 121 BC the Romans had made their strength known north of the Cevennes, and their alliance with the Aedui had already driven a wedge into the centre of Gaul, but for sixty years Gallia Comata ('Long-Haired Gaul') the vast region between the Cevennes, the Rhine and the ocean had been left to itself.

Choice must here be made whether to dismiss the story of the Gallic War, which has been told so often, in a couple of paragraphs or whether to recount briefly some of its main episodes. It is perhaps worth attempting the latter, firstly because it acquaints the reader with the location and history of the main tribes who play an important part in Roman Gaul, and secondly because it seems desirable to summarise what is known of the archaeology of the campaigns.

The story of the conquest is told in Caesar's *Bellum Gallicum*. After the long period of prehistoric anonymity we come upon this remarkable work, concise, sober, sophisticated, yet full of drama, which suddenly brings a generation to life. To Caesar we owe a picture-gallery of contemporary characters, the scheming pro-Roman Diviciacus, the heroes Vercingetorix and Ambiorix, the crafty and able German Ariovistus. In it the Gauls, with all their qualities, good and bad, step into the full light of history. Caesar's account has been argued over for generations, but no amount of criticism can alter the hard facts of the conquest. The broad details of the various campaigns are unassailable, though Caesar found it advantageous to alter the emphasis here and there, to telescope events or even to tamper with their sequence (Rambaud 1953). It is evident that he was stating a case, for his own political future was at stake, but he had to tell his story with a minimum of distortion, since he was dealing with events in which many men of importance in the Roman political world had shared. As for matters such as the works around Alesia, archaeology has vindicated his accuracy to a high degree. The archaeological record for Gaul during the conquest is otherwise thin. For a century the celebrated *Histoire de Jules César* of the Emperor Napoleon III, with its *Atlas* of plans drawn to illustrate the sites claimed to be identified, and the excavations of Colonel Stoffel, has had to suffice, although under fire from numerous critics. The truth seems to be that Napoleon's identifications of the major sites like Alesia, Gergovia and probably Uxellodunum, stand, but that too much haste and an excess of enthusiasm led to mistakes over a number of lesser places.

Caesar's consulship expired at the end of December, 59 BC, and he awaited his proconsulship of Illyricum, Cisalpine Gaul and Transalpine Gaul hopefully. Of late the German Suebi had been giving trouble in northeast Gaul. The astute Suebic king Ariovistus had no mind to fight unnecessarily but, like the Romans, he understood how to take advantage of the divisions among the Gauls. About 71 BC he had taken Upper Alsace from the Sequani as payment for having helped them

against the Aedui. In 61 he was again threatening trouble and the Aedui sent an embassy to Rome asking for help. The Senate passed a decree 'recommending the present governor of Transalpine Gaul and his successors to protect the interests of the Aedui and other friends of Rome as far as such protection might be compatible with his duty to his province (*BG* i, 35). Ariovistus in turn sent presents to Rome and was accepted as a 'friend of the Roman People' (*BG* i, 43). But there was another Gallic tribe in difficulties, the Helvetii, who, by the beginning of the century, had been driven by the Germans from their former lands between the Main and the upper Rhine and were now confined to the area between the Jura and the Alps. Cramped for space and threatened by further German advances, they decided to move out and seek a new home in the land of the Santones, in the west of Gaul.

We can watch the preparation of a folk migration which must resemble so many which had gone before it in the course of the previous millennium. The Helvetii took two years to get ready, collecting large stores of food to take with them, and building waggons to carry their possessions. At the appointed time the waggons were loaded up and the abandoned homes and all superfluous food were burned so that the expected German invaders should not benefit and so that the tribe should realise the irrevocableness of the move. News of the impending start reached Caesar in Rome in March 58. He left immediately and in eight days was at Genava (Geneva) where a legion awaited him. The Helvetii requested permission to pass through the Province in peace (i.e. to follow the Rhône to its confluence with the Saône and then to cross over into Gallia Comata). Caesar refused and they had to take a more northerly route. He hastened back to Cisalpine Gaul and brought up his main army with which he too entered free Gaul, a decisive step from which all his subsequent moves stemmed. The Aedui were eager for help, and Caesar, obeying the Senate's decree of 61 BC, followed and defeated the migrating host,[1] which was now on Aeduan territory. He commanded the surviving Helvetii to return to their former homes, to rebuild

---

[1] Caesar states (*BG* i, 29) that tablets, with names in Greek letters of the Helvetii and their allies taking part in the migration, were found among the booty taken after the final battle. The total given is 368,000 men, women and children, 263,000 being Helvetii. Caesar says that he sent back 110,000 at the end of the war, a census of whom was taken. These figures are now usually adopted, with reservations, by scholars, though they have been hotly disputed (Stähelin 1948, 73 n.1). Even the stout champion of Caesar's veracity, Rice Holmes (2nd edn., p. 241) thought the numbers 'enormous' and found that he could not share Stoffel's view that 143,000 could have died in the final battle. Grenier also (1945, p. 227) finds the numbers difficult to believe. If the figure is the total tribal number it might have been reduced by a good many slipping away at an early stage to return to their homes, or disappearing along the route. The approximate area of the Helvetian territory is known and it has been calculated that the figures given would work out at about thirteen persons to the square kilometre. The final figure of 110,000 is probably reliable, so we may guess that there had been at least 200,000 on the move.

them and to start afresh. The Allobroges were instructed to supply them with corn, so at least they were not to be allowed to starve. That a better future awaited them is shown by the economic and artistic activity of Roman Switzerland (Stähelin 1948).

A site of very great interest, the Engelhalbinsel near Berne (Müller-Beck 1962, 133), has yielded traces of the Caesarian period. A La Tène settlement of the early first century BC was destroyed about the middle of the century and rebuilt with new fortifications very shortly afterwards. The excavators have concluded that the earlier settlement was burnt and abandoned by its inhabitants when they joined the migration, and that the subsequent one was built by the returning survivors.

The result of the campaign electrified Gaul, and the tribes which had been menaced by the Helvetian march rejoiced at the outcome. A Council of Chiefs was summoned and Caesar was invited to rid Gaul of Ariovistus. By the end of the summer the German king had been outmanoeuvred and completely routed in Alsace. Caesar now left his army to winter in Gaul among the Sequani, an ominous sign for those with eyes to read it, probably choosing the *oppidum* of Vesontio (Besançon) as quarters for the legions. To the northwest were the Lingones, who gave no trouble to Caesar, but beyond them were the Belgae, who mistrusted his intentions and prepared to march against him in the following spring.

At this point (57 BC) Fortune handed Caesar (*BG* ii, 3) a supremely useful gift, the co-operation of the Remi, one of the Belgic tribes, who deliberately decided that their future lay with Rome and doubtless that it was also worth seeking Caesar's friendship for the immediate advantage that they would gain in being protected from their neighbours, the Suessiones. But the muster of the rest of the Belgae proceeded. Caesar advanced to meet them, crossing the Aisne near Berry-au-Bac and raising the usual entrenched camp. This is one of the Caesarian sites traced by Colonel Stoffel, a marching-camp of 41 hectares astride the present Pontavert-Guignicourt road, with *claviculae* at the gateways and a regularity which attests its Roman origin (Napoleon III *Atlas*, pl. 8 and 9; Grenier *Manuel* I, 191-3). After several minor engagements the Belgae withdrew. Like all barbarian hosts they had not the necessary organisation or supplies to remain long in the field. The Romans followed them, taking *oppidum* after *oppidum* and finally receiving the surrender of the Ambiani whose capital was Samarobriva (Amiens). Caesar had now, however, to meet the Nervii and the Atrebates who nearly overcame him in one of the fiercest battles of the war.

By the spring of 56 BC many of the tribes of the northwest, led by the Veneti of Brittany, were preparing for war. The ensuing campaign includes the first recorded battle in which the oaken sailing ships of the Atlantic seaboard took part. Despite the excellence of the Venetic ships, which greatly impressed Caesar, all the advantages went to the Roman side and a final disaster, a sudden calm, confounded the Veneti when they were attempting to escape.

Caesar describes the promontory forts which were the Venetic strongholds (*BG* iii, 12). From these in case of need escape might be made by taking to their ships, a tactic frequently carried out during the earlier part of the campaign. A number of these 'cliff castles' on the coasts of Morbihan and Finistère were examined in 1938-9 by Wheeler and Richardson (1957). They are defended across the narrow strips of land connecting them with the mainland by one to three banks and ditches, and hut-sites are visible on some of them. Iron Age pottery of 160-50 BC was found and also many sling-stones.

The disastrous defeat of the Veneti brought in its train the downfall of the neighbouring tribes. Coin hoards of the period are frequent in their territory (e.g. Colbert de Beaulieu 1956, *Osismii*) and also in Jersey, where it is thought that some of the fugitives took refuge. The exploration of some of the *oppida* has thrown light on the greatness of the effort made by neighbouring tribes. One of the most important is the 20-hectare (48-acre), multivallate *oppidum*, with *murus gallicus*, of Le Châtellier at Le Petit Celland in the land of the Veneti at the base of the Cotentin peninsula, excavated in 1939 (Wheeler and Richardson 1957). Its occupation had been short, and the main gate had been destroyed by fire; many coins of the Caesarian period were found. This tribal refuge has its counterpart in the still larger Camp d'Artus, Huelgoät (Finistère), identified as the main refuge of the Osismii, which had suffered the same fate.

The year 55 BC saw the first expeditions into Germany and Britain. It also saw the savage destruction of two German tribes, the Usipetes and Tencteri, who had hoped to establish themselves in new homes west of the

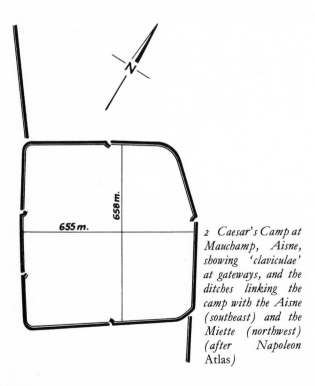

2 Caesar's Camp at Mauchamp, Aisne, showing 'claviculae' at gateways, and the ditches linking the camp with the Aisne (southeast) and the Miette (northwest) (after Napoleon Atlas)

655 m.

658 m.

Rhine. This constant pressure of would-be migrants into Gaul is Caesar's chief justification for his Gallic War, but the attack on the Usipetes and Tencteri while negotiations were proceeding was an act of bad faith against which Cato in Rome protested vehemently (Appian, *Celtica* XVIII; Plutarch, *Cato*, li).

More trouble was brewing among the ever active Belgae and in the late autumn of 54 BC Ambiorix, a chief of the Eburones, saw his chance and lured a Roman legion out of its winter camp, destroying it and its commanders. Caesar cruelly suppressed the Eburones the following spring but Ambiorix managed to disappear into the great forest of the Ardennes and was never found. In 1961, air photographs taken by M. Agache of a Gallo-Roman theatre site near Breteuil-sur-Noye (Oise), 36 km. south of Amiens, revealed two parallel ditches of a large camp, and an entrance protected by a *titulus*. Trial trenches were dug and the section of the ditches showed up clearly in the chalk. It is thought that this must be a Roman legionary camp of the Caesarian period, perhaps the camp of Crassus in 54 BC mentioned by Caesar (*BG* v, 46, 1; Noché and Dufour 1963).

88; VIII   In the fateful winter of 53–52 the uprising associated with the name of Vercingetorix, the Arvernian leader, began. Caesar had left his legions among the Treveri, Lingones and Senones, and, having provided for their supplies, had gone as usual to Cisalpine Gaul. The campaign of 52 BC is marked by the participation of the Arverni who had hitherto made no move, and towards

87   its end, by the defection of the Aedui. The Remi, who had freely made their choice six years previously, and his other faithful allies the Lingones, remained stubbornly on the side of Caesar. Most of the Belgae held aloof. The Treveri, who had troubles of their own with the Germans, were unable to move. Preparations for revolt began with the holding of a Council of the Gauls in the land of the Carnutes, and the first overt act was the massacre of Roman traders and business men in Genabum (Orleans), the usual accompaniment of such risings in the provinces of Republican Rome. The plan of the Gauls was to prevent Caesar from rejoining his army, a wise decision foiled by his unexpectedly early start and his usual celerity of movement. He re-took Genabum. A little later the full-dress siege of Avaricum (Bourges) followed, of special interest to us because his account contains the celebrated description of the *murus gallicus* (*BG* vii, 23), a timber-laced rampart, the timber framework consisting of beams laid along and across the line of the wall and nailed together (Cotton 1957; Dehn 1960, 43–55; Harmand 1967, 64). Caesar says that a distance of two feet separated the timbers and that between them blocks of stone were laid in regular courses, both on the outside and the inside of the wall. The centre was filled with rubble. He expresses admiration for it 'since the stone protects from fire and the timber from battering'. One of the first examples of the *murus gallicus* to be discovered was the rampart of

99   Vertault, and this has recently been re-examined by Joffroy. It seems, however, to be post-Caesarian (*Gallia*

1958, 348; 1960, 344). Earlier examples are the *oppida* of Huelgoät and Le Châtellier (p. 196).

Vercingetorix now withdrew southwards to his own territory and concentrated his forces on the hill of Gergovia, whither Caesar followed him. The ditches of Caesar's camps were found by the indefatigable Colonel Stoffel and were re-examined in 1936 and following years by Père Gorce (Napoleon *Atlas*; Gorce 1941).[1] Caesar failed to take the *oppidum* by assault and this definite check caused the anti-Roman party among the Aedui to gain the upper hand. He therefore had to leave Gergovia and hasten north to join his legate Labienus, who had meanwhile been conducting a successful but perilous campaign at Lutetia (Paris). Caesar, protector of Gaul from the Germans, was now reduced to sending over the Rhine for horsemen and in the next encounter this German cavalry turned the fortunes of the day. Vercingetorix withdrew to Alesia, where he had already collected supplies and arms. There follows the immortal story of the siege and of the Gallic cavalry sent to all the tribes to bring back a rescue force, while Caesar dug lines of contravallation to keep the besieged in and of circumvallation to keep the relieving army out. When this arrived, after at least six weeks, three successive battles were fought around Alesia, but it was all in vain. The relieving force, what was left of it, fled; Vercingetorix surrendered to save the starving defenders of the *oppidum*.

The excavations of Caesar's siege-works around Alesia carried out for Napoleon III in 1861–5 (Napoleon *Atlas*, pl. 25, 28; Grenier *Manuel* I) have acquired fresh interest through the recent discovery of contemporary documents (Le Gall 1959, 1961). Papers preserved by the families of Paul Millot, the Agent Voyer who supervised the digging, and of his assistant, V. Pernet, have come to light. Also, in 1957 M. Jean Harmand, Asst. Conservateur at Saint-Germain-en-Laye, discovered in the museum library store an album of drawings by Millot of the excavations of 1861 and 1862 carried out by the Commission de la Topographie des Gaules. This album contains 320 drawings, of which 280 are of the Caesarian works. In 1862 the direction of the excavations was transferred to Stoffel, and a number of his letters to Millot are among the finds. These documents between them show the extreme thoroughness and care with which the work was carried out. In addition to these discoveries there has been verification on the ground at several points of the trenches discovered by the early excavators and air photographs have been 3 taken which show traces of the circumvallation (*Gallia* 1954, 1956, 1957, 1958; *RAE* 1956; Le Gall 1959).

[1] Fr. M. Gorce looked for Caesar's camps on the sites marked by Stoffel. His trenches across the lines of the main camp showed clear sections of v-shaped ditches, some of which the present writer saw at the time of their excavation. His publication in the *Revue des Deux Mondes* (1941) unfortunately only gives rough sketches showing the position of his trenches, but a photograph of one of the sections was published in *Gergovie, Haut Lieu de France*, 'Auvergne', Clermont-Ferrand, 1943, p. 33. The excavations are noted briefly by Lantier in the *RA* 1937, I, p. 93, and following years.

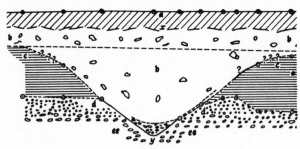

3 Alesia: section of one of the ditches of the double fosse at Grésigny. X-Y = 1 m.
a. arable soil; b. clay, gravel and stones; c. clay without intrusive elements; d. small fine gravel; e. coarser gravel (after Joly)

Weapons and other objects of the period of the siege can be seen at the Museum of Saint-Germain and at Alise-Sainte-Reine. The find on the battle-field of a fine silver drinking-cup such as might have been the property of a Roman officer has been confirmed by the newly-discovered records. The greatest number of finds was made near Grésigny at the foot of Mont Réa in the ancient ditches and in an area extending over hundreds of metres; there were large numbers of weapons and the bones of men and horses, also 619 Gallic and Roman coins which have been studied by J. B. Colbert de Beaulieu (1966). The 134 Roman and Italian coins, the inscriptions on most of which are legible, are all Republican, the two latest being of 54 BC. The Gallic coins are all of pre-51 types and among them is one inscribed with the name of Vercingetorix.

The archaeological picture of the *oppidum* itself is less clear. The plateau (407 m. above sea-level) covers 97 hectares but the small Mandubian settlement occupied only part of the western end. Remains of a dry-stone wall which may be Gallic were found at several points along the edge, but the sides are so steep that very formidable walls were not needed and they may not even have been continuous. Several short pieces of wall including some *murus gallicus* have been found at the east end of the *oppidum* but it is difficult to date them or to account for their position, and J. Harmand (1967) has suggested that the *murus gallicus* may simply be part of the enclosure wall of the Gallo-Roman sanctuary of Apollo Moritasgus. As for the traces of the camp of Vercingetorix which Napoleon thought he had found, these were already rejected as such by the excavators. There are thus still many puzzles to solve.

Vercingetorix had been vanquished, but there was still resistance. The Bellovaci were now preparing to move with their whole confederacy, six months too late. In the early spring of 51 BC Caesar marched to meet them as they made their way along the valley of the Oise towards the land of the Suessiones, and though they fought with spirit and cunning the campaign ended in the usual way. It was long customary to locate the campaign against the Bellovaci in the neighbourhood of Compiègne but since Matherat's work in the 1930s, Clermont-de-l'Oise has been accepted by many scholars

as the Bellovacan stronghold and they believe that Caesar's camps are the earthworks Matherat excavated on the hill of Nointel. Objections to this have been raised by Harmand who wishes to re-examine the two hills near Compiègne favoured by Napoleon (Matherat 1936, 1943; Harmand 1959; Napoleon *Atlas*).

The final campaign was in the southwest where two chiefs, Drappes and Lucterius, attempted an advance towards the Province but were forced to take refuge in Uxellodunum. In the end Caesar arrived and cut off the hill-fort's water-supply. The Puy d'Issolu near Vayrac (Lot) is usually identified as Uxellodunum (Isso-lu = Uxello?) with reasonable though not complete certainty (Grenier *Manuel* I, 203) the most telling point in favour being the existence of a spring on the west side of the hill where a subterranean gallery was found which could well be that of the Roman mine (Napoleon *Atlas*, pl. 31, 32). There has been no recent check on this, though a stretch of the *oppidum* rampart has been excavated (*Gallia* 1962, 593).

Thus Rome had conquered a new province, an acquisition of illimitable importance for the future of the Empire and of Europe. In *L'Histoire de la Gaule*, Camille Jullian, the great champion of the Gauls, has summed up the reasons why the Gallic cause was hopeless from the beginning, reasons only too apparent from the most superficial reading of the story: tribal jealousy, the inability to act in concert for any length of time, the headlong rush into action without proper thought against the better armed, better trained Roman forces. On top of that they had the misfortune to come up against one of the ablest generals and politicians that the ancient world produced. There was, too, the prestige of Rome, the city which had defeated all comers, whether barbarians or great powers, and the irresistible pull of the Mediterranean civilisation, which made many Gauls like the Remi ready to pay the price of submission in order to share in it. Yet there is the other side of the picture, the massacres and devastation, and there is something in Jullian's description of the war (iii, 568) as a gigantic slave raid.

The fashioning of Roman Gaul

GAUL AFTER CAESAR

Caesar had to wind up affairs in Gaul in a hurry. He made provision for its government and security for the time being, assigning legates and a minimum of troops and also a stipulated but not excessive *tributum* (Jullian iii, 571; iv, 302). He recruited into his army a number of Gauls, putting them mostly into cavalry regiments (iii, 571-2). The Gallic aristocracy had the Celtic aptitude for a soldier's life and a long tradition of mercenary service in distant parts of the world, and they went not unwillingly to war under the great general whose many successes had shown him to be a favourite of the gods. This removed from Gaul a large unruly element, not unlike the younger sons of the Frankish and Norman barons who, more than a millennium later, went to seek their fortunes on crusade. But the loss of life and the carrying into slavery of so many men, women and children also ensured a generation of forced calm. It is not surprising that Gaul lacked the strength to give serious trouble during the civil wars (though even so the Bellovaci rose in 46, the Aquitani in 38 BC). What is remarkable is its rapid recovery.

Caesar had brutally punished the Gauls who opposed him, but after peace had been established he dealt fairly with them. In the crisis in which he found himself he had no choice but to exercise his celebrated clemency. The pro-Roman Gauls also now had their reward. Caesar was liberal in grants of Roman citizenship and the numerous families in Roman Gaul with the *nomen* Julius testify to his generosity and to that of later members of his family. Strong links of loyalty to the Julian house were forged which survived the vicissitudes of the dynasty and several Gallic risings.

There was no radical alteration in Celtic society from its state as described in the *Commentaries*, though change gradually came about, the first thing being the final disappearance of kings, who had already been discarded by the greater tribes of Celtica before Caesar's day, in favour of elected magistrates called *vergobrets* (*BG* i, 16; *CIL* XIII, 1048). On the one hand there were still the powerful nobles, chiefs with broad lands and great wealth able to support large bands of followers or *clientes* on whom they could call in time of war. They remained as a powerful element that the government had to reckon with. We hear of such chieftains again, Julius Sacrovir the Aeduan who revolted in AD 21; Julius Vindex, Roman Senator and Governor of Celtica in AD 68, a descendant of Aquitanian kings; the rebellious Lingonian chief Julius Sabinus in AD 70. On the other hand there were the peasants who tilled the soil. The Gauls produced plenty of wheat for their own consumption and Caesar had been able to feed his armies during his campaigns without serious difficulty. As for craftsmen and traders, they already formed an important element in pre-Roman Gaul, and had a prosperous future before them. Of religion and Druids mention will be made later.

The first concern of the survivors of the conquest was to keep alive and therefore to produce enough food. Life went quietly on and they were left very much to themselves. They often stayed on in their hill *oppida* and even strengthened the fortifications to give security in a post-war era not without its minor turbulence. We know little of Gaul in this period, but where we can lift the veil, we meet a vigour, an enterprise, which is far from reflecting a people exhausted by war and calamity. As the generation of the conquest died out and new men grew up who had not known the old heroic days, the Roman world was emerging from the ordeal of the civil war between Octavian and Antony. The brunt of these wars had happily passed Gaul by and now its provinces could benefit from the reorganisation of the whole empire that Augustus was to achieve.

In the interval many of the chiefs still issued coinage (Colbert de Beaulieu 1962). One of the best known of

them is the pro-Roman Arvernian Epasnactus (*BG* viii, 44) who issued coins during and after the war inscribed EPAD, the later ones a Romanised type copied from denarii of the Gens Platoria. A certain Asedullus imitated a *denarius* of A. Licinius Nerva of about 47 BC and inscribed it with his name and those of two other Gauls, Connos and Epillos. Another pro-Roman chief, Duratius (*BG* viii, 26, 27) inscribed his coins DVRAT/IVLIOS which shows that he had received Roman citizenship. They are found in the territory of the Pictones (Poitou). The coins of Q. Julius Togirix, who seems to have come from east Gaul, perhaps from the Sequani, are very abundant. He is thought to have been the commander of an auxiliary regiment, because on some of the coins he appears in an unmistakable Roman helmet (Dayet 1962). A late example of the series is that of GERMANVS INDVTILLI L which was copied from a Lugdunum coin of about 15-10 BC.

These are but a few of the post-conquest Gallic coins, but they show chiefs still in positions of some power, even though that power might be only a shadow of its former state; none of them coined gold, few silver, and the bronze was often debased.

THE AUGUSTAN PROVINCES

The Augustan system was to last substantially for nearly three centuries. The whole area of the Gauls was divided into four provinces, Gallia Narbonensis (the old Gallia Transalpina), Lugdunensis (part of Celtica), Belgica and Aquitania. To the old Basque Aquitania south of the Garonne was added the properly Celtic territory from Garonne to Loire, which made for administrative symmetry and cut up the large area formerly known as Celtica. The strip of land west of the Rhine was under the control of the army but remained part of Gaul and

4 *The Provinces of Gaul in the time of Augustus*

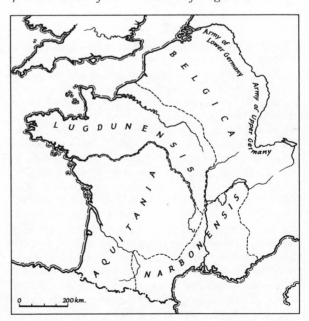

was not made into the provinces of Germania Superior and Germania Inferior until the Flavian period. In the early days all the Gallic provinces were governed by one man, often a member of the imperial family, such as Agrippa or Drusus, but when things settled down each province had its own governor. The finances of the Tres Galliae (Gallia Comata) were in the hands of two equestrian procurators, one at Lugdunum combining control of Lugdunensis and Aquitania, while the Procurator of Belgica, with his seat at Augusta Treverorum had, in addition to Belgica, the supervision of the Rhenish territory and thus the important function of controlling the pay and maintenance of the large armies stationed along the Rhine.

Little is known of the stations of troops within Gaul during the Civil War and Augustan periods, though a few military tombstones and legionary tiles have been found (Grenier *Manuel* I, 232 ff; cf. Ritterling *BJ* 1906, 172). It is possible that a military post existed at Néris-les-Bains (Allier).

From 12 BC to AD 16 Roman armies campaigned across the Rhine, but the attempt to establish a hold up to the Elbe was then abandoned and the Rhine became the permanent frontier except for minor adjustments later on. From the time of Tiberius until AD 70 there were four legions in Lower Germany, two at Vetera, one each at Novaesium and Bonna; and four in Upper Germany, two at Moguntiacum, one each at Argentorate and Vindonissa. In addition to the legions there were large numbers of auxiliary regiments. Troops were not stationed permanently in inner Gaul, save for an Urban Cohort at Lugdunum.

One of the basic tasks of Augustus was to put the finances of the provinces on a sound basis. Hence the importance of the census which provided the data on which taxation could be based. Taxation in some degree and customs dues had been levied by the more advanced tribes (*BG* i, 18) but the strict Roman methods were something new. With this unpalatable revolution the Gauls willy-nilly shouldered the burdens of civilisation. Nobody suffers taxation willingly, and the process was watched by the emperor with some anxiety; the census began in 27 BC and he went in person to start it off, though it must have taken a number of years to complete. The value of all landed property had to be recorded, the amount of arable and pasture land, of flocks and herds, the numbers of fruit-trees and, in the south, of olives and vines. Other forms of property were also listed and taxed. Augustus, following Caesar, retained the old tribe, or *civitas* as the Romans called it, as the basis of social and political organisation in Gaul, and indeed they could hardly have done otherwise. Tax-collection was left to the tribal magistrates. It followed that the headquarters where the business with the Roman State had to be transacted was the chief or most convenient tribal centre which now became a town if it were not one already. Indeed, the Romans deliberately encouraged the growth of town life and many important Gallo-Roman towns are Augustan foundations.

GALLIA NARBONENSIS:
the growth of towns

The proximity of the Greek cities had stimulated the development of a certain degree of town life before 125 BC, as has already been seen in the cases of Ensérune and Entremont. The small town of Glanum in the Alpilles is also of interest. Here Celts and Greek traders appear to have lived in amity and shared in the embellishment of the shrine of the healing goddess which gave Glanum a certain religious importance. But the most significant urban development of the first two generations of Roman rule had been that of the colony and port of Narbonne.

With the end of Caesar's campaigns there begins a new series of colonies and the Augustan peace ushered in a period of rapid growth, deliberately fostered by the Roman authorities. In the front rank were the five veteran colonies founded by Caesar and Augustus: Narbo, enlarged with veterans of the X Legion, Baeterrae (Béziers) and Arelate (Arles) – Caesarian; Forum Julii (Fréjus) and Arausio (Orange) – Augustan. Except possibly Forum Julii, they were set up in or alongside existing towns. Next came colonies with Latin rights, chief of them Vienna (Vienne) of the Allobroges and Valentia (Valence) of the Segovellauni, two native towns probably promoted in status by Caesar. These received new settlers who merged quickly with the local inhabitants. Colonia Nemausus (Nîmes), owing its colonial title to Augustus, is thought to have received a number of Egyptian Greeks after the war with Antony, the evidence being the coins of Nîmes showing a croco- 98 dile chained to a palm tree, and the large number of tombstones with Greek inscriptions found in the city (Grenier *Manuel* I, 314). Latin rights were liberally granted to the towns of Narbonensis, large and small. Their bestowal on a town meant that its magistrates became Roman citizens on taking up office, and transmitted the citizenship to their children, which resulted in a steady growth in the number of Roman citizens. The great *oppidum* of Ensérune survived through a final phase (30 BC–AD 25) but then became deserted. Cessero (St Thibéry), however, received Latin rights and was to live on, because of its position on the Via Domitia (p. 193). Tolosa, on the northwestern border of the province, had long been a place of importance. The site of the Celtic *oppidum* is Vieille-Toulouse (*Gallia* 1964, 450); the present city lies over the Gallo-Roman town that took its place.

When the colonies were laid out, allotments of land were measured on a grid system prepared by the *agrimensores*, the official surveyors. Traces of this grid, or centuriation, have been observed in a number of places (Grenier *Manuel* II, 12-23; Bradford 1957). In the centre of Orange nearly six hundred fragments of marble were unearthed, belonging to a monument on which was inscribed the official record of the property rights of the citizens. It is in the form of a map showing landholdings of both colonists and Gauls. This had been set up after the troubles of AD 70, but much of it must reflect the original settlement (Piganiol 1962).

Massilia, the ancient ally of Rome, had suffered heavily from the siege by Caesar after her mistake in espousing the cause of Pompey. Much of her commerce passed to the rising ports of Arelate (Arles) and Narbo. Her natural advantages began to reassert themselves in the first century AD though her chief renown now was as a centre of learning where Gauls could be taught the philosophy and literature of the Greek world and whither many young Romans were sent in preference to Athens.

It was the policy of Augustus and his associate Agrippa to foster the pride of the inhabitants of Narbonensis, native and colonist alike, in their cities, and these early years were a time of astonishing building activity which produced many of the famous Roman monuments of Provence. Augustus gave Nîmes its girdle of walls (16-15 BC), while Agrippa saw to the restoration of the fountain of the tutelary god Nemausus (*CIL* XII, 3153, 3154) and is often regarded, because of his interest in aqueducts, as the builder of the city aqueduct and thus of the Pont du Gard. He took no less interest in the smaller town of Glanum where he built a temple to Valetudo, the ancient goddess of the spring under her Latin name. The theatres of Arles and Orange, closely resembling one another and intimately bound up with the monumental layout of the two cities, are also attributed with virtual certainty to Augustus. The fine quality of the building in early Roman Provence has often been ascribed to the inherited skills of masons brought up to construct buildings in the Greek tradition, and the growing number of discoveries of Greek masonry makes this easy to believe (e.g. at St-Blaise, St-Rémy, Antibes; for Marseilles itself, see *Gallia* 1969, 423 ff.)

No pains were spared to express the might of Rome. On a hill above Monte Carlo stands the much-restored Tropaeum Augusti, the monument of 6 BC commemorating the subjugation in 25 BC of the Alpine tribes which for generations had made travel through the mountains or along the coast a hazard (Formigé 1949). Another trophy of the period was set up at Lugdunum Convenarum (St Bertrand-de-Comminges), celebrating in the old colony of Pompey the victories of Augustus. Caesar had placed an altar near Pompey's monument in the Pyrenees (Cass. Dio xli, 24).

The so-called 'triumphal arches' are normally monuments set up by communities to celebrate their municipal or colonial status or as tributes of loyalty to the emperor. Such an arch should lie just outside the city at the point where one of its axial roads cuts the *pomerium,* the ritual boundary. In Provence, five are still standing and the remains of eleven more are known. The most famous of them, the Orange arch, has recently been intensively studied by a team of eminent French scholars (Amy *et al.* 1962). It was found to have been built over the foundations of an earlier arch which may have been set up to commemorate the foundation of the colony shortly after 36 BC. The great three-bay arch still presents problems, but P.-M. Duval, summing up (*ibid.*), shows that it is later than has usually been thought and

must date from after AD 10 and most probably from between 21 and 26. The inscription to Tiberius was added after the arch had been completed. Above the side arches are sculptures with the familiar Celtic panoply of wild-boar standards, the carnyx, shields with Celtic decorations and names, etc., but careful study of the battle scenes by G. C. Picard and J.-J. Hatt (*ibid.*) has shown that the arms with which the Gauls are fighting Roman cavalrymen are Roman [1] and include the *gladius.* These Gauls are in fact already partially Romanised and the scene probably represents the defeat of Sacrovir in AD 21.

THE THREE GAULS
Towns
Caesar describes the Gauls as living in *aedificia*, isolated farms or other buildings, *vici*, villages, and *oppida*. The word *oppidum* may mean a temporary refuge or a fortified town, and it is sometimes difficult to make a distinction without archaeological evidence. The statement often found that there was no urban settlement in Gallia Comata before the Roman conquest implies a very rigid definition of urbanism, because there is plenty of evidence of stable if loose agglomerations. It must be admitted that the communities in the Tres Galliae had no knowledge of architecture in the Mediterranean sense; their houses or huts were of wood, often circular in plan, and covered with thatch or perhaps split-stone shingling. Their foundations might be of dry stone, but they had no knowledge of masonry. The question is, when does a large village become a town? The process is described for us just across the border, in Narbonensis, by Strabo's note (iv, i, 11) that the chief men of the Allobroges lived in Vienna 'formerly a village, but called, nevertheless, the "metropolis" of the tribe, and have built it up into a city'.

Among the *oppida* mentioned by Caesar there is first ʃ and foremost the hill-top town of Bibracte, on its 800 m. height, called by Caesar (*BG* i, 23) 'by far the largest and best-provided of the Aeduan towns'. Its military and political importance are clear from his narrative; it contained an important temple, and when it was excavated between 1865 and 1901, first by Bulliot and later by Déchelette, a considerable settlement was found, notable for its many workshops of iron-, bronze- and enamel-working. Most of the buildings traced belong, it must be admitted, to the period after 58, but there were some earlier structures (Cotton 1957; Déchelette *Manuel* 1st edn II, 948; 2nd edn IV, 453; Grenier *Manuel* II, 694; III, 343). Occupation continued until about 5 BC when Augustodunum (Autun) was founded in the valley below and the people of Bibracte moved down from their uncomfortable old stronghold. Alesia (407 m.) was a favoured site, not too high or cold or remote (Cotton 1957; Grenier *Manuel* I, II). The remnant of its people resumed life on the hill and their

---

1 The authors make the ingenious suggestion that the objects which have been regarded as *têtes coupées* are in fact simply Roman parade-helmets with visors used by cavalry regiments.

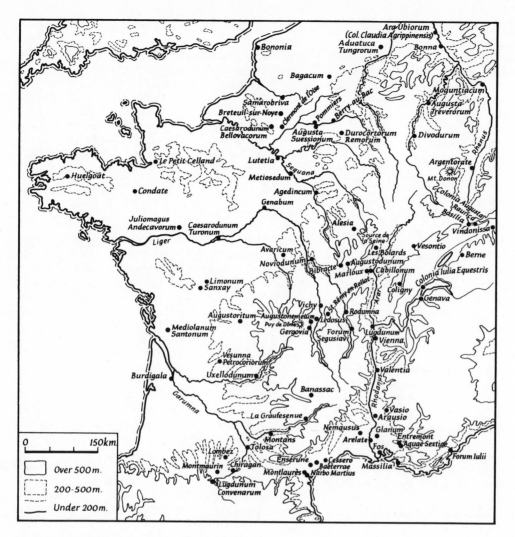

descendants remained there permanently. Its importance as a religious centre has been demonstrated by the excavation of several temples, Celtic shrines which lived on into the Gallo-Roman period.

Gergovia (600 m.) presents a number of unsolved problems (Hatt 1943; Labrousse 1948, 1950). No buildings that can be definitely dated to the period of Vercingetorix have so far been found and it would seem that the *oppidum* was then a refuge rather than a town. There had been plenty of inhabitants in the surrounding area. Hatt excavated an important La Tène III village at Aulnat east of Clermont-Ferrand (Hatt 1942, 1945) and recent extension of the work (by Périchon) shows that the settlement also flourished during the second century BC (La Tène II, see *Gallia* 1967, 304). On the other hand there is evidence of intensive occupation of Gergovia from about 30 BC to at least the Tiberian period. Other hill-tops in the vicinity, such as Corent, were also occupied, like Gergovia, in the post-conquest period. The pottery from all these sites is abundant and important, and dated by finds of imported pots (p. 208). Labrousse has wondered whether some adjustment in the dating system will become necessary which might

close the gap between 52 and 30 BC (Labrousse 1950, 32ff). A new town, Augustonemetum (Clermont-Ferrand), was founded in the valley below and thither the occupants of Gergovia in due course repaired, leaving a few farmers to occupy the plateau and to maintain the worship of the gods of the mountain in the pair of small Gallo-Roman temples near the east end of the plateau which may be presumed to have had Celtic predecessors.

Bibracte and Gergovia are by no means the only *oppida* that were replaced by Roman foundations. A large northern example is Pommiers on a height above the river Aisne. It is 40 hectares in extent, and may be Noviodunum (*BG* ii, 12) of the Suessiones. Dr J. B. Colbert de Beaulieu analysed 1900 coins found on the site and concluded: '1. It was heavily occupied from *c.* 70 to 51 BC; 2. Occupation continued in some measure into the principate of Augustus' (Wheeler and Richardson 1957, 130). It was replaced by Augusta Suessionum (Soissons), 5 kilometres to the southeast.

An example of a small *oppidum* is Chateaumeillant (Cher), identified as Mediolanum Biturigum, which appears to have been a centre of active commerce before Caesar. This was not seriously interrupted during Caesar's war, and life went on much as before after 52 BC. Two outstanding examples of refuges used only for the purpose of the war have already been noticed in the northwest (p. 196), the Camp d'Artus and Le Châtellier.

Oppida which were certainly towns when Caesar arrived are found in the major river valleys, generally on the river-banks, but here archaeological finds of the period are rare because the sites have been occupied continuously since antiquity. Avaricum (Bourges) was a place of unusual importance, a source of pride to the Bituriges, 'the safeguard and the ornament of their state' (*BG* vii, 15). Genabum (Orleans) on the Loire was an important commercial centre which commanded a bridge over the river (*BG* vii, 11). Agedincum of the Senones (Sens), used as one of Caesar's chief depots (*BG* vii, 10), occupied a nodal point on Gallic roads, later followed by the Roman road system initiated by Agrippa. In the east was Vesontio (Besançon), 'the largest *oppidum* of the Sequani' (*BG* I, 38). Caesar describes the citadel, saying 'this height is surrounded by a wall to form a citadel and join it with the town'. Lutetia of the Parisii was on the Ile-de-la-Cité, where the Seine was bridged (*BG* vii, 58). We first hear of it in 53 when Caesar summoned a Council of the Gauls to meet him there (vi, 3). The best evidence of its importance is furnished by the pre-conquest coinage of the Parisii, which is of outstandingly fine quality. Professor Duval thinks that these coins were issued not long before the Conquest; for one thing, because they did not have time to circulate to regions outside the immediate neighbourhood of Lutetia. On the other hand, many second- and first-century coins of the Seine valley tribes, Senones, Sequani and Meldi, were also found in Paris, which implies active trade in the area. The great number of boats, large and small, which Labienus was able to commandeer from Metiosedum (Melun) a short distance upstream, is the first hint that we get of the importance of the ship-owners on the Seine, who had become an organised corporation by the time of Tiberius.

Mediolanum Santonum (Saintes) on the Charente is an old Gallic *oppidum* which bloomed rapidly under the Roman régime. The Santones had helped Caesar with ships against the Veneti (*BG* iii, 11); this may have been because of old rivalry with the latter over maritime trade; they may also perhaps have felt gratitude for the defeat of the Helvetii who had had designs on their land. Some of their families were remarkably wealthy, such as that of the Gaius Julius Rufus who was priest at the altar of Lugdunum and who not only gave a monumental arch to decorate the approach to the bridge of his native city, dedicating it to Tiberius, Germanicus and Drusus, but who also built the first amphitheatre at the confluence of Rhône and Saône (p. 204).

Some of the towns created by Roman intervention have already been noted. Pride of place among the new tribal capitals must go to Augustodunum (Autun) 'the

stronghold of Augustus' which was given city walls by the emperor and the dignity these implied. Here also there was founded a school for the sons of Gallic notables, to further their romanisation. The new towns were normally given the name of the princeps or of his family, for example Caesarodunum Turonum (Tours), Juliomagus Andecavorum (Angers), Augustodurum Baiocassium (Bayeux), Juliobona Caletorum (Lillebonne). After the Latin name there is always a Celtic suffix, such as *dunum* (stronghold) or *magus* (market), which, with the name of the tribe, makes clear the Celtic character of the town.

In the far north towns developed more slowly than in central Gaul (cf. however Graff 1963 on *oppida*). The war-scarred Nervii had recovered and had their chief town at Bagacum (Bavai) an important road junction which goes back to Augustan times (*CIL* 3570, inscription to Tiberius). The Bellovaci too received a new capital, Caesaromagus Bellovacorum (Beauvais). The remnants of the Aduatuci, Condrusi and Eburones were welded into a composite tribe, the Tungri, and given a new town Aduatuca Tungrorum (Tongres). These new northern towns were to receive fresh impetus from the conquest of Britain (AD 43) and the consequent passage across their territory of traffic between Britain and the Rhineland.

The frontier zone was economically always part of Gaul and the large garrisons were strong forces of romanisation. Around the legionary fortresses towns inevitably grew up, or the pre-existing settlements were greatly increased; such were Moguntiacum, Bonna, Vindonissa, Argentorate. The chief city of the Rhineland was Cologne which was initially founded for the Ubii, a friendly German tribe installed on the west bank of the Rhine by Agrippa in 38 BC. In AD 50 its population was augmented by a number of Roman veterans and it was given the name of Colonia Claudia Arae Agrippinensium.

There are three Roman colonies in the Tres Galliae of which two certainly and one probably were founded on the instructions of Caesar. These are Colonia Copia Lugudunensium (Lyons) and Colonia Augusta Raurica (Augst, Switzerland), founded by L. Munatius Plancus, Caesar's appointee as Legate of Gaul in 44-43, and Colonia Julia Equestris Noviodunum (Nyon, Switzerland) which by its name must have been a foundation for cavalry veterans.

For the foundation of Lugdunum (more stricly Lugudunum) in 43, land was taken from the Segusiavi, who 94 occupied a large territory between the Saône and the Loire, and who had an *oppidum*, dedicated to the god Lug, on the heights of Fourvière, which was taken over for the new city. There is now a considerable body of knowledge of this unique Gallo-Roman city (Wuilleumier 1951; Audin *Gallia*, especially 1962, 1963, 1967 and 1968; Montauzan 1909). The grid pattern of the colony up on the hill begins to emerge, with the forum, the theatre, the odeum and a temple. Of the four aqueducts, Audin believes the Craponne to be the earliest, anterior to 12 BC about which time it is assumed that the second, that of Mont d'Or, was constructed for the buildings at the confluence. Audin has come upon traces of the forum of Plancus under the Augustan theatre (Audin 1967).

The colonists of Lugdunum were military – how chosen we are not told – and a century later their descendants still proudly upheld the military tradition that they were a part of the Roman army (Tacitus *Hist.* i, 65). Lugdunum was from the first very much a capital. It was, like Carthage, the garrison of an Urban Cohort; it held, with Pergamum and Rome itself, one of the three imperial mints, and it was the central point from which radiated the Roman road system which was one of the achievements of Agrippa. 'Lugdunum', says Strabo, 'is an acropolis, as it were, not only because the rivers meet there, but also because it is near all parts of the country. And it was on this account also that Agrippa began at Lugdunum when he cut his roads.' (iv, 6, 11).

In 12 BC, the country at peace, the census achieved, the organisation of the provinces completed, a great altar to Rome and Augustus was set up at the confluence of the Rhône and Saône. A new *Concilium Galliarum* was convened, all the sixty tribes of the Tres Galliae being invited to send representatives to the solemn inauguration performed by Drusus, stepson of Augustus. The president of the Council was the High Priest (*sacerdos*) of the Altar, and was on this occasion the leading Aeduan, an appropriate choice, since the Aedui were Rome's oldest allies in Gaul. This assembly provided a continuation, in a new guise, of the old Councils of the Gauls held in the days of independence, and it became an annual festival, held on 1 August, an essential part of the life of Roman Gaul. It was regarded as a great distinction to be a member of the council, and, still more, a priest; but the Council of the Gauls had practical as well as honorific value, for it provided a means whereby complaints about unjust governors could be brought to the notice of the emperor.

The site of the federal sanctuary at the confluence has been located. Coins issued in Lyons from 11-9 BC show the altar flanked by two Victories standing on columns. A few fragments of marble carved in the Augustan style and the letters RO (Roma) must belong to the altar, and Audin and Quoniam in 1962 made the very plausible suggestion that four columns in grey Egyptian syenite, now in the church of St Martin at Ainay, which are in fact a pair of tall pillars each cut in half, are those on which the Victories stood. By the site of the altar were found the bronze tablets on which the celebrated speech of Claudius advocating the admission of Gauls to the Senate was inscribed. The first amphitheatre at the confluence was constructed in the time of Tiberius by a Santonian high priest, Gaius Julius Rufus, and his family (*Gallia* 1964).

There is a third aspect of Lugdunum to consider – the commercial quarter, or rather quarters, which spread along both banks of the Saône and across the Île d'Ainay where the Gare de Perrache is today one of the nodal points for Common Market commerce. From the first, Lugdunum with its corporation of shippers and its position as a road centre, had a great influence on the commercial development of Gaul (see p. 208). Many of the Segusiavi must have remained to share in the prosperity of the new foundation, though they also had a capital of their own, Forum Segusiavorum (Feurs).

Vici and aedificia

A few small settlements have been excavated which may be claimed as *vici* of the Caesarian period that were still occupied in Gallo-Roman times. They generally appear to be villages which had grown up at convenient points along the roads of Gaul. That free Gaul had been well provided with reasonably good tracks is evident from the ease with which Caesar made his way from end to end of the country.

Marloux (*Gallia* 1944, 25-41; 1946, 426) 8 km. west of Chalon-sur-Saône on the road to Autun is a good example. It flourished at the end of the Gallic period and in the early Gallo-Roman period. Among the numerous finds the excavations of 1942-3 yielded were quantities of Gallic pottery of the Mont Beuvray type, painted ware, as well as many Gallic coins. They show that metal (iron and copper) was worked. An early Roman mosaic pavement was found overlying Gallic material, and the settlement had a long life. Chalon itself (Cabillonum) had been a trading settlement from early times, in relationship with Mont Beuvray. Les Bolards, immediately southeast of Nuits-Saint-Georges, within the same area, shows traces of the Gallic period and was certainly occupied from the first century BC to the fifth century AD, engaging in a considerable volume of trade at all times, especially with the south.

These examples of *vici* could be multiplied (cf. Grenier *Manuel* II), especially if some of the smaller *oppida* were counted in. They help to show the continuity of Gallic and Gallo-Roman society.

Of *aedificia* there is at present less to say, a lack that we can confidently hope will be remedied with the modern development of archaeological techniques and with the aid of air-photography. The most cogent example remains the farmhouse at Mayen near Andernach (Germany), which has been a classic example for forty years; a small Roman villa of about AD 100, the excavators found beneath it structures of two earlier periods, the first a large Celtic hut identified by the post-holes for the roof and wall supports (Grenier *Manuel* II, 784-95). There must have been many *aedificia* of this sort when Caesar invaded Gaul. There were also larger buildings, the villas of the nobles, such as the house surrounded by forest where Ambiorix was nearly captured (*BG* vi, 30). A few allusions to the villas of Gallo-Roman nobles in the early days are to be found in classical literature. In AD 21 the rebel Julius Sacrovir fled to his villa near Augustodunum, where he committed suicide after setting fire to the building (Tacitus *Ann.* iii 46), and we are told of Sabinus' villa in AD 70 (Tacitus *Hist.* iv, 67). For long the houses, large and small, as well as the huts of the poorer folk, were nearly all built of wood, except in very stony open areas. In many parts of France, especially in the northern half, there are hollows or ponds, known as *mardelles*, which on investigation prove to have been dug to take the foundations of wooden huts, often of considerable size. Excavation has revealed the wooden framework of the roofs and sides, and the contents show that they were built throughout the Iron Age and the Gallo-Roman periods. Some of them may represent isolated farms surrounded by their outbuildings, others are built in village groups (Grenier *Manuel* II, 752). Most of the known great country houses of Roman Gaul are dated to the second century or later, but a growing number of them has been shown, on excavation, to have been preceded by buildings of the early first century. The famous villa at Chiragan shows four successive phases, the first Augustan, extending over the whole of the first century. The first *villa urbana* at Montmaurin (Hte-Garonne) is not later than Claudius (Fouet 1969). At the Villa d'Antone (Hte-Vienne; *Gallia* 1952), finds of Gallic and early imperial coins suggest a first-century date. Many wealthy pro-Roman Gauls had survived the war of conquest and their families doubtless still lived on their estates.

Production and trade

The conquest of Gaul brought an economic revolution to the country, one which the Gauls, with their long tradition of craftsmanship, were well equipped and alert to put to best use. One of the most attractive characteristics of the Celts is their respect for men of skill. Certain gods and heroes in Irish lore (Powell 1958, 126) are venerated as 'masters of skill', among them Lug whom we know in Gaul. The craftsman, especially the smith, was a valued member of society in Ireland as in early Gaul. He it was who had brought Celtic art into being in the great days of the warrior kings; he fashioned the iron weapons which were the source of strength and domination, and decorated them with his equally masterly bronzework to please his patrons. The skill of the Gauls as miners is mentioned emphatically by Caesar (*BG* iii, 21, Aquitani; vii, 22, Bituriges). The metalwork of the Celts, of outstanding quality for several centuries, continued to be produced after the conquest. Key sites for the period immediately before and after Caesar are the *oppida* of Stradonitz in Bohemia and of Mont Beuvray where the metalwork shows close cultural links which did not disappear until Stradonitz was destroyed by the German Marcomanni in 12 B C.

A vast field of new activity opened for the inhabitants of Gallia Comata with the coming of Roman building techniques. Dressed stone, mortar, tiles and bricks now came into use; quarrying became important. In Gallia Narbonensis fine stone masonry, introduced by the Greeks, had long been familiar, and skilled artisans could be found on the spot for the erection of the great monuments of the Augustan period. A new phase of art had started under Greek influence (Benoît 1956) before the arrival of the Romans and produced the celebrated 79-80 sculptures of Entremont and La Roquepertuse, and many others. The Celts of Narbonensis took kindly to

6 Fragments of a bronze disc from Levroux, Indre, in Musée Bertrand, Châteauroux. Scale c. *2 : 3 (after Megaw)*

sculpture and we can detect the native element in the exuberant decoration of the early monuments of the Roman period such as the arches of St-Rémy and of Orange.

Metalwork

Metalwork with the traditional florid Celtic decoration was still produced in Britain and Ireland after the Roman conquest of Gaul, but the Gallic workers were by no means idle. Certain types of bronzework, characteristically Celtic in style, are found on Gallo-Roman sites of the first three centuries A D. They must be derived from the pre-conquest art, but the links are still not clear. For instance, the curvilinear Celtic decoration with its trumpet-like patterns reappears again in the *Trompetenmuster* decoration on brooches and openwork discs favoured particularly on military sites, which found its way all along the frontiers, even as far as Morocco. This is datable to the second and third centuries A D, but its Celtic character is obvious. Bronze openwork of Celtic type, though less pronouncedly so than the *Trompetenmuster*, is also known in the middle of the first century A D when a successful bronzeworker of Aquae Helveticae (Baden, Switzerland) specialised in openwork sheath-mounts on which his name, Gemellianus, and the name of his town, form part of the decorative whole (Stähelin 1948, 442). Other workers followed the same style.

Recently Megaw (1968) drew attention to some pieces of Celtic bronzework from Levroux (Indre) near Châ- *6* teauroux that were found in 1867 and are mentioned by Déchelette. They show certain resemblances to the decorations on the Aylesford bucket (early first century A D). Following Nylen (1958), who suggested that the Aylesford and Marlborough bronzework came from Gaul, Megaw has postulated a centre of Celtic art somewhere in north-central Gaul in the first century B C. If this can be substantiated it will help to bridge the gap.

The Celts too were noted for their gay enamelwork, which dates back to the third century B C. Before the conquest they used red enamel; by the second century A D they were producing numerous brooches and other articles decorated with other colours the use of which they seem to have learnt from the glass that came into Gaul from Syria and elsewhere. Mlle Françoise Henry wrote (1933) that in her opinion there was enough evidence to show the existence of Gallo-Roman workshops which, while developing the Celtic tradition, let it profit by the technical advances brought by the conquest. These centres blossomed anew in the second and third centuries A D in Gaul and Britain, as is shown by the great variety and beauty of the enamelled brooches and of such things as the bowl found in 1882 at Rochefort (Jura; cf. Forsyth 1950).

Celtic fibulae continued to be made in well-established forms, and new varieties were introduced. An interesting series is the type frequently bearing the name of the maker Aucissa, who is believed to have worked in Belgica about the middle of the first century A D, but his type of brooch goes back into the last years of the first century B C.

Gallic silversmiths were imitating Italian silver cups before the end of the Augustan period and some of the vessels in the hoard found at Hildesheim in Germany are regarded as of Gallic origin. A cup of the finest quality dated to the second half of the first century found at Lyons is decorated with scenes from Celtic, instead of the usual classical, mythology (Wuilleumier 1936).

Pliny, writing in the third quarter of the first century A D, refers to Gallic metalworking. He mentions the art of plating copper to make it look like silver (*HN* XXXIV, 162): 'A method discovered in the Gallic province is to plate bronze articles with tin so as to make them almost indistinguishable from silver; articles so treated are called *incoctilia*. Later they also proceeded in the town Alesia to plate with silver in a similar manner, particularly ornaments for horses and pack animals and yokes of oxen; this method also is found among the Bituriges.' A large number of metalworkers' establishments has been found at Alesia (Grenier *Manuel* II, 705).

An industry in which Gaul, like every other part of the Empire, participated, was the making of holy images, little bronze statuettes of gods and goddesses, bought by those who could afford something better than the popular clay figurines (p. 208). Near every famous sanctuary, every place of pilgrimage, the devout could buy these figures, mostly rather crude, but sometimes of fine quality.

The sources of the metal used in Gaul are discussed by Grenier (*Manuel* II, 961 ff.). The production of the Spanish and British mines was on a much greater scale than that of Gaul but there were nevertheless many deposits there which were worked during pre-Roman and Roman times. Iron was widely produced, though the mines of the Bituriges and the Petrocorii were the most famous. Copper, too, was common, but inferior in quality to that from Spain. The history of the British tin trade (Davies 1935) still presents problems, but the celebrated passages in Diodorus (v, 22 and 38) about the transport of the metal across Gaul to Narbo or Arelate points to its importance during the period in which we are interested. There were also tin mines in Gaul – in the Creuse, the Haute-Vienne and in Brittany – from which some gold was also extracted.

Lead, of little concern to the free Gauls, was of great importance in the Roman Empire for making pipes. It was used for parts of aqueducts where the water had to flow under pressure. Large quantities of lead piping have been found in the Rhône at Arles where the water of the aqueduct was carried across the river by syphon. To reach Fourvière the aqueducts of Lyons had to be piped across a deep valley in the same manner. In Pliny (*HN* XXXIV, 164) we read that 'Black lead which we use to make pipes and sheets is excavated with considerable labour in Spain and through the whole of the Gallic provinces, but in Britain it is found in the surface-stratum of the earth in such abundance that there is a law prohibiting the production of more than a certain amount.' The working of lead on a large scale was a new thing to the Gauls, and one may wonder about the source of the lead used in aqueducts built before the conquest of Britain. It would have been easy to supply the Narbonensian aqueducts from Spain. In the case of Lyons it may be observed that the Segusiavi, the local tribe, mined lead, and they may well have supplied some of that required for the aqueducts. A lead ingot of the Segusiavi has been found at Fréjus (*CIL* XII, 5700). There were important mines of argentiferous lead in the land of the Pictones, and these were probably already being exploited before the Romans came (Grenier *Manuel*, ii, 975-6).

Woodworking

Almost as important as the smith in the early Gallic communities was the carpenter who put up the wooden houses and barns and built the numerous carts and boats, and the finer woodworker who carved images or wooden domestic ware. The *muri gallici*, the remains of huts and houses, testify to master carpenters on the grand scale. The barrel is perhaps a Gallic invention. Of the smaller work there is naturally less to show, but carvings of human figures are known. Caesar tells us (*B G* vi, 17, 2) that there were many images of the god he equates with Mercury and these almost certainly will have been of wood, as were the most ancient and venerated of ancient Greek images. A wooden figure of a man more than 3 m. high wearing the Gallic cloak and hood was found in the ancient harbour of Genava on the Lake of Geneva (Stähelin 1948, 544) and one of the outstanding finds of the 1960s was that of nearly two hundred wooden votive images from the temple at 105-6 the source of the Seine (p. 210), dated to the later first century B C and the first century A D (Martin 1963, 1965; Deyts 1966; *Gallia* 1964, 302). They were votive offerings, mostly pilgrim goods, and though of no artistic value, some of them show a fineness of execution which has all the precision and mastery of a long-established craft. A few may justifiably be classed as works of art and the later ones were evidently influenced by classical models. These discoveries were followed in 1968 by the excavation of a comparable series of carvings at Chama- 107 lières to the south of Clermont-Ferrand. More than two thousand wooden votive offerings lay round a mineral-water spring which was still in use in the present

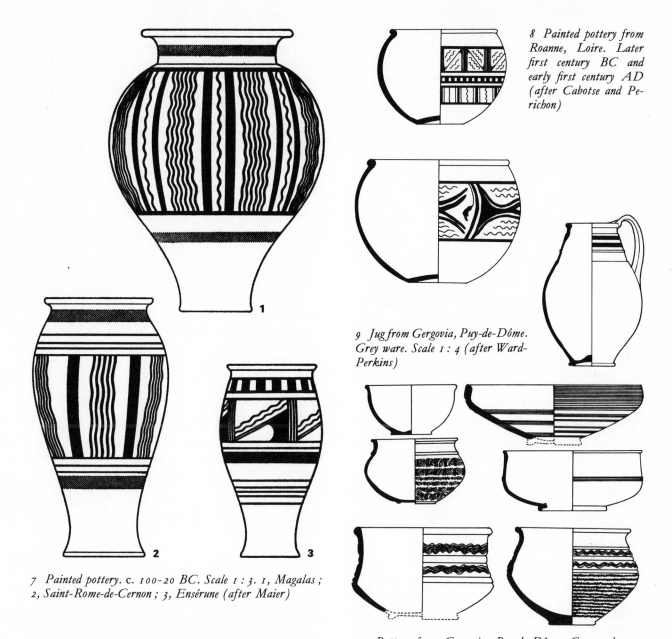

8 *Painted pottery from Roanne, Loire. Later first century BC and early first century AD (after Cabotse and Périchon)*

7 *Painted pottery.* c. *100-20 BC. Scale 1 : 3. 1, Magalas; 2, Saint-Rome-de-Cernon; 3, Ensérune (after Maier)*

9 *Jug from Gergovia, Puy-de-Dôme. Grey ware. Scale 1 : 4 (after Ward-Perkins)*

10 *Pottery from Gergovia, Puy-de-Dôme. Grey and grey-black wares. Scale 1 : 4 (after Ward-Perkins)*

century. They too are dated to the late first century BC and the early years of the first century AD. The best of 103 them are figures showing palpable classical influence and of considerable artistic quality (Vatin 1969, 320).

THE POTTERY INDUSTRY
Central and southwestern Gaul
Intense activity was displayed by the potters of Roman Gaul in the Augustan period, but less is known of the twenty years after the conquest, though there are many indications that inherited skills were carefully handed down. For instance, painted pottery of a distinctive 7-8 kind is found at Ensérune and across central and north-eastern France to Switzerland and beyond (Maier 1931, 1970). It is dated to the early and mid-first century BC and is found on sites like Mont Beuvray and Aulnat-Sud occupied in the last days of independence (Hatt

1945). In early Augustan times its place was taken by another, closely-related variety of painted pottery of which the 'bol de Roanne' is characteristic (Cabotse 8 and Périchon 1966). It is thought that some of this late painted pottery was made at Ledosus (Lezoux) in the valley of the Allier, 26 km. east of the future Augustonemetum.

A characteristic pottery of the region is the black and slate-coloured ware: bowls, jugs and plates, with distinctive roulette decoration found in quantity at Gergovia (Ward-Perkins 1940; Hatt 1943, 1949; Labrousse 1948, 1950). Some of this was made at Lezoux. The potters also turned their attention towards the end of the century to the production of a white-slip ware, imitated from Italian prototypes and used especially for attractive *ollae* and jugs, which were a pleasing, good-class household pottery. In a kiln excavated at Lezoux by the late Mme Mathonnière-Plicque (*Gallia* 1961), there was a black bowl with the impressed decoration of the Gergovia wares, and fragments of the white pots, while near by was a piece of painted pottery, and a large deposit of sherds, grey, black and white. The pottery of the Clermont area has been taken in hand with important results by H. Vertet (1961, 1962, 1965, 1967) who has found that *terra sigillata*, the familiar red ware made in Italy and then in Gaul, was being produced in Lezoux as early as A D 10, preceding the earliest known examples from Montans and La Graufesenque by several years.

Lezoux was not the only Arvernian pottery active at this period. Several other centres are known (Déchelette 1904, I, ch. 2). A little farther down the valley of the Allier were the important kilns of Saint-Rémy-en-Rollat, active from the end of the first century B C, producing beakers in the Aco style of north Italy, and developing a form of lead-glaze ware which had a considerable vogue and even reached Britain. There were also the Vichy ceramic workers who, besides making pottery, produced white terracotta figurines. The Allier provided a useful route for the distribution of these products.

Excavations at La Graufesenque have shown that before the manufacture of *terra sigillata* started, there was on the site a La Tène settlement (first or perhaps second century B C) using native pottery and also receiving Campanian ware and wine jars from Italy (*Gallia* 1953, 346; *RA* XXVII, 1951). At Montans, too, there are indications of earlier potters (*Etudes Celtiques* 1956, 256-68; *Gallia* 1957, 138), for a number of the white-and-red painted pots have been found, slightly different from those of Roanne. It is natural enough that at the three major sites, Lezoux, La Graufesenque and Montans, there should already have been kilns in view of the large local deposits of good quality clay, and the presence of ample wood in the vicinity.

Until recently it was believed that the earliest makers of *terra sigillata* in Gaul were the potters of Montans and La Graufesenque (about A D 15) and that Lezoux learnt the art from potters who had migrated from these centres. Now, as we have seen, it would appear that they started work, if anything, a few years later than Lezoux. In the early years, however, Lezoux potters lagged behind the Ruteni in the quality and quantity of their output, which was only locally important, whereas the Rutenian pottery was dispersed far and wide. The Ruteni had the advantage of nearness to the port of Narbo. It was they (from La Graufesenque and from Banassac which began production about A D 40) who became rivals of the Italian potters on their own ground, as the Flavian consignments of pottery found at Pompeii show. Their wares also preponderate for a time in the Arvernian country itself, at Roanne, in the Rhineland and in Britain, and their consciousness of

success is reflected on a stamp of the south Gaulish potter Scotius which was found in a stratum of A D 20 at the legionary fortress of Vindonissa: *Scotius fe(cit) Aretinu(m) (vas)* – 'Scotius made this Arretine pot' (Ettlinger *Germania* 1933, 367). Italian potters must have played a part in this massive development by themselves migrating or sending trained slaves. Some of the names of early potters at the Rutenian centres are foreign, such as Chrestus, Euhodus or Xanthus. Vertet has shown another way in which the potters set to work to 'make Arretine': the Italians prepared their moulds for the decorated forms by the use of specially made pattern-stamps. A vase would take the fancy of a Gaulish potter who would first make a mould of it and then make stamps from the various motifs in the mould; thereafter he could use these stamps to work out designs of his own choice to decorate new moulds.

Among the many new discoveries in the field of Gallo-Roman pottery is that of workshops in Lyons, on the left bank of the Saône, where Leglay and Vertet have reported beakers in the style of Aco, and large quantities of plain *sigillata* which they date to Tiberius. There are two groups of name-stamps, one of potters known to be Italian, the other of potters known to have worked in Gaul. It seems that Lyons may have played an appreciable part in the spread and development of the *sigillata* industry in Gaul which has not hitherto been known (Leglay 1968, 570-72).

Near the Pyrenees, Lombez (Gers) was a centre for the production of a thin-walled, orange pottery found all over southern Gaul, which appears to have been preferred even to *terra sigillata* in its early days. The decoration of these pots is surprisingly rich and varied; it may be in barbotine, or 'sanded' so that the fabric comes out with a rough surface, or, again, made in stamped moulds like *sigillata* (Mesplé 1951). As the excavator remarks, it can be seen that the makers manipulated their matrices with the joy of the creative artist. Coins on the site run from 50 B C to A D 50, and the pottery is ascribed to the first half of the first century A D.

Gallo-Belgic and related wares
Between the Massif Central and Belgica lay the tribes of the Aedui and the Lingones. On Mont Beuvray large quantities of grey and black wares resembling the pottery of Gergovia were found, and in the territory of the Lingones is more black pottery, this time closely linked with early Gallo-Belgic ware (Hatt 1949).

In northern Gaul the pottery known as Belgic had long been of high quality and at the time of the conquest many centres were still producing it. From about 10 B C the Belgic potters had begun to adopt a number of Italian forms and a characteristic pottery came to prevail all over the northern half of Gaul and along the Rhineland, which archaeologists now prefer to call Gallo-Belgic to distinguish it from its predecessor, the true Belgic ware of the La Tène period. It is influenced by *terra sigillata* though it retains strongly Celtic characteristics, including many La Tène forms. Already in

82 Gold coin of the Aulerci: *Obv.* Head, right. *Rev.* Charioteer with torc in right hand, driving human-headed horse.

82

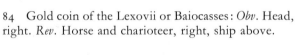

83

83 Bronze coin of the Remi: *Obv.* Three heads of a deity, left. *Rev.* Two-horse chariot, left. REMO.

84 Gold coin of the Lexovii or Baiocasses: *Obv.* Head, right. *Rev.* Horse and charioteer, right, ship above.

84

85

85 Bronze coin of unknown tribe of north-west or west central Gaul: *Obv.* Head with goatee beard, left. INDECOM. *Rev.* Horse, left. Wild boar standard below.

86 Reverse of bronze coin showing man carrying torc.

86

87   Bronze coin of the Aedui: *Obv*. Head, right; . . . ORB. *Rev*. Horse, right; DVBNOR.

87

88   Obverse of gold coin of the Arverni with helmeted head of Vercingetorix, left; . . . TORIXS.

88

89 Gold coin of the Arverni: *Obv*. Head of Vercingetorix, left; VERCINGETORIXS. *Rev*. Horse, left; wine jar below.

89

90   Silver coin of the Arverni: *Obv*. Head, right. *Rev*. Horse and rider, right; EPAD.

90

91   Bronze coin of the Arverni: *Obv*. Helmeted head, right; EPAD. *Rev*. Soldier with standard, spear and shield.

91

92   Bronze coin, Duratos-Julius: *Obv*. Female head, left; DVRAT. *Rev*. Horseman; IVLIVS.

92

93 Bronze coin of Togirix: *Obv.* Helmeted head, right. TOG. *Rev.* Lion, right. TOG.

94

94 Silver coin of the Segusiavi: *Obv.* Helmeted head. SEGVSIAVS. *Rev.* Hercules and wooden image. ARVS.

95 Silver denarius of Narbo, with serrated edge: *Obv.* Head of Roma, right. L COSCO MFX. *Rev.* Warrior (Bituitus) in two-horsed chariot, right, hurling spear and holding shield and carnyx. L LIC CN DOM.

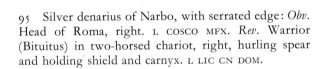

95

96

96 Silver coin of the Remi, Aulus Hirtius Imperator: *Obv.* Head, right. AθHDIAC. *Rev.* Lion, right. A HIRT IMP.

97 Reverse of bronze coin of Lugdunum, showing the Altar with pillars on either side bearing victories. ROM ET AVG.

97

98

98 Bronze coin of Nemausus: *Obv.* Heads of Augustus and Agrippa. IMP DIVI FILI. *Rev.* Crocodile chained to palm tree. COL NEM.

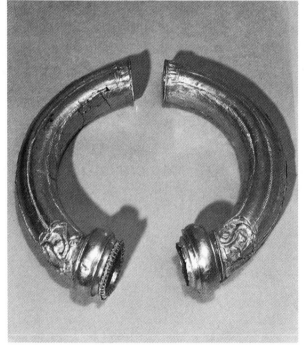

99 *Murus gallicus*, Vertault (Côte-d'Or).

100 Milestone of Cn. Domitius Ahenobarbus.

101 Gold torc from Mailly-le-Camp (Aube).

102 Gallic warrior wearing coat-of-mail. Vachères.

103

104

105

106

107

103 Wooden figure of pilgrim, Chamalières (Puy-de-Dôme).

104 Wooden figure showing internal organs, Chamalières.

105 Wooden figure showing internal organs, Saint-Germain-Source-Seine.

106 Wooden figure of woman, Saint-Germain-Source-Seine.

107 Wooden ex-votos in a spring at Chamalières.

108 Stone monster from Noves, holding severed heads.

108

109 Sculpture of the head of Cernunnos.   110 Sculptured relief of two severed heads from Entremont.

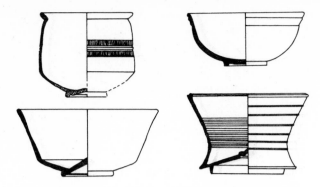

11 Gallo-Belgic ware. Terra nigra. Scale 1 : 4 (after Hawkes and Hull)

Augustan times there were two chief wares, the reddish, imitating Arretine, generally called *terra rubra*, and the
11 black or grey *terra nigra* (Hawkes and Hull 1947). From Gaul it spread to Britain, and pre-Roman Camulodunum contains many examples of imported Gallo-Belgic pots. The potters of the Argonne, destined to become large-scale producers of *terra sigillata* in the second century A D, were already at work in the first century B C near Lavoye; found there were kilns for Gallo-Belgic ware of high quality which continued to work through the first century A D. Even when *terra sigillata* production became important, the old native pottery continued to be produced, an instance of the continuation of Celtic modes which were to reassert themselves during the third century.

One of the best examples of kilns producing this ware comes from Vertault, near Châtillon, and thus in Lingonian and not Belgic territory. One practice imitated from Italian potters was that of using name-stamps. A very large number of these is known, 360 recognisable Gallo-Belgic stamps having been found at Camulodunum, while Vertault produced 42 different potters' names (Bohn 1922).

The Gallo-Belgic wares were purchased in quantity by the Roman army, as the excavation of early forts such as Urmitz, Oberaden, Basle, Haltern and Hofheim shows. Close relationship between native pottery workers and a military establishment is to be seen at Vindonissa, where large numbers of pots made locally in imitation of Arretine have been found.

Lack of space prevents the inclusion of many interesting examples, but mention must be made of the urns of Bavai with their striking decoration of embossed heads. These evidently represent gods and goddesses and sometimes a three-faced being is present, a favourite Celtic symbol of the threefold power of divinity. They were being produced by the mid-first century A D.

In the foregoing summary we have seen how the Gallic potters clung tenaciously to their craft and were determined not to be ousted by the products of Italy which poured into the country, especially into the northeast in the wake of the Roman armies and which were also bought by well-to-do Gauls. They answered the threat by learning to imitate the Italian work, and they were equally vigorous in pushing their wares in the expanding markets of Gaul itself and of neighbouring territories. Whether we regard this as romanisation of Gaul or celticisation of Mediterranean trade, it is one of the most important developments of early Roman Gaul. A contributory factor was the necessarily high cost of pottery brought all the way from Italy; if adequate vessels of the same kind could be produced nearer the markets they could be sold more cheaply and in greater quantity. This is, in fact, what happened, until the Gaulish industry grew strong enough to drive the Italian wares from the western markets and even to compete with them in Italy itself. Business enterprise was not, of course, confined to the Gauls. It seems clear that some of the Italian master potters were alive to the opportunities and either went themselves to Gaul to establish workshops, or sent their slaves. But in the long run it was the Gauls who profited.

When the industry had got into its stride the personnel engaged in making and designing pots was almost exclusively Gaulish. Close students of their work, after examining thousands of examples, are 'impressed with the artistic originality and excellence that they displayed' (Howard Comfort). The old Celtic flair was still active.

Agriculture

Metalworking and pottery are the two forms of economic activity most easy to discuss since there is plenty of concrete evidence. Concerning the highly productive Gallic agriculture there is a mass of information to be culled from ancient literature. Gaul was recognised from the first as 'outstanding for its wheat and rich in pastures' (Mela, iii, 2). Considerable quantities of wheat were exported to Italy under the supervision of the *Annona*, the imperial corn-supply organisation. The fields of northern Gaul were the source of wheat and fodder for the Rhine armies (Grenier, *Econ. Survey*, ed. Frank, iii, 1937, 579). Pliny (first century) writes of the agricultural skills of the Gauls and it is he who describes a reaping machine of the type depicted on a tombstone of the second-third century at Arlon. Strabo writes (iv, 197) of the sheep and pigs which were raised in such numbers by the Belgae that they exported woollen goods and salt pork in large quantities to Rome and all Italy. One of the major products of Gaul was in fact wool and woollen goods. The trade is shown on well-known tomb reliefs of the second and third centuries A D, but its importance in the first century is equally evident from the statement of Strabo.

Viticulture spread gradually but steadily. Already the Allobroges of the first century were producing a wine much appreciated by connoisseurs. The list of other products is long and cannot be attempted here, but mention should be made of the special Gallic product of soap, and the forest industry of resin extraction.

THE GAULISH CONTRIBUTION TO THE EMPIRE
The energies of this gifted, volatile but industrious

people had now found an outlet other than tribal quarrels, and in all aspects of life they made contributions to the well-being of the Empire of which they were a vital part. Whether the cheerful, often rather smug faces that look out at us from the tombstones of Gaul are the descendants of the tempestuous cavaliers who fought Caesar, we cannot tell. Certainly a new bourgeois aristocracy made its way up the social scale in the prosperous days of the first two centuries A D. Aristocracies have a way of dying out and being replaced, but the great and productive estates of many of the old families must have given them a good chance of survival. A proportion of these were still very much alive in the first century A D and some of them took the lead in the risings which from time to time showed that the old spirit of independence was not altogether forgotten. A good example of a rich and well established family entering with enthusiasm into the new state of affairs and using some of its wealth to embellish its local city is that of the Julii Rufi of Mediolanum Santonum (Saintes), who dedicated an arch at its bridge to the imperial family; on the inscription are mentioned four generations, C. Julius Rufus, his father C. Julius Otuaneunus Rufus, his grandfather C. Julius Gedemonius and finally his great-grandfather who only had the Celtic name Epotsorovidus and who must have been an elder contemporary of Vercingetorix.

Religion

Glimpses of the Celtic religion are to be found in the works of ancient authors, and for a good modern summary there is Powell's book (*The Celts* 1958). A great deal survived until Christianity swept the old native gods away along with Jupiter and Apollo. More than four hundred Celtic gods and goddesses are known from the inscriptions of Roman Gaul. The Gallo-Romans developed their own temple architecture, the well-known small *fanum* of square plan, surrounded by a portico, also square, and frequently set within a large temenos. Such temples have been found all over the Celtic provinces of the Empire. The ground plan may vary to the extent of being octagonal or circular instead of square, but the essence of the central cella with its portico appears throughout and it is quite distinct from the rectangular temples of classical type (Grenier *Manuel* III and IV). As a rule little more remains than the foundations, but the so-called Temple of Janus just outside Autun is the cella of one such temple, while the high circular tower at Périgueux is a temple of Vesunna, the city goddess. The complex of ruins excavated at Sanxay (Vienne) contains an octagonal temple.

There is a growing, if small, volume of material evidence of the survival of Celtic places of worship into Roman times. This is not surprising, for to a pagan the gods associated with a place are potent and belong with that place, be its inhabitants what they may. Though the Romans might bring the Capitoline triad with them they would not dream of turning out the gods already established. Nîmes, for example, remained the city of Nemausus, the god of the healing fountain, and far

from interfering with his shrine, the Romans from the beginning embellished it and added to it. This very rebuilding on the ancient sites has made it more difficult to collect evidence of Celtic temples, but it is in religion that we feel the essential unity of Narbonensis and the Tres Galliae which can act as a corrective to excessive insistence on the Italian character of the former. From this area have come the remarkable pre-Roman statues and other sculptures of Nîmes, Nages, Vachères, Entremont, etc., an art which owes its origin to the impulse derived from classical and Etruscan art (p. 190), though what it depicts is Celtic figures, gods and men.

A clear case of survival is to be found at Saint-Germain-le-Rocheux (Côte-d'Or) where, underneath the stone foundations of two successive temples of the Roman period, post-holes of an earlier wooden temple accompanied by Gallic and Augustan coins were found (*Gallia* 1960, 339). The Châtelard at Lardins (Basses-Alpes) has yielded large numbers of early finds, and the Gallic and Republican coins found at Monjustin (Haute-Saône) may also be significant (*Gallia* 1958, 343).

A well known site which has recently yielded evidence of the tenacity of Celtic cults is the temple at the source of the Seine, high among the hills northwest of Dijon. Excavations begun in 1836 showed that there was a Gallo-Roman temple here where a healing-goddess Sequana was worshipped, and among the remains were numerous stone votive offerings carved to represent parts of the body reputed to be cured by the goddess (Grenier *Manuel* IV, ch. v). In 1963, as we have seen above, a large earlier deposit of wooden figures was found.

Another site on which long and patient work has been abundantly rewarded is Les Fontaines-Salées *12* (Yonne) where there were medicinal springs whose use may go back as far as the sixth century B C. The early wells are made up of sections of trunks of oak-trees which had been burnt out in the middle. Over the remains of these primitive wells were found successive shrines and also baths of the Roman period. The foundations of a large circular enclosure wall (diameter 31 m.) believed to date from the first century A D were found round an area in which there had been several protohistoric wells. The wall is 45 cm. thick and accompanied by an exterior paving 3.50 m. broad, thought to belong to a portico (*Gallia* 1956, 317; 1962, 467).

Grenier was of the opinion that the standard square temple of good masonry was not built until after A D 70, but there appear to be some instances of earlier date, such as a Celtic-type temple at Val-Suzon (Côte-d'Or) which was destroyed in the rebellion of Civilis of A D 69-70. Grenier points out, however, that the essence of the Celtic holy place was not the temple but an enclosure for the gatherings of pilgrims and the performance of appropriate rites and sacrifices. The large circular enclosure of Fontaines-Salées would appear to be in this tradition. It has also recently been claimed that many small rectangular enclosures of La Tène and early Roman times in France and Germany hitherto unexplained are simply sanctuaries of this open type (Schwarz

1958). One instance of a long surviving custom is the *puits-funéraire*, a ritual or burial pit found on Gallic and Gallo-Roman sites in Aquitaine, dating in large numbers from 50-30 BC, but continuing as a practice until the fourth century AD. They are often about 10 m. deep and contain cremations covered with many funerary offerings, including pottery and animal bones among which are those of creatures like toads, suggesting magical practices and supporting the view that these are not ordinary burials (Fouet 1958; Piggott 1968).

The Romans respected Celtic religion but they also imported their own gods. There followed the familiar classical practice of giving Latin names to the native deities, carried out by their own worshippers rather than by any official action. Caesar's excursus on Gallic religion, necessarily a summary account of a complicated subject, is obscured and over-simplified by the use of Latin rather than Celtic names. The Celts probably had no clear-cut system of hierarchic relationships between their gods, and these gods had not been divided up with different functions to anything like the same extent as had the Olympian deities. But the *Interpretatio Romana* went on and most of the Gallic gods bear two names, a Latin and a native one, such as Apollo Moritasgus of Alesia. Often the Celtic name finished by dropping out, especially for gods, while goddesses more frequently retained theirs, so that we get divine couples such as Mercurius and Rosmerta, or Apollo and Sirona.

Healing gods tended to become Apollo, like Apollo Grannus, but Belenus, the god of sun and light, is also equated with Apollo. Mercurius is found on mountains, such as Mercurius Dumias of the Puy-de-Dôme, or the Mercurius of the Donon in the Vosges; he was also the patron of trade, and is associated with a variety of other gods, including Esus the forester. Jupiter is found as the god riding a horse supported by a strange serpent-legged being, a group which was frequently set up on columns. The Gallic gods are in fact extremely varied, and defy systematisation. The Celts ascribed a triple degree of power to divine beings and many representations have threefold attributes – the three-faced god of Soissons and Rheims, the statuettes of three-horned bulls. Another impressive deity is the god Cernunnos, with antlers springing from his brow, often seated cross-legged with a bag of coins between his knees. The cross-legged posture, also found on the early statues at Provençal sites, is probably simply the way that Gauls habitually sat.

It is, however, among the goddesses that we find the Celtic deity who achieved the widest renown in the Roman Empire, the horse-goddess Epona whose worship was carried to Rome by cavalrymen. Mother-goddesses, frequently in groups of three, are found all over Gaul and other Celtic provinces.

One religious element in Gaul had to go, and that was the Druids, the caste of wise men recruited from the ruling classes, who had first say in council, who managed ritual and who, with the bards, had kept alive the old Celtic myths and history. They were a potential focus for political unrest and, as priests presiding at rites of human sacrifice, they had power over life and death, a power which the Roman State would not allow out of its own hands. Roman citizens were forbidden by Augustus to take part in certain foreign cults, among which Druidism was counted. This automatically downgraded the Druids from their former aristocratic status, since it was among the aristocracy that the citizenship was most sought after. The edict of Tiberius against magicians and the like adversely affected the Druids, and finally came their suppression by Claudius, giving their bloody practices as a reason, no doubt truly, but not mentioning the still more cogent reason of their political undesirability. It is paradoxical that the only Druid with whom we have any real acquaintance is the half-romanised Aeduan character Diviciacus, who knew so clearly on which side his bread was buttered. Those Druids who remained went underground, to reappear sporadically in later years.

Such knowledge of reading and writing as the Gauls possessed was ascribed to the influence of the Druids. They were probably responsible for the longest document in Gaulish that has survived, the Calendar of Coligny (Ain) now in Lyons museum. This is a list of lunar months and their associated ceremonies, among which the festivals of Beltine (1 May) and Lugsanad (1 August) can be recognised. It is significant that 1 August, the birthday of Augustus and also the day of Lug's festival, was chosen as the day of the great annual gathering at the confluence of Rhône and Saône beside his old city of Lugdunum, which celebrated the participation of the Gauls in the *Pax Romana* and the classical civilisation which it was destined to preserve.

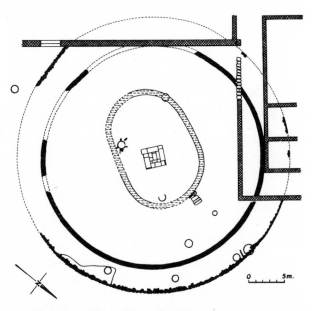

12 Fontaines-Salées, Yonne. Plan showing circular enclosure of first century AD round the sacred area. In the centre is a paved pool and round it are the remains of an earlier oval enclosure. The small circles are wells (mostly pre-Roman). The later buildings are second-century baths (after Chaumeil)

8
Summary and Conclusions
GLYN DANIEL
STUART PIGGOTT

The purpose of this book, when it was conceived many years ago, was to provide an up-to-date summary of what was known about France before Rome. It was not intended to be, and is not, a work of *haute vulgarisation* (that is to say of scholarly popularisation, to use Professor Thurstan Shaw's happily phrased translation), but a synthesis for students and scholars. It is a work of history and tells what we know of man's development in France until Gallia became a province of Rome. It is the first of those four volumes into which the history of a country is conventionally divided – Prehistory, Ancient History, Medieval History, Modern History. The word prehistory has always been a bit of a misnomer: English and Americans use it for that period of time before written history in the country concerned. The English and American contributors to, and editors of, this book certainly regard it as a prehistory of France. The French, however – and there is Gallic logic in this view – regard prehistory as ending all over the world when writing and therefore history *sensu stricto* began, which was roughly five thousand years ago in Egypt and Sumeria. They would therefore bring prehistory to an end in France at 3000 BC, and call from 3000 BC to the Roman conquest proto-history. They would therefore regard this book as the *préhistoire* and *protohistoire* of France. We mention this *en passant*: it was a convenient, though really indefensible, terminology when France before 3000 BC seemed to be the Stone Age, and from 3000 BC the Neolithic, Bronze and Early Iron Ages, but nowadays radiocarbon dating would suggest the beginning of the Neolithic in France to be in the fifth millennium BC – the arrival of writing in southwest Asia coincides with the last part of Bailloud's chapter, and 3000 BC is not a significant moment in the story of early France.

Because this book deals with the early history of man in France, even if it ends when written history begins, we have given chronological limits to the chapters and deliberately eschewed chapter headings such as Upper Palaeolithic or Early and Middle Bronze Age. Such phrases were widely used in archaeological literature until recently; they are derived from the epochal development of the technological model of man's past invented by C. J. Thomsen in Denmark in the early nineteenth century, and developed on a European basis by his pupil and successor, J. J. A. Worsaae. Archaeology could not have made the progress it did in the

nineteenth century were it not for the technological model, and for the gradual elaboration of the Danish three-age system into a five-age system of Palaeolithic, Mesolithic, Neolithic, Bronze Age and Early Iron Age. In the further elaboration of this system French archaeologists played a most notable part as may be seen by looking at Gabriel de Mortillet's *Formation de la Nation Française* (1897) and Joseph Déchelette's *Manuel d'Archéologie* (1908-14). The realisation that the epochs, or small subdivisions of the five age system, were only one way of looking at the material remains of the past, came in the years following the First World War, when Déchelette was killed. In England the non-epochal way of looking at the past was well exemplified by Gordon Childe and in France by Henri Breuil; writers on pre-Roman France from the mid-twenties to 1950 were happy writing about cultures (if they wrote in English, *civilisations* if they wrote in French). Since the discovery of radiocarbon dating it has become possible to speak with assurance of the prehistoric past in terms of accurately dated moments of time, and this is why an historical and chronological framework is now, it seemed to us, the best way of organising the archaeological material that survives.

But whether or not we find the concept of *préhistoire* and *protohistoire* a valid one, there remains one notable watershed dividing the subject-matter of this book into two very unequal parts. From a date probably before 400,000 years ago until the fifth millennium BC the human population of France, in common with the rest of Europe, had their subsistence-economies based on hunting and gathering, with all the social implications that such a mode of life entails. By the end of the period it appears that some communities in the south of France, and probably in the west as well, had achieved at least a degree of selective herding, if not full domestication, of the locally indigenous sheep surviving from the Pleistocene into temperate climatic conditions. This move towards a greater self-sufficiency in the provision of at least the protein element in a mixed diet was soon to be reinforced in the Mediterranean coastal areas by peoples who shared traditions of material culture (especially in their impressed pottery) with other coastal communities from the Dalmatian coast to Portugal and in north Africa, and also shared a fully agricultural economy which was to supplant that of the earlier hunters and gatherers.

A southern cultural province of stone-using agriculturists now comes into being, developing its own traditions of pottery and other elements of material culture. On its northeast boundaries France from the fifth and fourth millennia B C touched the fringe of the great central European province of earlier Neolithic culture, that of the makers of Linear pottery, and we now know that the influence of these peoples, or their actual territory, extended farther to the west than had hitherto been suspected, with characteristic pottery styles as far from the Danubian area as for instance the Channel Islands and, even more significant, the highly individual Linear pottery long house of massive timber-work has now been identified by excavation as far as the Yonne and the Seine.

If we take with this the emergence of further highly individual forms of Neolithic culture in the west, and especially in Brittany, we see that by the fourth millennium B C all Gaul was already divided into three parts, respectively Mediterranean, Atlantic and central European in tradition. Within this gross simplification other regional variants can already be perceived, and characteristically, as in other parts of Neolithic Europe, we see a tendency towards a developmental pattern which begins with basic uniformity in material culture over wide areas and by the Late Neolithic in the third millennium B C has split up into many distinctive regional forms. It is within such a pattern that we can recognise the likelihood that independent experimentation in technology combined with internal developments of the social order could produce new forms of tools or tombs whose features could be better explained by such local developments in the indigenous cultures, than by invoking long-range contacts with other centres.

We are well aware from the fourth millennium B C onwards of the southern and eastern elements in the personality of France as recognised many years ago by Vidal de la Blache. Was there also a western element? Were there early settlers along the west coast of France from Spain and Portugal? Much has been written about the Atlantic route in European prehistory, and Savory and others have talked of an Atlantic Bronze Age. These ideas are very relevant to the study of the prehistoric megalithic monuments of France. For the greater part of this century it has been maintained that the French megalithic tombs came from the Mediterranean: the Passage Graves or *dolmens à galerie* of France were derived from Spain and Portugal, and one of us argued for the dual origin of the French megaliths in the Mediterranean – the Passage Graves in Iberia and the Gallery Graves or *allées couvertes* in the long rock-cut tombs of the west Mediterranean (Daniel 1940, 1960). This latter view of the origin of the long stone tombs no longer seems convincing and it would appear that the *allées couvertes* of France, especially those of the Paris Basin, the Loire Valley, Brittany and Normandy should be regarded as lithic versions of long trench graves and long wooden tombs belonging to a widespread tradition extending from northern France to Poland and Scandinavia.

Could not the Passage Graves of northwestern France together with the similar monuments of Iberia and the British Isles represent a similar tradition of the translation into funerary architecture of round stone houses such as those that survive in the exceptionally well preserved settlement of Skara Brae in the Orkneys? After all, the round stone-built house has remained for centuries one of the common features of French and west Mediterranean peasant life, particularly in transhumantic regions. Radiocarbon dating of the west European megalithic tombs suggests that they are much earlier than all their claimed antecedents in the east Mediterranean. The west European Passage Grave would now seem to be an indigenous feature of life there in the fourth and third millennia B C. L'Helgouach still believes that the Breton monuments come from Iberia (L'Helgouach 1965) but at the moment the earliest dates come from Breton tombs. We want far more dates before this issue can be resolved.

It is one of the virtues of Bailloud's chapter that he sees little evidence for a special megalithic 'people' in prehistoric France. The megalithic monuments were built by the ordinary people of that country in the fourth and third millennia B C: they have attained a disproportionate position in our thinking about the prehistoric past because they were built of large stones, they have survived, and even in their decay are often grand and grotesque.

From time to time archaeologists and others in western Europe have speculated on the possible astronomical significance of megalithic monuments. It is many years since Marcel Baudouin wrote his *La Préhistoire par les Etoiles,* and until very recently this kind of astro-archaeology was unfashionable and seemed a part of the lunatic fringes of archaeology. But recently Professor Alexander Thom, as a result of long and careful surveys in Scotland, formed the opinion that many of the Scottish megalithic monuments were constructed to observe the movements of the moon. These views may be seen summarised in two books, namely *Megalithic Sites in Britain* (1967) and *Megalithic Lunar Observatories* (1971). In 1970 Thom visited the great megalithic monuments of Carnac and Locmariaquer in southern Brittany. He found that the same unit of measurement was used in Brittany as was used in Scotland, that the flattened ellipses at the west end of the three Carnac alignments took the same form as those of many of the Scottish monuments, and he argued that the Grand Menhir Brisé at Locmariaquer was used as a universal means of foretelling the rising and setting moon at the eight critical positions (see *The Listener,* 31 December 1970). Thom's views are certainly controversial but it begins to look as though the people of prehistoric France who were responsible for the dolmens and alignments and menhirs were not only skilled architects and builders, but had considerable mathematical and astronomical knowledge as well.

The second millennium B C opens in France, as in so many other areas of Europe, with a first-class problem, that of the origins and subsequent movements of people archaeologically represented by the Beaker style of pottery, known from the Tagus to the Danube, and from the Straits of Messina to the Pentland Firth. Here is a classic situation of competing claims from east and west, the question of diffusion as against independent invention, and of monogenetic or polygenetic origins. The Iberian Peninsula has for long been favoured as the area of origin for the whole complex, but central Europe has not been without its claimants, while ingenious compromise solutions have been advanced, ranging from Palliardi's half-forgotten suggestion of a dual origin to which both west and east contributed, to Sangmeister's complex pattern of an Iberian origin followed by a transmission of culture to Central Europe whence, after interaction with local late Neolithic cultures including that of Corded ware, intricate reflux movements took place, eventually to reach the Iberian homeland itself. We are hampered, over the whole Beaker province, by a lack of radiocarbon dates in sufficient quantity to enable an assessment in terms of absolute chronology to be made, nor has a proper corpus been produced whereby the pottery itself could be interpreted by the sophisticated analytical means Clarke has used for the British material.

Whatever the eventual outcome of the search for origins, in France as in many other areas the makers of Beaker pottery also appear to be associated with the earliest non-ferrous metallurgy in an otherwise Late Neolithic context, even if individual types such as the tanged copper daggers have no progeny, but are quickly replaced by the products of other schools of metallurgy centred on the Rhineland. From these there stem, first in copper and soon in tin-bronze, the types characteristic of the subsequent Bronze Age cultures of the earlier second millennium BC, and the Rhône province shows its affiliations to the main centre of innovation and development, the Únětice culture of Czechoslovakia.

Linked also to central Europe, and to Britain, was the culture responsible for the Breton Tumulus Graves, often strikingly rich in objects not only of copper or bronze, but in gold, silver, and occasionally amber. The manifest links between the earlier series of the graves with those of the so-called Wessex culture of southern England have led to variant interpretations, of which the old thesis of a Breton origin for the English culture seems now hardly tenable in its original form. Rather it would appear more reasonable to see Wessex and Brittany deriving their bronze types from a common central European source (which for Brittany would also provide the rite of tumulus burial, of earlier origin in Britain), with subsequent cross-Channel contacts. Most, perhaps all, the original assumptions as to the nature, chronology and outside contracts of the Wessex culture have recently been called in question, and the resolution of this problem, if achieved, will naturally have its repercussions on the Breton Tumulus Graves.

The subsequent story of bronze-using cultures in France (as in many other areas) has to be pieced together almost wholly from the products of the bronze industry itself, since before the Urnfield cultures burials are few

and settlement sites virtually unknown. With the advent of these cultures, reaching France from the east at the end of the second millennium BC, we can see the development of another east-west situation, with the intrusive traditions of the Urnfields in the east, while, in the Atlantic west, distinctive bronze industries are created, which, by the seventh century BC, can be seen affecting and contributing to the pattern of commerce and contact with Britain.

From the seventh century, too, we begin to have material – settlements and cemeteries such as those of Cayla de Mailhac – that fill out the picture of prehistoric culture in southern France, and with the founding of the Greek colony of Massalia around 600 BC we enter a new and exciting world, technologically cognisant of the use of iron for edge tools and weapons, and, along the north-south axis of the Rhône, effecting contacts between the Greek world and that of the Hallstatt princedoms from Burgundy to southern Germany. This is the world of Vix and Ste-Colombe, and of the hill-forts of Mont Lassois and its congeners, and, by the fifth century, Greek imports were to be the catalysts in releasing the great Celtic artistic achievement in the new kingdoms north of those of the Hallstatt leaders of a century or so before.

For the first time, after the faceless anonymity of the prehistoric millennia, we can glimpse at least a known and named language group, and see France coming within the ambit of Indo-European speech. Whether we can attach culture to language is always a problem: a new language can be adopted or imposed without any change in the material culture recognisable to the archaeologist. But Early Celtic art is so distinctive an expression of a cohesive aesthetic experience that we could hardly deny the artists and patrons who maintained it a similarly shared social tradition and structure, and to designate this too as Celtic.

It is on the borderline between prehistory (or proto-history!) and history with its literate documentation that many of us would feel that the most rewarding studies of ancient communities in Europe can be made. Celtic flesh is put on the archaeological skeleton when we begin to get the comments of such percipient ethnographers as Posidonius, and Roman Gaul provides us with one of the most complete pictures of later Celtic civilisation that we have. For an understanding of Celtic religion the naturalistic traditions of Roman art expressed in Gallo-Roman sculpture have been, since the beginning of such studies, an essential source, and now that stone sculpture is beginning to be supplemented by the extraordinary hoards of wooden figures from water-logged sanctuaries at spring-heads, a new dimension has been added both to Celtic iconography and Celtic art in its final phase. But, as this book shows, the Gauls – romantically favoured in nineteenth-century art, unromantically remembered in the character of Asterix today – have a long ancestry of culture and tradition behind them.

The archaeologist is always being told that it is not enough to describe and record, that chronicle by itself is unsatisfactory – what is also needed is explanation. This is easier said than done. Here in this book eight scholars who have worked extensively in differing fields of French prehistory have summarised the story of pre-Roman France as it appears to them at this moment of twentieth-century time, and as it can be deduced from the archaeological record. This is a very different story from that written by Déchelette at the beginning of this century, just as Déchelette's story was very different from that given by de Mortillet in his *Formation de la Nation française*, and both very different from the books of Cartailhac and Bertrand. The difference is partly the changing nature of the archaeological record: we now know far, far more about pre-Roman France than Bertrand, Cartailhac or de Mortillet dreamt would be possible, and, through geochronological techniques of which C14 dating is the most important, we have an independent and exact chronology of which archaeologists working as recently as twenty-five years ago had no knowledge or hope.

But the greatly enlarged body of archaeological facts and the exact dating of the prehistoric past does not make the explanation of the past all that easier. We can still only guess at the non-material aspects of the life of man in pre-Roman France. What religious ideas the builders of the megalithic tombs and alignments had is a matter of guesswork. When we come to the shrines of the Celts and Celto-Ligurians we are nearer to written history and we are assisted in part by the interpretation by Greeks and Romans of barbarian Celtic religion, and to some extent helped by their understanding, or misunderstanding, of what they saw. One of us has recently discussed what we can know and do know about the Druids (Piggott *The Druids*, 1968), using the archaeological and the literary evidence in conjunction.

The archaeological record demonstrates nothing more clearly than change: tools, weapons, pottery styles, tombs, houses, temples change and so does art. What is at the root of this change so clearly and obviously reflected? It was the fashion for a long time to invoke new people whenever there was change in material culture, and the invasion model was for many a standard and very proper way of interpreting prehistory. Nor should the existence of prehistoric invasions and migrations be dismissed entirely. We know only too well that the end of Roman France was followed by a period of migrations, and that it is as a result of the Migration Age that the romanised Gauls became the French. It is not only reasonable, but necessary, to postulate in pre-Roman France invasions similar to those of the Migration Period and these would be directly responsible for many of the major cultural changes that took place. The arrival of agriculturists in fifth-millennium France must represent some invading groups, and so must the Urnfields of the first millennium. But all change does not demand hordes of invaders.

All we can say, then, is that the Gauls who were Romanised and formed the basis of the French nation in the Dark Ages were a people whose traditions went back to the survivors of the hunting-fishing Mesolithic people, the first agriculturists from the Mediterranean and central Europe, and the Celtic warriors and artists of the Urnfield, Hallstatt and La Tène cultures. And when we look backwards, as anyone with historical curiosity must, we should remember that the painted and engraved caves of Lascaux and Font-de-Gaume, the megaliths of Carnac, the treasure of Vix, the shrine of Roquepertuse, the Amfreville helmet are alike part of the living past of France, part of the rich heritage of its pre-Roman, native days.

Bibliography

1
From the Beginnings of Man to *c*. 33,000 BC

ARKELL, W. J. *Geology of Oxford*. Oxford 1947.

AULT DU MESNIL, D. d'. Note préliminaire sur les terrasses fluviatiles de la vallée de la Somme. *Ann. Soc. Géol. Nord*, 1910, 196-9, 205.

— Note sur le terrain quaternaire des environs d'Abbeville. *Rev. Mens. Ecole d'Anthrop.*, 1896.

AUSTEN, R. A. C. On the bone caves of Devonshire. *Proc. Geol. Soc.*, III, 1838, 286-87.

BIBBY, G. *The Testimony of the Spade*. London 1957.

BIBERSON, P. *Le Paléolithique inférieur du Maroc atlantique*. 2 vols, 1961.

BINFORD, L. R. and S. R. A preliminary analysis of functional variability in the Mousterian of Levallois facies. *American Anthropologist*, 68, No. 2, Pt 1, 1966, 508-12.

BLOOM, A. L. Glacial-enstatic and isostatic controls of sea level. In Turekian, K.K. *Late Cenozoic glacial ages*. Yale 1972.

BORDES, F. L'évolution buissonante. *L'Anthropologie*, 54, 1950, 393.

— . L'Atelier Commont. *L'Anthropologie*, 57, 1953, 1-45.

— Les limons quaternaires du bassin de la Seine. *A.I.P.H.*, 26, 1954.

BORDES, F. and F. BOURGON. Le complexe moustérien. *L'Anthropologie*, 55, 1951, 1-23.

BORDES, F. *et al*. Observations sur le gisement de Combe Grenal. *Actes Soc. Linnéenne*, 103, sér. B, No. 10, 1966, 1-19.

BOUCHER DE PERTHES. *De la Création*. 5 vols, Abbeville 1838.

— *Antiquité Celtique*. 3 vols, Paris 1847.

BOURGON, M. *Les industries moustériennes et pré-moustériennes du Périgord*. Paris 1951.

BREUIL, H. Etude de stratigraphie paléolithique dans le Nord de la France, la Belgique et l'Angleterre. *L'Anthropologie*, 42, 1932, 28-47; 291-314.

— De l'importance de la solifluction dans l'étude des terrains quaternaires de la France et des pays voisins. *Rev. Géograph. Phys.*, VII, fasc. 4, 1934, 209-331.

— Somme et Charente. *Bull. Soc. Archéol. Hist. Charente*, XXX, 1938.

— La Préhistoire. *Rev. Cours. Confér.*, 31, 1, 1929-30, 97-113.

— The Pleistocene succession of the Somme Valley. *Proc. Prehist. Soc.*, V, 1939, 33-38.

CHERNYSH, O. P. Paleolitichna stoianka Molodova V. *Akad. Nauk. Ukraine*, 1961.

CLARK, J. D. *Kalambo Falls*. 2 vols, Cambridge 1969.

COMMONT, V. Les gisements paléolithiques de Saint-Acheul, coupe du Quaternaire dans la vallée de la Somme. *C.R. Assoc. Franç. Av. Sci.*, Compte rendu de la 37ᵉ Session (1908), 1909, 454-65.

— Note préliminaire sur les terrasses fluviatiles de la vallée de la Somme. *Ann. Soc. Géol. Nord*, XXXIX, 1910 (a), 185-293.

— Industries des graviers inférieurs de la haute terrasse de Saint-Acheul. *C. R. Assoc. Franc. Av. Sci.*, Compte rendu de la 38ᵉ Session (1909), 1910, 774-77.

DEPERET, C. Les anciennes lignes de rivage de la côte française de la Méditerranée. *Bull. Soc. Géol.*, VI, sér. 4, 1906, 207-30.

— Essai de coordination chronologique générale des temps quaternaires. *C.R. Acad. Sci.*, 25, No. 167, 1918, 979-84.

EMILIANI, C. Absolute dating of deep sea cores by the PA/Th method. *Jour. Geol.*, 69, 1961, 162.

FIRBAS, F. Vegetationsentwicklung..., *Naturwis.*, Berlin, Jahrgang 27, Heft 6, 1939, 81, 104.

FREEMAN, L. G. The nature of the Mousterian facies in Cantabrian Spain. *American Anthrop.*, 68 (special issue), 1966, 230-37.

GILEAD, D. Hand-axe industries in Israel. *World Arch.*, II, 1, 1970, 1-11.

HODSON, F. R. Searching for structure within multivariate archaeological data. *World Arch.*, I, 1, 1969, 90.

HOWELL, F. C. Early Man. *Life Nature Library*, 1965.

KERNEY, A. and G. DE G. SIEVEKING. Account of recent excavations at Bakers Hole. Paper read to the Prehistoric Society, 21 October 1970, unpublished.

LAMOTHE, L. DE. Les anciennes nappes alluviales et les lignes de rivage du bassin de la Somme. *Bull. Soc. Géol.*, XVIII, sér. 4, 1918, 3-58.

LUMLEY, H. DE. La Grotte du Vallonnet. *Bull. Mus. Anthrop. Prehist.*, No. 10, 1963, 5-20.

LYELL, SIR C. *The Antiquity of Man*. London 1863.

MELLARS, P. The chronology of Mousterian industries in the Perigord region. *Proc. Prehist. Soc.*, 35, 1969, 134-71.

PENCK, A. and E. BRÜCKNER. *Die Alpen im Eiszeitalter*. 3 vols, Leipzig 1901-09.

POSER, A. Auftautiefe Frostzerrung im Boden Mittel Europas. *Naturwis.*, Jahrgang 34, Heft 8, 1947 (a), 232-38.

— Dauerfrostboden der Würm-Eiszeits. *Naturwis.*, Jahrgang 34, Heft 1, 1947 (b), 10-18.

RIGOLLOT, A. Memoir on the mammalia of the valley of the Somme, 1819; quoted in Lyell, Sir C., 1863.

ROE, D. F. The British Lower and Middle Palaeolithic. *Proc. Prehist. Soc.*, 30, 1964, 245.

SHACKELTON, N. J. and OPDYKE, N. D. Oxygen isotope and palaeomagnetic stratigraphy. *Jour. Quat. Res.*, 3, 1973, 39-55.

SHOTTON, F. W. The problems and contributions of methods of absolute datting. *Quarterly Jour. Geol. Soc.*, 20, 1966.

WEINER, J. S. and B. G. CAMPBELL. The taxonomic status of the Swanscombe skull. In C. Ovey, *The Swanscombe skull: a survey of research on a Pleistocene site*. Royal Anthropological Institute Occasional Paper XX, 1964.

WEST, R. *Pleistocene Geology and Biology*. London 1968.

WRIGHT, W. B. *Tools and the Man*. London 1939.

ZEUNER, F. E. *The Pleistocene Period*. London 1945.

— *Dating the Past*. London 1946.

2
The Upper Palaeolithic:
c. 33,000-10,000 BC

ALLAIN, J. and R. FRITSCH. Le Badegoulien de l'abri Fritsch aux Roches de Pouligny Saint-Pierre (Indre). *Bull. Société Préhist. Franç.*, 64, 1967, 83-94.

BLANC, A. C. La stratigraphie de la plaine côtière... *Rev. Géographie phys.*, 9, 1936, 129-62.

BONIFAY, E. *Les terrains quaternaires dans le Sud-Est de la France*. Publications de l'Institut de Préhistoire de l'Université de Bordeaux, mémoire nº 2, Bordeaux 1962.

BORDES, F. 1954. *Op. cit.*

— Le passage du Paléolithique moyen au Paléolithique supérieur. *Neandertal Centenary 1856-1956*, Utrecht, 1958 (a), 175-81.

— Nouvelles fouilles à Laugerie-Haute: premiers résultats. *L'Anthropologie*, 62, 1958 (b), 205-44.

— Considérations sur la typologie et les techniques dans le Paléolithique. *Quartär* 18, 1967, 22-55.

— *The Old Stone Age*. London 1968.

BORDES, F., P. FITTE and P. LAURENT. Gravure féminine du Magdalénien VI de la Gare de Couze (Dordogne). *L'Anthropologie*, 67, 1963, 269-82.

BORDES, F. and D. DE SONNEVILLE-BORDES. Protomagdalénien ou Périgordien VII? *L'Anthropologie*, 70, 1966, 113-22.

BOUCHUD, J. Le Renne et le problème des migrations. *L'Anthropologie*, 58, 1954, 79-85.

— *Essai sur le Renne et la climatologie du Paléolithique moyen et supérieur*. Thèse de Doctorat es-Sciences, Paris 1959.

— L'évolution du climat au cours de l'Aurignacien et du Périgordien d'après la faune. *Bull Soc. méridionale de Spéléologie et de Préhistoire*, VI-IX, 1956-59, 143-53.

BOULE, M. and H. V. VALLOIS. *Les Hommes fossiles*, Paris 1952.

BREUIL, H. *Les subdivisions du Paléolithique supérieur et leur signification*. Geneva 1912 (second edition, Paris 1937).

— Les peintures et les gravures pariétales de la caverne de Niaux. *Bulletin de la Société préhistorique de l'Ariège*, 5, 1950.

— *Quatre cent siècles d'art pariétal*, Montignac 1952.

BREUIL, H. and R. JEANNEL. La grotte ornée du Portel à Loubens (Ariège). *L'Anthropologie*, 59, 1955, 197-204.

BREUIL, H. and R. DE SAINT-PÉRIER. *Les Poissons, les Batraciens et les Reptiles dans l'Art quaternaire*. Archives de l'Institut de Paléontologie humaine, mémoire nº 2, 1927.

CAPITAN, L. and J. BOUYSSONIE. *Limeuil: un atelier d'art préhistorique*. Publications de l'Institut international d'Anthropologie, mémoire no 1, 1924.

CAPITAN, L. and D. PEYRONY. *La Madeleine: son gisement, ses industries, ses œuvres d'art*. Publications de l'Institut international d'Anthropologie, No. 2, 1928.

CHEYNIER, A. Le Magdalénien primitif de Badegoule: niveaux à raclettes. *Bull. Soc. Préhist. Franç.*, XXXVI, No. 7-8, 1939, 354-96.

COMBIER, J. *Le Paléolithique de l'Ardèche dans son cadre paléoclimatique*. Publications de l'Institut de Préhistoire de l'Université de Bordeaux, mémoire No. 4, 1967.

DELPORTE, H. Le Paléolithique dans le Massif central: I, Le Magdalénien des vallées supérieures de la Loire et de l'Allier. *Bull. Soc. Préhist. Franç.*, 1966, 181-207.

ESCALON DE FONTON, M. Du Paléolithique supérieur au Mésolithique dans le Midi méditerranéen. *Bull. Soc. Préhist. Franç.*, 1966, 66-180.

GAUSSEN, J. *La grotte ornée de Gabillou (près Mussidan, Dordogne)*, Publications de l'Institut de Préhistoire de l'Université de Bordeaux, mémoire No. 3, 1964.

GOBERT, E.-G. Sur les 'Vénus aurignaciennes'. *La Préhistoire: problèmes et tendances*. Paris 1968.

LAVILLE, H. Recherches sédimentologiques sur la paléoclimatologie du Würmien récent en Périgord. *L'Anthropologie*, 68, 1964, 1-48, 219-52.

LEROI-GOURHAN, A. *Les religions de la Préhistoire*. Paris 1964

— *Préhistoire de l'art occidental*. Paris 1965. (English trans.: *The Art of Prehistoric Man*. London, 1967.)

— Les mains de Gargas: essai pour une étude d'ensemble. *Bull. Soc. Préhist. Franç.*, 1967, 107-22.

LEROI-GOURHAN, A. and Arlette. Chronologie des grottes d'Arcy-sur-Cure (Yonne). *Gallia-Préhistoire*, VII, 1964 1-64.

LEROI-GOURHAN, A. and M. BRÉZILLON. L'habitation magdalénienne nº 1 de Pincevent près de Montereau (Seine-et-Marne). *Gallia-Préhistoire*, IX, fasc. 2, 1966, 263-385.

LEROI-GOURHAN, Arlette. Le Badegoulien de l'abri Fritsch: climat et chronologie. *Bull. Soc. Préhist. Franç.*, LXIV, 1967, 95-9.

MÉROC, L. La conquête des Pyrénées par l'homme. *1er congrès international de Spéléologie, Paris, 1953*, IV, 4, 1956, 35-51.

— L'Aurignacien et le Périgordien dans les Pyrénées françaises et dans leur avant-pays. *Bull. Soc. méridionale de Spéléologie et Préhistoire*, 1963, 63-74.

MOVIUS, H. The Proto-Magdalenian of the Abri Pataud, Les Eyzies (Dordogne). *Bericht über den V Internationalen Kongress für Vor und Frühgeschichte, Hamburg, 1958*, 561-6.

— Radiocarbon dates and Upper Palaeolithic archaeology in central and western Europe. *Current Anthropology*, I, 1960, 355-91.

— More on Upper Palaeolithic archaeology, *Current Anthropology*, II, 1961, 427-54.

— The hearths of the Upper Perigordian and Aurignacian horizons at the abri Pataud, Les Eyzies (Dordogne), and their possible significance. *American Anthropologist. Recent studies in palaeoanthropology*, part 2, 68, No. 2, 1966, 296-325.

MOVIUS, H. and H. V. VALLOIS. Crâne proto-magdalénien et Vénus du Périgordien final trouvés dans l'abri Pataud, Les Eyzies (Dordogne). *L'Anthropologie*, 63, 1960, 213-32.

NOUGIER, L. R. *L'art préhistorique*. Paris 1966.

PALES, L. and M. TASSIN DE SAINT-PÉREUSE. Un cheval-prétexte. Retour au chevêtre. *Objets et Mondes*, VI, fasc. 3, 1966.

— *Les gravures de la Marche, t. I. Félins et Ours*, Publications de l'Institut de Préhistoire de l'Université de Bordeaux, mémoire nº 7. Bordeaux, 1969.

PÉQUART, M. and ST-JUST. Récente découverte de deux œuvres d'art magdalénien au Mas d'Azil (Ariège). *Revue scientifique*, 80e année, 1942, 91-5.

PEYRONY, D. Les industries aurignaciennes dans le bassin de la Vézère: Aurignacien et Périgordien. *Bull. Soc. Préhist. Franç.*, XXX, 1933, 543-59.

— La Ferrassie. *Préhistoire*, III, 1934, 1-92.

— Le Périgordien et l'Aurignacien: nouvelles observations. *Bull. Soc. Préhist. Franç.*, XXXIII, 1936, 616-19.

— Une mise au point au sujet de l'Aurignacien et du Périgordien. *Bull. Soc. Préhist. Franç.*, XLIII, 1946, 232-7.

PEYRONY, D. and E. *Laugerie-Haute*, Archives de l'Institut de Paléontologie humaine, mémoire nº 19. Paris 1938.

PIETTE, E. *L'art pendant l'Age du Renne*. Paris 1900.

— Le chevêtre et la semi-domestication des animaux aux temps pléistocènes. *L'Anthropologie*, 17, 1906, 27-53.

PIVETEAU, J. Paléontologie humaine. *Traité de Paléontologie*, VII, 1957.

— *L'origine de l'Homme*. Paris 1962.

PRADEL, L. La pointe des Cottés. *Bull. Soc. Préhist. Franç.*, LX, 1963, 572-90.

PRAT, F. *Recherches sur les Equidés pléistocènes en France*. Thèse de Doctorat ès-Sciences, Bordeaux 1968.

SAINT-PÉRIER, R. DE. *La grotte d'Isturitz, II : le Magdalénien de la Grande Salle*, Archives de l'Institut de Paléontologie humaine, mémoire 17. Paris 1936.

SCHMIDER, B. *Le Paléolithique supérieur en Ile-de-France*. Thèse de Doctorat de troisième cycle, Faculté des Lettres et Sciences humaines. Paris 1968.

SEMEENOV, S. A. *Prehistoric technology*. London 1964.

SMITH, P. *Le Solutréen en France*, Publications de l'Institut de Préhistoire de l'Université de Bordeaux, mémoire nº 5. Bordeaux 1966.

SONNEVILLE-BORDES, D. DE. Position stratigraphique et chronologique relative des restes humains du Paléolithique supérieur entre Loire et Pyrénées. *Annales de Paléontologie*, XLV, 1959, 19-51.

— *Le Paléolithique supérieur en Périgord*. Bordeaux 1960.

— Le Paléolithique supérieur de Belgique. *L'Anthropologie*, 65, 1961, 421-43.

— Le Paléolithique supérieur en Suisse. *L'Anthropologie*, 67, 1963 (a), 205-68.

— Upper Palaeolithic Cultures in Western Europe. *Science*, 142, No. 3590, 1963 (b), 347-55.

— Les industries des abris et grottes ornés du Périgord. *Bull. de la Soc. Hist. et Arch. du Périgord*, Centenaire de la Préhistoire en Périgord, 1965, 167-80.

— L'évolution du Paléolithique supérieur en Europe occidentale et sa signification. *Bull. Soc. Préhist. Franç., Etudes et travaux*, LXIII, 1966, 3-34.

— *La Préhistoire moderne*. Périgueux 1967.

THÉVENIN, R. *La faune disparue de France*. Paris 1943.

VALLOIS, H. V. Les maladies de l'homme préhistorique. *Revue scientifique*, 1934, 666-78.

— La durée de la vie chez les hommes fossiles. *L'Anthropologie*, 47, 1937, 499-532.

— Vital statistics in prehistoric population as determined from archaeological data, in *The application of quantitative methods in archaeology*, Chicago 1960, 186-222.

— The social life of Early Man: evidence of skeletons, in the Wenner-Gren symposium *Social life of Early Man*, Chicago 1961, 214-35.

VERNEAU, R. Les grottes de Grimaldi (Baoussé Roussé). *Anthropologie*, Monaco 1906-12.

ZERVOS, C. *L'art de l'époque du Renne en France*. Paris 1959.

3
From the End of the Ice Age to the First Agriculturists: 10,000-4000 BC

BAILLOUD, G. and P. MIEG DE BOOFZHEIM. *Les civilisations néolithiques de la France*. Paris 1955.

BARRIÈRE, G. *Les civilisations tardenoisiennes en Europe occidentale*. Bordeaux 1956.

BONIFAY, E. Recherches sur les terrains quaternaires dans le Sud-Est de la France. *Publications de l'Institut de Préhistoire de l'Université de Bordeaux*. Mém. 2, 1962, 194.

BORDES, F. and P. FITTE. Microlithes du Magdalénien supérieur de la gare de Couze (Dordogne). *Miscelanea en homenaje al Abate Henri Breuil*, 1964, 259-67.

BOURDIER, F. *Préhistoire de France*. Paris 1967.

BOURDIER, F. and H. DE LUMLEY. Existence d'une industrie Proto-Azilienne contemporaine du Renne en Dauphine. *Bull. Soc. Préhist. Franç.*, LI, 1954, 7.

— Magdalénien et Romanello-Azilien en Dauphiné. *Bull. Mus. d'Anthrop. Préhist. de Monaco*, 3, 1956, 123-87.

BREUIL, H. Cailloux gravés aziliens. *Quaternaria*, II, 1955, 29-34.

COMBIER, J. Informations archéologiques. *Gallia-Préhistoire* V, 1962.

— Informations archéologiques. *Gallia-Préhistoire* VII, 1965.

COULONGES, L. Le gisement préhistorique du Martinet à Sauveterre-la-Lémance (L.-et-G.). *L'Anthropologie*, 38, 1928, 495-503.

COURTIN, J. La Préhistoire récente de la vallée du Verdon. *Cahiers Ligures de Préhist. et d'Archéologie*, nº 10, 11, 1961.

DANIEL, M. and R. Le Tardenoisien classique du Tardenois. *L'Anthropologie*, 52, 5-6, 1949, 311-49.

DANIEL, R. Nouvelles études sur le Tardenoisien français. *Bull. Soc. Préhist. Franç.*, 1932, 420-8; 1946, 242-8.

— Les gisements préhistoriques de la forêt de Montmorency (S.-et-O.). *Bull. Soc. Préhist. Franç.*, LI, 11-12, 1954, 554-9.

— Le gisement mésolithique de 'Désert d'Auffargis' (S.-et-O.). *Bull. Soc. Préhist. Franç.*, 9, CCCVII-CCCXIV, 1965.

DANIEL, R. and J. G. ROZOY. Divers types d'armature tardenoisiennes à base non retouchée. *Bull. Soc. Préhist. Franç.*, LXIII, 2, 1966, 251-61.

DANIEL, R. and E. VIGNARD. Tableau synoptique des principaux microlithes géométriques du Tardenoisien français. *Bull. Soc. Préhist. Franç.*, L, 5-6, 1953, 314-22.

— Le Tardenoisien français. *Bull. Soc. Préhist. Franç.*, LI, fasc. 8, 1954, 72-3.

DUCOS, P. Le gisement de Châteauneufles-Martigues (B.-du-Rh.): les mammifères et les problèmes de la domestication. *Bull. Mus. d'Anthrop. Préhist. de Monaco*, 5, 1958, 119-33.

ESCALON DE FONTON, M. Préhistoire de la Basse-Provence: état d'avancement des recherches en 1951. *Préhistoire*, XII, 1956.

— Du Paléolithique supérieur au Mésolithique dans le Midi méditerranéen. *Bull. Soc. Préhist. Franç.*, LXIII, fasc. 1, 1966 (a), 66-180.

— A propos de quelques datations C.14 pour le Préhistoire du Midi de la France et de l'Italie. *Bull. Soc. Préhist. Franç.*, LXIII, 2, 1966 (b), L-LI.

— Le campement romanellian de la Valduc à Istres (B.-du-Rh.). *L'Anthropologie*, 70, 1-2, 1966 (c), 29-44.

— Problèmes posés par les blocs d'effondrement des stratigraphies préhistoriques du Würm à l'Holocène dans le Midi de la France. *Bull. Assoc. Franç. Étude du Quaternaire*, (A.F.E.Q.) nº 4 (1969).

— Les séquences sédimento-climatiques du Midi méditerranéen, du Würm à l'Holocène. *Bull. Mus. d'Anthrop. préhist. de Monaco*, nº 14 (1967), 1969.

GIRAUD, E. and E. VIGNARD. Un rendez-vous de chasse mésolithique 'Les Rochers' commune d'Auffargis (S.-et-O.). *Bull. Soc. Préhist. Franç.*, 7-8, 1946, 1-11.

HINOUT, J. Gisements tardenoisiens de l'Aisne. *Gallia-Préhistoire*, VII, 1964, 65-106.

LAPLACE-JAURETCHE, G. Les couches à escargot des cavernes pyrénéennes et le problème de l'Azilien de Piette. *Bull. Soc. Préhist. Franç.*, L, 4, 1953, 199-211.

LEROI-GOURHAN, A. La fonction des signes dans les sanctuaires paléolithiques. *Bull. Soc. Préhist. Franç.*, LV, fasc. 5-6, 1958 (a), 307-21.

— Le symbolisme des grands signes dans l'art pariétal paléolithique. *Bull. Soc. Préhist. Franç.*, LV, fasc. 7-8, 1958 (b), 384-98.

— Répartition et groupement des animaux dans l'art pariétal paléolithique. *Bull. Soc. Préhist. Franç.*, LV, fasc. 9, 1958 (c), 515-28.

MALVESIN-FABRE, G., L. R. NOUGIER and R. ROBERT. Le Proto-Azilien de la Grotte de la Vache (Ariège) et le genèse du harpon Azilien. *Bull. Soc. Préhist. de l'Ariège*, V, 1950.

MORI, FABRIZIO. *Tardrart Acacus : arte rupestre e cultura del Sahara preistorico*. Turin 1965.

PACCARD, M. L'Abri de l'Eglise (Methamis, Vaucluse). *Bull. Mus. d'Anthrop. de Monaco*, 4, 1957, 189-207.

— Le gisement préhistorique de Roquefure. Commune de Bonnieux, Vaucluse. *Cahiers Rhodaniens*, 10, 1963, 3-36.

PARENT, R. Gisements tardenoisiens de la Sablière de Fère-en-Tardenois (Aisne). *Bull. Soc. Préhist. Franç.* LIX, 9-10, 1962, 650-5.

— Le gisement tardenoisien de l'Allée Tortue, à Fère-en-Tardenois (Aisne). *Bull. Soc. Préhist. Franç.*, LXIV, fasc. 1, 1967, 187-208.

PEQUART, M. and ST J. Le Kjökkenmödding et les sépultures mésolithiques de l'île Hoëdic (Morbihan). *Congrès préhist. de France*, Périgueux 1934.

PIETTE, E. Une sépulture dans l'assise à galets coloriés du Mas d'Azil. *Bull. Soc. Anthrop. de Paris.*, III 1892; VI, 1895.

SONNEVILLE-BORDES, D. DE. *Le Paléolithique supérieur en Périgord*. Bordeaux 1960.

VIGNARD, E. and A. NOUEL. Présence de pics-planes dans certains gisements tardenoisiens. *Bull. Soc. Préhist. Franç.*, LIX, 5-6, 1962, 382-8.

VILAIN, R. *Le gisement de Sous-Balme à Culoz (Ain) et ses industries microlithiques*. Document Laboratoire Fac. Sciences Lyon, 13, 1966.

4
The First Agriculturists:
4000-1800 BC

ARNAL, J. La structure du Néolithique français d'après les récentes stratigraphies. *Zephyrus*, IV, 1953, 311-44.

— La grotte de La Madeleine. *Zephyrus*, VII, 1956, 33-79.

ARNAL, J., G. BAILLOUD and R. RIQUET. Les styles céramiques du Néolithique français. *Préhistoire*, XIV, 1960, 1-208.

ARNAL, J. and CL. BURNEZ. Die Struktur des französischen Neolithikums auf Grund neuester stratigraphischer Beobachtungen, 37-8. *Bericht der römisch-germanische Kommission, 1956-7*, 1957.

ARNAL, J. and H. PRADES. El neolitico y calcolitico franceses. *Ampurias*, XXI, 1958, 69-164.

AUDIBERT, J. *La civilisation chalcolithique du Languedoc oriental*. Bordighera 1962.

AUDIBERT, J. and M. ESCALON DE FONTON. Aperçus sur le Néolithique méridional. *Revue d'études ligures*, XXIV, 1958, 5-23.

BAILLOUD, G. Le mobilier néolithique de la grotte de Nermont à Saint-More (Yonne). *Revue arch. de l'Est et du Centre-Est*, VII, 1956, 97-113.

— Le Néolithique dans le Bassin parisien. IIᵉ supplément à *Gallia-Préhistoire*, Paris 1964.

BAILLOUD, G. and PH. COIFFARD. Le locus 5 des Roches à Videlles (Essonne). *Bull. Soc. Préhist. Franç.*, LXIV, 1967, 371-410.

BAILLOUD, G. and P. MIEG DE BOOFZHEIM. *Les civilisations néolithiques de la France dans leur contexte européen*. Paris 1955.

BARRAL, L. La grotte de La Madeleine (Hérault). *Bull. Mus. d'Anthrop. préhist. de Monaco*, 7, 1960, 5-73.

BOSCH-GIMPERA, P. and J. DE C. SERRA-RAFOLS. Études sur le Néolithique de l'Enéolithique en France. *Revue anthropologique*, 1925, 341-64; 1926, 318-45; 1927, 208-13.

BREA BERNABO, L. Il neolitico a ceramica impressa e la sua diffusione nel Mediterraneo. *Revue d'Etudes ligures*, XVI, 1950, 25-36.

BURNEZ, CL. *Le Néolithique et le Chalcolithique dans le Centre-Ouest de la France*. Cognac 1967.

BUTTLER, W. *Der donauländische und westische Kulturkreis der jüngeren Steinzeit*. Berlin 1938.

CAUVIN, M. C. Industrie de technique campignienne du Vexin et du pays de Bray. *L'Anthropologie*, 64, 1960, 493-511.

CHENET, G. Le village néolithique d'Ante (Marne). *Bull. Soc. arch. champenoise*, 1926, 113-34.

CORDIER, G. Inventaire des mégalithes de France, I, Indre-et-Loire. 1ᵉʳ supplément à *Gallia-Préhistoire*, vol. 1, Paris 1963 (a).

COURTIN, G. La grotte de l'Eglise à Baudinard (Var). *Gallia-Préhistoire*, X, 1967 (a), 282-300.

— Le Néolithique de la Provence. Marseille 1969.

DANIEL, G. *The prehistoric chamber tombs of France*. London 1960.

DUCOS, P. Étude de la faune du gisement néolithique de Roucadour (Lot). *Bull. Mus. Anthrop. préhist. de Monaco*, 4, 1951, 165-88.

— Le gisement de Châteauneuf-les-Martigues (B.-du-Rh.). Les mammifères et les problèmes de domestication. *Bull. Mus. Anthrop. préhist. de Monaco*, 5, 1958, 119-33.

ESCALON DE FONTON, M. Préhistoire de la Basse-Provence. *Préhistoire*, XII, 1956.

— Chasséen et Lagozien, *Congrès préhist. Fr., XVIᵉ session, Monaco, 1955*. 1959, 550-7.

— Les stèles de Trets (B.-du-Rh.). *Antiquités nationales et internationales*, III, 1962, 8-12.

— Origine et développement des civilisations néolithiques méditerranéennes en Europe occidentale. *Palaehistoria*, XII, 1966, 209-48.

— *Préhistoire de la Basse-Provence occidentale*. Martigues 1968.

FORRER, R. Le cimetière néolithique de Lingolsheim... *Cahiers d'archéologie et d'histoire d'Alsace*, XXIX, 1938, 191-206.

GALAN, A. La station néolithique de la Perte du Cros à Saillac (Lot). *Gallia-Préhistoire*, X, 1967, 1-71.

GIOT, P. R., J. L'HELGOUACH and J. BRIARD. *Brittany*. London 1960.

GLORY, A. *La civilisation du Néolithique en Haute-Alsace*. Strasbourg 1942.

GUERRESCHI, G. *La Lagozza di Besnate e il Neolitico superiore padano*. Como 1967.

GUILAINE, J. La grotte de Gazel à Sallèles-Cabardès (Aude). Note préliminaire sur les niveaux du Néolithique ancien. *Préhistoire-Spéléologie ariégeoises*, XX, 1965, 129-37.

IAWORSKY, G. La grotte du Pertus II à Méailles (Basses-Alpes) du Néolithique au Romain. *Bull. Mus. Anthrop. préhist. de Monaco*, 7, 1960, 81-152.

JEHL, M. and CH. BONNET. Contribution à l'étude du Néolithique en Haute-Alsace. *Cahiers alsaciens d'arch., d'art et d'hist.*, IX, 1965, 5-28; and X, 1966, 5-16.

KAHLKE, D. *Die Bestattungssitten des donauländischen Kulturkreises der jüngeren Steinzeit, I. Linienbandkeramik*. Berlin 1954.

KIMMIG, W. Zur Frage der Roessener Kultur am südlichen Oberrhein. *Badische Fundberichte*, 18, 1950, 42-62.

LOUIS, M. *Préhistoire du Languedoc méditerranéen et du Roussillon*. Nîmes 1948.

LUNING, J. Die Michelsberger Kultur, 48. *Bericht der römisch-germanische Kommission*, 1967, 1-350.

MAIER-ARENDT, W. *Die bandkeramische Kultur im Untermaingebiet*. Bonn 1966.

MAURY, J. *Les étapes du peuplement sur les Grands Causses*. Milan 1967.

NIEDERLANDER, A., R. LACAM and J. ARNAL. Le gisement néolithique de Roucadour (Thémines, Lot). 3ᵉ supplément à *Gallia-Préhistoire*, Paris 1966.

NOUGIER, L. R. *Les civilisations campigniennes en Europe occidentale*. Le Mans 1950.

PARRUZOT, P. Les influences danubiennes dans le Néolithique de la Basse vallée de l'Yonne. *XXVIIIᵉ congrès de l'Assoc. bourguignonne des Soc. savantes, Châtillon-sur-Seine, 1957*. 1958, 31-7.

PÉTREQUIN, P. Les influences danubiennes dans le Nord du Jura. *Bull. Soc. Préhist. Franç.*, LXIV, 1967, 327-38.

— *La grotte de la Baume à Gonvillars (Haute-Saône)*. Besançon 1969.

PIGGOTT, S. Le Néolithique occidental et le Chalcolithique en France. *L'Anthropologie*, 57, 1953, 401-43; 58, 1954, 1-28.

PRÉVOST, R. *L'habitat néolithique de la Montagne de Lumbres.* Arras 1962.

RIQUET, R. Essai de synthèse sur l'ethnogénie des Néo-énéolithiques en France. *Bull. Soc. Anthrop. Paris*, 1951, 201-33.

— Chassey où est-tu?. *Bull. Soc. Préhist. Franç.*, LV, 1959, 364-74.

— *Populations et races au Néolithique et au Bronze ancien.* Bordeaux 1967.

RIQUET, R. and CL. BURNEZ. Les cadres culturels du Néolithique des pays du Centre-Ouest. *Congrès préhist. Franç.*, XVᵉ session, Poitiers-Angoulême, 1957, 861-78.

SALMON, PH., D'AULT DU MESNIL and L. CAPITAN. Le Campignien. Fouille d'un fond de cabane au Campigny, commune de Blangy-sur-Bresle (Seine-Inférieure). *Revue Ec. d'Anthrop. Paris*, 1898, 365-405.

SOUDSKY, B. Étude de la maison néolithique. *Slovenska archeológia*, XVII, 1969, 5-96.

STROH, A. Die Roessener Kultur in Südwestdeutschland, 28. *Bericht der römisch-germanischen Kommission*, 1939, 8-179.

THÉVENOT, J. P. Éléments chasséens de la céramique de Chassey. *Rev. Arch. de l'Est et du Centre-Est*, XX, 1969, 7-95.

VENCL, S. Les instruments lithiques des premiers agriculteurs en Europe centrale. *Sbornik narodniho Muzea v Praze*, classe A, XIV, 1960, 1-91.

5
Bronze Age Cultures: 1800-600 BC

ABAUZIT, P. La question des Champs d'Urnes en Bourbonnais. *Rev. Arch. Centre*, 1962, 134.

ABAUZIT, P. and B. VANNIER. Découverte d'une nécropole des Champs d'Urnes... à Orval, Cher. *Rev. Arch. Centre*, 1965, 125.

ARNAL, J. and J. AUDIBERT. Enquête sur la répartition des vases de la Polada en France. *Bull. Mus. d'Anthrop. Préhist. de Monaco*, 3, 1956, 241.

ARNAL, J. and H. MARTIN-GRANEL. Le château préhistorique du Lébous... *Bull. Soc. Préhist. Franç.*, LVIII, 1961, 571.

AUDIBERT, J. Nouvelles recherches sur la céramique de la Polada dans le sud de la France. *Rev. d'Et. Ligures*, 1958, 331.

— Age des Métaux, Hérault-Gard. *Inventaria Archaeologica*, 1963, F7, F16.

BAILLOUD, G. L'habitat néolithique et protohistorique des Roches, commune de Videlles (Seine-et-Oise). *Mémoires Soc. Préhist. Franç.*, V, 1958, 192.

— Un habitat du Bronze Moyen Marion des Roches. *Bull. Soc. Préhist. Franç.*, LVIII, 1962, 99.

— La civilisation du Rhône et le Bronze Ancien du Midi de la France. *Rev. Arch. Est*, XVII, 1966, 131.

BAILLOUD, G. and CL. BURNEZ. Le Bronze Ancien dans le Centre-Ouest de la France. *Bull. Soc. Préhist. Franç.*, LIX, 1962, 515.

BOCQUET, A. *L'Isère Pré et Protohistorique.* Grenoble 1968.

BOUSQUET, N., R. GOURDIOLE and R. GUIRAUD. La grotte de Labeil, *Cah. Ligures, Préhist. Arch.*, 1966, 79.

BRIARD, J. *Les dépôts bretons et l'Age du Bronze atlantique.* Rennes 1965.

— Nouveaux dépôts de haches à talon en Bretagne. *Bull. Soc. Préhist. Franç.*, LXIII, 1966, 565.

BRISSON, A. and J. J. HATT. Les nécropoles hallstattiennes d'Aulnay-aux-Planches. *Rev. Arch. Est*, IV, 1953, 193.

— Fonds de cabanes...en Champagne. *Rev. Arch. Est*, XVIII, 1967, 7.

BURGESS, C. B. The later Bronze Age in the British Isles and North-Western France. *The Archaeological Journal*, CXXV, 1968, 1.

CHAPOTAT, G. Le char de la Côte Saint-André. *Gallia*, XX, 1962, 33.

CHARLES, R. P. and J. GUILAINE. Une grotte sépulcrale du Bronze Moyen en Languedoc... *Gallia-Préhistoire*, VI, 1963, 149.

CORDIER, G. Une nécropole de la civilisation des Champs d'Urnes à Chissay-en-Touraine. *L'Anthropologie*, 1961, 184.

COURTIN, J. Données nouvelles sur l'Age du Bronze dans le Sud-Est de la France. *Cah. Ligures Préhist. Arch.*, 12, 1963, 210.

COURTIN, J. and H. PUECH. La première phase de l'Age du Bronze en Basse Provence. *Cah. Ligures Préhist. Arch.*, 1963, 56.

COURTOIS, J. C. L'Age du Bronze dans les Hautes-Alpes. *Gallia-Préhistoire*, III, 1960, 47.

COWEN, J. D. The Hallstatt sword of bronze on the Continent and in Britain, *Proc. Prehist. Soc.*, XXXIII, 1967, 377.

DÉCHELETTE, J. *Manuel d'Archéologie*, II. Paris 1910.

GALAN, A. La grotte de Marsa, Beauregard, Lot, *Gallia-Préhistoire*, IV, 1961,

GIOT, P. R. and J. COGNÉ. L'Age du Bronze Ancien en Bretagne, IV, 91. *L'Anthropologie*, 55, 1951, 413.

GIOT, P. R. J. L'HELGOUACH and J. BRIARD. *Brittany*, London 1960.

GROSJEAN, R. *Filitosa et son contexte archéologique*, Fondation E. Piot, Paris 1961.

— *La Corse avant l'Histoire.* Paris 1966.

GUILAINE, J. Réflexions sur la chronologie des vases polypodes pyrénéo-aquitains. *Ogam*, XIV, 1962, 25.

GUILAINE, J. and J. ABÉLANET. La céramique poladienne du Roussillon..., IV. *Symp. Préhist. Peninsular*, Pamplona, 1966, 129.

GUILAINE, J. and G. RANCOULE. La cachette launacienne du Peyré à Sabarat, Ariège. *Bull. Soc. Préhist. Ariège*, XXI, 1966, 81.

HATT, J.-J. Chronique de Protohistoire, *Bull. Soc. Préhist. Franç.*, LII, 1955, 96.

HESSE, A. Néolithique danubien et Bronze Récent à Champs. Yonne. *Gallia-Préhistoire*, V, 1962, 157.

JOFFROY, R. Age des Métaux, France. *Inventaria Archaeologica*, 1954, F1, F6.

— Note sur deux sépultures du Bronze Final découvertes à Barbuise. Courtavant (Aube). *Bull. Soc. Préhist. Franç.*, LXVII, 1970, 28.

JULLY, J. J. and O. RAPPAZ. A propos de deux poignards en bronze inédits. *Ogam*, XII, 1960, 31.

KIMMIG, W. Où en est l'étude de la Civilisation des Champs d'Urnes en France? *Rev. Arch. Est.*, 1951, 65-81; 1952, 131-72: 1954, 7-28, 209-32.

KLEEMAN, O. Eine Neue Verbreitungskarte des Spangenbarren, *Archaeologia Austriaca*, 1954, 68.

LACROIX, B. *La nécropole préhistorique de la Colombine.* Paris 1957.

L'HELGOUACH, J. *Les sépultures mégalithiques en Armorique.* Rennes 1965.

LOUIS, M., O. and J. TAFFANEL. *Le premier Age du Fer languedocien.* 3 vols, Bordighera, 1955-60.

MILLOTTE, J. P. *Le Jura et les Plaines de Saône aux âges des Métaux.* Paris 1963.

MOHEN, J. P. Les Bronzes protohistoriques de Paris et de sa région au Musée de l'Armée (Invalides), *Bull. Soc. Préhist. Franç.*, LXV, 1968, 779-816.

— *Carte archéologique de la Lorraine.* Paris 1965.

PHILIPPE, J. Le Fort-Harrouard. *L'Anthropologie*, 1937, 253.

PIGGOTT, S. The Early Bronze Age in Wessex. *Proc. Prehist. Soc.* 1938.

— *Ancient Europe from the beginnings of agriculture to classical Antiquity.* Edinburgh 1965.

PIROUTET, J. Sur la coexistence des populations différentes en Franche-Comté. *Congr. Préhist. France*, 1914, 560.

RIQUET, R. L'Age du Bronze autour de l'estuaire girondin. *Bull. Soc. Etud. Scient. Angers*, 1959, 62.

RIQUET, R. and A. COFFYN. Les cadres culturels préhistoriques autour de l'estuaire de la Gironde. *Bull. Soc. Arch. Hist. Bordeaux*, 1964.

SANDARS, N. K. *Bronze Age Cultures in France*. Cambridge 1957.

SAVORY, H. N. The 'Sword Bearers' a reinterpretation. *Proc. Prehist.Soc.* 1948, 155.

SCHAEFFER, C. F. A. *Les Tertres Préhistoriques de la forêt de Haguenau*. Haguenau 1926.

SIREIX, M. and J. M. LARROQUE. Un vase du Bronze Ancien en Gironde. *Bull. Soc. Préhist. Franç.*, LXIV, 1967.

SOUTOU, A. La stèle de Substantion..., *Ogam*, XIV, 1962, 521.

SOUTOU, A. and J. ARNAL. Le dépôt de la Croix de Mus-Murvielles-Béziers (Hérault)... *Bull. Mus. Arch. Préhist. de Monaco*, X, 1963, 173.

UENZE, O. *Die frühbronzezeitlichen triangulären Vollgriffdolche*. Berlin 1938.

ZUMSTEIN, H. L'Age du Bronze dans le département du Haut-Rhin, *Rev. Arch. Est*, XV, fasc. 1-2, 1964, 7; fasc. 3-4, 161; XVI, 1965, 9-56.

6
From 600 BC to the Roman Conquest

The only comprehensive work covering this chapter is the *Manuel* of J. Déchelette, written before his death in the First World War and reprinted later (Déchelette 1914, 1927). Still of the greatest interest, this study was based on only a fraction of the evidence now available. A lead into the more recent, detailed literature mentioned in the bibliography would be given by: *The Celts* by T. G. E. Powell (London 1958); *Brittany* by P. R. Giot (London 1960) and by R. Joffroy's monographs on Vix/Mont Lassois (Joffroy 1954, 1960).

ALLEN, D. F. Monnaies-à-la-Croix. *Numismatic Chronicle*, 7th ser. IX, 1969, 33.

ALMAGRO, M. *Las necrópolis de Ampurias*. III, 1955.

ARNAL, J., H. PRADES and R. MAJUREL. A Lattes, près de Montpellier, un port retrouvé. *Archéologia*, 31, Nov.-Déc. 1969, 69.

BENOÎT, F. L'art primitif méditerranéen de la vallée du Rhône. *Pub. Ann. Fac. Lettres Aix*, N.S. 9, 1955.

— L'épave du grand Congloué à Marseille. *Gallia*, suppl. XIV, 1961.

— Recherches sur l'hellénisation du Midi de la Gaule. *Pub. Ann. Fac. Lettres Aix*, N.S. 43, 1965 (a).

— La statuaire d'Entremont. *7e Cong. Int. Arch. Class. (1963)*, 1965 (b).

— La topographie de Marseille. *Gallia*, 24, 1966, 1.

— Résultats historiques des fouilles d'Entremont 1947-67. *Gallia*, XXVI, 1968, 1.

BERGMANN, J. Entwicklung und Verbreitung der Paukenfibel. *Jahrbuch Röm.-Germ. Zentralmuseums Mainz*, 5, 1958, 18.

BOUSCARAS, A. Découverte d'une épave du premier âge du fer à Agde. *Revue d'Études Ligures*, 30, 1964, 288.

BRISSON, A. and J.-J. HATT. Nécropoles hallstattiennes d'Aulnay-aux-Planches. *Rev. Arch. Est.*, 4, 1953, 193.

— Fonds de cabanes de l'âge du bronze final et du premier âge du fer en Champagne. *Rev. Arch. Est.*, 18, 1967, 7.

CHAILLAN, M. L'oppidum de la Teste-Nègre, aux Pennes. *Ann. Fac. Sci. Marseille*, 24, 1917, 33.

CLERC, M. *Massalia, Histoire de Marseille dans l'Antiquité*, I, 1927.

COLBERT DE BEAULIEU, J.-B. Monnaies coriosolites et autres monnaies gauloises. *Ann. de Bretagne*, 72, 1965, 209.

— Umlauf und Chronologie der gallokeltischen Münzen. *Jb. Numismatik und Geldeschichte*, 16, 1966, 45.

CORDIER, G. Un nouveau tumulus à char hallstattien: Sublaines (Indre-et-Loire). *Ogam*, XX, 1968, 5.

COTTE, C. Découverte d'une oenochoe dans un tumulus de Provence. *L'Homme Préhistorique*, 1909, 7.

COTTON, M. A. Muri Gallici. *In* Wheeler and Richardson, 1957.

COURTOIS, J.-C. Essai sur la protohistoire des Alpes du Dauphiné. *Rev. Arch. Est.*, 12, 1961, 287.

— Une sépulture de chef sous tumulus à Chabestan (H.-A.). *Gallia*, XXII, 1964, 173.

— Un village protohistorique à Sainte-Colombe (H.-A.). *Gallia*, XXIV, 1966, 217.

DAYET, D. Recherches archéologiques au Camp du Château (Salins) (1955-9), *Rev. Arch. Est.*, 18, 1967, 52.

DÉCHELETTE, J. *Manuel d'archéologie préhistorique celtique et gallo-romaine: IV, Second âge du fer ou époque de La Tène*. 2nd ed. Paris 1927.

DEHN, W. Alter-latènezeitliche Marnekeramik im Rheingebiet. *Reinecke-Festschrift*, Mainz, 1950, 33.

— Die Bronzeschüssel aus dem Hohmichele, Grab VI, und ihr Verwandtenkreis. *Fundberichte aus Schwaben*, N.F. 17, 1965, 126.

DEHN, E. and O.-H. FREY. Die absolute Chronologie der Hallstatt- und Frühlatènezeit Mitteleuropas auf Grund des Südimports. *Atti VI Cong. Sci. Preist. e Protostoriche*, I, 1962, 197.

DRACK, W. Wagengräber und Wagenbestandteile aus Hallstattgrabhügeln der Schweiz. *Zeitschr. Schweiz. Arch. und Kunstgesch.*, 18, 1958, 1.

DRIEHAUS, J. Fürstengräber und Eisenerze zwischen Mittelrhein, Mosel und Saar. *Germania*, 43, 1965, 32.

DUMOULIN, A. Les fosses funéraires de Cucuron (Vaucluse). *Gallia*, XX, 1962, 323.

— Les puits et fosses de la colline Saint-Jacques à Cavaillon (Vaucluse). *Gallia*, 23, 1965, 1.

EUZENNAT, M. and F. SALVIAT. Marseille retrouve ses murs et son port grecs. *Archéologia*, 21, 1968, 5.

FABRE, G. *Les civilisations protohistoriques de l'Aquitaine*, 1952.

FAVRET, P.-M. Les nécropoles des Jogasses à Chouilly (Marne). *Préhistoire*, 5, 1936, 24.

FOURDRIGNIER, E. *Double sépulture gauloise de la Gorge-Meillet, territoire de Somme-Tourbe (Marne)*. 1898.

FREY, O.-H. Eine etruskische Bronzeschnabelkanne. *Ann. Lit. Univ. Besançon*, sec. ser. II, 1 (*Archéologie 2*), 1955.

— Die Zeitstellung des Fürstengrabes von Hatten im Elsass. *Germania*, 35, 1957, 229.

— Zu den 'rhodischen' Bronzekannen aus Hallstattgräbern. *Marburger Winkelmann-Programm*, 1963, 18.

— Der Ostalpenraum und die antike Welt in der Frühen Eisenzeit. *Germania*, 44, 1966, 46.

GALLET DE SANTERRE, H. Informations: circonscription de Languedoc-Roussillon. *Gallia*, XXIV, 1966, 449.

— Fouilles dans le quartier ouest d'Ensérune (insula no. X). *Rev. Arch. de Narbonnaise*, 1, 1968, 39.

GIOT, P. R., J. L'HELGOUACH and J. BRIARD. *Brittany*. London 1960.

GIRY, J. La nécropole préromaine de St-Julien (Cne de Pézenas, Hérault). *Rev. d'Ét. Ligures*, XXXI, 1965, 117.

GJØDESEN, M. Greek bronzes: a review article. *Amer. Jour. Arch.*, 67, 1963, 333.

GOBY, G. Histoire de l'origine de la découverte des cnémides grecques à Roquefort. *Rhodania*, 1929, 1352.

GOURY, G. L'enceinte et la nécropole d'Haulzy. *Étapes de l'Humanité*, I, fasc. II, 1911.

HENCKEN, H. O'N. *The Archaeology of Cornwall and Scilly*. London 1932.

HODSON, F. R. La Tène chronology: Continental and British. *Bull. Inst. Arch. University of London*, 4, 1964, 123.

— The La Tène cemetery at Münsingen Rain. *Acta Bernensia* V., 1968.

JACOBSTHAL, P. *Early Celtic Art*. Oxford 1944, repr. 1972.

JANNORAY, J. *Ensérune: Contribution à l'étude des civilisations préromaines de la Gaule méridionale*. Paris 1955.

JOFFROY, R. Le trésor de Vix. *Mon. Mém. Piot*, XLVIII, 1954, 1.

— Les sépultures à char du premier âge du fer en France, *Rev. Arch. Est.*, 7, 1957, 193.

— L'Oppidum de Vix et la civilisation hallstattienne finale dans l'est de la France. *Pub. Univ. Dijon*, XX, 1960.

JOFFROY, J. and D. BRETZ-MAHLER. Les tombes à char de La Tène dans l'Est de la France. *Gallia*, XVII, 1959, 5.

KIMMIG, W. Zur Urnenfelderkultur in Sudwesteuropa, *Festschrift für Peter Goessler*, 1954, 41.

LAGRAND, C. Massif de la Sainte-Baume. *Cah. Lig. Préhist. Arch.*, 8, 1959 (a), 219.

— Un habitat côtier de l'Age du Fer à l'Arquet, à la Couronne (B.-du-Rh.). *Gallia*, XVII, 1959 (b), 179.

— La céramique 'pseudo-Ionienne' dans la vallée du Rhône. *Cah. Rhod.*, 10, 1963, 37.

LARDERET, P. Les découvertes archéologiques de l'oppidum de La Roque. *Rev. d'Ét. Ligures*, 23, 1957, 69.

LEGLAY, M. Informations: Circonscription de Rhône-Alpes. *Gallia*, XXVI, 1968, 559.

LO PORTO, G. F. Una stazione dell'Età del Ferro nel Tortonese. *Rev. d'Ét. Ligures*, 20, 1954, 163.

LOUIS, M., O. and J. TAFFANEL. *Le premier âge du fer languedocien.* Institut International d'Études Ligures, Bordighera. I, *Les habitats*, 1955; II, *Les nécropoles à incinération*, 1958; III, *Les Tumulus: Conclusions*, 1960.

MILLOTTE, J.-P. Le Jura et les Plaines de Saône aux âges des métaux. *Ann. Lit. Univ. Besançon*, 59 (Arch., 16), 1963.

— Carte archéologique de la Lorraine. *Ann. Lit. Univ. Besançon*, 73 (Arch., 18), 1965.

MOREL, J.-P. Les Phocéens en occident: certitudes et hypothèses. *La Parola del Passato*, 21, 1966, 378.

PIROUTET, M. La Tène A ou La Tène Ia? *Cong. Préhist. France, 12 (1931)*, 1936, 832.

REIM, H. Zur Henkelplatte eines attischen Kolonettenkraters vom Uetliberg (Zürich). *Germania*, 46, 1968, 274.

ROBERT, A. Les Oppida du Gard. *Celticum*, XII, 1965, 207.

ROLLAND, M. H. (1951). Fouilles de Saint-Blaise (B.-du-Rh.). Suppléments à *Gallia* III, 1951.

— Fouilles de Saint-Blaise (1951-1956). Suppléments à *Gallia* VII, 1956.

— Saint-Blaise. *Gallia*, XXII, 1964, 569.

ROWLETT, R. M. The Iron Age north of the Alps. *Science*, 161, 1968, 123.

ROWLETT, R. M., E. S.-J. ROWLETT and M. BOUREUX. A rectangular Early La Tène Marnian house at Chassemy (Aisne). *World Archaeology*, I, 1969, 106.

SCHAAF, U. Versuch einer regionalen Gliederung frühlatènezeitlicher Fürstengräber. *Fundberichte aus Hessen*, Beiheft I (Dehn Festschrift), 1969, 187.

SCHAEFFER, F. A. Tertres funéraires préhistoriques dans la forêt de Haguenau: II, *Les tumulus de l'âge du Fer*, Haguenau, 1930.

SCHEERS, S. Le monnayage des Ambiani. *Rev. Belge Numis.*, 114, 1968, 45.

SCHIEK, S. Das Hallstattgrab von Vilsingen, *Festschrift für Peter Goessler*, 1954, 150.

SCHULE, W. Frühe Antennenwaffen in Südwesteuropa, *Germania*, 38, 1960 (a) 1.

— Probleme der Eisenzeit auf der Iberischen Halbinsel. *Jahrbuch RGZM*, 6, 1960 (b) 59.

— Vorformen von Fusszier und Armbrustkonstruktion der Hallstatt-D-Fibeln. *Madrider Mitteilungen*, 2, 1961, 55.

SCHWAPPACH, F. Stempelverzierte Keramik von Armorica. *Fundberichte aus Hessen*, Beiheft I (Dehn Festschrift), 1969, 213.

SCHWARZ, K. Zum Stand der Ausgrabungen in der spätkeltischen Viereckschanze von Holzhausen. *Jahresber der Bayerischen Bodendenkmalpflege*, 1962, 22.

SOUTOU, A. Contribution au classement chronologique des monnaies préromaines du Languedoc. *Ogam*, XVIII, 1966, 275.

SOUTOU, A. and J. ARNAL. Le dépôt de la Croix-de-Mus, et la datation du Launacien. *Bull. Mus. d'Anthrop. Préhist. de Monaco*, 10, 1963, 173.

SOUTOU, A. and J. VEZIAN. Mobilier d'une tombe à incinération de Mas-Saintes-Puelles (Aude). *Cah. Lig. Préhist. Arch.*, 13, 1964, 164.

STEAD, I. M. *The La Tène cultures of eastern Yorkshire.* York 1965.

TAFFANEL, O. Le 1er Age du Fer à Mailhac (Aude). *Cah. Lig. Préhist. Arch.*, 11, 1962, 159.

TAFFANEL, O. and J. TAFFANEL. Deux tombes de chefs à Mailhac (Aude). *Gallia*, XVIII, 1960, 1.

— Deux tombes de cavaliers du 1er âge du fer à Mailhac (Aude). *Gallia*, XX, 1962, 3.

VILASECA, S. La necropolis de Can Canyis, Banyeres, Taragona. *Trabajos* (Madrid), 1963, 8.

VILLARD, F. *La céramique grecque de Marseille.* Paris 1960.

WHEELER, R. E. M. and K. M. RICHARDSON. *Hill-Forts of Northern France.* Research Reports of the Society of Antiquaries, London, 1957, 49.

7
The Coming of Rome and the Establishment of Roman Gaul

References to classical authors are given in the text. Where quotations are used they have been taken from the Loeb translation.

The most important periodical today for the study of Roman Gaul is *Gallia, Fouilles et Monuments archéologiques en France métropolitaine*. Started in 1943, it has chronicled year by year the fieldwork and other research being conducted in its field. The older periodicals continue to make valuable contributions and two notable more recent ones dealing with Celtic matters, *Celticum* and *Ogam*, must also be mentioned.

Some of the standard works included are valuable for their full bibliographies as well as for their own texts.

AMY, R. *et al.*, L'Arc d'Orange. *Gallia*, supp. XV, 1962.

AUDIN, A. Fouilles en avant du Théâtre de Lyon. *Gallia*, XXV, 1967, 11-48.

AUDIN, A. and P. QUONIAM. Victoires, et colonnes de l'autel fédéral des Trois Gaules. *Gallia*, XX, 1962, 103-16.

BENEDICT, C.-H. Romans in Southern Gaul. *Amer. J. Phil.*, LXIII, 1942, 38-50.

BENOÎT F. *L'art primitif méditerranéen de la Vallée du Rhône.* Paris 1956.

— Résultats historiques des fouilles d'Entremont (1946-67). *Gallia*, XXVI, 1968, 1-31.

— *Art et Dieux de la Gaule.* Paris 1969.

BOHN, O. *Belgische Gefässe in Vertillum (Vertault, Côte-d'Or).* 1922, 123-5.

BRADFORD, J. S. P. *Ancient Landscapes*, Oxford.

CABOTSE, J. and R. PERICHON. Céramiques gauloises et gallo-romaines de Roanne. *Gallia*, XXIV, 1966, 29-75. Also *Cambridge Anc. Hist.*, vol. IX, 1932, ch. iii and ix, 1957.

COLBERT DE BEAULIEU, J.-B. Le Trésor de Guingamp. *Revue Belge de Numismatique*, CII, 1956, 81-141.

— Les Monnaies gauloises au nom des chefs mentionnés dans les Commentaires de César. *Coll. Latomus*, LVIII, 1, 1962, 419-46.

— Epilogue numismatique d'Alésia. *Mélanges Piganiol*, I, 1966, 321-42.

COTTON, M. Murus Gallicus. *In* Wheeler and Richardson, 1957.

DAVIES, O. *Roman mines in Europe.* Oxford, 1935.

DAYET, M. Qui était Togirix? *Rev. arch. de l'Est*, XIII, 1962, 82-98.

DÉCHELETTE, J. *Les Vases céramiques ornés de la Gaule romaine.* Paris 1904.

— *Manuel d'Archéologie, II, Archéologie celtique ou protohistorique*. Pt III, 2nd edn, 1927.

DEHN, W. Einige Bemerkungen zum *Murus Gallicus. Germania*, 38, 1960, 43-55.

DEYTS, S. Différents 'Styles' de sculptures en bois de la Seine. *Rev. arch. de l'Est*, XVII, 1966, 198-211.

DUVAL, P.-M. A propos du milliaire de Cneus Domitius Ahénobarbus trouvé dans l'Aude en 1949. *Gallia*, VII, 1949, 207-31.

FORMIGÉ, J. *Le Trophée des Alpes (La Turbie). Gallia*, suppl. II, 1949.

FORSYTH, W. H. Provincial Roman enamels recently acquired by the Metropolitan Museum of Art. *Art Bulletin*, XXXII, 1950, 296-307.

FOUET, G. Puits funéraires d'Aquitaine. *Gallia*, XVI, 1958, 115-96.

— *La villa gallo-romaine de Montmaurin (Hte-Garonne), Gallia*, suppl. XX, 1969.

GRAFF, Y. *Oppida* et *Castella* au pays des Belges. *Celticum*, VI, 1963, 113-70.

GRENIER, A. *Manuel d'Archéologie galloromaine*. 4 vols, Paris, 1931-60.

— *Les Gaulois*. Paris 1945.

HARMAND, J. Une question césarienne non résolue: la campagne de 51 contre les Bellovaques et sa localisation. *Bull. soc. nat. ant. Franç.*, 1959, 263-81.

— *Une campagne césarienne: Alésia*. Paris 1967.

HATT, J.-J. Découverte d'un village gaulois de La Tène III à Aulnat-Sud. *Bull. histor. et scientif. de l'Auvergne*, LXII, 1942, 36-48.

— Les fouilles de Gergovie, *Gallia*, II, 1943, 97-124.

— Essai d'une comparaison entre la céramique celtique d'Aulnat-Sud et la céramique gallo-romaine précoce de Gergovie. *Bull. hist. et scientif. de l'Auvergne*, LXIV, 1945, 36-48.

— Aperçus sur l'évolution de la céramique commune gallo-romaine, principalement dans le nord-est de la Gaule. *Rev. étud. anc.*, LI, 1949, 100-28.

HAWKES, C. F. C. and M. R. HULL. *Camulodunum*. Research Reports of the Society of Antiquaries, LXIV, London, 1947.

HENRY, F. Emailleurs d'Occident. *Préhistoire*, II, 1933, 65-143.

HUBERT, H. *Les Celtes, II: depuis l'Epoque de La Tène et la civilisation celtique*. Paris 1932.

JACOBSTHAL, P. *Early Celtic Art*. Oxford 1944, repr. 1972.

JANNORAY, J. *Ensérune: Contribution à l'étude des civilisations préromaines de la Gaule méridionale*. Paris 1955.

JOFFROY, R. Le torque de Mailly-le-Camp (Aube). *Monuments Piot*, LVI, 1969, 45-59.

JULLIAN, C. *Histoire de la Gaule*. 8 vols.: I (5th ed.), 1924; II (4th ed.), 1921; III (3rd ed.), 1920; Paris.

LABROUSSE, M. Les fouilles de Gergovie, 1943 et 1946. *Gallia*, VI, 1948, 31-95.

— Les fouilles de Gergovie, 1947 et 1949, *Gallia*, VIII, 1950, 14-53.

LE GALL, J. Récentes fouilles d'Alésia. *Bull. soc. nat. ant. franç.*, 1959, 257-61.

— Nouveaux aperçus sur les fouilles d'Alésia. *Comptes rendus l'Acad. Inscr.*, 1961, 73-9.

— Que pouvons-nous savoir actuellement des défenses gauloises d'Alésia? *Celticum*, VI, 1963, 181-92.

— Nouvelles découvertes à Alésia. *Comptes rendus l'Acad. Inscr.*, 1963, 294-300.

LEGLAY, M. Report of Circonscription de Rhône-Alpes. *Gallia*, XXVI, 1968, 589-72.

MAIER, F. Vindonissa-Roanne Grupper bemalter frühkaiserztl. Keramik. *Ann. Schweiz Altertumskunde*, XXXIII, 1931, 47.

— Die bemalte Spätlatène-Keramik von Manching. *Die Ausgrabungen in Manching*, ed. W. Kramer, vol. 3, *Röm. Germ. Kom.*, 1970.

MARTIN, R. Sculptures en bois découvertes aux sources de la Seine. *Rev. arch. l'Est*, XIV, 1963, 7-35.

— Wooden figures from the source of the Seine. *Antiquity*, 1965, 247-52, pls. xlv-li.

MATHERAT, G. Les 'Ponts-de-Fascines' de Jules César, à Breuil-le-Sec (Oise). *Rev. arch.* 6th ser., VII, 1936, 53-94.

— La technique des retranchements de César, d'après l'enseignement des fouilles de Nointel. *Gallia*, I, 1943, 81-127.

MATHONNIÈRE-PLICQUE, A. and A. GRENIER. Nouvelles fouilles à Lezoux (Puy-de-Dôme). *Gallia*, XIX, 1961, 55-69.

MEGAW, J. V. S. Les fragments de feuille de bronze décorés de Levroux (Indre), *Gallia*, XXVI, 1968, 33-41.

— *Art of the European Iron Age*. Bath 1970.

MESPLÉ, P. L'Atelier de potier gallo-romain de Galane à Lombez (Gers). *Gallia*, XV, 1951, 41-62.

MONTAUZAN, C. GERMAIN DE. *Les Aqueducs de Lyon*. Paris 1909.

MÜLLER-BECK, H. Die Besiedlung der Engelhalbinsel in Bern auf Grund der Kenntnissstandes vom Februar des Jahres 1962. *Berichte der Röm. Germ. Kom.*, XLIII-XLIV, 1962-3.

NAPOLEON III. *Histoire de Jules César*. 2 vols. and *Atlas*. Paris 1865.

NOCHÉ, A. and G. DUFOUR. Fossés romains d'Alésia et fossés récemment découverts sur les Châtelets près de Breteuil-sur-Noye (Oise). *Celticum*, VI, 1963, 201-14.

NYLEN, E. The remarkable bucket from Marlborough. *Acta Archaeologica*, XXIX, 1958, 1-20.

PICARD, G. C. *Les Trophées romains*. Paris 1957.

PIGANIOL, A. *Les Documents cadastraux de la colonie romaine d'Orange. Gallia*, suppl. XVI, 1962.

PIGGOTT, S. *The Druids*. London 1968.

— *Early Celtic Art*. Edinburgh 1970.

POWELL, T. G. E. *The Celts*. London 1958.

RAMBAUD, M. L'Art de la déformation historique dans les Commentaires de César. *Ann. Univ. de Lyon*, fasc. 23, 1953.

ROLLAND, H. *Fouilles de Glanum. Gallia*, suppl. I, 1946. *Fouilles de Glanum, 1947-56. Gallia*, suppl. XI, 1958.

SCHWARZ, K. Spätlatènezeitliche Viereckschanzen - keltische Kultplätze. *Neue Ausgrabungen in Deutschland*, *Röm. Germ. Kom.*, XII, 1958, 203-14.

STÄHELIN, F. *Die Schweiz in römischer Zeit*. 3rd edn, Basle 1948.

TAFFANEL, O. and J. Les Epées à sphères du Cayla à Mailhac (Aude). *Gallia*, XXV, 1967, 1-10.

VATIN, C. Circonscription d'Auvergne et Limousin. *Gallia*, XXV, 1967, 320 ff.

VERTET, H. Céramique de Saint-Rémy-en-Rollat (Allier). *Gallia*, XIX, 1961, 218-26.

— Vases caliciformes gallo-romains de Roanne et la chronologie des fabriques de terre sigillée de Lezoux au début du premier siècle. *Gallia*, XX, 1962, 351-80.

— Vases sigillés moulés de Lezoux au début du premier siècle. *Actes 88e Congrès des sociétés savantes, Clermont-Ferrand 1963*, 1965, 105-19.

— Céramique sigillée Tibérienne à Lezoux. *Rev. Arch.*, 1967, 255-86.

WARD-PERKINS, J. B. The pottery of Gergovia in relation to that of other sites in Central and South-Western France. *Archaeological Journ.*, XCVII, 1941, 37-87.

WHEELER, R. E. M. and K. RICHARDSON. *Hill-Forts of Northern France*. Research Reports of the Society of Antiquaries, XIX, London 1957.

WUILLEUMIER, P. Le Gobelet en argent de Lyon. *Rev. arch.*, 6th ser., VIII, 1936, 46-53.

— *Fouilles de Fourvière à Lyon. Gallia*, suppl. IV, 1951.

Sources of illustrations

Arabic numerals refer to half-tone illustrations and roman numerals to colour illustrations.
The maps and hand-lettered charts in this book were drawn by H. A. Shelley.

Chapter 2

I   The 'Venus' with horn, Laussel. Musée d'Aquitaine, collection Lalaune. Photo A. Roussot

II Grotte de Cougnac, Lot. Ibex painted in ochre. Photo J. Vertut

1   Laussel: detail of the 'Venus' with horn. Musée d'Aquitaine, collection Lalaune. Photo A. Roussot

2   Les Combarelles: reindeer engraved on the cave wall. Photo A. Roussot

3   *Equus caballus gallicus* (after Prat 1968). Magdalenian horse in black, Le Portel, Ariège. After Breuil and Jeannel 1955

4   *Saïga tatarica*: 1, present-day; 2, Magdalenian engraving at Gourdan, Hautes-Pyrénées. After Piette 1900

5   La Marche: human figure engraved on a rock. Musée des Antiquités Nationales, Saint-Germain-en-Laye. Photo A. Roussot

6   Heads of horses, with offset outline; Magdalenian, Isturitz, Basses-Pyrénées. After Nougier 1966

7   Wounded bison, painted in black. The two arrows at the side are red. Niaux cave, Ariège. After Breuil 1950

8   La Mouthe: sandstone lamp with engraved ornament on the back. Musée des Antiquités Nationales, Saint-Germain-en-Laye. Photo A. Roussot

9   Abri du Poisson: fish carved on the roof of the shelter. Photo A. Roussot

10 Raymonden, Chancelade: engraved bone. Musée du Périgord. Photo A. Roussot

11 Richard (alias Grotte des Eyzies): rib decorated with engravings of ibex, with detail. Collection Watelin. Photo A. Roussot

12 Mammoths and 'roof-shaped' signs (traps?) engraved in the Bernifal cave, Dordogne. After Breuil 1952

13 Rouffignac: paintings of mammoths, from the frieze of eleven. By permission of Mme Plassard. Photo A. Roussot

14 Rouffignac: central rhinoceros from the frieze of three. By permission of Mme Plassard. Photo A. Roussot

Chapter 3

15 Grand Abri de Châteauneuf. General view before excavation. Photo M. Escalon de Fonton

16 Grand Abri de Châteauneuf. View during excavation. Photo M. Escalon de Fonton

17 Grand Abri de Châteauneuf. Castelnovian bone industry and perforated shells. Photo M. Escalon de Fonton

18 La Baume de Valorgues: section. The Romanellian levels run from layers 8-25. The rock resting on layer 7 broke off during Dryas III. After M. Escalon de Fonton

19 La Baume de Valorgues: Middle Romanellian flint industry at the beginning of the Allerød interstadial (examples from layers 25-19). After M. Escalon de Fonton

20 La Baume de Valorgues: Flint tools and bone point (examples from layers 9-8). After M. Escalon de Fonton

21 La Baume de Montclus, General view taken from the west. Photo M. Escalon de Fonton

22 La Baume de Montclus. Mesolithic skeleton from layer 5: Epi-Castelnovian proto-Neolithic. Photo M. Escalon de Fonton

23 La Baume de Montclus. Partial view of the site. Photo M. Escalon de Fonton

24 La Baume de Montclus. Final Cardial Neolithic pottery (layer 4). After M. Escalon de Fonton

25 La Baume de Montclus. Epi-Cardial pottery (layer 3). After M. Escalon de Fonton

26 La Baume de Montclus. Epi-Cardial pottery (layer 2B). After M. Escalon de Fonton

Chapter 4

III Ménec alignments. Photo Jos Le Doaré

IV Mané-Kerioned passage graves. Photo Jos Le Doaré

28 Middle Neolithic of the Paris basin, Cerny culture: decorated sherds from Les Roches layer E. Photo Musée des Antiquités Nationales, Saint-Germain-en-Laye

29 Tombs of the Atlantic Middle Neolithic: passage grave in the La Hogue tumulus. Photo G. Bailloud

27 The giant tumulus of Saint-Michel. Photo Z. Le Rouzic

30 Megalithic art in the Atlantic Middle Neolithic: Tossen-Keler tumulus. Photo Laboratoire d'Anthropologie préhistorique de Rennes

31 Megalithic art: Gavrinis passage grave. Photo Musée des Antiquités Nationales

32 Middle Neolithic of west-central France, Peu-Richard culture: decorated sherd from Chaillot de La Gard. Photo Morel, Burnez and Coffyn

33 Head of a statuette in baked clay from Roanne. Photo Morel, Burnez and Coffyn

34 Neolithic dwellings: Middle Neolithic house (Cerny culture) at Les Gours-aux-Lions. Photo G. Bailloud

35 Stumps of houses from the Neolithic at Chalain. Photo G. Bailloud

36 Late Neolithic of the Paris basin, Seine-Oise-Marne culture: gallery grave of Blanc-Val. Photo E. Basse de Ménorval

37 Sculptured slab from the vestibule of the Dampmesnil gallery grave. Photo G. Bailloud

38 Statue-menhir at Puech-Réal. Photo Musée des Antiquités Nationales, Saint-Germain-en-Laye

39 Village of Conquette. Photo Cours

40 Chalcolithic of Languedoc, Fontbouïsse culture: fortified enclosure at Lébous. Photo de Gramont

Chapter 5

V   Kernonen barrow, Plouvorn. Wooden coffin with bronze dagger and flint arrowheads. Photo J. Briard

VI Kernonen barrow, Plouvorn. Bronze dagger decorated with minute gold nails. Photo J. Briard

41 Plouhinec tumulus, Finistère. Photo J. Briard

42 Vault of the Plouhinec grave, Finistère. Photo J. Briard

43 Hoard from Lessart, La Vicomté-sur-Rance. Photo Pitt Rivers Museum, Oxford

44 Bar-ingots from Les Fonts-Gaidons, Bourges. Photo Musée de Bourges

45 Morges type axe, Saône-et-Loire. Photo Musée de Bourges

46 1-2, Eguisheim, torc, dagger and roll-headed pin; 3, Serrigny, Côte-d'Or, gold pin; 4, Cessieu, Isère, Morges type axe; 5-6, Donauberg, pin, torc, bracelet and dagger. (1-2, after Zumstein; 3, after Déchelette; 4, after Bocquet; 5-6, after Schaeffer)

47 Excised pottery, Videlles 12. Photo G. Bailloud

48 Pottery with cordons and finger impressions, La Rousselerie, Loire-Atlantique. Photo P. R. Giot

49 Vase with imitation basketry decoration, Lesneven. Photo Laboratoire d'Anthropologie préhistorique de Rennes

50 Gold torc of Yeovil type, Cesson, Ille-et-Vilaine. Photo Laboratoire d'Anthropologie préhistorique de Rennes

51 Polypod vase, Lombives. Photo Sallis

52 Handled jug, Milhes, Clermont-sur-Lanquet. Photo J. Guilaine

53 Jar, Milhes, Clermont-sur Lanquet. Photo J. Guilaine

54 Statue-menhir, Filitosa V, Corsica. Photo R. Grosjean

55 Vase from the Chissay urnfield, Loir-et-Cher. Photo Cordier

56 Knives from Mehun and Vasselay. Musée de Bourges

57 Antennae sword, Lyons. Musée de Rennes

58 Pendants, La Prairie de Mauves, Nantes, Loire-Atlantique. Photo J. Briard

59 Swords from Bellevue, Loire-Atlantique. Photo Laboratoire d'Anthropologie préhistorique de Rennes

60 Armorican socketed axe, Le Trehou, Finistère. Photo J. Briard

61 1, Briod, Jura, sickle; 2-5, Le Bourget, pins; 6-11, Prairie de Mauves, Nantes, winged axe, carp's tongue sword, razor, scraper, bugle-shaped object. Launacian; 12, Mas-Granier, Tarn-et-Garonne, scraper; 13-15, La Croix de Mus, Hérault, conical butt, socketed axe, bracelet. 1-5, Musée de Rennes; 6-11, Musée de Nantes; 12-15, after Soutou and Arnal

Chapter 6

VII Basse-Yutz, Lorraine: Early La Tène wine flagon. Bronze with coral and enamel inlay. Photo British Museum, London

62 Roquefort. Bronze greaves, perhaps from a cremation burial. Musée Fragonard, Grasse

63 Three-hooked belt buckle in bronze of Mailhac III type. Musée Fragonard, Grasse

64 The Vix burial: imported gold collar. Musée de Châtillon-sur-Seine

65 The Vix burial: imported wine flagon of 'beaked' type. Probably made in Etruria in the second half of the sixth century BC. Musée de Châtillon-sur-Seine

66 Wine flagon of so-called 'Rhodian' type, probably made in Etruria c. 600 BC. From a cremation burial beneath a tumulus at Pertuis. Musée Borely, Marseilles

67 The Vix burial: imported bronze krater of Greek workmanship. Musée de Châtillon-sur-Seine

68 The Vix burial: imported Attic cup decorated in the Black Figure style, c. 525 BC. Musée de Châtillon-sur-Seine

69 Somme-Bionne, Marne: imported Attic cup from a chariot burial; decorated in the Red Figure style,

c. 415 BC. British Museum, London
70 La Gorge-Meillet, Marne: plan and section of the chariot burial as published by E. Fourdrignier in 1878. Musée des Antiquités Nationales, Saint-Germain-en-Laye
71 La Tène brooches (fibulae) from the Marne. Phases Ia, Ib, Ic, IIa, IIb, III British Museum, London
72 Developed La Tène art: motif on a cast bronze torc from the Aube. Fourth or third century BC. British Museum, London
73 Ensérune, Hérault. View of the *oppidum* from the southeast. Photo R. Hodson
74 Marnian pottery: dish (left) from Bergères-les-Vertus. Vase (right) from Marson. British Museum, London
75 Marnian pottery: pedestal urn (left) from Prosne. Vase (right) from Bergères-les-Vertus. British Museum, London
76 'Combed urn' from Les Pennes, Marseilles. Musée Borély, Marseilles
77 Roquepertuse, Bouches-du-Rhône: portico of a sanctuary with 'têtes coupées' pillars and sculpture. Musée Borély, Marseilles
78 Grézan, Nîmes. Torso in stone of a warrior. Perhaps fourth century BC. Musée Archéologique, Nîmes

79 Roquepertuse: double head in stone. Musée Borély, Marseilles
80 Entremont, Aix-en-Provence: hand with '*tête coupée*'. Photo F. Benoît
81 Celtic coins. Four gold coins from Gaul imitating staters of Philip II of Macedonia. British Museum, London

Chapter 7
The author wishes to thank Mr D. F. Allen for his kind help and advice in selecting the coins for illustration.

VIII Portrait of Vercingetorix, from the obverse of a gold stater. Cabinet des Médailles, Bibliothèque Nationale Paris
82 Coin of the Aulerci Cenomani. British Museum, London. cf. Muret 6493
83 Coin of the Remi. British Museum, London. cf. Muret 8040
84 Coin of the Lexovii or Baiocasses. Cabinet des Médailles, Bibliothèque Nationale, Paris. Muret 6927
85 'Indecom' coin. British Museum, London. cf. Muret 6342
86 Coin reverse of man carrying a torc. British Museum, London
87 Coin of the Aedui. British Museum, London. cf. Muret 4972
88 Coin with Vercingetorix wearing a

helmet. Cabinet des Médailles, Bibliothèque Nationale, Paris. Muret 3775
89 Coin of Vercingetorix. Cabinet des Médailles, Bibliothèque Nationale, Paris. Muret 3774
90 Coin of the Arverni. Hunterian Coin Cabinet, University of Glasgow, cf. Muret 3885
91 Coin of the Arverni. British Museum, London. cf. Muret 3900
92 'Duratos Iulios' coin. British Museum, London. cf. Muret 4478
93 Coin of Togirix. British Museum, London
94 Coin of the Segusiavi. National Museum, Copenhagen. cf. Muret 4622
95 Coin of Narbo. Fitzwilliam Museum, Cambridge. Sydenham (1952) No. 521
96 Coin of the Remi, Hirtius as Governor. The Hague Coin Cabinet. cf Muret 8086
97 Reverse of coin of Lugdunum. Fitzwilliam Museum, Cambridge. Mattingley and Sydenham (1923) Pl. IV; Muret 4744
98 Coin of Nemausus. Fitzwilliam Museum, Cambridge. cf. Mattingley and Sydenham (1923) p. 44; Muret 2806
99 *Murus gallicus*, Vertault. Photo courtesy of Musée des Antiquités Nationales, Saint-Germain-en-Laye

100 Milestone of Domitius Ahenobarbus. Narbonne Museum. Photo Sallis
101 Torc from Mailly-le-Camp, Aube. Musée des Antiquités Nationales, Saint-Germain-en-Laye. Photo Lauros-Giraudon
102 Statue of a Gaul from Vachères. Musée Calvet, Avignon
103 Wooden pilgrim statuette from Chamalières. Musée de Clermont-Ferrand
104 Wooden figure showing internal organs from Chamalières. Musée de Clermont-Ferrand
105 Wooden figure showing internal organs from Saint-Germain-Source-Seine. Musée Gallo-Romain Dijon. Photo Rémy
106 Wooden female figure from Saint-Germain-Source-Seine. Musée Gallo-Romain, Dijon. Photo Rémy
107 Wooden ex-votos as found around the spring at Chamalières. Photo Musée de Clermont-Ferrand
108 Stone monster statue from Noves. Musée Calvet, Avignon
109 Sculpture of the head of Cernunnos. Musée des Antiquités Nationales, Saint-Germain-en-Laye
110 Sculpture of two severed heads. Musée Calvet, Avignon. Photo CNRS

Index

Page numbers given in *italic* refer to in-text illustrations. Monochrome plates are referred to in **bold** and colour plates in Roman numerals.

Abbeville, 18, 147; Abbevillian, 15, 18
Achenheim, 152
Acheulean, 15, 16, 20, 28, 31
Aco ware, 208
Adaouste, *52*, *53*
Aduatuca Tungrorum (Tongres), 203
Aduatuci, 194, 203
aedificia, 201, 204-5
Aedui, 193, 197, 204, 208, **87**
Agde, *157*, 158
Agedincum (Sens), 203
agriculture, Bronze Age, 145, 154; Early Neolithic, 102, 104-5; Late Neolithic, 124, 126; Middle Neolithic, 111, 123-4; Roman Gaul, 209; La Tène, 192
Agrippa, 200, 201, 203, 204, **98**
Ahenobarbus, Cnaeus Domitius, 193, 194, **100**
Aisne, 106, 107
Aldène, *53*
Alesia, 195, 197-8, 201, 206
Algeria, 17, 19
Allauch, 136
Allerød interstadial, 43, 62ff, 94-5, 100
Allier valley, 52, 208
Allobroges, 193, 194, 196, 200, 201, 209
Alps, 102, 111, 128
Alsace, 106, 107, 109, 131, 134, 150ff, 182, 186
amber, 136, 145, 146, 182, 183
Ambiani, 196
Ambiorix, 195, 197, 204
Amboise, 121, 124
Ambrona, 18, 20
Ambrones, 194
Ampurias, 159, 188, 189
Angevin dolmens, 125
Angle-sur-l'Anglin, *53*, *57*
Angles, *48*, *50*
animal paintings and engravings, 47, 48, *50*, 51, 54
animals, Allerød interstadial, 94-5; Atlantic, 97; Boreal, 97; Bronze Age, 145, 147, 154; domestication, 72, 102, 103, 108; Early Neolithic, 104; Epipalaeolithic, 66-7; Late Neolithic, 126; Mesolithic, 68; Middle Neolithic, 110, 111; Pre-Boreal, 96; Roman Gaul, 209; Romanellian, 62; Upper Palaeolithic, 43, 53-4; *see also* fishing, hunting
Antibes, *157*, 159, 201
Antipolis, 159
Appian, 193
Aquae Helveticae (Baden), 205

Aquae Sextiae, 190, 193
Aquitaine, *82*, 86, 89, 191, 219
Aquitania, 199-200
Arausio (Orange), 194, 200, 201
Arcachon, 154
Arcy-sur-Cure, *32*, 43, 45, *53*
Ardèche, 45, 52, 127, *130*, 153
Arelate (Arles), 200, 201, 206
Argentorate (Strasbourg), 200, 203
Argonne, 155, 183, 209
Ariège, 133, 154, **7**
Ariovistus, 195, 196
Arisian, 81
Arles, 127, 201, 206
Arlon, 209
Armeau, *105*
Armorican Tumulus culture, 109, 110, 124, 125-6, 132, 136, 145, 147, 187
Arlay, *52*
armour, 153, 160, 166
arrowheads, Bronze Age, 132, 136, 145; Early Neolithic, 90, 104, 105, 108; Late Neolithic, 124, 125, 128, 130; Mesolithic, 67, 88; Middle Neolithic, 109, 110, 111, *112*; Upper Palaeolithic, 55
Arruda, 89
art, Cardial Neolithic, 90; Celtic, 192, 205ff; Epipalaeolithic, 64, 66, 67; Mesolithic, 71-2; Middle Neolithic, 122; La Tène, 183-4, 185; Upper Palaeolithic, 30, 31, 47, 53, 56, 57, 59; *see also* engraving, sculpture
Artenac, 127, 132-4
Arudian, 81
Arverni, 193, 194, 195, 197, **88-91**
Asedullus, 199
Asturias, 49, 52
Atelier Commont, 19-21
Atestine culture, 186
Atlantic Bronze Age, 153-4
Atlantic Middle Neolithic, 121-4
Atlantic Neolithic, 108-9
Atrebates, 196
Attic ware, 158, 160, *177*, *184*, 188; Black Figure pottery, 158, 160, *177*, 178-9, 180, 182, 188, **68**; Red Figure pottery, 158, 185, 188, 189, **69**
Aube, 109-10
Aube-Seine-Yonne group, 149
Aucissa, 206
Aude, 127, 130, 154
Aude-Rossillon, 127
Audincourt, 150, *151*
Augusta Suessionum, 202
Augusta Treverorum, 200
Augustan Provinces, 199-205
Augustodunum (Autun), 201, 203, 210
Augustodurum Baiocassium (Bayeux), 203
Augustonemetum (Clermont-Ferrand), 202
Augustus, 199ff, 219, **98**

Augy-Sainte-Pallaye, 109-10
Aulerci, **82**
Aulnat, 202, 207
Aulnay-aux-Planches, 152, 154, 182
Aulnay-la-Rivière, 152
Aurensan, *52*
Aurignac, *52*
Aurignacian, 30ff, 43, 44, 45ff, 54, 59
Avaricum (Bourges), 197, 203
Aven de Gage, 136
Aveyron, 127, 128, 153
awls, Bronze Age, 135, 136; Early Neolithic, 105; Epipalaeolithic, 64; Late Neolithic, 126, 128; Mesolithic, 71; Middle Neolithic, 111, *112*, 124; Upper Palaeolithic, 46
axes, Bronze Age, 134, 135, 136, 146, 147, 149, 153, 154; *see also* hand-axes
Azay-le-Rideau, 134, 154
Azilian, 31, 32, 53, 59, 64, 65-7, 100
Azilian points, *51*, 62, 63, 66, 82
Azilio-Sauveterrian lithic industry, 82ff

Baeterrae (Béziers), 188, 200
Badegoule, *32*, *52*; Badegoulian, 51
Baden, 109, 152, 205
Bagacum (Bavai), 203, 209
Baiocasses, **84**
Balme, 64
Banassac, 208
Bandkeramik (Linear) culture, 104-8, 109, 110; *see also* Linear pottery
Baou, Grotte du, 135
Baou-Roux, *157*
Barbirey-sur-Ouche, *107*
Barbuise-Courtavant, 149
Barcelonnette, 191
Barésia, 155
Barnenez, 108, *109*, 122
Basle, fort, 209
Basse-Yutz, *157*, VII
bâton de commandement, 54
La Baume de Montclus, 72, 81, **21-6**
La Baume de Valorgues, 62, 63, **18-20**
La Baume-Latrone, *53*
Baume-Longue, Abri de la, 68, *69*
Bavaria, 134, 150, 155
Bayol, *53*
Beachy Head, 154
'beaked' handles, 132-3, 148
Beaker culture, 109, 126-7, 128, 129-32, 136, 146, 148
Beauregard, *32*, 52, 133
Bédeilhac, *52*, *53*
Bègues, 134
Belcayre, 47
Belfort Gap, 106, 107
Belgae, 196, 197, 208-9
Belgica, 199-200, 206

Bellevue, **59**
Bellovaci, 198, 199
Bennwihr, 150
Berchon, 147
Bergerac, 126
La Bergère, 134
Bergères-les-Vertus, **74, 75**
Berneuil, *123*
Bernifal, 55, **12**
Berry, 52
Berry-au-Bac, 196
Bibracte, 201-2
Bignan, 147
Biharian, fauna, 18
Bischheim group, 109, 110
Bituitus, 193
Bituriges, 203, 206
Bize, *66*
bladelets, Epipalaeolithic, 62, 63, 66; Mesolithic, 67, 81; Middle Neolithic, 111; Upper Palaeolithic, 47, 48, 50, 51
Blanc-Val, Presles, **36**
Blanchard, Abri, *50*
Bobache, *52*, 64
Bois-du-Roc en Vilhonneur, 152
Les Bolards, 204
Bølling, 43
Bonhomme, hoard, 134
Bonna, 200, 203
Bonne-Nouvelle, *123*
Le Bono, *122*
Boquidet, 154
Bordes, F., 12, 15, 16, 19, 22, 23-8, 45
Boreal, 100
borers, 31, 45, 50, 51, 53, 54
Bouches-du-Rhône, *67*, *68*, 127
Bœufs, Abri des, Ventabren, *68*
Bougon or Luxé style of decoration, 121
Bounias, *128*
Le Bourget, 152, 154, **61**
Les Bourroches, Dijon, 135
bows, 55
Boyne Hill, 19
brain size, 29
Brassempouy, *32*, *48*
Brennilis, *122*
Breteuil-sur-Noye, 197
Breuil, Henri, 12, 13, 14-15, 16, 18, 22, 44, 45, 51, 59
Briatexte, Vielmur, 154
Briod, **61**
Brittany, Armorican Tumulus culture, 132, 136; Artenac culture, 133; change from bronze to iron, 154; Chassean, 111; exploitation of lead, 154; Médoc group, 147; Seine-Oise-Marne culture and, 125; Tardenoisian, 89, 97, 99; tombs, 108, 109, 122, 136; Urnfield culture, 150, 153
Bucey-les-Gy, 155
Buckland, Dean, 12
Bulliot, 201
Burgundy, Bischheim, 110; Chassean, 111, 112; Hallstattian, 180,

181, 182; Magdalenian, 52; Rössen, 107, 110; La Tène, 184; Urnfield, 152; Wauwil, 109

burials, multiple, 47, 124, 125; *see also* cremations, graves, tombs

burins, Early Neolithic, 105; Epi-palaeolithic, 62-3, 64; Meso-lithic, 67ff, 81ff; Upper Palaeo-lithic, 30-1, 45, 47ff

Bush Barrow, Normanton, 145

La Butte, 182

Cabillonum (Châlon-sur-Saône), 204

Caesar, 188, 192, 195-8, 199, 200, 203, 204, 206

Caesarodunum Turonum (Tours), 203

Caesaromagus Bellovacorum (Beauvais), 203

Calvados, 108

Cambous, 127

Camp d'Artus, Huelgoät, 196, 203

Camp de Chassey, *111*, 135

Camp de Château, *157*

Camp de Fort-Harrouard, Sorel-Moussel, 133

Camp des Matignons, *123*

Campanian ware, 208

Campignian, industry, 110, 121, 126

Camulodunum, 209

Les Canals, 154

Cannes, **63**

Canteperdrix, 127, *128*

Cap-Blanc, *50*

Capeau, Abri, 62-3

Capitaine shelter, *130*

Capucin, *128*

Carcassonne, 148, 154

Cardial culture, 109, 111, 112; Cardial pottery, 61, 71, 90-4, 103, 104, 106, 107, 108

Carn pottery, 108

Carnac, **27**, 121, 122, *123*, *130*, III

Carnoet, 145

Carnutes, 197

La Carrière, 86, 136

Carthage, 157, 204

Casablanca, 21

Les Cascades, 127

Castelnovian, 72, 81, 83, 90, 97, 104

Castelnovian Tardenoisian, 67-81

Castillo, 28

Catalonia, 49, 52, 154, 178, 191

Catumandus, 158

Causses, 111, 124, 127, 178

Cavaillon, *157*, 189, 190

cave dwellings, *see* habitation

Caversham Channel, 18

Cayla de Mailhac, 154, *157*, 158, 159-60, 177, 181, 183, 188, 194

Cayla de Frouzet, *157*

Cazevielle, *155*, 156, *157*, 178

Cellier, 47

Celts, 132, 145, 158; and Roman occupation, 192ff; *see also* La Tène

Cerny, 110, 121, 124, **28, 34**

Cessero (St Thibéry), 200

Cessieu, 146, **46**

Cesson, 148, **50**

Cévennes, 126

Chabot, *53*

Chadourne, 28

Le Chaffaud, *52*

Chaillot de La Jard, **32**

La Chaire à Calvin, *50*

Chalain, 125, **35**; Lac de, 135

Chalcolithic, 126-30

Challans, 154

Chamalières, 206, **103, 104, 107**

Chamant, *125*

Chambertrand, 152

Chambon, 110

Chambre des Fées, Coincy, 97

Champagne, 125, 151, 152, 182, 184-7

Champlan cist, 135

Champlay, 149

Champs, 149

Champs d'Urnes, 161

Chancelade, *32*, *52*, 59, **10**; Chancelade man, *30*, 53

Charente, 38, 45, 52, 54, 97, 109, 111, 122, 123, 124, 126, 132, 153

Charente-Maritime, 122, 132

chariot burials, 184, 185, 187; *see also* wagon burials

Charmoy, *105*, 106

Chassean culture, 109, 110, 111-21, 128

Chassemy, *157*, 185

Chassey ware, 91, *123*, 129

Château-sur-Salins, 179, 180-1, 184

Châteaumeillant, 202

Châteauneuf-de-Grasse, 153

Châteauneuf-les-Martigues, 68, *70*, *71*, *72*, 90-4, 97, 102, 103, **15, 16, 17**

Châteauroux, 205

Le Châtellier, Le Petit Celland, 196, 203

Châtelperron, *32*; Châtelperron points, 45, 49, 54

Châtillon, 209

Chats, Grotte des, St-Martin, 153

Chauzon, 127

Chellean, *see* Abbevillian

Chenon, 132, 147

Chéry, 150

Le Cheval, *52*

Chiragan 205

Chissay, 152, **54**

Chrestus, 208

Christy, *32*

Cicero, 194

Cimbri, 192, 193-4

Cimeuil, *52*

Cirque de la Patrie, *32*, 49

Cisalpine Gaul, 195, 197

Cissac, 147

Citeaux, 134

Civilis rebellion, 210

Clacton-on-Sea, 20; Clactonian, 15

Clairvaux, 135

Clapade, Grotte de, Millay, 153

Claret, *128*

Claudius, 204, 219

Clayeures mound, 155

Clermont-de-l'Oise, 198

Clermont-sur-Lanquet, **52, 53**

climate, Allerød interstadial, 94-5; Atlantic, 97-8; Boreal, 97; Dryas III, 95-6; Middle Neolithic, 124; present day, *94*; Upper Palaeo-lithic, 42-3; Würmian, *41*

clothing, Middle Palaeolithic, 26; Neolithic, 102; Upper Palaeo-lithic, 57

Coincy, 87, 97

coins, 187, 196, 198, 199, 200, 203, 204, 208, **81, 82-98**

Colbert de Beaulieu, J. B., 196, 198, 202

Collet-Redon, 127

Collier cave, 148

Collies, *135*

Colomb, 64

Le Colombier, *53*

La Colombine, 149, *150*, *151*

Colonia Augusta Raurica (Augst), 203

Colonia Claudia Arae Agrippinen-sium (Cologne), 106, 203

Colonia Copia Lugudunensium (Lyons), 203

Colonia Julia Equestris Novio-dunum (Nyon), 203

Colonia Nemausus (Nîmes), 200

Les Combarelles, **2**

La Combe-Bernard, 149, 151

Combe-Capelle, *32*, 36; Combe-Capelle man, 30

La Combe d'Ain, 155

Combe Grenal, 28

Commana, *125*

Commarque, *50*

Commont, V., 12, 13, 14, 19

communication, Upper Palaeo-lithic, 58-9

Compiègne, 198

Condrusi, 203

Congy, *125*

Connos, 199

Conquette, 127, **39**

copper industry, 102, 124ff, 145

Corbiac, 57

Corded ware, 131-2

Corent, 134

Cornille, Abri, 64, *65*, 68, 69, 71

Corno-Lauzo, 177

Cornwall, 136, 145, 154

Corrèze, 45, 47

Corsica, 148-9, **54**

Cortaillod, 112

Côte-d'Or, 109-10

Côte-Saint-André, 153

Cotentin, 136

Cotte de St Brelade, 28

Les Cottés points, *45*, 46, 49

Coucoules, 136

Cougnac, *53*, II

Courchapon, 151

La Couronne, 127, 128, 129, 148

Couronnian pottery, *69*

Court-Saint-Etienne, 155

Courtavant, *150*, 152

Couze, *48*

Craponne, 203

Crassus, Marcus Licinius, 193, 197

La Crau, 68, 96

Cravanche, 107

Crec'h-Quillé, *122*

Crécy-en-Brie, *125*

cremations, 131, 145, 151, 152, 160, 182, 185, 188, 189

Creuse, 206

Cro-Magnon race, *30*, 47, 48

La-Croix-de-Mus, 154, **61**

La Crouzade, 52, *66*, 81, 82

Crugou, *130*

Cruguel, *146*

Cuchulainn, 192

Cucuron, *157*, 189

Le Cuzoul de Gramat, 82, *84*, *85*

Cys-la-Commune, 106, 107

daggers, Bronze Age, 131ff, 145ff; La Tène, 186

Daleau, 147

Dampmesmil, **37**

Danubian culture, 104-7, 108, 109-11

Dauphiné, 53, 64, 128

Déchelette, J., 154, 201, 205

Deffends, 148

Deux-Sèvres, 122, 132

Deville-lès-Rouen, 154

Diodorus Siculus, 192, 206

disease, Upper Palaeolithic, people, 58

Diviciacus, 195, 219

Domitii, 194

Dompierre-sur-Besbre, *151*, 152

Donauberg, 134, **46**

Donon, 219

Dordogne, 32, 126, 153

Les Douattes, *52*

Drappes, 198

Druids, 192, 219

Drusus, 200, 203, 204

Dryas III, 95-6, 100; Dryas phases, 43

Du Chatellier, P., 136

Duchcov, 187

Dufour bladelets, 47

Duratos-Julius, **92**

Durban, 154

Ebbou, *53*

Eburones, 197, 203

Eemian period, 13, 28

Eguisheim, 134, **46**

Egypt, 148, 149

Elisyci, 193

Elven, 136

Emporion, 159, 178

end-scrapers, 30-1, 45, 47, 50, 62, 63, 66

Engelhalbinsel, 196

Enfants, Grotte des, Grimaldi, *30*, 46

engravings, Bronze Age, 132; Epipalaeolithic, 64, 66; Meso-lithic, 88; Middle Neolithic, 122; Upper Palaeolithic, 47, *50*, *51*, 53, 54, 56, 59; *see also* sculpture

Ensérune, *157*, 158, 188-9, 191, 192, 194, 200, 207, **73**

Entremont, *157*, 158, 189-90, 191, 193, 194, 205, 210, **80, 110**

Epasnactus, 199

Epi-Azilian, 81, 96-7

Epi-Gravettian culture, 61-2

Epillos, 199

Epipalaeolithic, 61-7

Epi-Perigordian, 49

Equus caballus gallicus, **3**

Er Lannic, 122

Erdeven, *122*

Eskimos, 25, 53, 54, 55, 56

Etcheberri, *53*

Etruria, **65, 66**

Etruscan imports, 158, 159, 160, 182, 185
Euhodus, 208
Eure, **37**
eustasis, *see* sea level fluctuation
Eyguières, *146*
Les Eyzies, *42*, 44, 45, 47, 59, **II**

Fabius Maximus, Quintus, 193, 194
Las Fados, Pépieux, 154
Farnborough, 18
Les Fées, Marcamps, *52*
Ferme de Grâce, 13-14
La Ferrassie, 28, 30, 31, 44, 45, *46*, 47
Ferrières, 127, 128, *129*
La Ferté-Hauterive, 152
fibulae, Hallstattian, 155, 179-82; Mailhac, 160, 166; La Tène, 188, 189, 191, 206
Le Figuier, *53*
Filitosa, 148-9, **54**
Finistère, 108, 136, 196
fishing, Boreal, 97; Early Neolithic, 104; Epipalaeolithic, 66; pre-Boreal, 96; Upper Palaeolithic, 53-7; *see also* hunting
Font de Gaume, 59
Font-Robert, *32*; Font-Robert points, *45*, 48-9, 54
Fontabert, 64
Les Fontaines-Salées, 210
Fontalès, *52*
Fontarnaud, *52*
Fontbouïsse, 127, 128, 129, **40**
Fonteius, 194
Fontenay-le-Marmion, 108, 122, **29**
Les Fonts-Gaidon, 134, **44**
Fontvielle, *128*
Fort-Harrouard, 133, 152
Forum Julii (Fréjus), 200, 206
Forum Segusiavorum (Feurs), 204
Fossae Marianae, 194
Fourneau du Diable, *32*, *46*, *50*, *52*, 57
Fourvière, 203, 206
Franche-Comté, 107, 109, 110, 111, 112, 125
Frasnes-lez-Buissenal, 192
Fresné-la-mer, 148
Frignicourt, 107
Fritzdorf, 145
Frouzet, 182

Gabillou, *52*, *53*, 56, 57
Gallia Comata, 195, 200, 201-5, 210
Gallia Transalpina, 192-4, 199
Gallic War, 192, 195-8
Gallo-Belgic ware, 208-9
Gard, *52*, 103, 127, 128
Gard-Ardèche, 50
Gardes, *135*, 136
Gardon, gorge, 111
Gare de Couze, *52*, 59
Gargas, *53*, 59
Garonne basin, 21, 24, 28, 50, 111
Garrigues, 178
Gavaudan, *46*
Gavrinis passage grave, **31**
Gemellianus, 205
Genabum, (Orleans), 197, 203

Geneva, 195, 206
geometric microliths, introduction, 96, 100
Gergovia, 195, 197, 202, 207, 208
Germanicus, 203
Gibraltar, Straits of, 17, 22
Gironde, 52, 54, 123
glaciations, 9-11, 13, 42
Glanum, 194, 200, 201
Glos, 64
gods, Roman Gaul, 210, 219
Golasecca group, 181, 186
gold, Bronze Age, 131, 134, 145, 148, 150; Early Iron Age, 180, 182
Gonvillars, 107, 109
La Gorge-Meillet, *157*, 185-6; **70**
Gourdan, *32*, *52*, **4**
Gours-aux-Lions, 110, **34**
Gouy, *52*, *53*
Grand Abri de Châteauneuf, 68, *70*, 90-4, **15, 16, 17**; *see also* Châteauneuf des Martigues
Le Grand Bassin, 154, 159, 160, 177
Grand Congloué wreck, 190
Grand Juyan de la Figarède, *128*
Grands Causses, 126, 127-8
Granges, 152
La Graufesenque, 208
graves, Bronze Age, 131, 134ff, 145ff, 155-6; Cardial-Neolithic, 91; Early Iron Age, 160; Early Neolithic, 105ff; Epipalaeolithic, 66; Jogassian culture, 182; Late Neolithic, 124ff, **36**; Mesolithic, 81; Middle Neolithic, 110, 111-12, 121-3; Roman Gaul, 219; La Tène, 184ff; Upper Palaeolithic, 31, 45-6, 47, 53, 58, 59-60
La Gravette, *32*, *45*
Gravette points, 45, 47, 48, 66, 82
Gravettian industry, 47-8
Greek colonisation, 158ff, 183, 188, 200
Grésigny, 198
Greux de Miège, 134
Grézan, *157*
Grézan warrior, 190,
Grimaldi, *30*, *32*, 47, 48
Gros-Guignon, *157*
Les Gros-Monts, *23*, *52*
Grotte-Murée, Basses-Alpes, *146*
Grotte Nicolas, *135*
Grotte Rey, *54*
La Groutte, 121
Gruisson, 66
Guardamonte, 189
Guerchy, 150
Gündlingen, 153

habitation, Bronze Age, 154; Early Neolithic, 103, 105; Epipalaeolithic, 64-5; Late Neolithic, 124, 127; Mesolithic, 81; Middle Neolithic, 110, 111, **34, 35**; Roman Gaul, 194, 200-5; La Tène culture, 187, 190; Upper Palaeolithic, 56-7
Habsheim, hoard, 134
Haguenau, 134, 145, *146*, 147
La Halliade, 148
Hallstatt culture, 153, 154-6, 160, 178, 179-82, 183, 188, 191

Haltern, fort, 209
Hanborough, 18
hand-axes, Lower Palaeolithic, 17-22; Middle Palaeolithic, 22ff, 110; *see also* axes
Hannibal, 192-3
Les Harpons, Lespugue, *52*
harpoons, 51, 53, 54, 65, 66; *see also* spears
Harthausen, *146*
Haulzy group, 183
Hauser, *32*
Haute-Vienne, 132
Hautes-Alpes, 147
Hautes-Bruyères, *105*
hearse burials, *see* chariot burials, wagon burials
hearth assemblages, 81, 189
Helvetii, 195-6, 203
Hérault, 111, 127, 128, 134, 154, **61**
Hervelighem, 145
Hesse Tumulus, 146
Heuneburg-Hohmichele, 182
Hildesheim, 206
Hoëdic, 89, 108
Hoenheim-Souffelweyersheim, *105*
Hofheim, fort, 209
La Hogue, **29**
La Hoguette, 108
Homo erectus, 19, 29
Homo habilis, 17, 18
Homo sapiens sapiens, 19, 30, 46
Horbourg, 146
horses, 55, 56, 130, 131
Les Hoteaux, *52*
houses, *see* habitation
Hoxne, 12, 19
Huelgoät, 196
Huelva, 154
Hungary, 50, 134, 187
Hunsrück-Eifel culture, 186
hunting, Early Neolithic, 104; Epipalaeolithic, 66-7; Mesolithic, 68; Pre-Boreal, 96; transition to reared animals, 103; Upper Palaeolithic, 53-7
hunting tallies, 50, 59
Hyères, *157*, 159

Iberian group, 153; ware, 154
L'Ile-aux-Maines, *123*
L'Ile Carn, *123*
Ile-de-France, 45, 48, 49, 53, 151, 182, 187
Illyricum, 195
Ionian ware, 158, 160, 179
iron, change from bronze to, 154-6
Isère, *136*, 146
Istres, 62, 67, 69
Isturitz, *32*, *50*, *52*, *53*, *57*, 59, **6**

Jaligny-sur-Besbre, 148
jasper tools, 49
Jaulny, 134
javelins, 54
Jean-Blancs, *32*, *52*
Jersey, 110, 196
jewellery, *see* ornaments, personal
Les Jogasses, *157*, 182
Jogassian, 182-3, 185, 187

Julian, 199
Juliobona Caletorum (Lillebonne), 203
Juliomagus Andecavorum (Angers), 203
Julius Gedemonius, Gaius, 210
Julius Otuaneunus Rufus, Gaius, 210
Julius Rufus, Gaius, 203, 204, 209
Juillac-le-Coq, *123*
Jura, 53, 102, 104, 112, 135, 155, 180, 184, 186
Justinius, 157, 158

Kakovatos, 148
Kent's Cavern, 12
Kerbschnitt ware, 145, 148, 150, 155
Keriaval, *130*
Kerlescan, 121
Kerloas en Plouarzel, 131
Kermaric, *122*
Kermeur-Bihan, *125*
Kernonen, Plouvorn, 136, V, VI
Kersoufflet, 131
Kerugou ware, 122, *123*, 126
Körös ware, 105
Kurzgeland, *146*

Labastide, *53*
Labeil, *146*, 148
Labienus, 197, 203
Lachaud, *52*
Les Lacs, 136
Lair, 134
Lalinde, *48*
lamps, stone, 56
Languedoc, Cardial Neolithic, 90; Chalcolithic, 124, 126, **40**; Chassean, 111; copper industry, 124, 126; Epi-Gravettian industry, 61; Fontbouïsse culture, 127, **40**; Hallstatt culture, 156; Iron Age, 159-60, 177-8; Polada ware, 148; Rhodanian daggers, 135; Roman occupation, 192; Sauveterrian, 83; La Tène culture, 189; tombs, 127, *128*; Urnfield culture, 154
Languidic, *122*
Lardins, 210
Lartet, *32*, 59
Las-Morts, 133
Lascaux, 56
Lattes, 188
Laugerie-Basse, *48*, 51, 54
Laugerie-Haute, 31, *32*, 42-50
Launac, 154, 183
Launacian, 154, **61**
Laure-Minervois, *128*
laurel-leaf points, 49, *50*, 54
Laussel, 43, **I**, I
Lavalduc, 62-3
Lavoye, 209
Layes, Abri des, 85, 86
lead resources, 154, 206
Leakey, L. S. B., 17
Lébous, 127, 129, 131, 135, **40**
Ledosus (Lezou), 207
Lehringen, 20
Len-Vihan en Arzon, 133
Lesconil, *130*
Lesneven, 147, **48**
Lespugue, *48*
Lessart, **43**

Lestours, 148
Leubingen, 132, 134
Levallois, 15, 16, 22, 23, 28
Levroux, 205
Lexovii, **84**
Limeuil, 57
Linear pottery, 88, 99, 104-7, 110
Lingolsheim, *107*, 152
Lingones, 196, 197, 208
Lipari islands, 112
La Liquisse, Nant, *128*, 136
Loir-et-Cher, 110, **55**
Loire valley, *Bandkeramik*, 104, 109; Chassean, 111, 121; Middle Neolithic, 110; Peu-Richard influence, 124; population, 52; Rössen influence, 109; spread of metalwork, 147; Tardenoisian, 86; tin trade, 187; tombs, 123, 125, 126; Upper Solutrean, 50; Urnfield culture, 152
Lombez, 208
Lombrives, **51**
Longueroche, 65
Longues, 145
Loriol, Drôme, 135, *136*
Lorraine, 106, 110, 125, 152, 155, 186
Lortet, *52*, *54*
Los Millares, 131
Lot, 52, 111, 126, 127, 128
Loucé, 145
Loudéac, 154
Lucterius, 198
Luern, 193
Lug, 205, 219
Lugasson, 133
Lugdunensis, 199-200
Lugdunum, 200, 203-4, **97**
Lugudunum Convenarum, 194, 201
lunates, 82, 83, 86, 89, 96
Lutetia, 197, 203
Lyons, 135, 203, 204, 206, 208, **57**

Maas group, 106
La Macelle, 136
Macon region, 48
La Madeleine, 46, 51-3, *54*, 60
La Madeleine, Villeneuve-les-Maguelonne, *112*
Magales, *207*
Magdalenian, 30, 31, 44, 51-3, 56, 58, 59, 61, 65
La Magdeleine, *48*, 50
magic, Epipalaeolithic, 67; Upper Palaeolithic, 57, 58, 59
Magny-Lambert, 149, 155
Mägstub, *146*
Mailhac, *129*, 154, 159-60, 177, 178, **63**
Mailly-le-Camp, 192, **101**
Main-Swabian group, 151, 152
Mandubian culture, 198
Mané-Bras, *122*
Mané-Kerioned passage graves, IV
Le Manio, 121, *122*
Les Marais, Marcilly, 110
La Marche, *48*, *52*, 56, **5**
Marcouline, Abri de la, Cassis, 63, 64
Marion des Roches, 147
Marius, 194

Marloux, 204
Marne culture, 184-7
Marnian ware, **74, 75**
marques de chasse, 46
Marsa, 127, 133, 148
Marseilles, *157*, 158-9, 178, 179; *see also* Massalia
Marson, **74**
Marsoulas, *52*
Le Martinet, *52*
Le Martinet de Sauveterre, 82, 83
Martroy-de-Feyrolles, 152
Mas d'Azil, *52*, *52*, 53, *55*, 56, *65*, 81
Mas-Granier, Tarn-et-Garonne, **61**
Massalia (Massilia), 157, 158-9, 179, 183, 188, 192, 193, 194, 201
Massif Central, Artenac culture, 127; Chassean, 111, 121; glaciation, 42; Hallstatt culture, 155, 156; Launacian industry, 154; Magdalenian culture, 52; Middle Neolithic, 102, 111, 121, tombs, 127
Les Matelles, *128*
Les Matignons, 109, 123, 124, 126
Mauer, 16, 17
Maurely, *128*
Mauthiers, *52*
Mayen, 204
Mayenne, 49
Mazuc cave, Penne, 133
Méaudre, *52*
Mediolanum Biturigum, 202-3
Mediolanum Santonum (Saintes), 203, 210
Mediterranean, Early Neolithic, 102-4
Médoc, 108, 147
Mehun, **56**
Meldi, 203
Mels-Rixheim, 150
Ménec alignments, III
Menneville, *105*, 109
Merxheim-Zapfenloch, *105*
Mesnay, 135
Mesolithic 67-90
metallurgy, introduction, 131-2
Metiosedum (Melun), 203
Meurthe-et-Moselle mound, 155
Michelsberg, culture, 109, 110, 111, 112, 124, 125
microgravers, 48
micro-Gravette points, 62, 63, 66, 82
Midi, agriculture, 102, 124; Atlantic period, 97; Beaker culture, 129-30; Chassean, 111, 112; development of metallurgy, 131, 148, 149; Late Neolithic and Chalcolithic, 126-9, 133; 'Neolithic Revolution', 102; Rhône culture, 134-6; Urnfield culture, 150, 151, 153
Milhes, **52, 53**
Millay, 153
Milles, 154
Millot, Paul, 197
Mindel, 18; Mindel-Riss Interglacial, 18, 19, 22
Minerve, 136
Mirabel, 135
Mireval, *135*
Moëlan, *125*

Moguntiacum, 200, 203
Moidons, Forêt des, 135
Molodova I, 27
Monceau-Laurent, *155*
Monéteau, 149
Mont Beuvray, 204, 205, 207, 208
Mont d'Or aqueduct, 204
Mont Lassois, *157*, 179, 180, 181, 182
La Montade, *135*, 136; Grotte de, 67, 68
Montadian, 67-81, 83, 96, 97
Montans, 208
Montauban, 111
Montaut, 49, 50
Montbani, 87, 88
Montbeyre, 111
Montclus, 72, 82, 90, 97; *see also* La Baume de Montclus
Monte Carlo, 201
Montespan, *53*
Montgaudier, *58*, *59*
Montière, 14
Montlaurès, 194
Montmaurin, 205
Montmorency, 106; Montmorency-Campignian, 108
Montmorentian, 89-90, 100, 110
Montpellier, 189
Montpezat, *130*, 148
Morbihan, 108, 110, 121, 122, 196, **27, 31**
Morges, 135, 136, **45, 46**
Mormoiron, 64, 65
Morvan, 193
Moselle valley, 106
Motes, Maluquer de, 148
La Motte-Saint-Valentin, *157*, 186
Mougau-Bihan, *125*
Le Moulin, 154, 159
Moulin-de-Vent group, 126
Mourez, Berneuil, *123*
Mousterian, 16, 22, 23, 25-8, 30, 31, 45-6, 50
Le Moustier, 28
La Mouthe, 56, **8**
Muge-Arruda, 89
Münsingen, 110
Murée cave, *130*, 148
Murus gallicus, 197, **99**
Mycenae, 145, 148

Nages, 210
Nantes, **57, 61**
Napoleon III, 195, 196, 197, 198
Narbo, 200, 201, 206, 208, **95**
Narbo Martius (Narbonne), 193, 194
Narbonensis, Gallia, 195, 200, 201-5, 210
natural environment, Allerød interstadial, 94-5; Atlantic period, 97-8; Boreal, 97, Dryas III, 95-6; Pre-Boreal, 96-7; Upper Palaeolithic, 42-4; *see also* animals, vegetation
Neandertal man, 29, 30
necklaces, 57 *58*, 60, 149
needles, bone, 50, *51*, 57
Nemausus, **98**
Néris-les-Bains, 200
Nermont cave, 110
Nerva, A. Licinius, 199
Nervii, 196, 203

Neyruz type of axes, 145
Niaux, *53*, **7**; Le Petit Caougne de, 133
Nicaea (Nice), 157, 159
Nicolaï, 63
Nîmes, 135, *157*, 189, 200, 201, 210, **78**
Noailles, *32*
'Noailles' burins, 31, 44, *45*, *46*, 48-9
Nohan, 134
Nointel, 198
Normandy, 147, 153, 182
'nosed' handles, 132-3
notched points, *50*, *51*
Notre-Dame-de-Londres, *155*, 156
Novaesium, 200
Noves, **108**
Noviodunum, 202
Nuits-Saint-Georges, 204
Nuraghic culture, 148

Oberaden, fort, 209
Oberfeld, 152
Oenochoe Tumulus, 178
Olbia, 159
Olduvai, 17, 19
Olette, 64
Olha, Abri, 28
oppida, Rhône valley, 178-9; La Tène, 188ff; Roman Gaul, 201-3
Orgelet, 146
ornaments, personal, Bronze Age, 128, 131, 132, 134, 135, 145, 148, 149, 150; Early Iron Age, 179, 183; Marne culture, 184; La Tène, 184; Upper Palaeolithic, 57, *58*
Orpièrre, *157*, 189
Orval, *151*, 152
Osismii, 196
Oullins, 52, *53*

Pair-non-Pair, 48, *53*
palstaves, 145-6, 147, 148, 149, 152
Paques, Grotte de, Collies, *135*
Parançot, Bois de, 135
Parc-Nehué, dolmen, Riantec, *123*
Paris basin, Acheulean, 20; arrowheads, 105; Aurignacian, 49; *Bandkeramik*, 104, 106-7; glaciation, 42; Late Neolithic, 124; Mesolithic, 86ff; 97; tombs, 125, 126, 127; Tumulus culture, 145, 147; Urnfield culture, 152
Parisii, 203
Parmilieu, 146
'parrot-beak' burins, 51
passage graves, 108, 122, 127, *128*
La Passagère, 64
Pataud, Abri, *45*, 47, 48
pebble-tools, 17-18
Pech de la Boissière, *32*, 52
Pech Merle, *53*, 59
Le Pègue, *157*, 178-9, 188
'pen-knife' blades, 62, 64
Penmarc'h, *130*
Les Pennes, *157*, 159, 189, 190, **76**
Pépinville, 153
percussion-flaking, 49
Périgord, 28, 32, 41ff, 50ff, 58, 66

Périgord-Corrèze, 49
Perigordian, 30ff, 44, 59
Périgueux, 59, 210
Perthes, Boucher de, 12, 15
Pertuis, *157*, 178
Le Petit Celland, *see* Le Châtellier
Le Petit-Morin, Marne, *125*
Petrocorii, 206
Peu-Richard, 109, 123, 126, 133, **32**
Peu-Richard ware, *123*, 124, 126
Pexton Moor, 186
Peynier, 191
Les Peyraoutes, Roquefort-les-Pins, *128*
Le Peyré, 154
Peyre-Haute, *157*
Peyroche II, cave, 127
Peyrony, D., *31*, *32*, 44, 45, 48; Elie, *32*
Pézenas, *157*
'Philippics', 187
'Phocaean' ware, 154, 158, 159, 160, 178, 180, 181, 189
Picard, G. C., 201
Picardy, 182
pic-planés, 89
picks, 89-90
Pictones, 199, 206
Pié-Miéjan, *128*
Piedmont, 189, 190, 191
Pincevent, *32*, *52*, 53, 57
pins, Bronze Age, 132ff, 145ff; poppy-head, 150; vase-headed, 154
La Pique, *52*
Piroutet, 112
Piscop, 87
Le Placard, *32*, *52*, 60
Plaine de Chambertrand, 152
Plancus, L. Munatius, 203
Plédéliac, *130*
Pliny the Elder, 206
Plobannalec, *130*
Plogoff, *123*
Ploubazlanec, 147
Ploudalmézeau, *123*
Plouhinec, **41, 42**
Ploumilliau, 145
Plouneventer, *146*
Plouvorn, 145, V, VI
Plovan, *130*
La Pluche, *52*
Poeymaü cave, *52*, 81
La Pointe Saint-Gildas, 89
points, 45, 49, 51, 54-5, 62, 86, 87; bone, *46*, 48-9, 54, 71; curved-back, 46, 53; laurel leaf, 49, *50*, 54; notched, 49, *50*, *51*; split-base, 46; unifacial, 49, *50*, 62; willow-leaf, 49, *50*
Poisson, Abri du, 47, 48, **9**
Poitou, *52*, 111, 199
Polada ware, 148
polishers, 46
Polybius, 191, 192
polyglacial theory, 13
Pommiers, 202
Pompeii, 208
Pompey, 194, 201
Ponteau, 68, *69*
population, Early Iron Age, 182; Middle Neolithic, 111, 123; Neolithic, 102, 104; Upper Palaeolithic, 57-8

Porcieu-Amblagnieu, 146
Le Portel, *53*, **3**
Portugal, 124
pottery, Bronze Age, 132ff, 145ff; Early Neolithic, 102, 103; Hallstattian, 155, 156, 179, 180-1; Jogassian, 182; Late Neolithic, 124ff; Marne, 184-5; Massalia, 158-9; Mesolithic, 61; Middle Neolithic, 110, 111, 112, *123*, 124; Roman-Gaul, 194, 204, 207-9; La Tène, 188ff, 208; Urnfield, 151-4, 178; *see also individual wares* e.g. Attic ware, Cardial ware
Pougues-les-Eaux, 151, 152
Les Pounches, Mons, 136
Le Pouyalet, Pouillac, 147
La Prairie de Mauves, Nantes, **57, 61**
Prépoux, 150
Presles, **36**
pressure-flaking, 49
Prosne, **75**
Provence, Beaker culture, 130; Cardial Neolithic, 90, 103, 111; Early Iron Age, 178-9; Late Neolithic groups, 126, 128; Magdalenian, 61; Montadian, 97; Polada ware, 148; reindeer-based culture, 62, 65, 95; Rhodanian culture, 135-6; Roman, 201; Solutrean, 49, 83; Tardenoisian, 83; tombs, 127, *128*
Prusly-sur-Ource, *155*
Puech-Réal, **38**
puits-funéraire, 219
Punic Wars, 193
Puy-de-Dôme, 134, 219
Puy d'Issolu, 198
Puymoyen, 28
Puyo-Hourmanio, 148
Pyrenees, Acheulean industry, 21; beaked handles, 133; as a boundary to occupation, 32; Chassean, 111; glaciation, 42; Launacian, 154; Middle Neolithic, 102; 'Noailles' burins, 48; Solutrean, 49, 50, 51
Pytheas, 158

quartz tools, 21
querelle du chevêtre, 56
querns, 91, 105
Quina, 28, 46
Quina index (Bordes), 24, *25*

raclette, 51, 52
Rame, 135, *136*
Rancogne, 152
Ras Shamra, 134
Ravin des Arcs, *155*, 156
Raymonden, *30*, 53, **10**
razors, 150, 153, 154, 155, 156
La Redoute, 154
reindeer, 56, 62, 63, 94, 95
religions, Roman Gaul, 201, 210, 219
Remi, 196, 197, 198, **83, 96**
Renne, Abri du, 47
Reteni, 208
Reverdit, *50*
Rhine valley, 87, 104, 105, 106, 109, 110, 130, 200

Rhodanian, 48, 134-6, 147
Rhodanian Sauveterrian, *85*, *86*, 96
Rhône valley, Acheulean, 20, 21; Aurignacian, 47; contacts with Greeks, 178; glaciation, 42; Hallstatt culture, 155, 156, 180; introduction of metals, 131, 132; Magdalenian, 61; Mesolithic, 83, 85, 101; Rhodanian, 48, 134-6, 147; Roman annexation, 158; Sauveterrian, 85, 96; Solutrean industry, 50; Tardenoisian, 97; Tumulus culture, 145
Richard (*alias* Grotte des Eyzies), **11**
Riedisheim, 134
Riegsee, 149, 151
Rillaton gold cup, 145
rilled ware, 152
Rippenbarren, 134
Riss, 16, 18, 19, 28
Rixheim, 106, 150, 153
Roaix, *129*
Roanne, 207, 208, **33**
Le Roc de Sers, *50*, 51
Roc-en-Pail, 28
Rocamadour, *53*
Roche-Chèvre, *107*
La Roche de Lalinde, *52*, *58*, 59
Le Rocher, *122*
Rochereil, *52*
Les Rochers d'Auffargis, 87, 88
Les Roches, 135, 147, **28**
Rodezian culture, 127, 128
Roh-en-Tallec, *123*
Roh-Vihan, *123*
Roman occupation, 158, 192ff
Romanellian, 62-5, 66-7
Les Ronces, *125*
La Roque, *157*, 189, 190
La-Roque-Saint-Christophe, 147, 153
Roquefort, 135, *157*, **62**
Roquefure, Abri de, 81, 82, 83, *85*
Roquepertuse, *157*, 189, 205, **77, 79**
Les Roseaux, Morges, 135
Rosmeur, *130*
Rosnoën, 150, *151*
Rössen culture, 107, 109, 110, 111
Roucadour, 108, 126
Rouet, *128*
Rouffach, 150
Rouffignac, 82, **13, 14**
La Rousselerie, **48**
Roussillon, 154
Royaumeix, 150
Ruscino, *157*, 188

Sabinus, Julius, 199, 204
Le Sablon, 64
Sacrovir, Julius, 199, 201, 204
Saïga tatarica, **4**
Saint Acheul, 13-14, 19
Saint-André, Salins, 135
Saint Antonin-sur-Bayon, *128*
Saint-Bernard, Ain, 152
Saint-Bertrand-de-Comminges, 194, 201
Saint-Blaise, 157, 159, 188, 190, 201
Saint-Brieuc-des-Iffs, 153
Saint-Denis-de-Pile, 153, 154
Saint-Estèphe, 147

Saint-Eugène dolmen, *128*
Saint-Germain-la-Rivière, *52*, *58*, 59, 60
Saint-Germain-le-Rocheux, 210
Saint-Germain-Source-Seine, **105, 106**
Saint-Gervais, Auxerre, 149
Saint-Gervais-les-Bagnols, *135*
Saint-Guyomard, *123*
Saint-Hypolithe du Fort, 136
Saint-Jean-de-Belleville, 191
Saint-Jean-de-Cas, *129*
Saint-Jean-de-Cuculles, 135
Saint-Julien, 147, 160
Saint-Just, 121
Saint-Laurent, 147
Saint-Laurent-du-Pont, 135
Saint-Marcel, *52*, 63
Saint-Martin-de-Londres, *127*, **39**
Saint-Mary, Charente, 132
Saint-Mathieu-de-Tréviers, *127*, **40**
Saint-Menoux, 134
Saint-Michel, Carnac, **27**
Saint-Michel-d'Arudy, *52*
Saint-Michel-du-Touch, 111, 112
Saint-Nazaire-de-Ladarez, 135
Saint-Paul-de-Varces, 146
Saint-Quay-Perros, *122*
Saint-Rémy, 201
Saint-Rémy-en-Rollat, 208
Saint-Roman, 64
Saint-Rome-de-Cernon, 207
Saint-Salvi-de-Carcaves, **38**
Saint-Vérédème, Sanhilac, 148
Sainte-Anastasie, *135*
Sainte-Baume, *157*, 178
Sainte-Colombe, *157*, 179, 181, 188, 189
Sainte-Croix-de-Verdon, *130*
Sainte-Pellaye, 109-10
La Salette, *151*
Salinelles, *128*
Salins, 112, 135, 180
Sallelès-Gabardès, *53*
La Salpêtre, 148
Saluvii, 193
Salzgitter-Lebenstedt, 27
Samarobriva (Amiens), 196
sanctuaries, Epipalaeolithic, 67; La Tène, 189-90; *see also* temples
sandstone tools, 89
Santones, 195, 203
Saran, 134
Sardinia, 136
Sassenay, 152, 154
Sauveterre-la-Guyenne, 147
Sauveterrian, 67, 81-9, 96-7, 100
sceptres, 145
Schoenensteinbach, *105*
Schussenried culture, 109
Schwieberdingen group, 109
Scotius, 208
scraper index (Bordes), 24, *25*
scrapers, Early Palaeolithic, 20-1; Epipalaeolithic, 62-3, 64, 66; Late Neolithic, 128; Mesolithic, 67, 81, 82, 83; Middle Neolithic, 124; Middle Palaeolithic, 22, *23*; Upper Palaeolithic, 30-1, 45ff, 50ff
sculpture, 48, 53, 59, 190, 205, 210; *see also* engraving
sea level fluctuation, 13-15, 17, 97
Sedlec, 18
Segovellauni, 200

Segusiavi, 203, 204, 206, **94**
Seine basin, 12, 15, 21, 53, 109; *see also* Paris basin
Seine-Oise-Marne, 124, 125, 126, 133, **36**
Senones, 187, 197, 203
Sept-Sault, 185-6
Sequani, 193, 195, 196, 199, 203
Sermoyer, 86
Serrigny, 134, **46**
Séry, Bois de, 135
settlements, *see* habitation
Sextius, 193
Seynes, Grotte de, Gard, *146*
Shardana, 148-9
sheep, 72, 97, 102, 147
shells, adornments, 46, 57, 71-2, 103, 134-5, 148; as currency, 134-5; impressed decoration, 90, 91, 103, 104
side-scrapers, 45, 50, 62, 67, 81, 124
Sinard, *136*
Singen, 153
Sireuil, *48*
Solliès-Pont, 135
Solutré, *32*, 49, 55
Solutrean, 30ff, 44, 49-51, 59
Solvieux, *52*
Somme basin, 12ff, 18, 19, 20-1, 28
Somme-Bionne, 185-6, **69**
Sonchamp, 87; Sonchamp points, 83, *85*, 88-9
sorcerers, 57
Sorde, *52*, 59, 60
Soubeyras, *52*
Le Souc'h vase, *123*
Le Soucy, *52*
Souhait Montagneux, 86
Sournan, *123*
Sous-Balme, Abri, 85, 86, 87
Sous-Vargonne, 86
Soyons, *130*
Spain, origins of Solutrean, 50; Polada ware, 148
Spangenbarren, 134
spear-points, 54, 64
spear-throwers, 55
spears, 20, 24, 25, 29, 46, 51, 54-5, 66, 188; *see also* harpoons
speech, Upper Palaeolithic people, 58-9
statue-menhirs, 127, 148-9, **38, 54**
Torri, 148-9
Steinheim an der Murr, 19
stock-raising, *see* animals
Strabo, 201, 204, 209
Stradonitz, 205
Strasbourg area, 106, 107
Straubing, 132
Substantion, 153
Suebi, 195
Suessiones, 196, 202
Suetonius, 192

Swanscombe, 19
swords, Bronze Age, 146, 148ff; Early Iron Age, 179; La Tène, 186, 188
Syngleyrac, 147
Syria, 132, 134

Les Taburles, Avançon, 135
talayots, 148
Tara-Yeovil torcs, 148
Tarbes, 154
Tardenoisian, 67, 81-9, 97, 98-9, 100-1, 105, 106, 108, 111, 112, 121
Tarn, 52, 127, 154
taxation, Roman, 200
Telamon, battle of, 192
temples, Roman Gaul, 210, 219
Tencteri, 197
Termo Pialat, 48
Ternay, 135
Ternifine, 19
terra sigillata, 208, 209
Teutones, 194
Téviec, 89, 108
Teyjat, *51, 52*
Thames, 16, 18, 19
Tharaux, *146*, 148
Tiberius, 201, 203, 208, 219
Tigurini, 194
tin industry, 131, 132, 136
Togirix, Q. Julius, 199, **93**
Tolosa, 192, 200
tombs, Bronze Age, 131, 134, 136, 145, 147, 149; Jogassian, 182; Late Neolithic, 124ff; Middle Neolithic, 121-3; *see also* graves
tools, Bronze Age, 134, 146, 150; Early Neolithic, 105; Epipalaeolithic, 62-6; Late Neolithic, 124, 126, 128, 199; Lower Palaeolithic, 17-22; Mesolithic, 67-71, 81, 82-90; Middle Neolithic, 110, 111, 121, 124; Middle Palaeolithic, 22-9; Upper Palaeolithic, 30-1, 44-53, 54; *see also* weapons, *and individual tools* e.g. axes, scrapers
torcs, 134, 148, **46, 50, 101**
Torri, 148-9
Tossen-Keler tumulus, Penvenan, **30**
Toulouse, 111, 189
Touraine, Grand-Pressigny floors, 124
La Tourasse, *52*
Tournal, 12
towns, Roman, 200-5
tranchets, 89, 106, 124
traps, hunting, 55-6

Tréboul, 147
Le Tréhou, 154, **59**
Les Treilles, 127
Trémargat, 147
trepanning, 58, 125
Tres Galliae, *see* Gallia Comata
Trévé, 131
Treveri, 197
Le Trilobite, 50
triumphal arches, Roman, 201
Les Trois Frères, *53, 55, 57*
Tropaeum Augusti, Monte Carlo, 201
Trompetenmuster decoration, 205
Tuc d'Audoubert, *50*, 53
Tumulus culture (*Hügelgräberkultur*), 145-7, 150, 151, 152, 155
Tungri, 203
Tursac, *48*
Ty-ar Boudiquet, *122*

Ubii, 203
Ugarit, 134
Únětice, 132, 134
Urmitz, fort, 209
Urnfield culture, 131, 148, 149, 150-3, 154, 178, 182-3, 191
Usipetes, 197
Ussat, **51**
Uxellodunum, 195, 198

La Vache, *52*, 65
Vachères, 210, **102**
Les Vachons, *32*
Val-Suzon, 210
Valentia (Valence), 200
Vallonet, 16, 17
Valorgues, 94; *see also* La Baume de Valorgues
Var, 103
vases-supports, 111-12, *121*
Vasselay, **56**
Vaucluse, *51*, 53, 103, *129*
Vayrac, 198
vegetation, Atlantic, 98; Bronze Age, 147; Dryas III, 96; Present day, 9; Upper Palaeolithic, 43-4
Vénat, 153
Vendée, 131
Venelli, 196
Veneti, 196, 203
Vensac, 147
Ventabren, *68*
'Venus', with horn, Laussel, **1**, I
Venuses, Aurignacian, 48, 59
Vercellae, 194
Vercingetorix, 195, 197, 198, **88, 89,** VIII
Verdon gorge, 111
Vernaison, 147
Vers, *128*

Vert-la-Gravelle, 107
Vertault, 197, 209, **99**
Vértesszöllös, 16, 17
Verzé, 134
Vesontio (Besançon), 196, 203
Vetera, 200
Veuxhaulles, 149
Veyrier, *52*
Vézère valley, 32, 45
Via Domitia, 193, 194, 200
Vichy ceramic workers, 208
Vici, 201, 204
Le Vicomté-sur-Rance, *43*
Videlles, 133, 147, 152, **28, 47**
Vielle points, 87
Vienna (Vienne), 200, 201
Vienne, 45, 49, 56, 110, 122, 132
Vienne-Charente group, 126
Vilhonneur, 132, 147
Villa d'Antone, 205
Villafranchian epoch, 16, 17, 18
Villegouge, **33**
Villepin, 66
Vindex, Julius, 199
Vindonissa, 200, 203, 208, 209
Vinets, 149
Vix, 179-82, 183, 185, **64, 65, 67, 68**
Vocontii, 194
Vosges, 104, 106, 109, 110, 219

wagon burials, 183, 184, 185; *see also* chariot burials
Waldalgesheim, 187
Wauwil group, 109, 112
wealth, Marnian, 186
weapons, Bronze Age, 131, 132, 136, 145ff; Acheulean, 20; Early Iron Age, 177, 179; Early Neolithic, 105; Epipalaeolithic, 66; Late Neolithic, 124; Middle Palaeolithic, 24, 25, 29; La Tène, 188; Upper Palaeolithic, 46, 51, 54-5; *see also* tools, *and individual weapons* e.g. daggers, harpoons
Wessex culture, 136, 145
Widensolen, 134
willow-leaf points, 49, *50*
Wolfgantzen, 150
women, Upper Palaeolithic, 59-60
woodworking, Roman Gaul, 206-7
'Wraith Painter', **68**
Würm, 16, 19, 28, 30-1, 42, 43, 44

Xanthus, 208

Yonne, 106, 109-10

Zambotti, Laviosa, 148